Media Ethics

Issues

&

Cases

Media Ethics

Issues & Cases

PHILIP PATTERSON
OKLAHOMA CHRISTIAN UNIVERSITY

LEE WILKINS
UNIVERSITY OF MISSOURI-COLUMBIA

Boston   Burr Ridge, IL   Dubuque, IA   Madison, WI   New York
San Francisco   St. Louis   Bangkok   Bogotá   Caracas   Kuala Lumpur
Lisbon   London   Madrid   Mexico City   Milan   Montreal   New Delhi
Santiago   Seoul   Singapore   Sydney   Taipei   Toronto

PATTERSON MEDIA ETHICS, 4E, JEAN H., 7/01

McGraw-Hill Higher Education
  A Division of The McGraw-Hill Companies

MEDIA ETHICS: ISSUES AND CASES
Published by McGraw-Hill, an imprint of The McGraw-Hill Companies, Inc. 1221
Avenue of the Americas, New York, NY, 10020. Copyright © 2002 by The McGraw-Hill Companies,
Inc. All rights reserved. No part of this publication may be reproduced or distribute in any form or by
any means, or stored in a database or retrieval system, without the prior written consent of The McGraw-
Hill Companies, Inc., including, but not limited to, in any network or other electronic storage or
transmission, or broadcast for distance learning.
Some ancillaries, including electronic and print components, may not be available to customers outside
teh United States.

This book is printed on recycled, acid-free paper containing 10% postconsumer waste.

3 4 5 6 7 8 9 0 DOC/DOC 9 8 7 6 5 4 3 2 1

ISBN 0-07-237388-1

Editorial Director: *Phillip A. Butcher*
Sponsoring Editor: *Valerie Raymond*
Developmental Editor: *Valerie Raymond*
Marketing Manager: *Kelly M. May*
Senior Project Manager: *Jean Hamilton*
Production Supervisor: *Carol A. Bielski*
Producer, Media Technology: *Jessica Bodie*
Freelance Design Coordinator: *David A. Tietz*
Cover freelance designer: *Design Solutions*
Cover Image: © *PhotoDisc.*
Typeface: *10/12 Times Roman*
Compositor: *Carlisle Communications, Ltd.*
Printer: *R.R. Donnelley & Sons Company*

Library of Congress Cataloging-in-Publication Data

Patterson, Philip
   Media ethics : issues and cases / Philip Patterson, Lee Wilkins. — 4th ed.
      p. cm.
   Includes bibliographical references and index.
   ISBN 0-07-237388-1
   1. Mass media—Moral and ethical aspects.   I. Title: Media ethics, issues and cases. II.
II. Wilkins, Lee.
P94.M36   1997
174—dc21
www.mhhe.com   2001030760

To Amy, Andrew, Miranda and Joshua
Four equally bright kids, unequally distributed between us

CONTENTS

CHAPTER IV
LOYALTY: CHOOSING BETWEEN COMPETING ALLEGIANCES   70

CASES

CHAPTER V
PUBLIC RELATIONS: ADVOCATE OR ADVERSARY?   95

CASES

CHAPTER VI
PRIVACY: LOOKING FOR SOLITUDE IN THE GLOBAL VILLAGE   119

CASES

CHAPTER VII
THE MASS MEDIA IN A DEMOCRATIC SOCIETY: KEEPING A PROMISE   147

CASES

CHAPTER VIII
MEDIA ECONOMICS: THE DEADLINE MEETS THE BOTTOM LINE   177

CASES

CHAPTER IX
PICTURE THIS: THE ETHICS OF PHOTO AND VIDEO JOURNALISM   203

CASES

CHAPTER X
ETHICS IN CYBERSPACE: NEW QUESTIONS AND NEW ROLES   237

CASES

CHAPTER XI
THE ETHICAL DIMENSIONS OF ART AND ENTERTAINMENT   260

CASES

CHAPTER XII
BECOMING A MORAL ADULT   287

FOREWORD

CLIFFORD G. CHRISTIANS
RESEARCH PROFESSOR OF COMMUNICATION
University of Illinois–Urbana

The playful wit and sharp mind of Socrates attracted disciples from all across ancient Greece. They came to learn and debate in what could be translated "his thinkery." By shifting the disputes among Athenians over earth, air, fire, and water to human virtue, Socrates gave Western philosophy and ethics a new intellectual center (Cassier 1944).

But sometimes his relentless arguments would go nowhere. On one occasion, he sparred with the philosopher Hippias about the difference between truth and falsehood. Hippias was worn into submission, but retorted at the end, "I cannot agree with you, Socrates." And then the master concluded: "Nor I with myself, Hippias. . . . I go astray, up and down, and never hold the same opinion." Socrates admitted to being so clever that he had befuddled himself. No wonder he was a favorite target of the comic poets. I. F. Stone likens this wizardry to "whales of the intellect flailing about in deep seas" (Stone 1988).

With his young friend Meno, Socrates argued whether virtue is teachable. Meno was eager to learn more, after "holding forth often on the subject in front of large audiences." But he complained, "You are exercising magic and witchcraft upon me and positively laying me under your spell until I am just a mass of helplessness. . . . You are exactly like the flat stingray that one meets in the sea. Whenever anyone comes into contact with it, it numbs him, and that is the sort of thing you seem to be doing to me now. My mind and my lips are literally numb."

Philosophy is not a semantic game, though sometimes its idiosyncracies feed that response into the popular mind. *Media Ethics: Issues and Cases* does not debunk philosophy as the excess of sovereign reason. The authors of this book will not encourage those who ridicule philosophy as cunning rhetoric. The issue at stake here is actually a somewhat different problem—the Cartesian model of philosophizing.

The founder of modern philosophy, René Descartes, preferred to work in solitude. Paris was whirling in the early seventeenth century, but for two years even Descartes's friends could not find him as he squirreled himself away studying mathematics. One can even guess the motto above his desk: "Happy is he who lives in seclusion." Imagine the conditions under which he wrote *Meditations II*. The Thirty Years' War in Europe brought social chaos everywhere. The Spanish were ravaging the French provinces and even threatening Paris, but Descartes was shut away in an apartment in Holland. Tranquility for philosophical speculation mattered so much to him that upon hearing Galileo had been condemned by the Church, he retracted parallel arguments of his own on natural science. Pure philosophy as an abstract enterprise needed a cool atmosphere isolated from everyday events.

Descartes's magnificent formulations have always had their detractors, of course. David Hume did not think of philosophy in those terms, believing as he did that sentiment is the foundation of morality. For Søren Kierkegaard, an abstract system of ethics is only paper currency with nothing to back it up. Karl Marx insisted that we change the world and not merely explain it. But no one drew the modern philosophical map more decisively than Descartes, and his mode of rigid inquiry has generally defined the field's parameters.

This book adopts the historical perspective suggested by Stephen Toulmin:

> The philosophy whose legitimacy the critics challenge is always the seventeenth century tradition founded primarily upon René Descartes. . . . [The] arguments are directed to one particular style of philosophizing—a theory-centered style which poses philosophical problems, and frames solutions to them, in timeless and universal terms. From 1650, this particular style was taken as defining the very agenda of philosophy (1988, 338).

The seventeenth-century philosophers set aside the particular, the timely, the local, and the oral. And that development left untouched nearly half of the philosophical agenda.

> Indeed, it is those neglected topics—what I here call "practical philosophy"—that are showing fresh signs of life today, at the very time when the more familiar "theory-centered" half of the subject is languishing (Toulmin 1988, 338).

This book collaborates in demolishing the barrier of three centuries between pure and applied philosophy; it joins in reentering practical concerns as the legitimate domain of philosophy itself. For Toulmin, the primary focus of ethics has moved from the study to the bedside, to criminal courts, engineering labs, the newsroom, factories, and ethnic street corners. Moral philosophers are not being asked to hand over their duties to technical experts in today's institutions, but rather to fashion their agendas within the conditions of contemporary struggle.

All humans have a theoretical capacity. Critical thinking, the reflective dimension, is our common property. And this book nurtures that reflection in communication classrooms and by extension into centers of media practice. If the mind is like a muscle, this volume provides a regimen of exercises for strengthening its powers of systematic reflection and moral discernment. It does not permit those aimless arguments that result in quandary ethics. Instead it operates in the finest traditions of practical philosophy, anchoring the debates in real-life conundrums but pushing the discussion toward substantive issues and integrating appropriate theory into the decision-making process. It seeks to empower students to do ethics themselves, under the old adage that teaching someone to fish lasts a lifetime, and providing fish only saves the day.

Media Ethics: Issues and Cases arrives on the scene at a strategic time in higher education. Since the late nineteenth century, ethical questions have been taken from the curriculum as a whole and from the philosophy department. Recovering practical philosophy has involved a revolution during the last decade in which courses in professional ethics have reappeared throughout the curriculum. This book advocates the pervasive method and carries the discussions even further, beyond freestanding courses into communication classrooms across the board.

In this sense, the book represents a constructive response to the current debates over the mission of higher education. Professional ethics has long been saddled with the dilemma that the university was given responsibility for professional training precisely at the point in its history that it turned away from values to scientific naturalism. Today one sees it as a vast horizontal plain given to technical excellence but barren in enabling students to articulate a philosophy of life. As James Carey concludes,

> Higher education has not been performing well of late and, like most American institutions, is suffering from a confusion of purpose, an excess of ambition that borders on hubris, and an appetite for money that is truly alarming (1989, 48).

The broadside critiques leveled in Thorstein Veblen's *The Higher Learning in America* (1918) and Upton Sinclair's *The Goose Step* (1922) are now too blatantly obvious to ignore.

But *Media Ethics: Issues and Cases* does not merely demand a better general education or a recommitment to values; it strengthens the communications curriculum by equipping thoughtful students with a more enlightened moral awareness. Since Confucius we have understood that lighting a candle is better than cursing the darkness, or, in Mother Teresa's version, we feed the world one mouth at a time.

PREFACE

As you glance through this book, you will notice its features—text, illustrations, cases, photos—represent choices the authors have made. I think it's as important to point out what's missing as what's there, and why. I'll begin with what's been left out and conclude with what you'll find in the text.

First, you'll find no ethics codes in the book. Several media organizations have codes that are well thought out. Some media ethics texts include them. However, we agree with Anthony Insolia of *Newsday* when he says, "Rules and guidelines, unfortunately, cover only the pat situations," and with Arnold Rosenfeld, of the *Dayton Daily News and Journal–Herald* when he says, "The decisions straight out of the book are easy. It is unfortunately the 2-to 3 percent for which there are no book rules that we earn our pay—and reputations."

Second, you'll find no media bashing in this book. There's enough of that already, and besides, it's too easy to do. This book is not designed to indict the media; it's designed to train its future employees. If we dwell on ethical lapses from the past, it is only to learn from them what we can do to prevent similar occurrences in the future.

Third, you'll find no conclusions in this book—neither at the end of the book nor after each case. No one has yet written the conclusive chapter to the ethical dilemmas of the media, and I don't suspect that we will be the first.

What, then, is in the book?

First, you'll find a diverse, up-to-date, and classroom-tested compilation of cases in media ethics. Authors from more than thirty institutions and media outlets contributed real-life and hypothetical cases to this text to help students prepare for the ethical situations they will confront in whatever areas of the media they enter. The authors believe case studies are the premiere teaching vehicle for the study of ethics, and this book reflects what we think are the best available.

Second, binding these cases together and providing a philosophical basis from which to approach them constitutes the text. While it intentionally has been kept succinct, the text introduces students to the relevant ethical theory that will help eliminate "quandary ethics," which often results when cases are used as a teaching strategy.

Third, you'll find built-in discussion starters in the questions that follow each case. The questions at the end of the cases were written by the authors of each case, with the instructions that they were to be like concentric circles. The tightest circle—the micro issues—focuses only on the case at hand and the dilemmas it presents. The next circle—middle-range issues—focuses on the problem in its context, and sometimes manipulates the facts slightly to see if the decisions remain the same. The most abstract level—the macro issues—focuses on issues such as truth, equity, responsibility, and loyalty. Properly used, the questions can guide discussion from the particular to the universal in any case in a single class period.

The book may be used either as the main text for a media ethics course or as a supplementary text for ethics modules in courses on newswriting, media and society, advertising and public relations, and photojournalism. The book works well for teachers who like to use the Socratic method in their classes, or as resource material for lecture classes.

Our approach in this text is best illustrated by an anecdote from a class. One student had the last hand up after a particularly heated case study. When I called on her, she asked, "Well, what's the answer?" I was surprised that she asked the question, and I was surprised that I didn't have a ready answer. I joked my way out of the question by asking if she wanted "The Answer" with a capital "a" or a lowercase one. If she asked today, I'd respond differently. I'd tell her that the answer exists within her, but that it won't emerge in any justifiable form without systematic study and frequent wrestling with the issues.

That's what this book is about. The chapters direct you in some systematic way through the philosophy that has explored these questions for centuries. The cases will make you wrestle with that knowledge in scenarios not unlike ones you might encounter while working. Together, they might not enable you to find "The Answer," but they might help you find *your* answer.

For the authors and contributors,

Philip Patterson

ACKNOWLEDGMENTS

The ethical dilemmas that challenge us require a "moral compass" to help us find our way down the winding paths of life. My compass was given to me by my parents at an early age, and it has worked for more than four decades. No one can ask for a better gift than that, and I thank them for their part in placing me where I am today.

No book of this type is a solo effort, and this book is certainly the result of hard work and encouragement by many people. To begin, each of the authors in the text has been a pleasure to work with. Lou Hodges, Cliff Christians, Ralph Barney, Jay Black, Deni Elliott and others listened patiently to the idea in its many stages and offered advice along the way. Over the years I have been privileged to attend workshops on ethics sponsored by the Poynter Institute, the Freedom Forum and the University of Nebraska. To Bob Steele, Ed Lambeth, Steve Kalish, and Robert Audi I owe a debt of gratitude for helping me continue to learn about ethics as I seek to teach my students.

A special thanks goes to the Ethics and Excellence in Journalism Foundation and to McGraw-Hill Higher Education for grants to cover photographs and illustrations in this edition of the text. Thanks to Valerie Raymond for believing in the project enough to give it a fourth edition. Finally, I thank my wife, Linda, and my children, Amy, Andrew and Joshua: I love you all.

p.d.p.

When ethics entrepreneur Michael Josephson opens his public speeches, he asks audience members to think of the most ethical people they know. Those people set ethical standards for others, by who they are and by what they inspire. It's fair for readers of this book to know who's on my list.

First, my mother, whose sense of human connection and compassion has been only incompletely copied by her daughter. Second, my father, who is the most principled human being I have ever met. Third, my stepmother Carrie, who's managed to love the family she's married into—a feat worthy of far more than a Kantian sense of duty. My dissertation advisor and friend, Jim Davies, affirmed for me the ethical connection between people and politics. My former colleagues at the University of Colorado, Russ Shain, Steve Jones, Sue O'Brien, and Risa Palm, have proved that connection to be a very human one, as have my colleagues at the University of Missouri. They have also been willing to listen—*another ethical activity that too often goes unmentioned.* Barrie Hartman and the staff of the *Boulder Daily Camera* were wonderful reality checks.

I've received intellectual help as well. I've attended a number of conferences designed to teach me about ethics. The Hastings House, Gannett, the Poynter Institute, and the University of Nebraska have done their best to educate me in this field. The people connected with those efforts deserve special mention. Among them, Ed Lambeth, Ted Glasser, Deni Elliott, Cliff Christians, Lou Hodges, Martin Linsky, Roy Peter Clark, Don Fry, Sharon Murphy, Jay Black, Ralph Barney, Steve Kalish, and Robert Audi have helped most profoundly. Many of them you will find mentioned in various contexts on the pages that follow. All of them have a special place in my intellectual psyche.

Two sets of acknowledgments remain.

For the past 20 years, my students at the state universities of Missouri and Colorado have taught me much more about ethics than I have taught them. They have suffered through portions of this manuscript with me. Their questions and their insights are evident on every page of this book.

Then there are Miranda and David—my daughter and my spouse. For the smiles, the hugs, the reading of first drafts, the talking, the listening, the suggestions, the lecture about using "skin" names, the films, and all of the rest that being a family means. Love and thanks. I could not have done this without you.

l.c.w.

CHAPTER I

An Introduction to Ethical Decision Making

By the end of this chapter, you should be able to:

- **recognize the need for professional ethics in journalism.**
- **work through a model of ethical decision making.**
- **identify the five philosophical principles applicable to mass communication situations.**

Making Ethical Decisions

Few people must make ethical decisions in public. Though all professionals make occasional ethical mistakes, only journalists have the courage or misfortune to display them to the public. And when those ethical decisions are faulty, public reaction is swift and critical.

Attempting to gain public acceptance or prevent public outcry isn't the only reason for advocating ethical professional practice—and it's not a very profound one at that. The most compelling reason for making ethical choices, other than internal personal satisfaction, is what ethical behavior can contribute to the profession. Ethical journalism is better journalism. Not only is it journalism that sustains reader confidence, an important consideration in these days of waning media credibility, but ethical journalism also sets a standard by digging deeper, including necessary context, and providing a variety of sources without undue regard to any particular set of special interests, including the journalist's own.

Too many books insist that ethics can't be taught. It's situational, they say—every message is unique, leaving no real way to learn ethics other than by daily life. This analysis is partially correct. Most of us, outside of church or parental teachings, have learned ethics by the choices we've made or seen others make.

Ethics, it is argued, is something you have, not something you do. But, while it's true that reading about ethics is no guarantee you will perform your job ethically, thinking about ethics is a skill anyone can acquire. It first requires some background about the study of ethics, which you will be introduced to in this chapter. Then you should learn a decision-making model that allows you to make ethical choices systematically. The model we've adopted was developed by philosopher Sissela Bok. She has written about the ethical choices many professionals, among them lawyers, doctors and journalists, have to make.

While each facet of mass communication has its unique ethical quandaries, thinking about ethics is the same, whether you make your living writing advertising copy or obituaries. Each day at work, journalists make ethical choices, and some days those choices will have an influence far beyond a single broadcast or one newspaper's circulation area. Thinking about ethics won't make many of those choices easier, but, with practice, your ethical decision making can become more consistent. Ethics will then become not something you have, but something you do. A consistently ethical approach to your work as a reporter, photographer, or copywriter in whatever field of mass media you enter can improve that work as well.

Contemporary professional ethics revolves around these questions:

• What duties do I have, and to whom do I owe them?
• What values are reflected by the duties I've assumed?

Ethics takes us out of the world of "This is the way I do it" or "This is the way it's always been done" into the realm of "This is what I should do" or "This is the action that can be rationally justified." Ethics in this sense is "ought talk." The dual questions of duty and values can be answered a number of ways as long as they are consistent with each other. For example, if a journalist sees her primary duty as that of informing the public, she will place a high value on truth telling, tenacity in the pursuit of a story, etc. If a public relations practitioner sees his duty as promoting a cause, his choices would change accordingly.

It is important here to distinguish between *ethics,* which is a rational process founded on certain agreed-on principles, and *morals,* which are in the realm of religion. For example, the Ten Commandments are a moral system in the Judeo–Christian tradition, and Jewish scholars have expanded this study of the laws throughout the Bible's Old Testament into the Talmud, a 1,400-page religious volume. The Buddhist Eightfold Path provides a similar moral framework.

But moral systems are not synonymous with ethics. *Ethics begins when elements within a moral system conflict.* Ethics is less about the conflict between right and wrong than it is about the conflict between equally compelling (or equally unattractive) values and the choices that must be made between them.

Immanuel Kant, the most influential philosopher of the eighteenth century, described this famous ethical dilemma: What should you do when a man carrying a gun arrives at your front door, asking the whereabouts of a second man (who is hiding in your closet) because he wants to kill him? Do you lie, or do you tell the truth? The Judeo–Christian moral system says that both killing and lying are wrong. Yet, you are being asked to make a choice between the two, and Kant's question is a surprising and perplexing one.

When elements within a moral system conflict, ethical principles can help you make tough choices. We'll review several ethical principles briefly after describing how one philosopher, Sissela Bok, says working professionals can learn to make good ethical decisions.

A Word About Ethics

The concept of ethics comes from the Greeks, who divided the philosophical world into three parts. *Aesthetics* was the study of the beautiful and how a person could analyze beauty without relying only on subjective evaluations. *Epistemology* was the study of knowing, debates about what constitutes learning and what is knowable to the human mind. *Ethics* was the study of what is good, both for the individual and for society. The Greeks were concerned with the individual virtues of courage, justice, temperance, and wisdom, as well as with societal virtues, such as freedom.

Two thousand years later, ethics has come to mean learning to make rational choices between what is good and bad, what is morally justifiable action and what is not. Ethics also means distinguishing among choices, all of which may be morally justifiable, but some more so than others. Rationality is the key word here, for the Greeks believed, and modern philosophers affirm, that people should be able to explain their ethical decisions to others. That ability to explain ethical choices is an important one for journalists, who, in the course of reporting a single story, may have to make separate ethical decisions when dealing with sources, colleagues and, ultimately, the public. When an angry viewer telephones to ask why you broadcast the name of a rape victim, "It seemed like the right thing to do at the time" becomes a personally embarrassing and professionally unsatisfactory explanation.

Bok's Model

Bok's ethical decision-making framework was introduced in her book, *Lying: Moral Choice in Public and Private Life.* Bok's model is based on two premises: that we must have empathy for the people involved in ethical decisions and that maintaining social trust is a fundamental goal. With this in mind, Bok says any ethical question should be analyzed in three steps.

First, consult your own conscience about the "rightness" of an action. *How do you feel about the action?*

Second, seek expert advice for alternatives to the act creating the ethical problem. Experts, by the way, can be those both living or dead—a producer or copywriter you trust or a philosopher you admire. *Is there another way to achieve the same goal that will not raise ethical issues?*

Third, if possible, conduct a public discussion with the parties involved in the dispute. These include those who are directly involved, i.e., the reporter or the source, and those indirectly involved, i.e., a reader or a source. If they cannot be gathered, conduct the conversation hypothetically. The goal of this conversation is to discover *How will my action affect others?*

Let's see how Bok's model works on the following sample scenario. In the section after the case, follow the three steps Bok recommends and decide if you would run the story.

HOW MUCH NEWS IS FIT TO PRINT?   In your community, one of the major charities is the United Way. The annual fund-raising drive will begin in less than two weeks. However, at a late-night meeting of the board of directors at which no reporter is present, the executive director resigns. Though the agency is not covered by the Open Meetings Act, you are able to learn most of what went on from a source on the board.

According to her, the executive director had taken pay from the agency by submitting a falsified time sheet while he was actually away at a funeral of a college roommate. The United Way board investigated the absence and asked for his resignation, citing the lying about the absence as the reason, though most agreed that they would have given him paid leave had he asked.

The United Way wants to issue a short statement, praising the work of the executive director while regretfully accepting his resignation. The executive director will also issue a short statement citing other opportunities as his reason for leaving. You are assigned the story by an editor who does not know about the additional information you have obtained but tells you to "see if there's any more to it (the resignation) than they're telling."

You call your source on the board and she asks you, as a friend, to withhold the damaging information because it will hinder the United Way's annual fund-raising effort that is just underway and jeopardize services to needy people in the community for years to come because faith in the United Way will be destroyed. You confront the executive director. He says, if you run the story you will ruin his chances of a future career.

What do you do?

The Analysis

Bok's first step requires you to *consult your conscience.* When you do, you realize you have a problem. Your journalistic responsibility is to tell the truth, and that means providing readers with all the facts you discover. You also have a larger responsibility not to harm your community, and printing the complete story about the United Way director's actions might well cause at least some short-term harm. Clearly, your conscience is of two minds about the issue.

You move to the second step: *alternatives.* Do you simply run the resignation release, figuring that the person can do no further harm to the community and therefore should be left alone? Do you run the whole story but buttress it with board members' quotes that such an action couldn't happen again, figuring that you have restored public trust in the agency? Do you sit on the story until after the fund-raising drive and risk the loss of trust from readers if the story circulates around town as a rumor? Again, there do seem to be alternatives, but they are not without some cost.

In the third step of Bok's model, you will attempt to *hold a public ethical dialogue* with all of the parties involved. Most likely you won't ask the executive director, the story's source, average readers of the newspaper, a United Way donor, and your editor into the newsroom for a lengthy chat about the issues involved when you are on deadline. Instead you can conduct an imaginary discussion among the parties involved. Such a discussion might go like this:

Executive Director: "I think my resignation is sufficient penalty for any mistake I might have made, and your article will jeopardize my ability to find another job. It's really hurting my wife and kids, and they've done nothing wrong."

Reporter: "But shouldn't you have thought about that *before* you decided to falsify the time sheet? This is a good story, and I think the public should know what the people who are handling their donations are like."

Reader 1: "Wait a minute. I am the public, and I'm tired of all of this bad news your paper focuses on. This man has done nothing but good in the community, and I can't see where any money that belonged to the poor went into his pocket. Why can't we see some good news for a change?"

Reader 2: "I disagree. I buy the paper precisely because it does this kind of reporting. It's stories like this that keep the government, the charities, and everyone else on their toes."

Publisher: "You mean like a watchdog function."

Reader 2: "Exactly. And if it bothers you, don't read it."

Publisher: "I don't really like to hurt people with the power that we have, but if we don't print stories like this, and the community later finds out that we withheld the news, our credibility is ruined, and we're out of business." [To source] "Did you request that the information be off the record?"

Source: "No. But I never thought you'd use it in your story."

Reporter: "I'm a reporter. I report what I hear for a living. What did you think I would do with it? To use the same argument he used a minute ago, it's stories like these that allow me to support my family."

Executive Director: "So it's your career or mine, is that what you're saying? Look, no charges have been filed here, but if your story runs, I look like a criminal. Is that fair?"

Publisher: "And if it doesn't run, we don't keep our promise to the community. Is that fair?"

Needy Mother: "Fair? You want to talk fair? Do you suffer if the donations go down? No, I do. This is just another story to you. It's the difference in me and my family getting by."

The conversation could continue, and other points of view could be voiced. Your imaginary conversations could be more or less elaborate than the one above, but out of this discussion it should be possible to rationally support an ethical choice.

There are two cautions in using Bok's model for ethical decision making. First, it is important to go through all three steps before making a final choice. Most of us make ethical choices prematurely, after we've consulted only our consciences, an error Bok says results in a lot of flabby moral thinking.

Second, while you will not be endowed with any clairvoyant powers to anticipate your ethical problems, the ethical dialogue outlined in the third step is best when conducted in advance of the event, not in the heat of writing a story. For instance, an advertising copywriter might conduct such a discussion about whether advertising copy can ethically withhold disclaimers about potential harm from a product. A reporter ght conduct such a discussion well in advance of the time he is actually asked to ithhold an embarrassing name or fact from a story. Since it is likely that such dilem-.nas will arise in your chosen profession (the illustration above is based on what happened to one of the authors the first day on the job), your answer will be more readily available and more logical if you hold such discussions either with trusted colleagues in a casual atmosphere or by yourself; well in advance of the problem.

Bok's model forces you to consider alternatives. It's in the pursuit of these alternatives that journalistic technique improves.

Guidelines for Making Ethical Decisions

Since the days of ancient Greece, philosophers have tried to draft a series of rules or guidelines governing how to make ethical choices. Obviously, in most ethical dilemmas such as the one above, you will need principles to help you determine what to do amid conflicting voices. While there are a number that work well, we will review five.

Aristotle's Golden Mean

Aristotle, teaching in the fourth century B.C., believed that happiness—which some scholars translate as "flourishing"—was the ultimate human good. By flourishing, Aristotle meant to exercise "practical reason" in the conduct of any particular activity through the setting of high standards.

Aristotle believed that practical reason was exercised by individuals. The *phrenemos,* or person of practical wisdom, was that human being who demonstrated ethical excellence through daily activity. For Aristotle, the highest virtue was citizenship, and the highest form of citizenship was exemplified by the statesman, a politician who exercised so much practical wisdom in his daily activity that he elevated craft to art. In contemporary terms, we might think of a *phrenemos* as a person who excels at one of a variety of activities—flautist Jean Pierre Rampal, poet Maya Angelou, filmmakers George Lucas and Steven Spielberg. They are people who flourish in their professional performance, extending our own vision of what is possible.

This notion of flourishing led Aristotle to assert that people and their acts, not particular sets of rules, are the moral basis of activity. His ethical system resulted in the creation of what is now called *virtue ethics.* Virtue ethics flows both from the nature of the act itself and the moral character of the person who acts. In the Aristotelian sense, the way to behave ethically is that (1) you must know (through the exercise of practical reason) what you are doing; (2) you must select the act for its own sake—in order to flourish; and (3) the act itself must spring from a firm and unchanging character.

It is not stretching Aristotle's framework to assert that one way to learn ethics is to select heroes and to try to model your individual acts and ultimately your professional character on what you believe they would do. An Aristotelian might well consult this hero as an expert when making an ethical choice. Asking what my hero would do in a particular situation is not necessarily a poor form of ethical analysis. The trick, however, is to select your heroes carefully and still think for yourself rather than merely copy behavior you have previously seen.

Figure 1.1
Aristotle's Golden Mean

Unacceptable behaviors	Acceptable behaviors	Unacceptable behaviors
Cowardice	Courage	Foolhardiness

Aristotle's philosophy is often reduced to the somewhat simplistic *"golden mean": Virtue lies at the mean between two extremes.* Courage, for example, is a mean between foolhardiness on one hand and cowardice on the other. But to determine that mean for yourself, you have to exercise practical wisdom, act according to high standards, and act in accordance with firm and continuing character traits. *In reality, therefore, the middle ground of a virtue is not a single point on a line that is the same for every individual.* It is instead a range of behaviors that varies individually, while avoiding the undesirable extremes, as shown in Figure 1.1.

Continuing with the example of courage, this principle can be illustrated by considering two witnesses to a potential drowning. If one onlooker is a poor swimmer yet a fast runner, then it would be foolhardy for him to attempt to jump into the water and attempt a rescue, just as it would be cowardly for him to do nothing. For him, the courageous thing might be to run for help. If, on the other hand, the second onlooker is a good swimmer, it would not be foolhardy for her to attempt a rescue; in fact, it would be cowardly for her not to jump into the water. In each instance, both onlookers have done the courageous act, yet in radically different ways.

Seeking the golden mean implies that individual acts are not disconnected from one another, but rather that they form a whole that a person of good character should aspire to. In this age of questions about character, Aristotle's concept of virtue ethics has been rediscovered by a variety of professions.

Kant's Categorical Imperative

Immanuel Kant's *categorical imperative* asserts that an individual should act on the premise that the choices one makes for oneself could become universal law. Furthermore, he states that you should act so that you treat humanity always as an end and never as a means only. Kant called these two maxims "categorical" imperatives, meaning that their demands were not subject to situational factors. Many readers will recognize the similarity between Kant's categorical imperative and the Bible's Golden Rule: Do unto others as you would have others do unto you. The two are quite similar in their focus on duty.

Kant's ethical theory is based on the notion that it is the act itself, rather than the person who acts, in which moral force resides. This theory of ethics is unlike Aristotle's in that it moves the notion of what is ethical from the actor to the act itself. This does not mean that Kant did not believe in moral character, but rather that people could act morally from a sense of duty even though their character might incline them to act otherwise.

For Kant, an action was morally justified only if it was performed from duty, and in Kant's moral universe there were two sorts of duties. The strict duties were generally negative: not to murder, not to break promises, not to lie. The meritorious duties were more positive: to aid others, to develop one's talents, to show gratitude. Kant spent very little time defining these notions, but philosophers have generally asserted that the strict duties (i.e., not to harm) are somewhat more morally mandatory than the meritorious duties (e.g., to render aid).

To some, Kant's ethical reasoning indicates that as long as you perform the right act based on what the categorical imperative and duty demand, the consequences of that act are not important. We prefer a somewhat less austere reading of Kant. While Kant's view is that the moral worth of an action does not depend on its consequences, those consequences are not irrelevant. For example, a surgeon may show moral virtue in attempting to save a patient through an experimental procedure, but the decision about whether to undertake that procedure requires taking into account the probability of a cure. This framing of Kantian principles allows us to learn from our mistakes.

The test of a moral act, according to Kant, is its universality—whether it can be applied to everyone. For instance, Kant would insist that the ethical person drive at a speed and in a manner that would be appropriate for everyone else on the same highway. Under Kant's categorical imperative, journalists can claim few special privileges, such as the right to lie or the right to invade privacy in order to get a story. Kant's view, if taken seriously, reminds you of what you give up—truth, privacy, etc.—when you make certain ethical decisions.

TABLE 1.1 The Shifting Focus of Ethics from Aristotle to Mill

PHILOSOPHER	KNOWN FOR	POPULARLY KNOWN AS	EMPHASIZED
Aristotle	Golden mean	Virtue lies between extremes.	The actor
Kant	Categorical imperative	Act so your choices could be universal law; treat humanity as an end, never as a means only.	The action
Mill	Utility principle	An act's rightness is determined by its contribution to a desirable end.	The outcome

Utilitarianism

The original articulation of *utilitarianism* by Englishmen Jeremy Bentham and later John Stuart Mill in the nineteenth century introduced what was then a novel notion into ethics discussions: *The consequences of actions are important in deciding whether they are ethical.* In the utilitarian view, it may be considered ethical to harm one person for the benefit of the larger group. This approach, for example, is the ethical justification for investigative reporting, the results of which may harm individuals even as they are printed or broadcast in the hope of providing a greater societal good.

With its focus on the consequences of an action, utilitarianism completes a cycle begun with Aristotle (see Table 1.1). Aristotle, in developing the golden mean, focused on the *actor.* Kant, in his categorical imperative, focused on the *action,* while Mill, in his utilitarian philosophy, focused on the *outcome.*

Utilitarianism has been condensed to the ethical philosophy of the greatest good for the greatest number. While this pithy phrase is a very rough-and-ready characterization of utilitarian theory, it also has led to an overly mechanistic application of the principle: Just tally up the amount of good and subtract the amount of harm. If the remaining number is positive, the act is ethical. However, when properly applied, utilitarianism is not mechanical.

In order to do justice to utilitarian theory, it must be understood within a historical context. Mill wrote during the earliest years of the Enlightenment, when the principle of democracy was fresh and untried, and when the thought that the average person should be able to speak his mind to those in power was novel. Utilitarianism as Mill conceived of it was a profoundly social ethic; Mill was among the first to acknowledge that the good of an entire society had a place in ethical reasoning.

Mill was what philosophers call a *valuational hedonist.* He argued that pleasure—and the absence of pain—were the only intrinsic moral ends. Mill further asserted that an act was right in the proportion in which it contributed to the general happiness, wrong in the proportion in which it contributed to general unhappiness or pain. Utilitarianism can be subtle and complex. Mill acknowledged that the same act can make some happy but cause others pain. Mill insisted that both sets of consequences be valued simultaneously, a precarious activity but one that forces discussion of competing stakeholder claims.

Utilitarianism can be applied in both the specific and the general, what some philosophers have referred to as "act utilitarianism" as opposed to "rule utilitarianism."

For instance, one way of evaluating the ethical impact of investigative reporting is through the application of *act utilitarianism.* A producer might reason that an investigative report, while it would hurt the subject of the investigation, might further the general welfare. Crooks and cheats could be exposed, general societal problems aired. When the methods of obtaining information are ethical, investigative journalism can be justified because it contributes more to human happiness than it extracts in the pain it causes some individuals.

Rule utilitarianism, on the other hand, might be applied as follows. Take the assertion sometimes made that advertising itself is unethical. The rule utilitarian would note that in contemporary American culture advertising provides needed information about a variety of products and services. It is often entertaining, and, it supports the media we enjoy. Of course, advertising sometimes can be in poor taste, it can be intrusive, and it can sometimes provide false or misleading information. When balancing the societal good against the societal harm, the rule utilitarian might well conclude that while the practice of advertising is ethical, certain forms of the activity—advertising products to children or advertising certain substances such as alcohol—should be regulated. Utilitarian theory does allow the sort of ethical reasoning that approves of particular activities while rejecting specific acts.

In utilitarian theory, no one's happiness is any more valuable than anyone else's—quantity and quality being equal. In democratic societies, this is a particularly important concept because it meshes well with certain social and political goals. In actual application, utilitarianism uniformly applied has a way of puncturing self-interest, although critics have argued that, when badly applied, it can actually promote selfishness.

Utilitarianism also suggests that moral questions are objective, empirical, and even in some sense scientific. Utilitarianism promotes a universal ethical standard that each rational person can determine. However, utilitarianism is among the most criticized of philosophical principles because it is so difficult to accurately anticipate all the ramifications of a particular act. Different philosophers also have disputed how one calculates the good, rendering any utilitarian calculus fundamentally error prone.

While we recommend utilitarianism as a theory, we do caution you against exclusive reliance on it. Taken to extremes, the act of calculating the good can lead to ethical gridlock, with each group of stakeholders having seemingly equally strong claims with little way to choose among them. Sloppily done, utilitarianism may bias you toward short-term benefit. And a view to the short term, in an ethical sense, can often be shortsighted.

Pluralistic Theory of Value

Modern philosopher William David Ross (1930) bases his ethical theory on the belief that there is often more than one ethical value simultaneously "competing" for preeminence in our ethical decision making. In this, he differs from Kant or Mill, who proposed only one ultimate value. To Ross these competing ethical claims, which he calls duties, are equal, providing the circumstances of the particular moral choice are equal. Further, these duties do not gain their moral weight from their consequences, but from the highly personal nature of duty.

Ross proposed six types of duties:

1. Those duties that rest on previous acts of my own: duties of *fidelity*, based on my implicit or explicit promise, and duties of *reparation*, arising from a previous wrongful act.
2. Those duties of *gratitude* that rest on previous acts of others.
3. Those duties of *justice* that arise from the necessity to ensure the equitable and meritorious distribution of pleasure or happiness.
4. Those duties of *beneficence* that rest on the fact that there are others in the world whose lot we can better.
5. Those duties of *self-improvement* that rest on the fact that we can improve our own condition.
6. One negative duty: the duty of *not injuring others.*

We would recommend two additional duties that may be implied by Ross's list but are not specifically stated:

7. The duty to tell the truth, *veracity* (which may be implied by fidelity).
8. The duty to *nurture,* to help others achieve some measure of self-worth and achievement.

Ross's typology of duties works well for professionals who often must balance competing roles. It also brings to ethical reasoning some affirmative notions of the primacy of community and relationships as a way to balance the largely rights-based traditions of much Western philosophical theory.

Ross's concept of multiple duties allows the ethical decision maker to appreciate and consider important aspects of a situation without losing the value of following some rules. Like Kant, Ross divided his duties into two kinds. *Prima facie duties* are those duties that seem to be right because of the nature of the act itself. *Duty proper* are those duties that are paramount given specific circumstances. Arriving at your duty proper from among the prima facie duties requires that you consider what ethicists call the *morally relevant differences.*

Let's take an example using one of Ross's prima facie duties: keeping promises. In your job as a reporter, you have made an appointment with the mayor to discuss a year-end feature on your community. On your way to City Hall, you drive by a serious auto accident and see a young child wandering, dazed, along the road. If you stop to help you will certainly be late for your appointment and may have to cancel altogether. You have broken a promise.

But is that act ethical?

Ross would probably say yes because the specific aspects of the situation had a bearing on the fulfillment of a prima facie duty. You exercised discernment. You knew that your commitment to the mayor was a relatively minor sort of promise. Your news organization will not be hurt by postponing the interview, and your act allowed ou to fulfill the prima facie duties of beneficence, avoiding harm, and nurturing. Had the interview been more important, or the wreck less severe, you could have analyzed the situation differently. Ross's pluralistic theory of values may be more difficult to apply than a system of absolute rules, but it reflects the way we make ethical choices.

Ross's concept of multiple duties "helps to explain why we feel uneasy about breaking a promise even when we are justified in doing so. Our uneasiness comes from the fact that we have broken a prima facie duty even as we fulfilled another. It helps explain why even the good consequences that might come from a failure to tell the truth or keep a promise do not always seem to us to justify the lie or breach of confidence" (Lebacqz 1985, 27).

Communitarianism

Classical ethical theory places its dominant intellectual emphasis on the individual and individual acts by emphasizing concepts such as character, choice, liberty and duty.

But contemporary politics points out the intellectual weakness in this approach. Consider the environment. On many environmental questions, it is possible for people to make appropriate individual decisions—today I drive my car—which taken together promote environmental degradation. My individual decision to drive my car doesn't matter very much; but when individual decisions are aggregated, the impact is profound. Furthermore, this environmental impact has consequences not for a single generation but for geologic time. Individual human beings cannot opt out of participation through daily living in the physical environment—unless they decide to live on the moon. While classical ethical theory acknowledges such problems, it provides little guidance for determining individual action or in understanding how individual actions fit within a larger whole.

Communitarianism, which has its roots in political theory, seeks to provide ethical guidance when confronting the sort of society-wide issues that mark current political and business activity.

Communitarianism spotlights society understood holistically and dynamically. Communitarianism returns to Aristotle's concept of the "polis"—or community—and invests it with moral weight. People begin their lives, at least in a biological sense, as members of a two-person community. Communitarian philosophy extends this biological beginning to a philosophical worldview. "In communitarianism, persons have certain inescapable claims on one another that cannot be renounced except at the cost of their humanity" (Christians et al. 1995, 14). In modern parlance, communitarians assert that when issues are political and social, community trumps individuals but does not trample them.

Communitarianism focuses on the outcome of individual ethical decisions, understood not as disconnected choices but analyzed as the impact of the sum of the choices on society. "Nurturing communitarian citizenship entails, at a minimum, a journalism committed to justice, covenant and empowerment. Authentic communities are marked by justice; in strong democracies, courageous talk is mobilized into action. . . . In normative communities, citizens are empowered for social transformation, not merely freed from external contraints." (Christians et al. 1995, 14).

Communitarianism asserts that social justice is the predominant moral value. While communitarians recognize the value of process, they are just as concerned with outcomes. They formally acknowledge one of history's more difficult lessons, that "good" process—for example, democratic elections or the writing of constitutions—can produce "bad" outcomes—for example, the 1933 takeover of Germany by a minority party headed by Hitler or the inclusion in the original U.S. Constitution of the three-fifths clause (African-Americans were equal to three-fifths of a single European, Caucasian colonist for purposes of population count to determine the number of representatives each state would have in the U.S. Congress). Communitarians measure individual acts against the normative standard of their impact in creating a more just society.

Communitarian thinking allows ethical discussion to include values such as altruism and benevolence on an equal footing with more traditional questions such as truth telling and loyalty. Indeed, empirical testing of the concept of community through game theory has demonstrated that cooperation, one of the foundation stones of community, provides a robust (in other words, long-lived) rejoinder to competition (Axelrod 1984). Cooperation is particularly powerful when something called the "shadow of the future" looms sufficiently large. The "shadow of the future" means that people understand they will encounter the outcome of their decisions, in the form of their impact on others, in readily foreseeable time.

Communitarian philosophy lacks a succinct summation of its general propositions. Amitai Etzioni, one of the movement's leaders, suggests that communitarianism emphasizes responsibilities "to the conditions and elements we all share, to the community." Political theorist Michael Sandel arranges communitarianism as both an extension of and a counterpoint to traditional political liberalism. Like traditional political liberalism—as expressed in this book by the philosophy of John Rawls and, to a lesser extent, the utilitarians—a communitarian community would be manifest in the aims and values of its individual participants. But it would differ from a traditional community in the sense that community members would include, as part of their understanding of self, their membership in the community. "For them, community describes not just what they have as fellow citizens but also what they are, not as a relationship they choose (as in a voluntary association) but an attachment they discover, not merely an attribute but as a constituent of their identity" (Sandel 1982, 150). Communitarian community resembles family more than it resembles town.

We believe that communitarianism is most helpful in discussing ethical issues that revolve around the journalistic role.

Viewed this way, journalism cannot separate itself from the political and economic system of which it is a part. Communitarian thinking makes it possible to ask whether current practice (for example, a traditional definition of news) provides a good mechanism for a community to discover itself, learn about itself, and ultimately transform itself into a more just and cohesive entity. Communitarian reasoning allows journalists to understand their institutional role and to evaluate their performance against shared societal values. It mutes the competition among journalistic organizations while amplifying the collective effect that journalists and their organizations have on society and culture. Communitarian thinking can provide journalists with an effective justification for sometimes placing family before work, for including mobilizing information in a story about the local rape crisis center, or for inviting viewers and readers to help determine the sort of political stories in which they are most interested and then providing ample coverage of them.

Because communitarianism is a philosophy of ideals, it is difficult to find concrete journalistic examples of the theory in action. Many writers have linked communitarian philosophy with the civic journalism movement. But, we believe perhaps the best example of communitarianism at work is in the ethic of the Internet. That ethic, as it has evolved since about 1990, emphasizes equality of access, cooperation and sharing (particularly of software known as freeware), global communication, decentralized control and a fierce devotion to communication as an activity between equals in which all have a chance to participate and benefit. While it remains to be seen whether the cooperative community of electrons will survive the assault of media conglomerates and government supervision, the Internet itself is a working example of a community that comes before—is axiologically and ontologically prior to (Christians et al. 1995, 14)—its individual members.

The "Science" of Ethics

Life in the Twenty-first Century has changed how most people think about issues, such as what constitutes a fact and what does or does not influence moral certainty. We will explore those changes, and the changes they have led to in the lives of mass-communication professionals, in more detail in the next chapter. But for now, it suffices to say that ethical theory, with its apparent uncertainties and contradictions, appears to have taken a back seat to science in much of modern life. Part of the reason people have become so concerned with ethics is that they seek "the answer" to ethical dilemmas in the same way they seek "the answer" in science. In such an endeavor, the vagaries of ethical choice as contrasted with scientific knowledge seem unsatisfactory.

We'd like to offer you a different conceptualization of "the facts" of both science and ethics. Science, and the seeming certainty of scientific knowledge, have undergone vast changes in the past hundred years. After all, before Einstein, most educated people believed that Sir Francis Bacon had accurately and eternally described the basic actions and laws of the physical universe. But Bacon was wrong. Scientific inquiry in the Twentieth Century searchingly explored a variety of physical phenomena, almost always uncovering new relationships, new areas of knowledge, and most importantly, new and expanding areas of ignorance. What modern humanity regarded as the certainty of scientific truth has changed fundamentally in the last hundred years, and humanity has every reason to expect similar changes in this century. Science and certainty are not synonymous, despite our tendency to blur the two.

Contrast these fundamental changes in the scientific worldview with the developments of moral theory. Aristotle's writing, more than two thousand years old and with no fundamental changes, still has much to recommend it to the modern era, although, of course, there will continue to be new interpretations. The same can be said of utilitarianism and of the Kantian approach—both subject to more than a hundred years of critical review. Certainly, new moral thinking has emerged—for example,

John Rawls's work on utilitarian theory (Chapter VI). But such work tends to build on rather than radically alter the moral theorizing that has gone before. This is not to assert that ethical philosophers do not have fundamental debates but rather to suggest that these debates have, in general, tended to deepen and enlarge previous insights rather than to "prove" them incorrect in some epistemological sense.

From this viewpoint, there is a continuity in thinking about ethics that is lacking in the development of scientific thought. Further, thinking about ethics in a global way uncovers some striking areas of agreement. We are aware of no ethical system, for example, that argues that murder is an ethical behavior, or that lying, cheating and stealing are the sorts of activities that human beings ought to engage in on a regular basis. Applying the various ethical theories outlined in this chapter will deepen your understanding of these principles and the complexity of application, but they are unlikely to change your views about the ethical correctness of murder or lying.

When the average person contrasts ethics with science, it is ethics that tends to be viewed as changeable, unsystematic and idiosyncratic. Science has rigor, proof, and some relationship to an external reality. We would like to suggest that such characterizations arise from a short-term view of the history of science and ethics. In our view, ethics as a field has at least as much continuity of thought as developments in science. And while it cannot often be quantified, it has the rigor, the systematic quality, and the relationship to reality that moderns too often characterize as the exclusive domain of scientific thinking.

Suggested Readings

Aristotle. *The Nicomachean ethics.*

Bok, Sissela. 1978. *Lying: Moral choice in public and private life.* New York: Random House.

Christians, Clifford, Kim Rotzoll, and Mark Fackler. 1993. *Good News: Social ethics and the press.* New York: Oxford University Press.

Gert, Bernard. 1988. *Morality: A new justification of the moral rules.* New York: Oxford University Press.

Mill, John Stuart. *On liberty.*

Pojman, L. 1998. Ethical theory: Classical and Contemporary Readings. Belmont, CA,: Wadsworth Publishing Co.

CHAPTER I ESSAY

Cases and Moral Systems

DENI ELLIOTT

University of Montana

Case studies are wonderful vehicles for ethics discussions. Some of their great strengths include helping discussants

1. appreciate the complexity of newsroom decision making;
2. understand the context within which difficult decisions are made;
3. track the consequences of choosing one action over another; and
4. learn both how and when to reconcile and how and when to tolerate divergent points of view.

However, when case studies are misused, these great strengths become their fundamental weaknesses. Case studies are vehicles for an ethics discussion, not its ultimate destination. The purpose of an ethics discussion is to teach discussants how to "do ethics"—that is, to teach them processes by which they can practice and improve their own critical decision-making abilities. Each discussant should, through the use of the case-study vehicle, reach the end point: a reasoned response to the issue at hand.

When the discussion stops short of this point, it is often because the destination has been fogged in by one or more myths of media case discussions:

Myth 1: Every opinion is equally valid.

Not true. The best opinion (conclusion) is the one that is best supported by judicious analysis of fact and theory. In an ethics discussion, it is the one that best addresses the morally relevant factors of the case. An action has morally relevant factors if it is likely to cause some individual to suffer an evil that any rational person would wish to avoid (such as death, disability, pain, loss of freedom or pleasure), or if it is the kind of action that generally causes evil (such as deception, breaking promises, cheating, disobedience of law, or neglect of duty) (see Gert 1988).

Myth 2: Since we can't agree on an answer, there is no right answer.

It's tough to take into account all of the various points of view when working through a case. One way people avoid doing this is to refuse to choose among the different perspectives. But this retreat to fatalistic subjectivism is not necessary. It may be that there are a number of acceptable answers. But there will also be many wrong answers—many approaches that the group can agree would be unacceptable. When discussants begin to despair of ever reaching any agreement on a right answer or answers, it is time to reflect on all of the agreement that exists within the group concerning the actions that would be out of bounds.

Myth 3: It hardly matters if you come up with the "ethical thing to do" since people ultimately act out of their own self-interest anyway.

The point of ethical reflection is to find and deal with those situations when one should not simply do that which benefits oneself. Acting ethically means to refrain from causing unjustified harm, even when prudential concerns must be set aside.

Any institution supported by society, manufacturing firms or media corporations, as well as medical centers, provides some service that merits that support. No matter what the service, practitioners or companies that act only in the short-term interest, for instance to make money, will not last long. Free-market pragmatism, as well as ethics, dictates that it makes little sense to ignore the expectations of consumers and of the society at large.

The guidelines below can serve as a map for an ethics discussion. They are helpful to have when working through unfamiliar terrain toward individual end points. They can also help detour around the myths discussed earlier.

While discussing the case, check to see if these questions are being addressed:

1. What are the morally relevant factors of the case?
   (a) Will the proposed action cause an evil—such as death, disability, pain, loss of freedom or opportunity, or a loss of pleasure—that any rational person would wish to avoid?
   (b) Is the proposed action the sort of action—such as deception, breaking promises, cheating, disobedience of law, or disobedience of professional or role-defined duty—that generally causes evil?
2. If the proposed action is one described above, is a greater evil being prevented or punished?
3. If so, is the actor in a unique position to prevent or punish such an evil, or is that a more appropriate role for some other person or profession?
4. If the actor followed through on the action, would he be allowing himself to be an exception to a rule that he thinks everyone else should follow? If so, then the action is prudent, not moral. One way to test this out is for journalists to ask how they would react if a person in another profession did what they are thinking of doing. Would the journalists applaud the action, or would they write an exposé?
5. If, at this point, the proposed action still seems justified, consider if a rational, uninvolved person would appreciate the reason for causing harm. Are the journalists ready to state, explain and defend the proposed action in a public forum?

CHAPTER II

Information Ethics: A Profession Seeks the Truth

By the end of this chapter, you should be familiar with:

• both the Enlightenment and pragmatic constructions of truth.
• the development and several criticisms of objective news reporting as a
    professional ideal.
• why truth in "getting" the news may be as important as truth in reporting it.
• how to develop a personal list of ethical news values.

Introduction

Each of the traditional professions has laid claims to one of the central tenets of philosophy. Law, ideally, is equated with justice; medicine with the duty to render aid.
Journalism, too, has a lofty ideal: the communication of truth.

But the ideal of truth is problematic. In routine interaction we consider truth a
stable commodity: it doesn't change much for us on a day-to-day basis, nor does it
vary greatly among members of a community. While we are willing to accept some
cultural "lies"—for example, the existence of Santa Claus—we stand ready to con-
demn others—for example, income tax evasion or fraud. Most of the time, we seem
to know what the boundaries are, at least when we deal with one another face to face.

However, the concept of truth has changed throughout human history. At one
level or another, human beings since ancient times have acknowledged that truth may
vary depending on individual points of view. Since Plato's analogy of life as shadows
on the wall of a cave 3,000 years ago, people have grappled with the amorphous nature of truth.

Compounding the modern problem of the shifting nature of truth is the changing
media audience. When a profession accepts the responsibility of printing and broadcasting the truth, facts that are apparent in face-to-face interaction become subject to
different interpretations among geographically and culturally diverse viewers and
readers. Ideas that were once readily accepted are open to debate. The whole concept
of telling the truth becomes not merely a matter of possessing good moral character
but something that requires learning how to recognize truth and how to convey it in
the least distorted manner possible.

A Changing View of Truth

One pre-Socratic Greek tradition viewed truth–*alethea*—as encompassing all that humans remember, singled out through memory from everything that is destined for Lethe, the river of forgetfulness (Bok 1978). Linking truth and remembrance is essential in an oral culture, one that requires information be memorized and repeated so as not to be forgotten. Repeating the message, often in the form of songs or poetry, meant that the accumulated ideas and knowledge were kept alive or true for subsequent generations. Homer's *Iliad* and *Odyssey* or much of the Bible's Old Testament served this function.

This oral notion of truth, as noted in Table 2.1, was gradually discarded once words and ideas were written down. However, it has come to the fore again with the advent of television. Television allows viewers to hear the words of the president rather than wait for those words to be passed down orally or in writing. When we see something on television, we assume that it closely corresponds to reality—that it is in some sense true. The maxim "Seeing is believing" reminds us that truth has somehow become tangled up with pictures and presence. It is an oral concept of truth that has been a dormant form of knowledge for hundreds of years.

While the other ancient Greeks tied truth to human memory, Plato linked truth to human rationality and intellect. In *The Republic,* Plato equated truth with a world of pure form, a world to which human beings had only indirect access. In Plato's vision, there was an ideal notion of a chair—but that ideal chair did not exist in reality. What people thought of as a chair was as similar to the ideal chair as the shadows on the wall of the cave are to objects illuminated by the fire. Truth was knowable only to the human intellect—it could not be touched or verified.

Plato's metaphor has had a profound influence on Western thought. Not only did Plato link truth to rationality, as opposed to human experience, but his work implies that truth is something that can be captured only through the intellect. Platonic truth is implicit within a thing itself; truth defined the "perfect form." Plato's concept of truth separated the notion of something as true from the external world in which that thing existed.

Subsequent centuries and thinkers adhered to Plato's view. Medieval theologians believed truth was revealed only by God or by the Church. The intellectual legacy of the Reformation centered on whether it is possible for the average person to ascertain truth without benefit of a priest or a king. About two hundred years later, Milton suggested that competing notions of the truth should be allowed to coexist, with the ultimate truth eventually emerging (see Table 2.1).

Milton's assertions foreshadowed the philosophy of the Enlightenment, from which modern journalism borrows its notion of truth. The Enlightenment cast truth in secular terms and developed what is now called a "correspondence theory" of truth. The correspondence theory asserts that truth should correspond to some external set of facts or observations. The Enlightenment concept of truth was linked to what human beings could perceive with their senses harnessed through the intellect. Truth acquired substance. It was something that could be perceived, and ultimately perception of truth was something that could be replicated.

TABLE 2.1 A PHILOSOPHY OF TRUTH EMERGES

SOURCE	TRUTH EQUALS
Ancient Greeks	What is memorable and is handed down
Plato	What abides in the world of perfect forms
Medieval	What the king, Church, or God says
Milton	What emerges from the "marketplace of ideas"
Enlightenment	What is verifiable, replicable, universal
Pragmatists	What is filtered through individual perception

This Enlightenment notion of truth has remained with us and is essential to what contemporary scholars refer to as the scientific method. Truth has become increasingly tied to that which is written down, to that which can be empirically verified, to that which can be perceived by the human senses, and to that which does not vary among people or among cultures. It is a truth uniquely suited to the written word, for it links what is written with what is factual, accurate, and important in the most profound of senses.

This Enlightenment view of truth undergirds the journalistic ideal of objectivity. Objectivity has its intellectual roots in the previous three hundred years. While objectivity has many definitions, it may be considered, most simply, a mechanism that allows journalists to divorce fact from opinion. Journalists view objectivity as refusing to allow individual bias to influence what they report or how they cover it. It is a journalism in which all facts and people are regarded as equal and equally worthy of coverage. Culture, an individual sense of mission, and individual and organizational feelings and views do not belong in objective news accounts. An Enlightenment view of truth allowed objectivity to be considered an attainable ideal.

However, philosophy was not the only reason, and some scholars have argued not even the most important reason, that objectivity became a professional standard in the early 1900s. The libertarian press of the Enlightenment was not really a mass press, and it garnered most of its financial support from political advertising and most of its readers through partisan political reporting. As the United States became urban in the late 1800s, publishers realized that to reach this large urban audience; they needed more support from a wider variety of advertisers. To convince potential advertisers that their advertising would be seen and possibly acted upon by a large audience, publishers had to make certain their publications would be read. Partisan publications could not ensure that, for strong views offended potential readers.

What publishers of the day needed was a product that built on an Enlightenment philosophical construction that guaranteed that facts would be facts, no matter who was doing the reading. Opinion would be relegated to specific pages. Both facts and opinion could be wrapped around advertising. Objective news reporting was born (Schudson 1978).

Objectivity came along at an advantageous time for yet another reason. The mass press of the early 1900s was deeply and corruptly involved in yellow journalism. Fabricated stories were common; newspaper wars were close to the real thing. Although many of the specific events of the era (for example, the apocryphal story that William Randolph Hearst began the Spanish-American War so he would have something to photograph) have been exaggerated, the excesses in pursuit of circulation tarnished the profession's image. Objectivity was a good way to clean up journalism's act with a set of standards where seemingly none had existed before. It fit the cultural expectations of the Enlightenment that truth was knowable and ascertainable. And it made sure that readers of news columns would remain unoffended long enough to glance at the ads.

The Enlightenment view of truth also was compatible with democracy and its emphasis on rational government. People who could reason together, who could arrive at some shared "truth" of how their political lives ought to function, could govern themselves. Information was essential to such a form of government, for it allowed citizens to scrutinize government. As long as truth was ascertainable by the rational being, government could function. Under this view, information—written, logical, linear—provided the social glue as well as the grease of such a society. Citizens and government need information in order to continue their rational function. Information, and the notion that it corresponded in some essential way with the truth, carried enormous promise.

Twentieth-century pragmatists—most notably Americans John Dewey, George Herbert Mead, Charles Sanders Pierce, and William James—challenged the Enlightenment view of truth. They held that the perception of truth depended on how it was investigated and on who was doing the investigating. Further, they rejected the notion that there was only one proper method of investigation—i.e., the scientific method. Borrowing from Einstein's insights, pragmatists argued that truth, like matter, was relative.

Specifically, the pragmatists proposed that knowledge and reality were not *fixed by*, but instead were the *result of*, an evolving stream of consciousness and learning. Reality itself varied based on psychological, social, historical, or cultural contexts. Additionally, reality was defined as that which was probable, not as something intrinsic (the Platonic view) or something determined by only one method of observation (the Enlightenment view).

Pragmatism found a comfortable home in the twentieth-century United States. Under pragmatism truth lost much of its universality, but it was in remarkable agreement with the American value of democratic individualism. Soon pragmatism filtered through literature, science, and some professions, such as law.

Pragmatic notions of truth provided a philosophical basis to challenge objectivity. At roughly the same time that the journalistic community was embracing Enlightenment standards of objectivity, the culture itself was adopting more pragmatic notions of truth. That clash fueled criticism of objectivity on both a scholarly and a popular level. Several questions surfaced. If truth is subjective, can it be best obtained and reported by an impassive, objective, and detached reporter? Does such a reporter exist? Is truth a construct that relies on the context of the source, the message, and the receiver?

Postmodern philosophy (see *The Matrix*) has taken these questions to their logical extension, suggesting that the concept of truth is devoid of meaning. Postmodernism asserts that context is literally everything, that meaning cannot exist apart from contextual understanding. This philosophical approach is antithetical to fact-based journalism, but designers and other visual journalists have employed it in everything from layout to typography.

The last thirty years have added yet another level of complexity to the problem: the information explosion. Not only do we as a culture now question the meaning of the terms *fact* and *truth,* we literally cannot sort them all out. Facts and truth come to us quickly from all over the globe. Our ability to attend to these various messages, let alone construct rational meaning from them, is on the verge of being overwhelmed.

In short, the concept of objectivity, which was once equated with printing the truth, has been deeply undermined by both philosophical shift and technological innovation (Christians, Ferré, and Fackler 1992). Telling your readers and viewers the truth has become a complicated business.

> Telling the "truth" therefore is not solely a matter of moral character; it is also a matter of correct appreciation of real situations and of serious reflection upon them. . . .
> Telling the truth, therefore, is something which must be learnt. This will sound very shocking to anyone who thinks that it must all depend on moral character and that if this is blameless the rest is child's play. But the simple fact is that the ethics cannot be detached from reality, and consequently continual progress in learning to appreciate reality is a necessary ingredient in ethical action. (Bok 1978, 302–303)

It is to the issue of learning to appreciate reality that we will now turn. First, we will review some of the scholarly findings about news coverage and what the news does and does not reflect. Then we will ask you to apply these scholarly findings, as well as a question or two, to case studies that deal with the links between news and the truth.

The Matrix: A postmodern examination of truth

"Do you ever have that feeling where you're not sure whether you are awake or still dreaming?"
"Yeah, all the time. . . . It just sounds to me like you might need to unplug, man . . . get some R&R?"

Thus begins Neo's journey down the rabbit hole (like Lewis Carroll's Alice) where reality literally turns inside out on itself. A computer wizard, and unknown genetic mutation, Neo—who is awakened to the possibilities courtesy of Morpheus—literally unplugs himself from the reality of a computer simulation where human beings serve as batteries for artificially intelligent machines that now run the world. The reality that most people know is nothing more than a computer code invented by the artificial intelligence and inserted electronically into billions of human neural systems from infancy onward. Neo, as his name suggests, is the person who has the capacity to crack and overcome the code.

The Matrix set the standard in the latter part of the last century for smart films about the potential of the computers that increasingly power, and in some subtle ways govern, the information age. The film was also stylish; in fact, the long, black trench coats Keanu Reeves and Carrie-Anne Moss wore were eerily predictive of the attire worn by the Columbine High School shooters. The special effects and set design, based as they were on a comic book reality, gave form to one vision of hyper-reality, as did the film's otherworldly and sometimes violent content.

More importantly for our purposes, the film provides an accessible discussion of the postmodern approach to truth.

Postmodernism is a logical outgrowth of pragmatism. Instead of suggesting that truth varies with receiver, or sender, or context, postmodernism suggests that truth—if it exists at all—is unknowable. Those who believe they know the truth, like Neo at the beginning of the film, discover that their "reality" is merely false consciousness, founded on invalid assumptions that shift constantly in a chaotic environment.

Postmodernism rejects such concepts as the correspondence theory of truth, or even the Platonic ideal that truth is knowable only as an intellectual construct. In postmodernism, revealed truth, as medieval scholars understood it, does not exist, and the marketplace of ideas yields either false understandings or babble. In the film, dreams are real, reality shifts, and absolutely nothing is what it seems. Control, in the form of computer programs (malleable by both the programmers and the programmed), and death, in the form of biological waste, remain.

Almost all journalistic endeavors by their very nature reject this postmodern way of thinking. Some philosophers, for example Clifford Christians, reject postmodernism on the grounds that the essence of humanity itself provides an irrefutable challenge to the postmodern premise. Others have noted that postmodernism too easily falls into the trap of solipsism—or the notion that it is impossible to know anything outside of one's individual thoughts and perceptions. Solipsism, of course, negates any attempt at social ethics where values, principles, and other people exist independently of individual thought and biological function.

While traditional theory may reject postmodernism, contemporary culture itself sometimes embraces what Morpheus calls "the desert of the real." Magazine designers employ postmodern sensibilities to create designs that play with the entire concept of text. Media critics argue that a media-generated reality, subject to no counter-argument from other messages or critical examination by audiences, is not so different from the matrix that Neo encounters. And, digitizing and editing visual images and sounds through sophisticated computer programs is the stuff of elementary school play.

So, if postmodernism is an appropriate worldview, does that mean journalists and persuasion professionals should abandon their jobs or their ancient foundations in the face of overwhelming information overload? We think not.

Neo and Morpheus still have to act. They learn to think in new ways, but their actions remain centered on their belief in human independence and the "rightness" of thinking about and connecting with others. Even in this postmodern vision, ethical thinking still has a place. Neo's goal, after all, is to dismantle one matrix so humanity can make its own choices.

And, as befits postmodern sensibilities, as of this writing two sequels are in production.

Who's Doing the Talking Anyway?

The pragmatic's critique of objectivity has called attention to the question of who writes the news. Journalists—who themselves are primarily male, Caucasian, well-educated, and middle to upper class—are often asked to cover issues and questions for which their life experiences have not prepared them. Stephen Hess (1981) noted that journalists, in terms of their socioeconomic status, look a great deal more like the people they cover than the people they are supposedly writing for. While the eastern, elite press provides an extreme example of this tendency, other work on the national press corps has shown similar results (Weaver and Wilhoit 1986).

In the past twenty years, almost every professional journalistic organization has developed programs specifically to attract and retain women and minorities, many with limited success (Sanders and Rock 1988). The broadcast industry provides an excellent example. "Sixty-one percent of the broadcasting work force is made up of men and 39 per cent of women; 80.9 percent of the workers are white, 11.8 are black, and 5 percent are Hispanics. Other minority groups are represented to a much smaller degree . . . males have 68.6 percent of the managerial positions, women 31.4 percent and only 6.1 percent of TV station presidents are women." (Lont 1995, p. 179). Journalism education itself still reflects a Caucasian, male reality (Beasley and Harlow 1988) even though students in schools and departments of journalism and mass communication are predominantly female (Becker et al., 2000).

This lack of access to the engines of information has not been lost on a variety of minority groups—from religious fundamentalists, who have in some cases established their own broadcasting networks, to racial minorities, who fail to find themselves either as owners or managers of media outlets or in front of the cameras and with front-page bylines. They argue that the result is news about middle-class Caucasians, for middle-class Caucasians, about a political-economic system that systematically excludes everyone but middle-class Caucasians.

1993, Washington Post Writers Group. Reprinted with permission.

How individual journalists and the corporations they work for should remedy the situation is unclear. But many editors and publishers as well as their corporate bosses worry that as the demographics change us from a culture that is predominantly Caucasian to one that is not, the mass media, particularly newspapers, will play an increasingly minor role unless journalists find a way to report news that is of interest to the new majority of their readers. Some are changing as a result. For instance, Gannett, the nation's largest newspaper chain, initiated the Gannett 2000 project in the early 1990s, a mechanistic attempt to ensure ethnic diversity and reader input in its news pages through formulas and heavy reliance on reader polls. The more recent civic journalism movement is another reflection of such efforts.

Seeing Isn't Believing

Another assumption embedded in the concept of objectivity centers on how the news is perceived. More than eighty years ago, journalist Walter Lippmann (1922) foreshadowed what modern psychology has now documented when he said, "For the most part, we do not first see, and then define, we define first and then see." He added that we tend to pick out what our culture has already defined for us, and then perceive it in the form stereotyped for us by our culture.

A New York journalism professor, blind since birth, performed an experiment on stereotyping with startling results (Rainville and McCormick 1977). The professor, an avid football fan, wanted to see if he could predict the race of football players being described in the play-by-play sports commentary by what was being said about them. He theorized Caucasian athletes would be described as intellectually gifted, literally examples of heads-up play. African-American athletes would be praised for their physical prowess and described as physically gifted but not as smart. An experiment proved the professor correct. In a culture that values brains over brawn, African-American football players were the subject of repeated stereotypical insults—all couched as praise in the play-by-play.

Groups such as women, the elderly, and the gay community have conducted studies with similar results. Their conclusion has been that while journalists maintain that they are objective, they (like their readers and viewers) bring something to the message that literally changes what they see and, hence, what they report (Lester 1996).

Journalists also bring technology to the message, and the technology of television has led scholars to question the role of objectivity in news reporting. Two famous studies provide an indication of the questions scholars have asked in the past five decades.

The first study centered on the difference between the reality of a parade to welcome General Douglas MacArthur home from the Korean War and what people saw on television. The researchers stationed observers along the parade route to record what they saw. They saw what anyone would have predicted: several hours of waiting followed by a few minutes of excitement as the dignitaries passed. But television didn't present the event that way. On television were expectant crowds and little boredom, and the dignitaries did not pass from the screen in just a few minutes, even though MacArthur returned to the United States in 1951 prior to a television era of videotape, sound enhancement, remote crews, and satellite feeds.

Any journalist who has ever covered a city council meeting can confirm these results. Council members yawning, digressing, or receiving endless explanations from earnest city staff members seldom make the newspaper pages. The event itself is condensed and packaged into an inverted pyramid. The reader can learn in five minutes what it took a reporter four hours to sift through.

All of this is accepted media practice. But, it also says something about journalistic notions of truth. Was the "mediated reality" people saw on television the truthful account of the parade? Or was the truthful account the eyewitness reports of the observers standing at the curb? Which standard is the objective one? Which standard is worth professional aspiration?

A second study shows how pictures can interact with the story in an unintended way. In 1960, when a relatively unknown Democrat from Massachusetts debated the vice president of the United States during the presidential campaign, political scientists examined whether television itself would make a difference. They found two groups of people—one group had heard the first Kennedy–Nixon debate only on radio and the second group had watched the event on television. They made certain that the two groups were in all other ways similar to each other. Then they asked those who had seen and listened to the debates who won and discovered that the medium and not the message was what had made a difference.

Those who heard the debate on radio said that Richard Nixon won. They heard his words and the arguments of a practiced debater. People who saw the debate as well as heard it said that John F. Kennedy had won. They saw a tan young man who looked at the camera instead of at his opponent. They saw Nixon sweat. And the visual image—which conveyed information of a sort that is not easily put into words—was compelling. In an election that was decided by less than 1 percent of the total votes cast, television acquired enormous political power.

Years ago, Marshall McLuhan commented that the next war will be fought not with bullets but with images. He was proven right in 1991 when the U.S. Army packaged the visual images of the Persian Gulf War with the help of a New York public relations firm. Today, a variety of political rhetoric, from campaigning to revolutions, is being packaged for the media in an attempt to tap into the enormous persuasive power of the supposedly objective news format.

Defining and Constructing the News

News reflects certain cultural values and professional norms. Those values and norms, often at odds with an Enlightenment concept of truth, lend themselves to a pragmatic version of the news, provided you remember who's doing the writing and story selection.

One professional norm that plays an important role in shaping the news is the journalistic imperative to tell a story to make a point. Often this leads to predictable narratives, many of them centering on crisis and politics (Nimmo and Combs 1985; Bennett 1988). Sociologist Herbert Gans (1979) studied how stories became news at *Newsweek* and CBS and found that almost all news stories reflected these six cultural values: ethnocentrism, altruistic democracy, responsible capitalism, individualism, an emphasis on the need for and maintenance of social order, and leadership. These dominant values not only helped to shape which stories were printed, but also what they said.

News stories about middle-class or upper-class people, those who tend to successfully adopt the culture's values, made the American news "budget," according to Gans, while stories about minorities, blue-collar Americans, and those sharply critical of governmental policy got lost on the cutting-room floor.

While Gans focused on journalism about the United States, other scholars have noted the same phenomenon, called *domesticating the foreign,* in international coverage (Gurevitch et al. 1991). Journalists working for U.S. media outlets tell stories about international events in cultural terms Americans can readily understand but which also sacrifice accuracy and a non-American point of view. For example, routine coverage of elections in Britain or Israel is conveyed in horse-race metaphors even though both countries employ a parliamentary system where governing coalitions are common and who wins the horse race not nearly so important.

The goal of telling a "good story" also raises other ethical questions, specifically those that focus on packaging to highlight drama and human interest. Ethical questions about packaging began with newspapers but have intensified with television. Television demands video, and television's video imperative has been found to dominate both story selection and placement (for example, Epstein 1974). If television arrives at a disaster before print journalists, it is television that frames the stories for the written word (Smith 1992). Photo availability sometimes contradicts the classic notion of objectivity that each story should stand on its own merits, but it certainly reflects the professional norms of particular media. *USA Today*'s graphic impact on the newspaper industry has not been applauded by everyone. Some see the paper as a further indication of the trivialization of news, with an emphasis on packaging. Political ads have helped journalists to frame news stories about the same issue (Jamieson 1992) to some extent because of compelling visuals in the ads.

Journalists also need something to package, which has led to a professional drive to find an "event" to report and to be there first. The need to find an event has meant journalists have missed some important stories because they were not events but rather historic developments with both a past and a future. For example, major social developments such as the women's movement (Mills 1989), the civil rights movement, and the anti-Vietnam War movement were undercover until their leaders created events such as sit-ins and demonstrations for the media to report. More recently, director Michael Moore said he began his wickedly funny 1989 film *Roger and Me* about the devastation of General Motors layoffs on his hometown of Flint, Michigan, because he "didn't see on the silver screen or the television screen what happened to people like us. It was a story then (in the mid-1980s) and it's a story now and that's part of the reason I did the movie" (Smith 1992).

This preoccupation with events affects coverage of several types of stories. Science is most frequently reported as a series of discoveries and "firsts" rather than as a process of discovery (Nelkin 1987). We are treated to stories about the next cancer or AIDS cure without the necessary context to interpret the latest research results. The socioeconomic, scientific, and political causes of a disaster, such as the one that claimed thousands of lives in Bhopal, India, were seldom mentioned in news coverage that focused on the picture-friendly event (Wilkins 1987). Finally, phenomena not linked to specific events, such as the greenhouse effect or the growth of an American underclass, often go unreported or underreported until an appropriate news peg arrives to supply the needed event the coverage requires.

Elections become horse races with one candidate the "front-runner" and the "rest of the pack" struggling to narrow the gap with each new poll. But reporting an election as a contest fails to focus on the policy issues, which is what democratic elections are supposed to be about. Perhaps this pattern was nowhere more apparent than in coverage of the 2000 U.S. presidential election, where media reports tended to focus on who was ahead in the polls rather than on issues. Even after the "too close to call" result, journalists devoted more time to "dimpled" ballots than to the sort of programs and policies that eventual President George W. Bush was likely to enact.

The drive to get to the event first has led to another sort of horse race, one chronicled in the film *The Front Page* and later recounted in Timothy Crouse's book *The Boys on the Bus* (1974) and Sabato's *Feeding Frenzy* (1992). All emphasize journalistic excesses and an unwillingness to engage in independent thought that would disturb enlightened and pragmatic philosophers alike. Yet the twin problems of pack journalism and the scoop mentality still dominate much reporting and editing. Because of this, important stories have been killed, while some poorly researched stories have been aired or published.

Journalists have also been cowed by the threat of litigation. The film *The Insider* presents a fictionalized but nonetheless fact-based account about the impact of litigation on reporting stories critical of big tobacco. Seymour Hersh's original reporting of the My Lai massacre during the Vietnam War, which eventually appeared in the *New York Times,* was held up because no other reporter had a similar story and a particular media outlet was afraid to stick its neck out.

On the other hand, the *New York Times* resorted to quoting the supermarket tabloid the *National Enquirer* in its coverage of the O. J. Simpson case largely in an effort to keep up with media competition. Equally significant, the *Enquirer* had the story right. And, the entire Washington press corps was confounded when Internet gadfly Matt Drudge, who styles himself a political reporter, published what became the first mention of the President Bill Clinton/Monica Lewinsky scandal. Drudge has said that he prints rumor as well as fact; traditional journalists, who want to separate the two, remain deeply troubled by the impact of the speed of the Internet on the need to check facts before more traditional publication.

Truth is more than just a collection of facts. Facts have a relationship to one another and to other facts, forming a larger whole. Yet analytic coverage of American institutions, of science and technology, of politics, and of social movements is rare. If the role of the mass media is not only to detail events and issues, but to do so in a way that relationships among them are clear, is merely retelling of a story sufficient? Or do we need to do it better?

Stephen Hess (1981) has argued that journalists need to engage in reporting that looks more like social science than storytelling. Gans argues for news that is labeled as originating from a particular point of view. If readers and viewers are alerted to the worldview of those who have selected the news, just as they were during the era of the partisan press, they would be better able to place news in context. Other scholars argue for news that is analytical rather than anecdotal, proactive rather than reactive, and contextual rather than detached. And on a practical level, working reporters and editors insist that individual journalists need to do a better job of understanding their own biases and compensating for them.

These findings, from studies about how the media decide what is news to analyses of how individual audience members interpret the same news message, strike at the core of objectivity and its relationship to the complex truths of this century. Intellectually, we are living in a pragmatic era, but professionally we seem to be unable to develop a working alternative to the Enlightenment's view of truth.

The Means to the End

In a profession that values the truth, is it ethical to lie to get a story? This seemingly simple question has layers of meaning. The first is generally phrased like this: What if there is no other way to get the story? Some forms of journalistic deceptions—for example, serving time in a prison to do a story on conditions there—have resulted in real social good. On the other hand, the well-known Mirage Bar scam in which a Chicago newspaper set up a phony bar to document government corruption was denied a Pulitzer prize because of the methods used to obtain the story. In both instances, what journalists worry about is the impact such reporting methods have on the believability of news accounts and on journalists' ability to cover subsequent stories.

The second layer of questions revolves around the issue of whether it is ethical to lie to liars. If I know that a politician is going to lie to me, am I justified in lying to him or her, providing a larger social good is served? A second question is this: If we lie are we willing to be lied to? Or do we expect what Bok (1978) calls "free rider" status—gaining the benefits of lying without incurring the risks of being lied to?

Many philosophers have asserted that lying is a way to get and maintain power. Those in positions of power often believe they have the right to lie because they have a greater than ordinary understanding of what is at stake. Lying in a crisis (for instance, to prevent panic) and lying to enemies (for instance, to protect national security) are two examples. In both circumstances journalists can be, either actively or without their knowledge, involved in the deception. Do journalists have a right to counter this lying with lies of their own, told under the guise of the public's need to know?

The act of lying also raises the question of "omission vs. commission." Investigative and other sorts of news reporters sometimes consider it ethical to obtain information from unsuspecting sources who fail to ask whether they are speaking with a journalist or are speaking for publication. Reporting via the internet has given new urgency to the issue of lying by omission. In most instances failing to identify yourself as a reporter when collecting information electronically from news groups, chat rooms, or other modes of public discussion the Internet makes possible is considered problematic. Journalists, when pressed, note that the U.S. Supreme Court has ruled Internet transmissions are public. The ethical issue emerges when most of those involved in the discussion are not aware of the legal standards and expect, instead, the more ethically based relations of face-to-face interactions.

Ethical thought leaves journalists with difficult choices. Bok asserts that a genuinely white lie may be excusable on some grounds, but that all forms of lying must stand up to questions of fairness and mutuality. Even lying to liars can have its downside.

> In the end, the participants in deception they take to be mutually understood may end up with coarsened judgment and diminished credibility. But if, finally, the liar to whom one wishes to lie is also in a position to do one harm, then the balance may shift; not because he is a liar, but because of the threat he poses. (Bok 1978, 140)

Since so many of the lies journalists are told emanate from powerful sources, the issue of telling some form of lie to report a socially beneficial story remains a troubling and important one. Another ethical issue centers on exactly how much truth journalists ought to tell. Completeness and accuracy are sometimes used synonymously with truthfulness and objectivity, but important ethical distinctions can be made among the concepts. If truth itself is relative, then how should a journalist balance getting the story against providing his or her readers with the essential information needed to evaluate it? Again, the issue becomes one of the means to a specific end, both now and in the long run.

Ethical News Values

Most mass media courses present a list of qualities that, collectively, define news. Most such lists include proximity, timeliness, conflict, consequence, prominence, rarity, change, concreteness, action, and personality. Additional elements may include notions of mystery, drama, adventure, celebration, self-improvement, and even ethics.

While these lists are helpful to beginning journalists, they probably will not help you decide how to recount the news ethically.

We suggest you expand your journalistic definitions of news to include a list of ethical news values. These values are intended to reflect the philosophic tensions inherent in a profession with a commitment to truth.

If news values were constructed from ethical reasoning, we believe the following elements would be emphasized by both journalists and the organizations for which they work.

Accuracy—using the correct facts and the right words and putting things in context. Journalists need to be as independent as they can when framing stories. They need to be aware of their own biases, including those they "inherit" as social class, gender and ethnicity, as well as learned professional norms. Their news organizations need to trust journalists when they report independently rather than expect them to act as part of a pack.

Tenacity—knowing when a story is important enough to require additional effort, both personal and institutional. Tenacity drives journalists to provide all the depth they can regardless of the individual assignment. It has institutional implications, too, for the individual cannot function well in an environment where resources are too scarce or the corporate bottom line too dominant.

Dignity—leaving the subject of a story as much self-respect as possible. Dignity values each person regardless of the particular story or the particular role the individual plays. Dignity allows the individual journalist to recognize that news gathering is a cooperative enterprise where each plays a role, including editors, videographers, designers, and advertising sales staff.

Reciprocity—treating others as you wish to be treated. Too often, the journalistic enterprise is defined as "writing for the lowest common denominator." Reciprocity eschews the notion of journalism as a sort of benevolent paternalism— "We'll tell you what we think is good for you"—and recognizes that journalists and their viewers and readers are partners both in discovering what is important and in gleaning meaning from it.

Sufficiency—allocating adequate resources to important issues. On the individual level, sufficiency can mean thoroughness, for example, checking both people and documents for every scrap of fact before beginning to write. On an organizational level, it means allocating adequate resources to the news-gathering process.

Equity—seeking justice for all involved in controversial issues and treating all sources and subjects equally. Like the ethical news value of accuracy, equity assumes a complicated world with a variety of points of view. Equity demands that all points of view be considered, but that not all be framed as equally compelling. Equity expands the journalistic norms of "telling both sides of the story" to "telling all sides of the story."

Community—valuing social cohesion. On the organization level, a sense of community means that media outlets and the corporations that own them need to consider themselves as citizens rather than mere "profit centers." On the individual level, it means evaluating stories with an eye first to social good.

Diversity—covering all segments of the audience fairly and adequately. There appears to be almost overwhelming evidence that news organizations do not "look like" the society they cover. While management can remedy part of this problem through changing hiring patterns, individual journalists can learn to "think diversity" regardless of their individual heritages.

Like all lists, ours should not be considered inclusive or without some measure of internal contradiction. We believe those contradictions, however, provide an important continuum within which informed ethical choice can be made.

Suggested Readings

Bennett, Lance. 1988. *News: The politics of illusion.* Longman: New York.

Gans, Herbert. 1979. *Deciding what's news: A study of CBS Evening News, NBC Nightly News, Newsweek and Time.* New York: Vintage.

Jamieson, Kathleen Hall. 1992. *Dirty politics.* New York: Oxford University Press.

Lester, Paul M. 1996. *Images that injure.* Westport, CT: Greenwood Press.

Lippmann, Walter. 1922. *Public opinion.* New York: Free Press.

Plato. *The republic.*

Sabato, Larry. 1992. *Feeding frenzy: How attack journalism has transformed American politics.* New York: Free Press.

CHAPTER II CASES

CASE II-A
News as Persuasion: The New York Times vs. Wen Ho Lee
LEE WILKINS
University of Missouri–Columbia

On March 6, 1999, under the headline "Breach at Los Alamos: A Special Report; China Stole Nuclear Secrets for Bombs, U.S. Aides Say," the *New York Times* began a front-page, 4,000-word piece detailing how workers—specifically one worker—at the Los Alamos laboratory had leaked sensitive nuclear secrets to the People's Republic of China. The story, written by two of the *Times*'s investigative reporters, James Risen and Jeff Garth, a Pulitzer Prize winner, linked the leaks with "breakthroughs" in Chinese weapons technology, posing a clear national security risk to the United States.

The reporters relied heavily on unnamed sources and one named source, Notra Trulock, a former Energy Department Director of Intelligence, who was described as a "star witness" in Congressional investigations. The story described Trulock as a "whistleblower" and said that the weapons leaks had become "one of the most damaging spy cases in recent history."

In the same story, the reporters said that the Clinton-administration Justice Department had failed to respond appropriately to the case. "A reconstruction by the *New York Times* reveals that throughout the Government, the response to the nuclear theft was plagued by delays, inaction and skepticism." The story also noted that while the investigation had continued for three years, no arrests have been made, and that the unnamed key suspect had been allowed to keep his high security clearance for more than a year after he had become the target of the investigation. "Only in the last several weeks, after prodding from Congress and the Secretary of Energy, have government officials administered lie-detector tests to the main suspect, a Los Alamos computer scientist who is Chinese-American."

The unnamed, but clearly identified suspect, was 59-year-old Wen Ho Lee.

In an April 28, 1999, article written by the same reporters, the *Times* noted that Lee had improperly downloaded computer files containing nuclear codes. The lead on the story read, "A scientist suspected of spying for China improperly transferred huge amounts of secret data from a computer system in a government laboratory, compromising virtually every nuclear weapon in the United States arsenal, government and lab officials say."

The government finally arrested Lee in December 1999—more than eight months after the *Times*'s original story. By the time of the arrest, other reporters at the *Times* were questioning some conclusions in the original pieces. The *Times* reporter assigned to the nuclear weapons beat, for example, reported five months after the original allegations that the information Lee was supposed to have disseminated was widely available at the time the "leaks" supposedly occurred.

There were other problems with the original *Times* story. For example, the *Times* reporters never independently investigated Trulock. Had they done so, they might have uncovered other sources, equally expert, who would have told them that Trulock had been building a case against Lee for almost four years, in part because Lee was ethnic Chinese. That was the content of an affidavit filed with the court that ultimately released Lee.

"Based on my experience and my personal knowledge, I believe that Mr. Trulock improperly targeted Dr. Lee due to Dr. Lee's race and national origin," said Charles Washington, former acting director of counterintelligence at the Energy Department who filed an affidavit in the case. The two reporters also appeared to discount sources and statements that did not support their allegations against Lee. For example, the reporters either did not know or decided not to run information from the CIA that concluded the charges against Lee, which were based on an "intelligence windfall from Beijing," actually were the work of a double agent trying to impress the government of Taiwan with Beijing's nuclear weapons progress.

The reporters also apparently failed to check with, or discounted, other experts in the nuclear weapons field who asserted that the alleged massive "jump" in mainland China's nuclear capacity was really little more than minimal progress, readily accounted for by hard scientific work instead of spying. Perhaps most telling, the two reporters also failed to inform their readership that the original leak came from a Congressional committee chaired by California Republican Christopher Cox. That committee had, as did much of the Republican-controlled Congress during 1998 and 1999, a distinct political agenda: the impeachment and conviction of President Bill Clinton.

There were other fact errors in the story: Lee had passed a lie detector test (the *Times* said he had not), he had not taken a secret trip to Hong Kong (the *Times* said he had), and the documents he was accused of downloading into his computer were not classified as "secret" until after formal charges were brought (the *Times* was silent on this issue, which means the reporters either did not know, had been misled, or did know but decided not to print the information). The *Times* coverage, of course, set the tone for much of the rest of the media reporting on the case, what some critics have described as a return to Cold War rhetoric and the most bogus set of spy charges since those that resulted in the deaths of Julius and Ethel Rosenberg at the height of the McCarthy era of U.S. history.

Meanwhile, Lee, a cancer survivor, was placed in solitary confinement without bail for nine months. On the day Lee was released "for time served" with the government's agreement, Judge James Parker told him, "I sincerely apologize to you, Dr. Lee, for the unfair manner you were held in custody by the executive branch."

When it became evident that the case against Lee was collapsing, the news organization did acknowledge that it had ignored problems with the government's case, failed to humanize Lee, and discounted a political agenda that pushed to narrow the pool of suspects before dispassionate analysis would have suggested a tight investigative focus. The September 26 article noted that a review of the totality of the paper's coverage "found careful reporting that included extensive cross-checking and vetting of multiple sources, despite enormous obstacles" but "In those instances where we fell short of our standards in our coverage of this story, the blame lies principally with those who directed the coverage, for not raising questions that occurred to us only later."

Other media critics were not nearly so kind. Bill Mesler, in an article entitled "The Spy Who Wasn't" accused the *Times* of launching a witch hunt that ended in Lee's incarceration. Robert Scheer, who wrote more than twenty columns and articles about the journalistic work in the case, called the *Times*'s transgressions startling. "I don't know if it makes the all-time Top Ten list [of low points in the history of this nation's journalism], but the trial and conviction of Lee in the pages of the *Times* . . . is certainly right up there."

Micro Issues:

1. What is the responsibility of journalists to investigate elements of their stories that run "counter" to their theories of events?
2. Evaluate the apology from the *Times* editors? Do you believe it was appropriate? What were the editors' responsibilities in relation to those of the reporters?
3. Should investigative reporters treat "whistle-blowers" differently than other sorts of sources? How about those sources who wish to remain anonymous?

Mid-range Issues:

1. Should journalists include political context in stories? Can news reporters do this without making it seem like bias?
2. Should news organizations develop policies about how to handle leaks, particularly from political sources?
3. How much do you think Dr. Lee's ethnicity influenced the reporting in the case?

Macro Issues:

1. The reporting in the Wen Ho Lee case came less than a year after the Monica Lewinsky story was broken by Matt Drudge on the Internet—without benefit of any official sources. Evaluate the impact of the journalism in the Lewinsky case on subsequent reporting, including the case of Wen Ho Lee.

CASE II-B
The Spouse Is Squeezed: A South Carolina TV Reporter's Attempt to Conceal Her Source
SONYA FORTE DUHÉ
University of South Carolina

It seems like a typical news day.

A man telephones WIS-TV Senior Reporter Heather Hoopes, claiming to possess a "bombshell videotape" that she must see.

The source tells the Columbia, South Carolina, NBC affiliate reporter the tape is available to her only if she comes to his house to get it. He says he won't mail it or drop it off at the station. If she wants it, she *has* to come and get it.

Concerned for her safety, Hoopes asks her husband, Jim Matthews—who, for more than twenty years has worked with the Department of Justice's Drug Enforcement Administration and now heads the local Columbia office—to drive her to the caller's home. He agrees.

Matthews has no idea that the videotape contains a privileged conversation between a murder defendant and his lawyer, secretly videotaped by a local sheriff's deputy. Hoopes isn't exactly sure what she is getting either.

After reviewing the tape, she broadcasts a story about the videotaping of the privileged conversation. To Hoopes and colleagues, the tape is a clear violation of the prisoner's rights.

Hoopes's move to have Matthews drive her to retrieve the videotape from this confidential source leads to numerous court battles and thousands upon thousands of dollars in legal costs for her, her husband and her employer.

Context

In 1995, Lexington County Sheriff's detectives arrested B. J. Quattlebaum and charged him with the murder of William Swartz. Quattlebaum was taken to the Lexington County Jail, where he called his attorney.

The men used a small room to talk. Unknown to them, a deputy sheriff was secretly and illegally videotaping their meeting.

At a later time, the same confidential source, who was subsequently identified as Columbia attorney Jack Duncan, called Hoopes at WIS to alert her to this alleged wrongdoing. Hoopes, her news director, and editors decided to use a portion of the videotape to expose the illegal action. However, in an attempt to protect the arrested man's rights, the news team didn't use the audio portion of the tape.

The FBI attempted to obtain the name of Hoopes's confidential source but could not meet Justice Department protocol because of First Amendment questions. When the FBI's efforts to subpoena WIS ran into roadblocks, it attempted to make Matthews reveal the person's identity.

In a May 10, 1999, story in *The Washington Post,* Hoopes was quoted as saying, "I consider it a backdoor tactic. I don't understand why the Justice Department is doing this. It's very stressful for me and my husband. I carry an extra burden because I put him in the situation."

Prosecutors subpoenaed Matthews, and a federal grand jury demanded that the DEA agent testify about the case.

Matthews's lawyer, along with the WIS legal team, filed motions with U.S. District Court asking that Matthews not be forced to testify. Lawyers argued that forcing him to be a witness would violate his First Amendment rights. These motions were dismissed. Written pleas to Attorney General Janet Reno, FBI Director Louis Freeh, and Justice Department official Beneva Weintraub also did not recuse Matthews from a court appearance.

Radio Television News Director Association is the world's largest professional organization devoted exclusively to electronic journalism. The organization represents local and network news executives in broadcasting, cable, and other electronic media in more than thirty countries. In those letters, RTNDA President Barbara Cochran called on the Justice Department to end FBI attempts to force Matthews to testify.

"On behalf of the 3,400 members of the RTNDA, I am writing to express our grave concern about FBI attempts to force the husband of a South Carolina television station reporter to reveal to a grand jury what he knows about his wife's confidential source," wrote Cochran.

"Efforts to force Mr. Matthews to betray the confidence of his spouse not only raise compelling questions about marital privilege, but they represent a blatant attempt to circumvent the reporter's privilege recognized by the Constitution, the state, and the Justice Department," she continued.

"It is well recognized that news-gathering activities are protected under the First Amendment of the United States Constitution. This protection extends to information given in confidence to a reporter, including the source of that information. The South Carolina legislature has also expressed a strong public policy of protecting news-gathering activities, enacting a shield law whose aim is to protect the free flow of information to the public. Moreover, Department of Justice regulations expressly recognize that: Because freedom of the press can be no broader than the freedom of reporters to investigate and report the news, the prosecutorial power of the government should not be used in such a way that it impairs a reporter's responsibility to cover as broadly as possible controversial public issues."

Cochran continued, "RTNDA is certainly aware of no case where a reporter's spouse has been ordered to disclose a confidential source. If prosecutors are allowed to obtain confidential news information from a third party where efforts to obtain the same information from the reporter have failed, then the protections afforded by the First Amendment and state press shield statutes would be meaningless."

Hoopes said, "I would have thought they (authorities) would have applauded the efforts of my source and WIS to bring this to light. Instead it seems like we're the criminals."

Quattlebaum was later convicted of first-degree murder and sentenced to death. In January 2000, the South Carolina Supreme Court overturned Quattlebaum's conviction, due in part to the videotape incident.

A federal judge ordered the deputy who videotaped the conversation to pay a $250 fine for civil rights violations. As for Hoopes's confidential source, he was sentenced to and spent several months in jail for lying to a federal grand jury and was disbarred.

Micro Issues:

1. Should the reporter have taken the videotape? Why?
2. Should the reporter have asked someone to accompany her to pick up the videotape? If so, who?
3. Was it okay for the reporter to air the videotape?
4. Should the reporter have aired the audio from the videotape?

Mid-range Issues:

1. Does the reporter have the right to air videotape of an illegal act? When would it be inappropriate?
2. Was it the journalist's responsibility to expose this illegal taping of a privileged conversation?
3. Did the journalist breach her source's confidentiality by allowing her husband to accompany her to pick up the videotape?

Macro Issues:

1. Should reporters be allowed to keep sources confidential if a criminal act has occurred?
2. What responsibilities do reporters have to law enforcement officials? Why?
3. Should spouses of reporters have the same First Amendment rights that reporters possess?
4. What role should non-journalists play in the news-gathering process?

CASE II-C
When Is Objective Reporting Irresponsible Reporting?
THEODORE L. GLASSER
Stanford University

Amanda Laurens, a reporter for a local daily newspaper, covers the city mayor's office where yesterday she attended a 4:00 P.M. press conference. The mayor, Ben Adams, read a statement accusing Evan Michaels, a city council member, of being a "paid liar" for the pesticide industry. "Councilman Michaels," the mayor said at the press conference, "has intentionally distorted the facts about the effects of certain pesticides on birds indigenous to the local area." Mr. Michaels, the mayor continued, "is on the payroll of a local pesticide manufacturer," and his views on the effects of pesticides on bird life "are necessarily tainted."

The press conference ended at about 5:15 P.M., less than an hour before her 6:00 P.M. deadline. Laurens quickly contacted Councilman Michaels for a quote in response to the mayor's statement. Michaels, however, refused to comment, except to say that Mayor Adams's accusations were "utter nonsense" and "politically motivated." Laurens filed her story, which included both the mayor's accusation and the councilman's denial. Laurens's editor thought the story was fair and balanced and ran it the following morning on the front page.

The mayor was pleased with the coverage he received. He thought Laurens had acted professionally and responsibly by reporting his accusation along with Michaels's denial. Anything else, the mayor thought, would have violated the principles of objective journalism. The mayor had always believed that one of the most important responsibilities of the press was to provide an impartial forum for public controversies, and the exchange between him and the councilman was certainly a bona fide public controversy. Deciding who's right and who's wrong is not the responsibility of journalists, the mayor believed, but a responsibility best left to readers.

Councilman Michaels, in contrast, was outraged. He wrote a scathing letter to the editor, chiding the newspaper for mindless, irresponsible journalism. "The story may have been fair, balanced, and accurate," he wrote, "but it was not truthful." He had never lied about the effects of pesticides on bird life, and he had "never been on the payroll of any pesticide manufacturer," he wrote. "A responsible reporter would do more than report the facts truthfully; she would also report the truth about the facts." In this case, Michaels said, the reporter should have held off on the story until she had time to independently investigate the mayor's accusation; and if the accusation had proved to be of no merit, as Michaels insisted, then there shouldn't have been a story. Or if there had to be a story, Michaels added, "it should be a story about the *mayor* lying."

By way of background: The effects of pesticides on bird life had been a local issue for nearly a year. Part of the community backs Mayor Adams's position on the harmful effects of certain pesticides and supports local legislation that would limit or ban their use. Others in the community support Councilman Michaels's position that the evidence on the effects of pesticides on bird life is at best ambiguous and that more scientific study is needed before anyone proposes legislation. They argue that pesticides are useful, particularly to local farmers who need to protect crops, and because the available evidence about their deleterious effects is inconclusive, they believe that the city council should not seek to further restrict or prohibit their use. The exchange between Mayor Adams and Councilman Michaels is the latest in a series of verbal bouts on the subject of pesticides and the city's role in their regulation.

Micro Issues:

1. Did Laurens do the right thing by submitting her story without the benefit of an independent investigation into the mayor's accusations about Councilman Michaels?
2. Is the mayor correct in arguing that Laurens acted responsibly by providing fair and balanced coverage of both sides of a public controversy without trying to judge whose side is right and whose side is wrong?
3. Is the councilman correct in arguing that Laurens acted irresponsibly by concerning herself only with reporting the facts truthfully and ignoring the "truth about the facts"?

Mid-range Issues:

1. Is it sufficient when covering public controversies to simply report the facts accurately and fairly? Does it matter that fair and accurate reporting of facts might not do justice to the truth about the facts?
2. Does the practice of objective reporting distance reporters from the substance of their stories in ways contrary to the ideals of responsible journalism?
3. If reporters serve as the eyes and ears of their readers, how can they be expected to report more than what they've heard or seen?

Macro Issues:

1. What distinguishes fact from truth? For which should journalists accept responsibility?
2. If journalists know that a fact is not true, do they have an obligation to share that knowledge with their readers? And if they do share that knowledge, how can they claim to be objective in their reporting?
3. Justify or reject the role of objectivity in an era where more media outlets are available than ever before.

CASE II-D
Columbine: News and Community—A Balancing Act
LEE WILKINS
University of Missouri

According to police, there was very little specific warning about the shootings that would occur on April 20, 1999, at Columbine High School in Littleton, Colorado. Certainly, there was no warning the day of the event in newsrooms across Denver, where the big story of the day was the latest developments in the ongoing JonBenet Ramsey case. But the events of April 20, 1999, would disrupt life not only in Columbine, but across the nation as well.

The psychological inner workings of killers Eric Harris and Dylan Klebold will probably never be completely understood. A videotape released months after the shooting revealed two students who had viewed themselves as complete outsiders in a high school scene dominated by athletes, popular teens, and minority students whom, they believed, received some sort of special treatment. In short, life at Columbine High School was not very different from life at many successful, suburban high schools where most students go on to college and where parents are generally economically comfortable.

At about 11:20 A.M., the scanners in newsrooms throughout the Denver metropolitan area picked up a transmission about a "kid at a school with a gun." Such reports are all too common in metropolitan areas, as are bomb threats. In many newsrooms, the general policy is to downplay the reports to prevent the spread of rumors and to avoid copycat acts. However, journalists soon realized this report was not routine. By just before noon, every newsroom in Denver was scrambling to get pictures and reports about what would become the worst school shooting in history.

At 11:55 A.M., KUSA, the NBC affiliate, removed the talk show "Leeza" from the air to go live continuously. Other stations soon followed. Meanwhile, newsroom phones were busier than anyone could remember. Not only were community residents calling about the story, but already the national media were demanding information for their own special reports.

Shortly after noon, the KUSA satellite truck began a live video feed. The first time news director Patti Dennis saw images of children on stretchers, she reacted as a parent, not a journalist. "No tight shots," she told field crews. "I don't want to see any faces. It's not appropriate. Too many parents are wondering what's happening. I don't think it's right to show anyone injured seriously. That compromises their privacy."

At almost exactly the same time, the sheriff's command post asked permission for a deputy to fly over in the helicopter of KMGH-TV (another Denver affiliate) to get an aerial view of the school. The station agreed.

Almost simultaneously, the station received a call from Columbine student Jonathan Ladd who was outside the school. After a brief vetting, KMGH put him on the air. A few minutes later the station aired information from another student who called from the school. He was breathing hard and sounded scared. One of the co-anchors encouraged the student to call 911; the student called back about thirty minutes later to report that the police lines were jammed and that the two gunmen, whom he had seen, appeared to be dressed in black. At 1:00 P.M. a third student—this one hiding in the school—called the station. He was also told to call 911, but about ten minutes later he called back reporting that police lines were jammed and that students were running up and down the halls screaming.

Meanwhile, at Columbine police and ambulances descended on the area. Police cordoned off streets near the school. One camera crew was temporarily prevented from returning to its satellite truck, which had inadvertently been roped off within the crime scene boundaries. Other journalists abandoned their cars blocks from the school and sprinted on foot to the scene. They shouted questions to police, who said very little. About 1:00 P.M. students—some of them wounded—began escaping from the high school. These shots were captured and sent out live. Calls from students continued to pour in to the local stations.

At about this time, the sheriff's office also asked the news media for help, requesting that the stations decline to air live footage of SWAT team activity for fear it would provide information to the gunmen, whom police believed were still inside the school. By 2:00 P.M. journalists covering the story were speculating much less about specific actions taken by the police and about the activities—and casualties—inside the school. However, at about 3:00 P.M. one station inadvertently revealed a death through live coverage. The station aired footage of an obviously dead body being dragged from the school. Seconds afterward, the station cut away from the live footage. The on-air anchor noted, "I'm very reluctant to characterize what that was."

At about 4:00 P.M. the Jefferson County Sheriff's office held its first press conference and announced an unknown number of casualties, including some teachers and students, and that the department believed the suspects had been found dead inside the building.

The initial reports from the sheriff's department greatly exaggerated the number of dead, saying as many as twenty-five had died in the attack. As it turned out, the eventual death toll was twelve. (In the ensuing months, one other student who was at the school at the time committed suicide.) However, the wrong information was part of the initial national broadcasts of the event.

Also at the scene was a KUSA reporter who summed up the situation: "Bleeding. Screaming. I needed to talk to some kids to see what they saw or heard. But you didn't know how to approach them. I tried to be really sensitive and understanding. I meticulously approached the kids asking nicely, 'Do you mind if I ask you some questions?' Surprisingly, most of them agreed."

Her camera operator faced equally difficult decisions. "When we pulled up, I saw kids lying on the grass; I saw blood on the driveway. I went to the truck, pulled out my tripod and knew that I had to stay back from the people. I stayed away from the families and victims. What was important to me as a member of the community was to stay away from becoming a part of the story and just capture what was happening—as opposed to putting my camera on my shoulder and walking into it."

As sensitive as the camera operator tried to be, the national media took some decision-making power out of his hands. The camera operator had shot some close-ups of the kids, thinking the footage might air later, when emotions weren't so raw. However, the footage was being fed into the newsroom, where CNN had access to it. When CNN got the footage, the local affiliate lost all control. It aired nationally the same day. The same thing continued throughout the remainder of that first day. At one point ABC's *20/20* aired the same footage of an obviously dazed student falling out of the second floor of the school building four times within twenty minutes.

Journalists who covered the story that initial day had enormous emotional reactions. Several reported getting home and beginning to cry and not being able to stop. Others said tears came later. One Denver newsman admitted on the air that, after Columbine, he was treated for depression. Managers noted that an essential part of the job for many became taking care of the emotional and mental health of the various newsroom staffers.

Micro Issues:

1. Should the Denver media have gone live at the scene? Were there other alternatives?
2. How should the news media have handled what became the incorrect reports from the sheriff's department?
3. Should other programming have been shelved during the event? What about during the hours when there was little new to report?
4. How should the stations have handled the calls from students outside the school? Inside the school?

Mid-range Issues:

1. Is the role of the national media different from that of the local media in stories such as Columbine? Critique the actions of CNN in airing the footage meant to be aired later.
2. Should the stations have cooperated with police at the scene?
3. When would it be appropriate to air comments critical of the emergency response or other official activities at Columbine?
4. Is Columbine a story a year later? Why?

Macro Issues

1. How would you respond to a viewer who asserts that coverage such as this only promotes more school violence?
2. What is the news media's overall responsibility in combating societal problems such as the violence at Columbine? What are the sorts of stories that might be a part of this response?
3. Which ethical theory would support the decisions made by the various journalists. Which do you find to present the most ethically compelling arguments?

CASE II-E
A Hometown Hero Takes a Spill
M. W. MULCAHY
Former editor, Cape Cod Times

Todd Eldredge was a major contender in the 1996 Olympic Games figure skating competition. As he went into his final routine, he had a good chance of taking home the gold medal. Many in his hometown community of Chatham, Massachusetts, and throughout Cape Cod, had been following his progress for years.

Then came the fall that dashed his hopes at the gold and pushed him back to fourth place.

In designing the front page of the next-day's Sunday *Cape Cod Times*, night production editor Ron Sikora said the decision was a simple one. It was the biggest story of the day for the community and an Associated Press photograph of the fall told the story best. The photo was played big across the top of the page. While none of the key editors were in the newsroom that Saturday night, all later agreed that they supported Sikora's call. The paper ran the photo of Eldredge sprawled on the ice.

By Monday morning the phone calls, E-mails, and letters were all pouring in from irate readers who wanted to know how the editors could be so insensitive as to show one of Cape Cod's local sons in his very moment of defeat. Why couldn't the paper show more support for Eldredge by picking a more upbeat photo?

The consensus at the paper was supportive of Sikora's decision, saying this photo best conveyed what happened and the agony on Eldredge's face showed that in that split second he realized that the fall meant defeat. In the newsroom, it came down to the issue of telling the truth. Based on callers' responses, it appeared the community felt the issue was more one of failing to support a local hero in his darkest hour. As the paper's news editor, I fielded many of these calls. While some simply wanted to complain about our insensitivity or to suggest we had made the photo smaller or played it in the sports section, one caller started off the conversation with the question "What were you thinking?" When I told her the editors felt a responsibility to tell the truth and that photo did the best job of conveying what really happened to Eldredge's Olympic dream, the caller still disagreed with the decision but felt some consolation in understanding the reasoning behind it.

Shortly after that call, the editors at the *Times* held a meeting to discuss how to best address the public outcry. There was general agreement that we must run as many of the letters as we could fit on the editorial page, but editor Cliff Schechtman dismissed the idea of an editorial, explaining our position by stating it would come off as being too defensive. The letters would run. The readers would have their say and that would be that.

But the caller's question, "What were you thinking?" kept pestering me after the meeting. Don't we have a responsibility to our community to explain our decisions? Aren't they entitled to understand the logic and philosophy used to defend the use and play of the photograph? By staying silent, I felt we were essentially saying, "It's our newspaper, and we do what we want, and we don't have to explain ourselves to anyone."

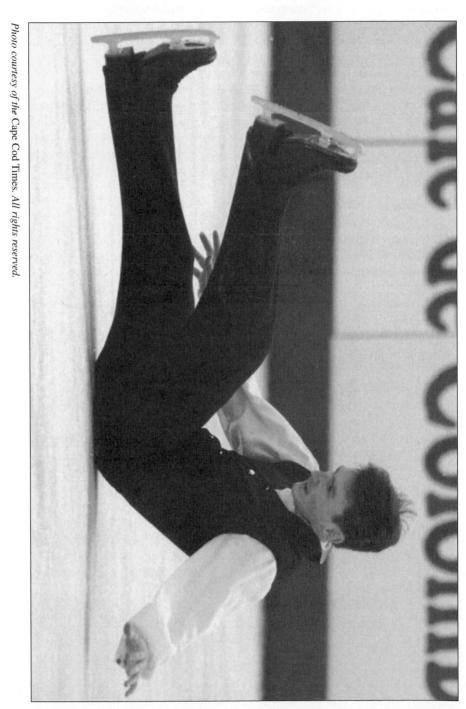

45

I wrote up a short explanation of the thought process that went behind the decision and gave copies to Schechtman and managing editor Alicia Blaisdell-Bannon. Schechtman made some changes but agreed to run it as a note from the editor to explain what we were thinking. Although a few calls and E-mails still trickled in the next day, it appeared that the note to our readers served the community by helping them to understand the reasoning behind our actions.

While the editors at the *Cape Cod Times* stood behind Sikora's decision, there was an interesting epilogue weeks later when Eldredge was in another skating competition. When it looked as though he was going to win a gold medal in that competition, the editors agreed they would reserve a spot on page one for the story—and a photo reflecting his victory—in the event that he took home the gold. Unfortunately, he came in third and the story and photo were pushed back to the sports section.

Micro Issues:

1. Should the newspaper have featured the fall as its main photo of Eldredge?
2. If a photo of Eldredge skating in the competition had been used, what different "truth" would have been told?

Mid-range Issues:

1. Could the fall have been better covered in an inside photo?
2. When is it appropriate in news coverage to show a person in tragedy? In triumph?
3. What type of official response did the public outcry warrant?
4. Even though Eldredge's fall happened at a public event, his feelings were private, but they were made public by the circumstances and magnified by the photo. Balance the competing values of his privacy and the interest of his fans in what had happened to him.

Macro Issues:

1. When a local newspaper reports on the athletic efforts of one of its own favorites, are the standards of reporting different? What if the local celebrity is a politician?
2. Critique the decision by Schechtman to not write an editorial on the basis that it might look too defensive.

CHAPTER III

Advertising Ethics: From Let the Buyer Beware to Empowerment

By the end of this chapter, you should be familiar with:

- **why both advertising and news can be evaluated as symbol formation.**
- **the balance and cognitive dissonance persuasion theories and their role in advertising.**
- **the issues surrounding the interaction between ads and vulnerable audiences.**
- **the TARES test for evaluating the ethics of individual ads.**

Introduction

Since the days of ancient Greece, a major function of communication has been to persuade. Greek citizens used the art of rhetoric to their advantage in the Greek city-states where democracy was practiced through an elaborate court system. Eventually, the courts of Athens became crowded with those who sought to use their persuasive powers for gain. Today's airwaves and printing presses are likewise filled with messages designed to increase the influence and wealth of their sponsors.

But ancient Athens has morphed into a Twenty-First-Century democracy that runs on the engines of capitalism, fueled in large part by advertising. While the ancient Greeks overtly attempted to persuade, contemporary advertising employs elements that act on the human psyche in more subtle ways. Indeed, communication theory has evolved in an attempt to discover how it is that some messages persuade and others do not. And, although the ancient Greeks accepted all speech as persuasion, contemporary understandings have separated advertising from news.

We think the Greeks had the right idea some 3,000 years ago. We suggest that both advertising and news be understood as elements of the same activity: symbol formation (Wilkins and Christians, 2001). Both news and advertising are rooted in culture. Both make some assumptions about the relationship between mediated messages and the individuals who receive them. Most important, if news and advertising really are different parts of the same process, then the same ethical tools—and standards—can be applied.

The similarities between advertising and news are particularly important when the lines between the activities blur (as they do in advertorials) or when advertising about newsworthy issues, such as who should be elected president, becomes an important way people learn about those questions. A set of ethical standards shared between both activities will give contemporary practitioners a better chance at "doing the right thing" in an increasingly competitive media environment.

But before we talk theory, let's talk some economic fact.

Pay When You Wash, Not When You Watch

Anyone in the management end of a media business understands this truth: the role of programming on television (either news or entertainment) and the role of copy (news, features or editorials) in newspapers is to deliver an audience to advertisers.

The United States is the only country in the world that has chosen to fund its media system almost exclusively through private dollars. The public broadcasting system receives a tiny fraction of 1 percent of the U.S. budget; requirements for the publication of legal advertising may keep weekly newspapers alive, but those revenues are insignificant to such media behemoths as the *New York Times*. While Americans may find advertising intrusive, seriously misleading, and environmentally unfriendly (think of the trees we could save if McDonald's didn't have to package every burger and fry with its own logo), it funds the world's most robust media system. As George Gerbner (1987) says, "You pay when you wash, not when you watch."

Contrary to what news journalists believe, most people regard advertising as another form of information. Experiments have shown that people prefer newspapers with advertising to newspapers that lack ads. Auction Web sites, one of the most popular kinds of Internet activity, provide further evidence that an audience with a purpose will seek out advertising to help make an informed choice.

These facts of media life do not blunt some of the deepest criticisms of advertising. The nature of the advertising message itself—short, highly visual, and intentionally vague—supports criticism about advertising's reliance on stereotypes, its glorification of consumerism at the expense of community, and its apparent willingness to indulge in any excess to "make a buck." Indeed, some of the most compelling evidence that advertising works has arisen from studies of the impact of tobacco advertising on children under eighteen. The United States—and the rest of the world—have the cancer rates to prove it.

As a nation, the United States has chosen to regulate some of advertising's most egregious excesses, but we have also chosen to continue this method of paying for news and information. If advertising practitioners are ever to be ranked above the bottom of the occupational trustworthiness scale, then ethical thinking needs to become every bit as much a part of the advertising process as market research and strategic communication plans.

Thinking About the Audience: From Persuasion Theory to Philosophical Anthropology

Psychologists first began to try to understand persuasion by working with a stimulus–response model. This early behaviorist approach led many to believe that the media could act as a "hypodermic needle" or a "magic bullet," sending a stimulus/message to an unresisting audience. These researchers, called "powerful effects theorists," found examples to support their theory in the public panic after Orson Welles's "War of the Worlds" broadcast on October 30, 1938, and in the success of propaganda during both world wars.

But, the stimulus-response model proved a poor predictor of much human behavior. By the 1940s, most researchers were concluding that media effects were limited or nonexistent. However, by studying only behavior change (i.e., changing my vote) the researchers overlooked the true power of the media in the cognitive (knowledge) and affective (emotional) realms.

Later, communication theorists focused on cognitive psychology. Rather than analyzing persuasion as a simple behavioral reaction to a sufficient stimulus, these scholars theorized that how people think helped to explain persuasion. According to these theories, people strain toward cognitive balance. Simply put, we are most comfortable when all of our beliefs, actions, attitudes, and relationships are in harmony, a state theorists called "symmetry."

Such theories have become known as "balance theories," since they stress the tendency of people to strive for cognitive balance in their lives. A person achieves balance only when his or her attitudes, information, and actions are in harmony. Leon Festinger (1957) coined the term cognitive dissonance to describe the state where a message and an action give conflicting and uncomfortable signals. The desire to eliminate that dissonance is a strong one, strong enough to influence purchasing behavior and voting habits or opinions—at least some of the time.

Doonesbury Copyright G. B. Trudeau. Reprinted with permission of Universal Press Syndicate. All rights reserved.

Advertisers use this theory. A frequent scenario in advertising copy is to knock a consumer off balance early and to promise restoration of that balance through the purchase of a product. For instance, the headline of an ad might suggest that your dandruff is making you a social outcast, and the subsequent copy promises you social approval if you use the correct shampoo. A television ad might suggest that the wrong choice of tires means you don't care about your family's safety, while the correct choice of tires restores peace of mind by providing needed protection.

This social science-based approach to understanding advertising helped in creating ads and, to a more limited extent, explained their effectiveness. However, the social science approach makes some assumptions about the nature of people that advertising itself calls into question. For example, advertising scholars have tried to outline how people cognitively "process" or think about ads. Yet the same studies indicate that people are often irrational, emotional, and not necessarily well-informed about the various claims made in ads. Despite the equivocal findings of social science-based research, the ultimate practical justification for advertising was summed up in the ancient Roman phrase, *caveat emptor*, "Let the buyer beware." In other words, the creators of the ads were willing to assume little responsibility for the impact of their work, and academic studies gave them partial cover: if you can't prove that something's been effective, then it's unreasonable to suggest you take some responsibility for it.

Philosophical anthropologists assert that human rationality exists on equal footing with human beings who explain themselves through daily experience, language and symbols. Culture and experience balance rationality (Wilkins and Christians, 2001). If philosophical anthropology is correct, then ethical analysis of advertising founded in "Let the buyer beware" is morally untenable. Instead, the ethical goal of advertising should be the empowerment of multiple stakeholders. If the concept of human being as creator of culture and dynamic user of symbols becomes an ethical foundation for thinking about the audience, then advertising practitioners could be expected to operate within the following framework:

- Clients and the public need information that gives them "a good reason to adopt a course of action" (Koehn 1998, 106). The reason needs to be nonarbitrary and capable of helping people support one action instead of others.
- Rather than offering only expert opinion, advertising should foster ongoing discussion so that people can explore when options are sound and when practical knowledge (common sense) is superior.
- Advertising, just like news, can help foster reflective community, including the community of consumers.
- Advertising needs to take seriously the role of culture in our lives. That means that advertising must authentically reflect the diverse voices that comprise our culture.
- Advertising will speak to the role of organizations in our lives. Questions of history and background can be conveyed in ads, but that must be done accurately and in context.

Given these general guidelines, let's explore a specific framework that puts ads to an ethical test.

Thinking About the Message: The TARES Test

The TARES test (Baker and Martinson, 2001) suggests the creators of every ad to ask themselves a series of questions. If the answers are "yes" the ad passes the test. If the answers to some or all of the questions are "no" then the creator must justify—in the sense that Bok discusses—the ad content decisions. While the TARES test will not solve all ethical problems in creating ads, it does give creative people, marketing directors, and strategic communication planners a tool.

The first element of the test—**T**—stands for **truthfulness.** Are the ad claims, both verbal and visual, truthful? If the message communicates only part of the truth (and many ads do this), are the omissions deceptive? Conversely, an ad would pass the test if it meets a genuine human need to provide truthful information, even if some facts are omitted.

The Cheerios television ads that emphasize eating Cheerios as part of a heart-healthy lifestyle could easily pass the first element of the TARES test. People do have to eat, and the ads provide needed information. The ads also omit some information—for example, the other components of a heart-healthy lifestyle or the fact that other breakfast cereals also meet these requirements. But the omitted information does not lead the mature consumer to make false assumptions and bad choices.

Step two in the TARES test—**A** for **authenticity**—is closely linked to step one. Authenticity suggests that it's important not only to do the right thing, but also "to do it with the right attitude" (Pojman 1999, 158). We link this notion to the concept of sincerity. First, is there a sincere need for this product within the range of products and services available? Second, are the reasons given the consumer purchasing the product presented in such a way that they also would motivate the person who developed and wrote the ad?

Let's take a set of ads about products designed to help elderly or infirm people live more independently. Although some of these products—for example, devices that turn on lights in response to a hand clap—may seem little more than high-tech toys, anyone with a grandparent in a wheelchair, a sibling crippled by an illness like rheumatoid arthritis, of even a young person suffering from the imposed immobility of a broken leg can readily understand the need for such devices. But if, in order to make this point, the ads stereotype elderly people as frail, helpless, weak, or easily panicked, they do not authentically reflect the reality of life beyond age sixty-five. Indeed, such stereotypical and fear-filled appeals omit a substantial number of consumers who might benefit from the product. The ad lacks authenticity. Thus, the TARES test would suggest rethinking the specific appeal in the ad to one that scares and stereotypes less and informs more. For creative people, such a switch is readily accomplished. Just as important, a fresher approach might well sell more.

The **R** in the TARES test stands for **respect,** in this case, respect for the person who will receive the persuasive message. However, as a shorthand way of thinking through this element of the test, it might be appropriate for advertising practitioners to ask themselves, "Am I willing to take full, open, public and personal responsibility for the content of this ad?" As Aristotle might add, a *phrenemos* respects himself as well as others. Mutuality is an ethical virtue. It's to this notion of mutuality that the TARES test now turns.

The **E** in the TARES test stands for **equity.** We conceptualize mutuality as follows: is the recipient of the message on the same, level playing field as the ad's creator? Or, in order to correctly interpret the ad must that person be abnormally well-informed, unusually bright or quick-witted, and completely without prejudice? Advertising copy that takes advantage of these common human frailties would not pass the equity portion of the TARES test. Phrased another way, the ad would not survive a trip behind John Rawl's veil of ignorance (see chapter VI).

Think about this corporate image ad for Mobil Oil—the one with the pristine scenery, glorious sunset, and an oil tanker. The ad claims that Mobil has the best interest of the environment at heart by building tankers with double hulls. While Mobil's claim—that it builds double-hulled tankers—is literally true, correctly interpreting the ad requires a rapid and thorough recall of recent legislative history. Mobil, and all other oil companies, were required by Congress to build double-hulled tankers after the single-hulled tanker, the *Exxon Valdez,* ran aground and spilled an enormous amount of oil in Alaska, an environmental disaster of the first magnitude. For the image ad to work, it counts on the average person not knowing—or not being able to connect—legislative requirements with corporate behavior. In fact, the ad assumes an unequal relationship between the knowledge of the person who created the ad and the consumer. It flunks the concept of equity.

Finally, the **S** in the TARES test. Is the ad **socially responsible?** This is perhaps the most difficult element of the test for the simple reason that advertising practitioners have duties to many groups, among them their clients, the agencies for which they work, consumers, people who see the advertising but do not buy a particular product, and society at large. Because this text emphasizes social ethics, we suggest interpreting this portion of the TARES test in the following fashion:

- If everyone who is financially able to purchase this product or service did so and used it, would society as a whole be improved?
- If there are some groups in society who would benefit from using this product as advertised, are there others that could be significantly harmed by it? Are there ways to protect them?
- Does this ad increase or decrease the trust the average person has for persuasive messages?
- Does this ad take the notion of corporate responsibility, both to make money and to improve human life and welfare, seriously and truthfully?

Using this concept of social responsibility should enable you to think ethically about television's decisions to air condom advertising. MTV, the network targeted at teenagers, chose to air such ads in 2000. More traditional network television outlets did not. Which decision do you believe is more ethically justified? Why? Has the notion of social responsibility any place in your analysis?

We acknowledge that the TARES test is a demanding one. But we believe asking these questions, particularly during the process of creating an ad, can also be a spur to better, more creative execution and be rewarded in the capitalistic marketplace. We also suggest that the TARES test may help advertising practitioners warn their corporate clients about the kind of advertising that could do them, as well as society at large, great long-term harm.

Advertising's Special Problems: Vulnerable Audiences

One of the contemporary quandaries for advertising practitioners are the twin pulls of target marketing and the reality that much advertising is carried by mediums that reach large, heterogeneous audiences. The unfortunate result is that advertising intended for one group is seen by and influences another. Sometimes the results are humorous, and maybe even a little embarrassing, as when radio ads for "adult theaters" run during times when parents are driving their children, and maybe other children in the carpool, to school in the morning.

However, in the case of the tobacco and the motion picture industries, this "confusion" of intended audience with actual recipients appears quite deliberate. Congressional hearings into Hollywood's advertising practices in 2000 produced internal documents that proved that the motion picture industry targets children between the ages of twelve and seventeen with ads for movies carrying the advisory "No one under 17 admitted without parent or guardian." The tobacco industry agreed to withdraw its cartoon spokesperson "Joe Camel" from magazines and billboards after internal documents revealed the industry targeted underage smokers. In other cases—for example the beer industry—advertising intended for adults is often seen by those who cannot legally drink but do remember the catchy commercials and the presentation of drinking as something connected with fun and good times. Even young children know about the Budweiser lizards, and most adult alcoholics report having had their first drink when they were underage.

These examples revolve around the same ethical question: are there certain types of audiences who deserve special protection from advertising messages? In keeping with thousands of years of ethical thinking, U.S. law has answered this question in the affirmative, particularly in the case of children. Thus, there are a number of legal restrictions on advertising targeted at children, in everything from Saturday morning television programming to the sorts of messages and characters that advertisers may employ. The reason is that children, unlike adults, are not assumed to be autonomous moral actors. They reason about advertising imperfectly, and in an attempt to protect them American society has accepted some regulation of commercial speech.

However, the issue gets murkier when the target audience is formed of adults—for example, ethnic consumers. Exactly when advertisers began to actively court ethnic consumers is uncertain. Brooks (1992) quotes a 1940 *Business Week* article that reported an organization was established in Los Angeles to help guide advertisers who wished to garner the patronage of African-American consumers. The businesses were cautioned against using words such as "boss," "boy," and "darkey" in their advertisements. Instead, the advertisers were urged to refer to African-American consumers as "Negroes" who want the same things as other shoppers.

The real attempt to court ethnic audiences began when those audiences acquired buying power. By the time you read this sentence, Hispanics will be the largest minority in the United States; the buying power of African-American consumers will be more than $300 billion. The Asian-American market has also increased substantially. Yet, a relative handful of advertisements reflect this emerging demographic reality, and commercials designed to appeal to this market segment sometimes employ troubling stereotypes or encounter other difficulties. For example, R. J. Reynolds Tobacco Company, which has spent millions developing Uptown cigarettes aimed at African-Americans, had to pull the product when consumer outrage over the impact of tobacco on the health of African-Americans became public.

Other tendencies in advertising combine, in troubling ways, cultural understandings and product sales. Magazines pointed at teenage girls seldom reflect the reality of teenage bodies. Scholarly studies have shown that women, when exposed to advertising images, find their own bodies less acceptable. The same goes for facial features. Scholars have noted that the ideal image of beauty, even in magazines targeted at African-Americans, is a Caucasian one of small noses, thin lips, and lighter skin tones. African-American women simply don't see themselves in these advertisements. Scholars in the cultural studies tradition argue that the impact of these repeated images is cumulative—the culture itself comes to accept without question what is, in reality, nothing more than a gender or a racial stereotype.

Few scholars have suggested that adults who are members of minority communities need special protection from advertising. What they have noted is that ads that abuse the trust between consumer and product have both short-term and long-term consequences. In the short term, products may not sell or may find themselves the target of regulation. In the long term, the load of cynicism and societal distrust increases. People sense they are being used, even if they can't explain precisely how. The buyer may learn to beware of advertising itself rather than to use advertising to help make better-informed decisions.

Suggested Readings

Baker, S. and Martinson, D. 2001. "The TARES Test: Five Principles of Ethical Persuasion." *Journal of Mass Media Ethics* Vol. 16, No. 2 & 3, in press.

Festinger, L. 1957. *A Theory of Cognitive Dissonance.* Stanford, CA: Stanford University Press.

Koehn, D. 1998. *Rethinking Feminist ethics.* New York: Routledge.

Leiss, William, Stephen Kline, and Sut Jhally. 1986. *Social communication in advertising: Person, products and images of well being.* New York: Methuen Publications.

O'Toole, John. 1985. *The trouble with advertising.* New York: Times Books.

Patterson, Thomas E., and Robert D. McClure. 1972. *The unseeing eye.* New York: G. P. Putnam's Sons.

Pojman, L. 1998. *Ethical Theory: Classical and Contemporary Readings.* Belmont, CA: Wadsworth Publishing Company.

Schudson, Michael. 1984. *Advertising: The uneasy persuasion.* New York: Basic Books.

CHAPTER III CASES

CASE III-A
Superman's Super Bowl Miracle
RENITA COLEMAN
Louisiana State University

In 1995 actor Christopher Reeve, best known as Superman, was paralyzed from the neck down in a horseback riding accident. Five years later, he "walked" across a stage to receive an award. This was no miracle of modern medicine; rather it was a miracle of computer animation. And, the occasion was an advertisement rather than a real awards ceremony or fund-raising effort for spinal cord research.

Reaction to the commercial for Nuveen Investments was swift. The phones started ringing at the National Spinal Cord Injury Association. Paralyzed people fooled by the image wanted to know where Reeve went to get cured. People with spinal cord injuries and physicians saw the commercial as either heartwarming or contemptible. Reeve was portrayed as either a saint or snake-oil salesman, pedaling false hopes or raising hope and money for research.

More than 131 million viewers saw the sixty-second spot that aired twice during the Super Bowl. It featured an auditorium full of people gathered to present an award for research that cured spinal cord injury. No specific date is given, and narration in the beginning puts the gathering sometime after 2006. The New York skyline has a few new, futuristic skyscrapers, and there are two outdoor shots of a subway train and a newsstand with a TV screen hanging overhead. But, once the screen moves inside the auditorium, there are no clues that this is a "flash forward." Reeve looks barely older than he does today.

An announcer in a tuxedo talks about the advances science has made against AIDS and cancer and tells the audience that someone special is to present the awards for some amazing breakthroughs in spinal cord injuries. The camera focuses on the lower body of a man getting up from a chair and walking stiffly to the stage; it is a beaming Christopher Reeve. The special effects are achieved with a computerized image of Reeve's head grafted onto another man's body. He walks haltingly to the stage with the help of canes and walkers. A voice-over says, "In the future, so many amazing things will happen in the world. What amazing things can you make happen?" The screen fades to black and three taglines read, "Invest well." "Leave your mark." "Nuveen Investments."

Was this commercial misleading or creative?

Many disabled people and their advocates were aghast. It cruelly offered false hope and unreasonable expectations to people who should be adapting to life with disabilities, they said. It was not just psychologically harmful, but practically harmful too, especially to young people, said one doctor with a spinal cord injury of his own. People could end up spending untold hours each day preparing their bodies for the time when the cure comes instead of preparing themselves for the realities of their new world. Others felt the commercial left the impression that people with spinal cord injuries were consumed by a quest for a miracle cure. Reeve's own wife was against the commercial. "I didn't like it because I worried that the commercial would result in disabled people being carried away by this fantasy of dramatic recovery," Dana Reeve told the *New York Daily News*. Some accused Reeve of parading his own fantasies in public to convert others. The *New York Times's* advertising column called it "crass and more than a little creepy."

However, not everyone connected with spinal cord injury was upset. It offered much needed hope, some said, and it helped focus attention on the need for research. Reeve himself defended it, saying breakthroughs are imminent and getting people interested and investing in research is paramount. In fact, since his injury Reeve has worked tirelessly for a cure, raising millions, setting up a research center, and persuading Congress to add $10 million for research. There is a genuine reason for optimism, Reeve said, citing scientific information he was given before it was published in academic journals.

Some doctors agree that a cure is in the foreseeable future; others caution any cure is more likely to benefit the newly injured, not people like Reeve.

In a released statement, Reeve called the commercial a "vision" and likened it to John F. Kennedy's setting a goal to land astronauts on the moon. "I was pleased to be involved in this spot because the message is that all of us must give back to society and leave our mark in some unique way."

The firestorm obscured one question: what was this commercial selling? Nuveen Investments is a 101-year-old Chicago-based company that has been shifting from municipal bond underwriting to money management for brokers and financial advisers. The company had a net income in 1999 of $97.3 million. Some speculated that Reeve's endorsement would boost the company's name recognition and credibility.

The connection between a cure for paralysis and investing money is unclear in the $4 million ad. Nuveen spokesman Chris Allen said the point of the ad was "to inspire a dialogue on money, to have a new dialogue and get away from buying bigger boats and bigger cars and think about the impact that money can have on the future."

Many viewers didn't know what the commercial was advertising then and still don't today. Less in doubt was the immediate effect of free publicity. The commercial was rebroadcast as news by hundreds of television stations and it dominated radio and television talk shows and newspaper columns for weeks.

Additionally, there is the issue of how visual images can fool even media-savvy viewers. The commercial was filmed to look like news coverage. There was no explicit statement that this was a futuristic vision, no visual cues that this was a flash forward. The visual image of Reeve walking was laced with emotional appeal. Reeve himself told *Adweek* that seeing a paralyzed person walking is "very emotional and almost overwhelming. So, it created a visceral response." Finally, there was the claim by some that the ad helped to raise money for spinal cord research.

Micro Issues:

1. Ethicists suggest that the claims made in an advertisement should be open to rational discussion. What are the claims in this ad? Could a consumer rationally respond to them based on information in the ad?

2. Should this ad have included visual cues about its hypothetical nature?
3. Since the goal of advertising is to sell something, how would you evaluate this ad's effectiveness?
4. Is this ad like or unlike ads in which now-dead film stars are inserted through use of digital animation to sell products such as Diet Coke or Coors beer? Why or why not?

Mid-range Issues:

1. Should news journalists have run stories about this commercial? Why or why not? What should those stories have said?
2. Research indicates that visual information and emotional responses tend to circumvent the brain's logic centers. For what sort of products might such ads be appropriate? Are there products or causes for which such an approach is inappropriate?
3. Do you believe this ad passes the TARES test? Justify your decision.

Macro Issues:

1. Do the ends justify the means in this ad? Does the possible good of increased awareness and funding for spinal cord injury justify what many said was a deception?

CASE III-B
Breaking Through the Clutter: Ads That Make You Think Twice
FRITZ CROPP IV
University of Missouri

Controversial advertising campaigns were nothing new for Benetton when it unveiled its spring–summer 2000 worldwide communication campaign. In January 2000, "We, on Death Row," a statement against the death penalty featuring U.S. death row convicts, brought Benetton an unprecedented level of criticism, complete with an apology from its president and the loss of a potentially lucrative contract with a mainstream American retailer.

Benetton, the Italian clothing company, had a fifteen-year record of concerning itself with social issues including peace, war, AIDS awareness, and multiculturalism. Previous imagery featured a dying AIDS patient surrounded by his anguished family, a picture of a black horse and a white horse copulating, an unwashed newborn baby with an uncut umbilical cord, a buttock branded with an HIV-positive stamp, a priest and a nun kissing, the blood-soaked uniform of a dead Bosnian sniper, a white baby nursing at a black breast, and the like.

Such ads invite controversy. The Vatican criticized the ad featuring a nun and priest kissing, and a French court ruled that the company had exploited human suffering in a campaign depicting dying AIDS patients and ordered it to pay damages to French citizens infected with the HIV virus. Yet Benetton seemed to invite the controversy, proclaiming its approach "looks reality in the face" (Hyperlink: http://www.benneton.com) by tackling social issues. Company president Luciano Benetton said ten years ago that "Our campaigns are an attempt to get away from traditional advertising in the belief that it has no power and no value any more." Adds Oliviero Toscani, Benetton's photographer and creative director, "My brief is not to concern myself with commercial images to sell more T-shirts but rather to create an image for the company that touches people in all of the countries in which Benetton is present" (Mondow 2000, 61)

While one cannot directly or singularly credit the advertising, Toscani's work has coincided with Benetton's worldwide growth. While critics decry the seeming vacuum between the provocative campaigns and the relatively mainstream Benetton stores and products, the company enjoyed a steady increase in worldwide sales and net profits through the 1990s. Benetton now sells clothes, accessories, and sporting goods in more than 7,000 stores in 120 countries, with 70 percent of its sales originating in Europe (Conley 2000).

"We, on Death Row" began when Toscani began working with freelance journalist Ken Shulman to photograph and interview twenty-six U.S. prisoners on death row. The work culminated in a ninety-six-page supplement in the January, 11, 2000, edition of *Talk* magazine, followed by a series of individual pictures of the prisoners in selected U.S. magazines and on billboards in major U.S. cities.

"The campaign is about the death penalty," proclaims the Benetton press release on the company's Web site. "Leaving aside any social, political, judicial or moral consideration, this project aims at showing the public the realities of capital punishment, so that no one around the world will consider the death penalty neither as a distant problem nor as news that occasionally appear (sic) on TV."

The *Talk* magazine supplement included pictures and comments from the prisoners, along with quotes from Pope John Paul II and the Dalai Lama. Questions were decidedly soft. Shulman asked inmates about their families, prison food, what they dream, and what they miss, with no mention of the victims, no discussion of current feelings of remorse.

Given space limitations, the advertisements, which Benetton claims were decided upon after the pictures and interviews had been taken and completed, were limited to a picture of an inmate, a description of his crime, the method by which he would be killed, the words "Sentenced to Death" and the "United Colors of Benetton" logo. Seven inmates agreed to allow their photographs to be used for this campaign. Even less context is provided in this format. There was no warning for the victims' families that the pictures were about to appear.

When they did, criticism came from many angles.

Sears, Roebuck and Company cancelled a franchising contract it had recently signed with Benetton. The contract was forged to help Sears with its declining clothing sales and help Benetton reestablish itself in the United States, which accounts for just 5 percent of the company's business. Further, Sears pulled from its shelves all brands owned by the global parent company.

California House Leader Scott Baugh drafted a resolution urging all California residents to boycott Benetton until the campaign disappeared. The bill passed 59 to 8. Pennsylvania Attorney General Lynne Abraham called for a nationwide boycott. Activists from Parents of Murdered Children staged a protest outside Benetton's U.S. office in New York City. The company also was targeted in Texas by Justice for All, the New York group Center for the Community Interest, and the International Union of Police Associations. Missouri Attorney General Jay Nixon filed a circuit court suit, saying that representatives form Benetton tricked their way into Missouri's jails by pretending to be journalists. "Selling sweaters on the back of death row inmates is sick and wrong," he said.

Advertising critics were equally appalled. Bob Garfield, a columnist at *Advertising Age,* wrote, "There is no brand—not a single one—that has the right to increase its sales on the backs, on the misery, on the fates of condemned men and women, much less their slaughtered victims" (Steuver 2000, C01).

In April 2000, Benetton announced that Toscani, who once said there is no such thing as going too far (Hughes 2000) was leaving after eighteen years. The company did not address whether the "We, on Death Row" campaign was a factor.

In the end, it is difficult to assess the cost or benefits to Benetton of "We, on Death Row." The $1.8 million in royalties to have been generated by the Sears deal represents a fraction of the company's $2 billion in annual sales. Similarly, the $15 million the company said it spent on global distribution, combined with the undisclosed production costs, may be balanced by the resulting publicity, which continues to build upon Benetton's edgy image among its young target as a socially conscious company. "A substantial number of consumers seem to sense genuine integrity and principle behind Benetton's actions," notes Patrick Allossery of the *Financial Post* (2000. C3).

Micro Issues:

1. The twenty-six prisoners interviewed by Toscani and Shulman were convicted of thirty-seven murders. Should Benetton have considered the victim's families before running its campaign? Should the company have given them advance warning that the images would appear?
2. Responding to 144 consumer complaints, the British Advertising Standards Authority accepted Benetton's explanation that the campaign was intended to encourage debate and remind people that even death row prisoners have human rights. Thus, it ruled that its duty was to uphold an advertiser's freedom of speech. When a clothing company exploits shocking issues in its advertising, is it an abuse of that freedom?
3. Was it okay for Benetton to expand its campaign to print advertisements and billboards without seeking the same type of permission it was granted prior to interviewing the prisoners for the *Talk* magazine insert?

Mid-range Issues:

1. It's been said that there's no such thing as bad publicity. Do the ends justify the means?
2. Does this type of campaign illuminate the issues—or potentially trivialize them?
3. If the point of "We, on Death Row" was to raise awareness of issues surrounding the death penalty, is a one-sided approach appropriate? Should Benetton have sought opinions from people in favor of the death penalty?

Macro Issues:

1. Should the definition of advertising be altered to include efforts such as "We, on Death Row," or should such campaigns be considered differently by review boards and by the media outlets that sell time and space?
2. Should standards be developed to prevent advertisers from insensitive or potentially irresponsible actions, or does paying for space or time supersede the need for balance, fairness, or objectivity?
3. Benetton claims to "tear down the wall of indifference, contributing to raising the awareness of universal problems among the world's citizens." However, there are cultural chasms to be addressed. In this case, the company's belief that the death penalty is inherently wrong is consistent with European opinion on the issue, but inconsistent with what many Americans believe. Should advertisers—or companies paying for space to espouse their own

commentary—be sensitive to cultural differences? If so, what guidance should be provided for them?

4. Jim Faulds, an advertising executive in Edinburgh, says ads that go beyond the boundaries of good taste also push back those boundaries. People become numbed to the shock tactics, and the only recourse is to shock further. Asks *Scotsman* reporter Michael Kerrigan (2000, 22), "As we recall the outrage that greeted those late 1990s campaigns we do indeed seem to be harking back to an age of innocence, long gone by. Have we, too, been implicated in Benetton's little habit?"

CASE III-C
The Plagiarism Factory
JOHN P. FERRÉ
University of Louisville

Terry had not long been advertising manager for the *Louisville Cardinal* when she received camera-ready copy of an advertisement for ready-made research papers. "RESEARCH PAPERS," it announced, "16,278 to choose from—all subjects. Custom research also available—all levels. COD or Visa/MasterCard." The ad urged students to send two dollars or to call a toll-free hotline for a catalog. With the camera-ready advertisement, the company enclosed a check for a year's space in the weekly university newspaper.

Because the *Cardinal* is an independent student paper, Terry was not compelled or prohibited from running by university administrators questionable advertisements. Furthermore, the newspaper had run the advertisement weekly for years. Tradition was on the side of publishing the ad, yet Terry felt uneasy about it. She voiced her uneasiness at the next staff meeting, and the staff agreed to reject the ad. Terry mailed the following letter:

I am sorry to inform you that we cannot run your advertisement for research assistance. The staff of the *Louisville Cardinal* reserves the right to refuse any advertisement it feels could be harmful or insulting to the students of this university. Therefore, out of respect for the integrity of the student body and for the protection of the ethical policies of the University of Louisville, I am returning your check for $111.36. I apologize for any budgeting inconveniences this may have caused you.

Although Terry lost a commission and the newspaper lost some revenue, the staff of the *Cardinal* felt confident that they had made the right decision. The mail-order research paper firm contacted the newspaper a couple of years later to no avail.

At least one of the newspaper's advisers was highly critical of the staff's decision. "Newspapers should print ads, not reject them," he argued, "especially since the *Cardinal* is the only newspaper on campus. It should not act as a censor. Its advertising columns should be open to anyone who is willing to pay for the space, whatever the product or service. Editorial judgments should be made only in regard to news and feature stories."

Despite the adviser's fear that the student newspaper was beginning a campaign of advertising censorship, the *Cardinal* has refused space to no other national advertiser. It prints advertisements for alcoholic beverages, for instance, even though alcoholism and drunk driving are arguably more dangerous for students than academic dishonesty. Apparently, the *Cardinal*'s primary moral criterion for the acceptance of advertisements is honesty. All ads that neither deceive nor encourage others to deceive are acceptable in the pages of the *Cardinal*.

Micro Issues:

1. If the research paper company queries the newspaper once again, should the newspaper reconsider its decision, or should it stand firm?

2. Is the financial health of the paper an ethically relevant factor? If the paper's budget was in the red, could an argument be made that it is better for the student body to have a newspaper with offensive ads than it is to let the paper die?
3. At some time in the future, the paper receives an ad for *Cliffs Notes*. The staff knows that some students are tempted to rely on plot summaries rather than read whole novels that are assigned in various courses in the humanities. Furthermore, the campus bookstore stocks a wide variety of *Cliffs Notes*. What should the newspaper do? If your answer differs from your decision on the research-paper ad, distinguish between the two products.

Mid-range Issues:

1. What types of advertisements should student newspapers reject? Community newspapers?
2. Should papers decide advertising policy in advance, or should they make these decisions on a case-by-case basis? What would such a policy look like?
3. Suppose your campus newspaper receives an advertisement from a local nightclub for a "Drink or Drown" promotion—all the beer you can drink for one price. Do you accept the ad? Suppose the campus radio station has refused air time to the advertiser. Is the newspaper under any obligation to reject it in light of the radio station's decision?

Macro Issues:

1. Are a newspaper's advertising columns a common carrier—selling space without discrimination—or should they operate with the same editorial freedom that applies to news and feature stories?
2. Is a newspaper morally responsible for everything it prints, whether or not the content originated at the newspaper?
3. Is it right to impose one's standards on information others receive? Is the newspaper doing so in this case?

CASE III-D
If You Let Nike Play . . .
RENITA COLEMAN
Louisiana State University

It takes you by surprise. A television commercial without a product. Just a half dozen or so preteen girls of various ethnic backgrounds in a working class playground. With the rhythm and cadence of a song, they voice the refrain "If you let me play; if you let me play sports." The verse goes like this:

> I will like myself more.
> I will have more self-confidence.
> I will be 60 percent less likely to get breast cancer.
> I will suffer less depression.
> I will be more likely to leave a man who beats me.
> I will be less likely to get pregnant before I want to.
> I will learn what it means to be strong.

At the end of thirty seconds, the screen goes black and the familiar Nike logo appears with the slogan "Just Do It."

Unusual, certainly. Only a few advertisements have departed so radically from standard practice. Is this commercial socially responsible or ethically questionable? Is its audience children or their parents? This thirty-second commercial is startlingly effective precisely because of its ambiguity. It grabs your attention with its rapid-fire visuals; it makes you sit up and pay attention with its hard-hitting issues; and it makes you curious to know what this unusual ad is all about. The net effect is that this subtle pitch of a sportswear company becomes all the more memorable.

The Nike "If you let me play" ad makes unique use of the time-honored advertising technique of cognitive dissonance. It knocks the viewer off balance with the incongruous image of preteen girls discussing such adult subjects as spouse abuse, breast cancer, and depression. It is emotionally and cognitively unsettling to hear children discussing such things because we assume youth equals innocence. We would rather not have to face the fact that many children today are intimately acquainted with such topics. Perhaps a mother or other family member has battled depression or even lost a fight with breast cancer. More unsettling yet, perhaps children have seen daddy hitting mommy.

Even absent firsthand knowledge, children today are subjected to such situations via the news and entertainment media. Who really thinks children have been shielded from the facts of O. J. Simpson's battering of his ex-wife Nicole? From Columbine High School? And the trend is for family secrets to be less concealed than they once were. Children today are not the innocents of the past or the innocents we would still like to believe they are. This Nike ad is an in-your-face testimonial to that. And true to the formula of ads that use cognitive dissonance as a tool, Nike proposes a solution to restore the viewer to balance: let me play, and inferentially, let me do so in Nike apparel.

"Our goal wasn't to be alarmist, just direct," said Andrea Bonner, who helped create the "If you let me play" commercial. "We just wanted to be real." She acknowledges that this issue-oriented commercial is "a different kind of animal for Nike." In fact, she says, it "borders on being a pro bono message."

Nike has been questioned on ethical grounds in the past. In 1994, a commercial featuring basketball's bad boy, Dennis Rodman, was criticized for reinforcing an ends-justifies-the-means mentality when Santa Claus grants Rodman his Christmas wish of expensive new shoes despite his unsportsmanlike conduct. African-Americans criticized the company for using Rodman as a role model when other, more positive African-American role models were available. Nike has similarly been criticized for advertising its shoes on billboards located in poor, inner-city neighborhoods where parents can ill-afford $100 shoes.

The company was even accused of helping to cause thefts and violence in ghettos where the apparent reason for the assault was the victim's expensive sports shoes. The children in the "If you let me play" ad appear to be from working-class families. While it is rather ambiguous, the appearance of the playground and the children's clothes provide visual cues to suggest this. Perhaps Nike tried to avoid being accused of marketing expensive products to socioeconomic groups that either cannot afford them or would do without necessities in order to purchase them.

The subject of target markets also brings up the issue of advertising to children. The poor and elderly as well as the young have often been singled out as audiences deserving special sensitivity and responsibility from advertisers. Because they are potentially more vulnerable, less experienced and adept at sorting out product claims, and more subject to peer pressure and advertising's influence, children's advertising must assume a greater sensitivity than advertising to the general population, an audience considered to be active and autonomous.

Research by Carol Gilligan and others has shown that adolescence is a particularly formative time for a girl's self-esteem. Adolescence is a time for issues of attachment for girls, and identity formation takes place within relationships. There is special vulnerability for girls in finding a way of caring for themselves while maintaining connections to others. The topics in this commercial are all of a connective nature—pregnancy involves a male and a child; domestic violence involves a relationship with a male, at least; strength, self-confidence, depression, and even breast cancer, with its strong ties to feminine issues, are all issues of self-caring and identity formation.

Another controversy centers on the source of the statistics in the ad. In "If you let me play," Nike claims it got its statistical information from the Women's Sports Foundation (WSF), a nonprofit organization that collects studies regarding athletics and women and girls. However, a representative of the WSF said the foundation would never knowingly provide its research to Nike because it is sponsored by Reebok, Nike's chief competitor. The advertising agency that created the commercial also claims that the information was obtained from WSF.

Micro Issues:

1. Is Nike guilty of using "scare tactics" to sell its clothing line?
2. Nike claims the message borders on being a pro bono message, in other words a free public service ad for a worthy cause. Critique that claim.

Mid-range Issues:

1. Would the same commercial have been any less arresting had it featured adult women? Would it be less effective?
2. Nike never produced a similar ad for boys, although there are documented health and social benefits for males who play sports. Why do you think there was not an "If you let me play" ad made featuring young boys?

Macro Issues:

1. The Women's Sports Foundation gets its research data from a variety of academic and not-for-profit sources. Given its goals of promoting fitness through sports for women, why would it consider the statistics in the Nike ad to be proprietary information? Shouldn't the foundation be pleased at the larger audience generated by the Nike ad?
2. Obviously many girls who do not play sports do not suffer any of the maladies mentioned in the ad later in life either. Is Nike guilty of portraying women as more vulnerable than they are in order to sell clothing?

CASE III-E
A Sobering Dilemma
BEVERLY HORVIT
University of Texas–Arlington

The music of "Pomp and Circumstance" plays as puppies cross the stage at their graduation from obedience school. One dog, the class valedictorian, carries a bottle of Canadian Crown Royal whiskey. The images are part of a Seagram's television commercial that first aired June 9, 1996, on a television station in Corpus Christi, Texas. The airings continued for a month. By running the ad, Seagram's ended an almost fifty-year, self-imposed ban on the television advertising of distilled spirits. Although beer and wine commercials are routinely seen on television, ads for "hard" liquor had not been visible since 1948.

Why break the ban in the summer of 1996? For one thing, there is the opportunity to enlarge Seagram's stake in the $98 billion per year alcoholic beverage market. More specifically, Seagram's spokeswoman Bevin Gove pointed to the changing times and the changing media landscape. She said the distinctions between types of media are not as clear-cut as in the past, making old policies that allow print but not broadcast ads outdated. "The industry code is outdated," Gove told *USA Today*.

Not mentioned by Gove is the fact that sales of distilled spirits were down. While beer consumption had been flat for years, liquor sales had fallen 32 percent since 1979. Seagram's chose Texas as a test because the Crown Royal brand had been selling well there, with sales doubling since 1980.

Seagram's actions were almost immediately decried by consumer groups, the president of the United States, and a bipartisan group of lawmakers. The same week the commercial first appeared, former U.S. Representative Joe Kennedy introduced legislation to ban television and radio advertising of hard liquor.

For the television station and Seagram's, the decision to run the ad was largely fueled by the profit motive and justified with free speech concerns. T. Frank Smith, owner of KRIS-TV, the independent NBC affiliate in Corpus Christi, was eager to line up advertising for hard liquor and discussed the ad with Seagram's for months. For her part, Gove said the company believes the distiller has the same right to "responsibly access electronic advertising" as do beer and wine manufacturers. She claimed Seagram's products are at a competitive disadvantage compared to beer and wine when they are not advertised on television.

From the perspective of Seagram's and the Distilled Spirits Council of the United States (DISCUS), there is no legitimate reason why beer and wine makers should enjoy free speech protection while the manufacturers of distilled spirits do not. Twelve ounces of beer, five ounces of table wine, and 1.5 ounces of distilled spirits (the council's preferred term) in a mixed drink contain the same amount of alcohol. "There is no beverage of moderation, only a practice of moderation. It's not what you drink that's important, but how much you drink that counts," the Council says. Similarly, DISCUS and other groups say the notion of "hard" liquor is a misnomer, pointing out that beer and wine can lead to drunkenness just as easily as distilled spirits can.

Walter Wurfel, a spokesperson for the National Association of Broadcasters (NAB), argues that because "alcoholic beverages are a legal product, there should be a legal right under the First Amendment to advertise them." However, Wurfel adds the NAB has cautioned individual broadcast stations that they should consider the impact of such advertising within their own communities.

The problem with the advertising, Rep. Kennedy said, is that it comes "at a time when our society is trying to curb the impact of alcohol abuse." Thousands of people are killed in alcohol-related crashes each year and those deaths account for nearly half of the traffic fatalities each year. In addition, nearly one-quarter of all teen drivers killed in traffic accidents have a blood alcohol content of .10 or higher, above the legal minimum for driving in every state. Alcohol abuse takes other tolls as well. According to the National Council on Alcoholism and Drug Dependence, alcohol contributes to 100,000 deaths annually, making it the third leading cause of preventable mortality in the United States, after tobacco and diet/activity patterns.

Seagram's and KRIS-TV's Smith countered that they are acting responsibly. Seagram's, Gove says, has a sixty-year history of promoting the responsible use of alcohol, including a slogan advising moderation in drinking and programs to encourage parents to talk to their children about alcohol. Smith said his station airs frequent public service announcements, including one featuring the station's news anchor, that warn viewers against drunken driving. Smith estimated the station ran the spots about forty times a month.

Those most critical of the Seagram's ad say it targets the young. The commercial, says George Hacker of the Center for Science in the Public Interest, "features the gracious and familiar strains of music that millions of teenagers will hear during the high school graduation ceremonies." Hacker argues that teens "already get an overdose of ads on television teaching them that drinking beer is fun, that it's cool, that it will help them score with girls. The last thing they need is another avalanche of powerful electronic messages assuring them that liquor will make them successful—even valedictorians—and that drinking should be a part of their lives." KRIS-TV owner Smith says he is not worried about children seeing the ad, because "a kid can't buy liquor. A kid can't even go into a liquor store."

Despite the national publicity, Smith received only about seventy-five letters, more than half from a local church, and fewer than twenty phone calls. In addition, the station conducted an unscientific poll asking viewers to call in to say whether they opposed or approved of the ad. According to Smith, more than 6,000 people called in, 70 percent of whom said they had no problem with the commercial and 30 percent of whom were opposed to it. While the poll was not scientific, Smith believes it's a pretty accurate reflection of the community's feelings.

Micro Issues:

1. Should the makers of distilled spirits be subject to different standards for broadcast advertising than the makers of wine and beer? If so, on what basis?
2. Does the ad described seem to target children, as Hacker claims? Does the ad imply that drinking Seagram's will make one more academically successful?

3. Gove claims that Seagram's started to advertise again because the distinction between print and electronic ad policies no longer made sense. Do you agree or disagree with that?
4. Does Gove's justification lose any of its validity in light of the shrinking sales of "hard" liquor?

Mid-range Issues:

1. If the community survey had revealed that 70 percent of those responding wanted the commercial off the air, what should Smith have done?
2. Would it make any difference in the controversy if the ads had been moved to the late evening hours when presumably fewer children could see them?
3. What should be the role of the FCC (Federal Communications Commission) in policing or prohibiting liquor ads on television?
4. You are the copywriter at the agency that is developing a similar campaign. Do you agree to work on the campaign? What can the agency demand of you as an employee?

Macro Issues:

1. Should station policy be dictated or even backed up by nonscientific polls?
2. The makers of distilled spirits have a strong case for free speech. However, the opponents of advertising of alcohol claim that alcohol contributes greatly to our society's problems. Does a product lose First Amendment rights because it has a potential to harm? What products other than alcohol can you draw a parallel to?

CHAPTER IV

Loyalty: Choosing Between Competing Allegiances

By the end of this chapter, you should:

- understand why the articulation of loyalties is important in professional ethics.
- know Royce's definition of loyalty and at least one of the major problems with that conceptualization.
- understand how journalists' role in society provides them with an additional set of loyalties to consider.
- be familiar with and able to use the Potter Box as a justification model for ethical decision making.

Loyalty as Part of the Social Contract

Decisions involving loyalty occur routinely for media professionals. When journalists make a decision to air or not to air a story, they have decided to whom they will be loyal. When recording executives cancel the contract of a controversial artist to avoid a boycott, they have chosen a loyalty. Most ethical decisions come down to the question "To whom (or what) will I be loyal?"

The original discussion of loyalty in Western culture was written by Plato in *The Trial and Death of Socrates* (see Russell 1967). In Plato's *Phaedo*, Socrates bases his defense against the charges brought against him on his unwavering adherence, or loyalty, to divinely inspired truth. When asked by his accusers if he will stop teaching philosophy, Socrates responds:

Men of Athens, I honor and love you: but I shall obey God rather than you, and while I have life and strength I shall never cease from the practice and teaching of philosophy, exhorting any one whom I meet. . . . For know that this is the command of God; and I believe that no greater good has ever happened in the State than my service to God.

While the word "loyalty" is not present in English translations of the *Phaedo*, the overall tone of the work is a tribute to loyalty, in this case a willingness to die for a cause. This willingness to make one of the ultimate sacrifices has troubled those who wrote about loyalty in subsequent centuries.

Social-contract theorist Thomas Hobbes was the first major Western philosopher to assert that God did not have to be the focus of loyalty and that people could have competing loyalties. In his historic work on the theory of the state, *The Leviathan*, Hobbes asserted loyalty is a social act, that it is the core of the agreement that allows people to form the social contract that is the basis of political society. However, Hobbes, unlike Socrates, admitted loyalty has its limits. Loyalty to the ruler stops when continued loyalty would result in a subject's death. One has a higher loyalty to self-preservation in this instance than to the ruler. The turmoil surrounding U.S. involvement in the Vietnam War is a classic example of this type of conflict of loyalties.

Hobbes made two central alterations in the Socratic notion of loyalty. First, he emphasized its social nature. Second, he acknowledged that people could have more than one loyalty and might, at certain times, be forced to choose among them. These two elements, in addition to the original insights of Socrates and Plato, provide the basis of contemporary philosophical discussion of the concept.

The Contributions of Josiah Royce

American theologian Josiah Royce, who taught at Harvard in the early 1900s, believed that loyalty could become the single guiding ethical principle. In *The Philosophy of Loyalty* (1908), Royce wrote, "My theory is that the whole moral law is implicitly bound up in one precept: 'Be loyal.'" Royce defined loyalty as a social act: "The willing and practical and thoroughgoing devotion of a person to a cause." Royce would be critical, therefore, of the stereotypical journalist found in Ben Hecht's *The Front Page*—a cynic of everything and everyone, a professional who gets a story at all costs and whose only loyalty is to himself. In Royce's view, loyalty is an act of choice. A loyal person, Royce asserted, does not have "Hamlet's option"—or the leisure not to decide. For in the act of not deciding, that person has essentially cast his loyalty.

Loyalty also promotes self-realization. Royce spent much of his academic career fascinated with what were then the new insights of Freudian psychology, and he viewed loyalty in a psychological and developmental light. As a person continued to exercise loyalty, Royce believed, he or she would develop habits of character that would result in systematic ethical action. Like other aspects of moral development, loyalty can be learned and honed, Royce believed.

Loyalty—and the ability to be loyal—was a virtue, one that could be exercised and strengthened by continuing devotion to a cause. Yet loyalty as an ethical guide has problems. *First*, loyalty, incompletely conceived, can be bias or prejudice cloaked in misleading language. *Second*, few people maintain merely a single loyalty, and if loyalty is to become a guiding ethical principle, we need to develop a way to help distinguish among competing loyalties. *Third*, with the advent of a mass society, the entire concept of face-to-face loyalty has lost much of its power to compel ethical action. *Finally*, one of the most troubling questions arising from the concept of loyalty is whether an ethical person can be loyal to an unethical cause, for example racism or genocide.

However, Royce suggested a way to determine whether a specific cause was worthy of loyalty. A worthy cause should harmonize with the loyalties of others within the community, which can be defined in a number of ways. For instance, the loyalty of the journalist should be in harmony with the loyalty of the reader. The loyalty of the advertising agency should not conflict either with the loyalty of its client or the consumer. Surely, loyalty to the concept of free and unfettered political discussion—the basis of modern democracy and journalism—would meet Royce's test of loyalty.

A true understanding of loyalty allows people to reject unethical causes, Royce believed. The true problem was not a poor choice of loyalties but failure to adhere to chosen loyalties: "The ills of mankind are largely the consequence of disloyalty rather than wrong-headed loyalty" (Royce 1908). The cause that is capable of sustaining loyalty, Royce noted, has a "super-individual" quality, one that is apparent when people become part of a community. A spirit of democratic cooperation is needed for Royce's view of loyalty to result in ethical action. For instance, advertising agencies are demonstrating an ethical loyalty when they view their role as providing needed information for intelligent consumer choice, but more often they opt for loyalty to the bottom line.

Royce's thought has been criticized on a number of grounds. First, some philosophers assert that Royce's concept of loyalty is simplistic and that the adoption of loyalty as a moral principle may lead to allegiance to troubling causes. For instance, the advertising copywriter who scripts distorted television spots about an opponent in the belief that she must get her candidate elected is demonstrating a troubling allegiance to a politician over the democratic process. Similarly, a reporter who must get the story first, regardless of its completeness or accuracy, would be demonstrating a misplaced loyalty to the professional ideal of the scoop.

Second, others have noted that Royce provides no way to balance among conflicting loyalties other than his assertion that loyalty to a particular cause should evoke a similar response in others. Who the others are, in this case, becomes an important question. The executive producer who relegates all but the most important foreign news to the end of the broadcast because Americans aren't interested in hearing about activities in other nations may have an excessively narrow definition of who the viewers are concerned about.

Third, it is unclear how Royce's ethical thinking would balance majority notions against minority views. Royce's notion of loyalty could inspire adherence to the status quo or strict majority rule. For instance, advertisements that stereotype groups of people despite evidence to the contrary help perpetuate incorrect images. The ads work because they appeal to the majority, but by stereotyping they have crowded out more accurate impressions.

Yet despite these criticisms, Royce's thought has much to recommend it. First, Royce speaks to the development of ethical habits, something most modern ethical theorists believe is necessary for continuing ethical behavior. Second, Royce reminds us that the basis of loyalty is social, and loyalty requires we put others on an equal footing with ourselves. In this sense, his view of ethics is not a purely rational one, but one that is founded in a concept of relationships. When you acknowledge loyalties, you are also acknowledging that things could have been otherwise. Most important is the overriding message of Royce's work: *when making ethical choices, it is important to consider what your loyalties are and how you arrived at those loyalties.* We believe this is particularly pertinent when people are acting in a professional role in a society that has given the profession both rights and responsibilities.

Journalism as a Profession

Loyalty is not a fixed point but a range within a continuum. In *Loyalty: An Essay on the Morality of Relationships*, George Fletcher identifies two types of loyalty. The first is minimal loyalty: "Do not betray me." The second is maximum loyalty: "Be one with me." Between these two poles is a range of possibilities for allegiance and for corresponding media behavior. The location on the continuum for *Spy* magazine will differ from that of *The Nation* magazine.

One of the problems that the modern news media face is that a large percentage of the U.S. public subscribes to the notion that if the media are not maximally loyal— i.e., one with government, the military, etc.—then they are traitorous. The public believes this mainly because big institutions assert it is true. The media have been called disloyal by more than one politician on the election trail, often for no greater sin than fulfilling the watchdog role.

Loyalty can be linked to one's role. A role is a capacity in which we act toward others. It provides others with information about how we will act in a structured situation. Some roles are occupationally defined—account executive, screenwriter, editor. Others are not: mother, spouse, daughter. We all play multiple roles, and they help us sort out situations and know what to expect from others.

When the role you assume is a professional one, you add ethical responsibilities. Philosophers claim that "To belong to a profession is traditionally to be held to certain standards of conduct that go beyond the norm for others" (Lebacqz 1985, 32), and journalism qualifies as one of those professions with a higher expected norm of conduct.

However, not all journalists agree in practice. Hodges (1986) makes the distinction in this manner: When asked what she does for a living, one journalist says, "I am a journalist" while another says "I work for the *Gazette*." Hodges claims the first speaker is a journalist who recognizes her responsibility as a professional while the latter merely acknowledges her loyalty to a paycheck. The first would be expected to be loyal to societal expectations of a journalist, the second may or may not.

Journalists and their employers have debated whether journalism should be considered a profession. For some, the concept of professionalism itself is not inherently positive. Advocates of professionalism assert that professionalism among journalists will provide them with greater autonomy, prestige, and financial rewards. Critics see the process of professionalization as one that distances readers and viewers from the institutions that journalists often represent.

Despite these debates, we intuitively sense that journalists have two central responsibilities that are distinct because of the role journalists play in modern society. First, they have a greater responsibility to tell the truth than most professions. Second, journalists also seem to carry a somewhat greater obligation to foster political activity than the average person.

Philosophers note that while specific ethical dilemmas are transitory, roles endure. Role expectations carry over from one situation to another. Most of the time, loyalty to the profession means loyalty to the *ideals* of the profession. To Aristotle, loyalty to a profession also would mean being loyal to and maintaining high professional standards. The Aristotelian notion of virtue means being the best television producer or advertising executive you can be in the belief that you are being loyal to the profession and its abstract ideals.

Conflicting Loyalties

As the foregoing discussion indicates, we are no longer talking about merely a single loyalty. We live in an age of layers of loyalties, creating added problems and complications.

Sorting through competing personal and professional loyalties can be difficult, particularly when loyalties in one role appear to conflict with the loyalties of another. However, those concerned with professional roles and the loyalties they generate have done some thinking about this issue. We have adapted one such framework from

Ed Stein. Reprinted courtesy of the Rocky Mountain News.

William F. May who outlined these layers of loyalties for college professors. We suggest a similar approach for those who work in the media.

1. Loyalties arising from shared humanity:
   - demonstrate respect for each person as an individual.
   - communicate honestly and truthfully with all persons.
   - build a fair and compassionate social and cultural environment that promotes the common good.
2. Loyalties arising from professional practice:
   - fulfill the informational and entertainment mission of the media.
   - understand your audience's needs.
   - strive to enhance professional development of self and others.
   - avoid the abuse of power and position.
   - conduct professional activities in ways that uphold or surpass the ideals of virtue and competence.
3. Loyalties arising from employment:
   - keep agreements and promises, operate within the framework of the law, and extend due process to all persons.
   - do not squander your organization's resources or your public trust.
   - promote compassionate and humane professional relationships.
   - foster policies that build a community of ethnic, gender, and socioeconomic diversity.
   - promote the right of all to be heard.
4. Loyalties arising from the media's role in public life:
   - serve as examples of open institutions where truth is required.
   - foster open discussion and debate.
   - interpret your professional actions to readers and viewers.
   - serve as a voice for the voiceless.
   - serve as a mirror of society.

The problem of conflicting loyalties is evident in the media employment reality of today. Most media practitioners work for a corporation. They owe at least some loyalty to their corporate employers. However, such loyalty is tenuous because it seldom involves a face-to-face relationship. Modern corporations often demand employee loyalty but are much less willing to tell employees their corporate loyalties or responsibilities. These mutually understood promises are essential to corporate loyalty, where the fear is that one's allegiance to the organization will advance the interest of the organization without reciprocal loyalty to the employee.

In the final analysis, most ethical decisions are not about loyalties to corporations or abstract concepts such as freedom of the press. They are about how you treat the subject of your interview or the consumer of your advertising. An element that is essential in such ethical decisions is the notion of *reciprocity*. Simply articulated, reciprocity requires that loyalty should not work against the interest of either party.

Even in an era of sometimes shifting loyalties, there are some loyalties that should only be most reluctantly abandoned. We recommend you give further consideration to two of them: loyalty to humanity and loyalty to truth. *Virtually no situation in media ethics calls for inhumane treatment or withholding the truth.* Maybe you can think of other loyalties you would rarely, if ever, break. Even if you can't devise a list of every conceivable conflict of loyalties, knowing where your ultimate loyalties lie isn't a bad place to start.

The Potter Box

In Chapter I, we introduced you to an ethical decision-making model developed by Sissela Bok, one that could help you make an ethical choice. In this chapter, we introduce you to a second decision-making model, one that incorporates articulation of loyalties into the reasoning process.

The model was developed by Harvard theologian Ralph Potter and is called the Potter Box. Its initial use requires that you go through four steps to arrive at an ethical judgment. The case below will help familiarize you with the model.

> You are the assistant city editor for a newspaper of about thirty thousand circulation in a western city of about eighty thousand. Your police reporter regularly reports on sexual assaults in the community.
>
> While the newspaper has a policy of not revealing the names of rape victims, it does routinely report where such assaults occurred, the circumstances surrounding the attack, and a description of the assailant, if police can provide it.
>
> Tonight the police reporter is preparing to write a story about a rape that occurred in the early morning hours yesterday on the roof of the downtown bus station.
>
> Police report that the young woman who was raped went willingly to the roof of the bus station with her attacker. Although she is twenty-five, she lives in a group home for the educable mentally handicapped in the city. She is one of seven women living in the facility.
>
> She could not describe her assailant, and police have no suspects.
>
> Your reporter asks you for advice about how much detail, and what detail, he should include in the story.

The Potter Box has four steps (see Figure 4.1) that should be taken in order. They are (1) understanding the facts, (2) outlining the values inherent in the decision, (3) applying relevant philosophical principles, and (4) articulating a loyalty. You pro-

---

Figure 4.1
The Four Steps of the Potter Box

Facts	**Loyalties**
Values	**Principles**

ceed through the four steps in a counterclockwise fashion, beginning with the factual situation. We will examine each step individually.

Step One: *Understanding the facts of the case.* In the scenario, the facts are straightforward. You, the newspaper editor, have the information. Your ethical choice rests with how much of it you are going to print.

Step Two: *Outlining values.* "Values" is a much abused word in modern English. People can value everything from their loved ones to making fashion statements. In ethics, however, values takes on a more precise meaning. In this sense, when you value something—an idea or a principle—it means you are willing to give up other things for it. If, as a journalist, you value truth above all things, then you must sometimes be willing to give up privacy in favor of it. In the foregoing case, such a value system would mean that you would print every detail, because you value truth, and would risk invading the privacy of a person who is in some important ways unable to defend herself. If, as a journalist, you value both truth and privacy, then you may be willing to give up some truth, the printing of every detail, to attempt to preserve the victim's privacy.

Values often compete, and an important element of using the Potter Box is to be honest about what you really do value. Both truth & privacy are lofty ideals. Lest lofty, most of us value keeping our jobs. Journalists often value getting the story first. A forthright articulation of all the values wrapped up in any particular ethical situation will help you see more clearly the choices that you face and the potential compromises you may or may not have to make.

Step Three: *Application of philosophical principles.* Once you have decided what you value, you need to apply the philosophical principles outlined in the first chapter. For example, in the previous scenario, a utilitarian might argue that the greatest good is served by printing a story that alerts the community to the fact that some creep who rapes women who cannot defend themselves mentally or physically is still out there. Ross would argue that a journalist has duties both to the readers and to the victim, and they must be weighed before making a decision.

Aristotle's Golden Mean would counsel a middle ground that balances printing every detail against printing no story at all. Kant would suggest that the maxim of protecting someone who cannot protect herself is a maxim that could be universalized, making a decision to omit some information justifiable.

In this case, application of several ethical principles leads to the same general conclusion: the newspaper should print some story, but not one that inadvertently reveals the victim's identity or that makes her out to be hopelessly naïve in her trust of strangers.

However, you should be alert that while application of different ethical principles in this scenario leads to the same conclusion, other ethical dilemmas may not produce such a happy result. This is precisely why use of the Potter Box demands the application of more than one ethical principle, for if ultimate judgments may vary, you need to be able to explain why.

Step Four: *Articulation of loyalties.* Potter viewed loyalty as a social commitment, and use of the Potter Box will reflect that sort of ethic. In the fourth step, you need to articulate your loyalties—and to decide whether any of them conflict. In the foregoing case, you may have a loyalty to telling the truth, to alerting the community to a potential danger, to protecting individual privacy, or to doing your job well. Again, in this case, your loyalties are not in severe conflict with one another unless you adopt an absolutist view of the truth the community needs to know. It is possible to counsel your reporter to write a story that tells the truth but omits some facts (for example, the woman's residence in a group home and her mental retardation), alerts the community to a danger (there's a creep out there who police haven't caught), protects the victim's privacy (you won't print her name or where she lives), and allows you to take pride in the job you've done (you've told the truth and not harmed anyone).

However, use of the Potter Box often highlights a conflict between loyalties. In these instances, we refer you to Royce's conception of loyalty itself. What you choose to be loyal to should be capable of inspiring a similar loyalty in others who are both like and unlike you. Journalists are often accused of being "out of touch" with their viewers or readers, and it is at precisely this point of idiosyncratic loyalties that the profession is most highly criticized. Nowhere was that more evident than in the Persian Gulf War when the majority of the press chafed at military restrictions out of a loyalty to freedom of the press, yet the majority of the public didn't care about the sanctions—demonstrating a loyalty to patriotism instead. However, you should be warned that loyalties are not subject to popular opinion, and that you might often hold unpopular loyalties in your particular professional role in society.

Our experience with the Potter Box has been that the vast majority of ethical decisions will allow you to sustain a variety of loyalties. Those decisions that are truly most troubling are ones in which loyalty to one particular cause or principle becomes so dominant in your reasoning process that you are forced to abandon a variety of other loyalties that once seemed quite essential to you.

While you may initially find the stepwise process of the Potter Box somewhat cumbersome, as you learn to use it you will become fluent in its application. You may also discover that you can go through the Potter Box on different levels of abstraction.

The following case study, "The Pimp, the Prostitute, and the Preacher," illustrates how you might use the Potter Box when making an ethical decision.

The Pimp, the Prostitute, and the Preacher

You are the court reporter for a daily newspaper in a city of about 150,000 in the Pacific Northwest. About a year ago, the local police force began to crack down on prostitutes working the downtown mall. However, the stated goal of the department's activities was to limit prostitution by arresting pimps—men who make money from prostitutes— rather than by arresting either the prostitutes or their customers. The first of those arrests has now come to trial, and your paper has assigned you to cover the story on a daily basis.

In his opening statement, the local assistant district attorney tells the jury that in order to convict a person of pimping under state law, the state must prove first that money was exchanged for sexual favors, and second that the money was then given to a third party, the pimp, in return for protection, continued work, etc. During the first two days of the trial, he calls as witnesses four young women, ages fourteen to sixteen, who admit they have worked as prostitutes in the city but are a great deal less clear on the disposal of their earnings. Your story after the first day of the trial encapsulates the police activities, the prosecutor's goals in the case, and the public testimony of two of the young women without disclosing their names.

Near the end of the second day in the trial, the prosecuting attorney begins to call as witnesses men who say they paid one or more of the four young women to have sex with them. Among those who testify is a middle-aged man who in an almost inaudible response to a question lists his occupation as a minister at one of the more conservative Protestant churches in the city. He admits to having paid one of the young women for sex, and that day's portion of the trial ends soon after his testimony is complete.

About forty-five minutes later you are back in the office to write the story of that day's testimony when the newsroom secretary asks you if you have a few minutes to speak with "Reverend Jones." The name itself doesn't register, but you look up and realize you are facing the minister who testified earlier in the day. In the open newsroom he begs you, often in tears and at one point on his knees, not to print his name in your story. He even holds out a copy of the story you wrote, which appeared on page one of this morning's paper, outlining why the names of the prostitutes had not been used. He asserts that, should a story with his name appear, his marriage will crumble, his children will no longer respect him, and he will lose his job.

After a few minutes and a whispered conversation with the newsroom secretary, the paper's managing editor realizes what is happening and calls you, the minister, and the news editor into his office for a conference. What do you say?

Using the Potter Box, determine how you would report this story. Your decision will reflect a set of loyalties as well as the values and principles you have chosen. Others may choose differently. A justification model such as Potter's or Bok's (introduced in Chapter I) does not eliminate differences. What it will do, ideally, is ensure that your choices are grounded in sound ethical reasoning.

When you are finished, the final casting of loyalties will inevitably create another fact for the first quadrant of the box. For instance, in this case, if the decision is to run the name, anything that might subsequently happen to the minister as a result—firing, divorce, even possible suicide—is now an additional "fact" for the first quadrant of the Potter Box. If you decide not to run the minister's name and his parishioners discover his indiscretion anyway, the loss of credibility the newspaper suffers from those who find out the name was withheld is also a "fact" to be entered into the first quadrant of the Potter Box. Considering these additional "facts," (even though they are at present hypothetical), you may want to go through the process again to see if your decision will remain the same.

Now that you've made a concrete decision about revealing the name of the minister based on the facts, we'd like to introduce you to additional facts. After you read them, go through the Potter Box again while focusing less on the minister and more on larger issues that affect how the story is written and how it is run in the newspaper. This time, think about the notions of stereotyping, how members of minority communities are portrayed in news reports, and the idea of what exactly we mean by the journalistic watchwords "objectivity" and "truth."

As the trial continues, it becomes increasingly clear to you that there are other factors at work. In your largely Caucasian community, the only people arrested for pimping have been African-American. All the young women who work as prostitutes are Caucasian, as are the customers who testify. As far as prostitution goes, your Pacific Northwest version is relatively mild. There are no reports of drug use among the prostitutes and their customers, and none of the prostitutes has complained of physical violence. Further, the prosecuting attorney cannot make any of the young women admit under oath that they ever gave the pimps any money. The jury verdict in this case is not guilty.

Do the new facts change your loyalties articulated in the first application of the model to the facts?

We recommend that you try using both the Bok and Potter justification models at various times in your ethical decision making. Becoming a competent practitioner of both methods will provide you with greater flexibility and explanatory power. We also recommend, regardless of the approach you use, that an unvarnished and critical discussion of loyalty becomes part of your ethical dialogue. We believe it will enable you to anticipate situations as well as react to them.

Suggested Readings

Fletcher, George P. 1993. *Loyalty: An essay on the morality of relationships.* New York: Oxford University Press.

Fuss, Peter. 1965. *The moral philosophy of Josiah Royce.* Cambridge, Mass.: Harvard University Press.

Hanson, Karen. 1986. "The demands of loyalty." *Idealistic Studies,* 16, pp. 195–204.

Hobbes, Thomas. 1958. *Leviathan.* New York: Bobbs-Merrill.

Oldenquist, Andrew. 1982. Loyalties. *Journal of Philosophy,* 79, pp. 173–93.

Powell, Thomas F. 1967. *Josiah Royce.* New York: Washington Square Press, Inc.

CHAPTER IV CASES

CASE IV-A
"Where Everybody Knows Your Name: Reporting and Relationships in a Small Market"
GINNY WHITEHOUSE
Whitworth College

Everybody is a source when you're covering an agricultural town with a population under 12,000.

But Sunnyside Police Sgt. Phil Schenck had not been a source for Jessica Luce when he asked her out for a date during a Halloween party in 1999. Luce had worked as a general assignment reporter at the *Yakima Herald–Republic* for almost a year. Sunnyside, Washington, was one of four communities she covered in this first job out of college. The two spent time together infrequently over the next two months.

"I was interested in him, we had fun, but if I had been asked what was going on I would have said we were friends," Luce said.

Nonetheless, a coworker was incredulous. Luce remembers him saying, "You can't go out on a date with a source. It's one of the biggest taboos in journalism!"

The *Herald–Republic's* four-page code of ethics advises staff to avoid conflicts of interest and to disclose those that are unavoidable. Prohibition of gifts and free travel is clearly explained. However, no specifics are given describing personal relationships that might cause conflicts of interest.

Luce decided to keep her relationship with Schenck, however it might be defined, quiet. Even with all the police stories she had written, she had never needed Schenck as a source and never thought the occasion would arise.

Schenck's boss, however, was another matter. Sunnyside Police Chief Wallace Anderson had been accused of shooting a great blue heron outside the police station, storing explosives at the station house, and of having a threatening temper. Following a lengthy and expensive investigation, Anderson resigned in November.

By New Year's Day, Luce and Schenck decided they were definitely dating. "I kept my relationship under wraps save for a few confidants at work. I felt the relationship would be perceived as something wrong," Luce said. "But I didn't see it interfering with my job. Phil and I didn't talk about work as much as normal couples might. We knew it wasn't fair to either one of us."

In mid-February, Schenck was named acting captain, giving him the number two position in the Sunnyside police department and making him the official media spokesman. Luce realized she needed to be pulled off the Sunnyside police beat immediately. Her editors agreed.

"It was hard to talk with them about my private relationship, and I was forced to define things about the relationship that I hadn't even done for myself," Luce said.

Craig Troianello, her city editor, sat her down for a long conversation. "Jessica made it easy because she was straightforward. We didn't ask intimate questions— that's irrelevant in this case," Troianello said. "By taking the proactive ethical stand that she did, it was easy for us to deal with this."

Luce said Troianello emphasized that his concern did not mean he was questioning her integrity. However, he had to make sure he hadn't overlooked something that could be perceived as a conflict by readers.

"This was a lesson on perception versus reality," Luce said. Luce's reporting did not affect Schenck's promotion, nor had Schenck ever implied that a story should or should not have been covered. Nonetheless, Schenck benefited from the chief's departure.

Troianello said he was never worried that Luce's reporting was compromised, but he wanted to make sure the newspaper was above suspicion. "Issues involving the police department were in the forefront of the news," Troianello said. "People could read anything into it—that she was protecting the chief, that she was trying to bring the chief down. Those kinds of spins drove my concern."

On the other hand, Schenck questions whether a strict conflict of interest standard is realistic in a small town. "Everybody is a potential source—even the clerk at the grocery store. We eat food. If her husband or boyfriend is a farmer, you could say she is promoting eating. This is an ideal that might be somewhat impractical," Schenck said. "If you can't be a real person, how can you report on real people?"

Luce says if she had to do it all over again she would not have kept the relationship a secret as long as she did. Nonetheless, it would still be hard to talk to a supervisor about dating. Troianello said he understands the complexities of a journalist's personal life but would rather Luce had brought the relationship to the newspaper's attention by New Year's Day when the two began dating.

However, he understands the dynamic of the situation. "She's in a small town where the number of people with four-year degrees and professionals is small," Troianello said. "It seems like there will be some mixing at some point. Relationships could occur as naturally as it does in the newsroom. I married a copy editor."

Once their relationship went public, Luce was surprised at how supportive the community and city officials were, including the new police chief (someone other than Schenck). "What we as journalists see as an ethical problem and conflict of interest isn't necessarily going to be seen as an ethical problem by the public."

However, Luce never heard comments one way or another from the former chief or his supporters. On several occasions, city officials have questioned whether Schenck leaked information to Luce or *Herald–Republic* reporters. Schenck simply explained that he had not. "I deal with stuff every day that Jessica would love to get her hands on," Schenck said. "But we just don't talk about it."

Luce now covers education in the city of Yakima. She and Schenck have set a wedding date.

Micro Issues:

1. Did Luce have a responsibility to tell her editors about her relationship with Schenck? If so, when should Luce have informed them?
2. What responsibility did the *Yakima Herald–Republic* editors have to explain expectations on conflicts of interest? Is spelling out those expectations necessary or appropriate in a code of ethics?

3. How would the ethical questions have changed if Schenck worked in another capacity for the city, such as being a teacher?
4. How would the ethical questions have changed if Luce and Schenck had remained only friends?

Mid-range Issues:

1. What aspects of their lives should journalists be able to keep private?
2. Is public perception of an ethical problem truly relevant?
3. Journalists spend most of their time with two groups: their sources and their coworkers. Considering those limitations, is dating possible or advisable?

Macro Issues:

1. Can journalists cover communities effectively if they are expected to remain remote and removed?
2. How specific should codes of ethics be on conflicts of interest?

CASE IV-B
She Chose Before Losing the Choice
TOM LYONS
Sarasota Herald–Tribune

Authors' note: Columnist Tom Lyons had talked with Lorraine Orr previously for a column on the Hemlock Society, an organization that advocates the right to end one's life. While Florida law allows for persons to enact living wills and "do not resuscitate" orders, Orr wanted the law to go a step further to decriminalize voluntary euthanasia. The seventy-nine-year-old Orr called Lyons shortly after suffering a mild stroke—her second—that left her temporarily incapacitated earlier in the week. At that point, she had decided to end her life before she was no longer able to make such choices for herself. What follows is the column Lyons wrote about their conversation.

"It's time for me to go," Lorraine Orr told me by phone Tuesday morning.

During the 10-minute conversation, she sounded completely rational, as well as crystal clear and calmly committed to her plan.

That plan would have sounded drastic and even crazy to many people and was terribly sinful by the teachings of some religions.

But suicide simply made good sense to Orr.

Given her assessment of her medical condition, Orr's intention was in perfect harmony with her beliefs about life and death. It fit with the right-to-die philosophy that she had been promoting for years, most recently as a Sarasota member of the Hemlock Society.

Her views had been shaped years ago, as she watched her husband die slowly of a cancer that led to removal of both sides of his jaw in multiple surgeries, only to have doctors insist on other operations as death approached—long after he had lost the power to refuse.

Because I had talked to her in 1994, I already knew Orr believed strongly that our laws should be changed. They should allow people to arrange for [a] doctor's help in ending their lives, she had said, when advanced age, medical problems and failing mental abilities made existence on Earth a painful and pointless horror.

But I never expected the phone call I got Tuesday morning.

Orr and her minister called to say that Orr had made preparations to end her life. She planned to start in just a few hours and to be dead that afternoon.

She sounded mentally competent. She even seemed cheerful. She still had a sense of humor, a ready laugh.

I asked her how old she was and she told me, "I'll be 80 next month." The irony of her words struck me, and I remarked in all seriousness: "No, it doesn't look like you will."

She just laughed, quietly, and agreed with me.

Orr had already told me that she had gathered drugs that would do the job.

"I've been collecting them one way and another for quite a while," she said. She would not give details for fear of getting other people into trouble.

That was just about the only concern she had about her decision, it seemed. She said she was not afraid of death. If the information she had gotten from the

Hemlock Society was correct, she should be able to end her life painlessly, she said.

"This is her morning to self-deliver," said George Exoo, the Unitarian–Universalist minister there with her. He is a Hemlock Society chaplain, and an old friend of Orr. He had flown down from Pennsylvania to be with her in her last hours.

He said he planned to read poetry to her and pray with her as she died.

Was Orr depressed, hopeless, feeling lost in an uncaring world?

No, not at all, judging by her words and her tone of voice.

"I'm fine," she assured me. She had led a colorful life, and she had friends, though her only close relative was a sister living in Canada. Orr didn't say whether she had called her sister, but did say she certainly didn't want to be a burden to that woman.

Orr said she had been feeling pretty good, actually. She said she would actually prefer to wait on this suicide plan.

If Florida's laws were more tolerant of her wishes, she explained, she wouldn't be taking her life just now.

"I could have had more nice times," she said. "I'm not desperately sick. But I can't take that chance."

She needed to act while she was still mentally and physically able to, she said.

That is what she wanted everyone, especially Florida's legislators, to understand. It shouldn't have to be this way, she said.

In February, while already coping with emphysema, she had had a stroke. It had left her in fairly good shape, considering, despite some memory problems. But she believed that more strokes were probable. She thought it all too likely that sooner or later she would be paralyzed, seriously brain damaged, maybe unable to talk.

Then, she thought, she might face years of existence in a nursing home bed with no control over her life, and no way out.

No matter what she wrote in her living will, Florida law would not allow a doctor to end her life when that time came. A simple injection can be used to put a beloved pet to death, but people are forced to suffer, she said.

That had to change, she said.

On Monday, she had what she thought was a second stroke. It left her unable to talk for a while. When she could talk again a few hours later, she still couldn't think of some words and names she knew well.

That had passed by Tuesday morning. But she saw the episode as a clear warning. She believed it was time to act, while she still could.

"I couldn't take the chance of being paralyzed and stupid in the head," Orr said.

She made one point very clear: Her minister was there at her request, and he shared her belief in the right to die. But he would not be administering the drugs or doing anything of the sort. Assisting her, they both knew, could mean a manslaughter charge.

"He won't be helping," she emphasized. "He's just sitting with me."

Then she summed it all up in understated words that seemed full of her love for life, as well as optimism about whatever lies ahead.

"It's time for me to go," she said. "I've had a nice time."

Lorraine Orr's minister friend called late Tuesday afternoon and told me it had gone as planned.

Talking through tears at times, Exoo said Orr had eaten a bitter mix of applesauce and drugs, and washed it down with a gulp of whiskey. She died peacefully sometime after a long discussion of her life, and after he had read her Emerson's essay on self-reliance and the 23rd Psalm.

It wasn't the first suicide he had witnessed, but it was the hardest for him, he said. He said he kept reading to her long after she stopped breathing.

Eventually, he left to join mutual friends at their home.

That evening, they all went back to Orr's house and then called 911 to report Orr's suicide.

Sarasota County sheriffs investigators questioned Exoo and the friends at length. The death, though still under investigation, is listed as a suicide.

Exoo hopes that people will realize that this suicide wasn't the act of someone who was depressed and miserable. He said it was the act of an optimistic, courageous woman who wanted to keep control of her life, and hoped that her final act might help her right-to-death cause.

Lorraine Orr would still be alive, he said, if the law had allowed her to make her own choice about her own death.

Micro Issues:

1. What were Lyons's options after he received the call?
2. Should the newspaper have run the column? Justify your answer.
3. Are there other stories that should also have been run, such as stories about where to go for help, etc.?
4. Would your answer be different if the caller had been a teenage girl who advocated the right to end her life? If so, in what way?

Mid-range Issues:

1. How would you answer the charge that Lyons was "used" by a reader who wanted her death to generate publicity for her cause?
2. Would you run the column if the caller were committing suicide to protest a cause like abortion?
3. What is the difference, if any, in publicizing this suicide and publicizing a hunger strike? Publicizing a physician-assisted suicide?

Macro Issues:

1. In a situation like this, where should a reporter's loyalties lie?
2. Can you anticipate other situations similar to this where a reporter might be brought into an ongoing story?
3. Is the ideal reporter a detached observer and recorder of events or a participant? Do the rules change for columnists or commentators?

CASE IV-C
One Person's Tragedy, Another Person's Prize
PHILIP PATTERSON
Oklahoma Christian University

July 22, 1975, was a busy day for *Boston Herald* photographer Stanley Forman. Early in the day he climbed towers and rode elevators all over Boston to get pictures of the city's skyline for a Sunday magazine feature. During that time, he remained on call for other daily assignments.

After returning his film to the newspaper, he was hoping to leave for the day when a call came about a fire in one of the city's older sections of Victorian row houses. The dispatcher mentioned that some people might be trapped in the burning structure. Forman followed the fire engine to the scene and heard on his scanner an SOS ordering a ladder truck to the scene. When he arrived, he followed a hunch and ran down the alley to the back of the row of houses.

There he saw firefighter Bob O'Neil and two people, a two-year-old girl and her nineteen-year-old godmother, on the fifth-floor fire escape. The fireman was calling for help from a fire truck below. The truck raised its aerial ladder to the trio. Forman climbed aboard the bed of the truck to get a better angle on what he anticipated would be a routine rescue.

Meanwhile the WBZ radio traffic helicopter had landed on the next roof, and the pilot was offering to take the child. Though he is visible in most of the photos, he never got a chance to help.

As Fireman O'Neil reached for the ladder of the fire truck below, there was a loud noise—either the sound of a scream or the shriek of metal bending. The fire escape gave way, sending the two victims falling and leaving O'Neil clinging for his life to the ladder. Forman saw it all through his 135 mm lens and took four photos as the two were falling, before turning away to avoid seeing them hit the ground. The woman, Diana Bryant, broke the fall of the girl, Tiare Jones, who survived. Bryant sustained multiple head and body injuries and died hours later.

O'Neil was shaken by the experience. "Just two more seconds. I would have had them," he said repeatedly. Though Forman took a few more pictures, he was shaking too much to hold the camera still.

Returning to the newspaper, he waited anxiously to see if he had the photos that he thought he had. When it was obvious he did, he stayed to help with some of the prints and went home, exhausted. At 8:00 P.M. he learned that Bryant had died. He wondered if the newspaper would still run the photos.

He saw the first morning edition of the paper shortly after 2:00 A.M. and was surprised to see that the key photo in the sequence (the one reprinted here) was printed on page one and measured 11½ inches by 16½ inches—virtually the entire tabloid page. A full sequence of the four photos ran on page three.

By 4:00 A.M., Forman had made a set of prints for the Associated Press, which gave the pictures worldwide distribution that same day. Tearsheets on the photos came from 128 U.S. papers and several foreign countries.

Stanley J. Forman. Used by permission.

Within twenty-four hours, action was taken in Boston to improve the inspection and maintenance of all existing fire escapes in the city. Fire-safety groups around the country used the photos to promote similar efforts in other cities.

Numerous awards came as well. The Pulitzer prize committee gave Forman its 1976 news photo prize. The National Press Photographers Association named the photo Picture of the Year. Several other groups, including the Society of Professional Journalists, honored the photo as well. Forman went on to win the Pulitzer prize again the following year, making him the only photographer to win consecutive Pulitzer prizes for news photography. His awards earned him a Nieman Fellowship at Harvard and lecture engagements around the world.

Micro Issues:

1. What are the rights of victims of a tragedy such as this one? Should they have protection from being photographed? Being interviewed?
2. Forman's instincts and resourcefulness enabled him to capture photos that no other photographer got. Is the exclusive nature of the photos a factor in whether to run them?
3. Forman said that when he heard Bryant had died, he assumed that the photos would not run. Should the death of one of the girls have affected the treatment of the photos?
4. Did the newspaper sensationalize the photo shown in this case by its size or placement?
5. Do the rights of the other people pictured—O'Neil and the helicopter pilot— enter into the decision of whether to use the photos?

Mid-range Issues:

1. Is the repair of aging fire escapes a morally justifiable reason for running the photos?
2. Many newspapers outside of Boston ran the photos as well. When the local news peg (the fire) is absent, what is the ethical reasoning for running the photos?

Macro Issues:

1. Photos such as Forman's are often singled out for awards within the industry. In fact, more than half of all photos that have won the two major prizes in photojournalism have involved tragedy. Should one person's calamity be a photojournalist's good fortune?
2. Are prizes too important to the profession of journalism? Are they ethical in a field such as journalism?

CASE IV-D
Keeping Secrets: A Public Relations Dilemma
JAY BLACK
University of South Florida

Nancy B. is public affairs officer in Jonesville for the city's largest employer, the National Steel Corporation (NSC). In her middle-management position she has access to her firm's immediate and long-range plans. She has attended a meeting of top management and the company's board of directors at which it was decided that economic conditions have made it absolutely necessary to close down permanently NSC's Jonesville plant. Factors include a glut of inexpensive, imported steel, which is diminishing the market for NSC's products, plus the government's insistence that the Jonesville plant's forty-year-old blast furnaces and scrubbers are environmental hazards that will cost $10 million to remedy.

Jonesville is in a sensitive economic position. It is a town of twenty thousand, located eighty miles south of the state's capital and economic center. There are few job possibilities for Jonesville's unemployed, who would probably have to sell their houses and move. Until a generation ago, the region was primarily agricultural, with only a moderate amount of manufacturing. After World War II, the NSC plant's growth changed the economic balance. The sons of farmers became ironworkers or developed skills in fields allied to the steel mill, and the numerous family farms were consolidated into several larger farms, with far fewer employment possibilities. Today, three thousand people work at the NSC plant. The plant has paid decent wages, and most of its workers own their own homes in or around Jonesville.

Nancy B. is a single parent of two high school children. She owns her own home and has been saving money to send her children to a moderately expensive out-of-state college. She has a sister, Elizabeth, who is the mother of three children and works part-time as a real estate salesperson. Elizabeth is very excited about having five "hot" prospects for house sales in town; the deals should go through in about three weeks. Elizabeth's husband, Frank, has been employed by NSC for fifteen years and now has a good-paying job as a shift foreman. Elizabeth and Frank have been very close to Nancy, especially since ten years ago when Nancy's husband died in an industrial accident at the NSC plant.

At the board meeting where the decision was reached to close down the plant, arguments were made that a great deal of harm would come to the company—its reputation, its inability to fill a final set of orders for one last major contract, and the response of the stock market—if word about the impending closure got out. All persons attending the meeting were asked to promise not to say anything to anyone about the closure, nor to act in any way that would set off either rumors or a panic.

Nancy B. was among those who were told by top management that NSC would make every effort to secure equivalent employment for them at another division of the corporation. In her case, her immediate supervisor reminded her of how well the firm had treated her upon her husband's death a decade earlier: she had gone from secretary to executive secretary to public relations assistant to public relations officer in quick succession.

Micro Issues:

1. Should Nancy protect herself by searching for a job and putting her home on the market?
2. Should she help Frank and Elizabeth by giving them the information?
3. Are her duties or responsibilities in this matter changed in any way by the fact that she is a single parent?

Mid-range Issues:

1. If Nancy acts out of loyalty to family and tells Elizabeth the news, can Elizabeth then claim the same loyalty to her clients who might need to sell their homes quickly? Do you see any difference in the situations?
2. What should Nancy do if she gets a call from the press attempting to confirm a rumor that the company is closing the plant and leaving?
3. Nancy will be offered a chance at another job and probably will get her relocation costs paid. Frank and Elizabeth, however, will not. Nancy has information that they need, but she badly needs to keep her job. Is she protecting her own comfort at their expense?

Macro Issues:

1. The request to remain quiet about the move was unilateral: Nancy listened to the request but did not make a promise to abide by it. Does this silence free her to do as she pleases, or is it implied that she understood the request and agreed to abide by it? Can a duty be assumed by failure to object to it?
2. Is it ever justifiable to lie to the media? If so, under what circumstances?
3. If you were in Nancy B.'s position, can you think of arguments that would persuade management to be more forthright with employees? How would the concept of proactive public relations help or hurt in this regard?

CASE IV-E
Standing Behind a Reporter: The CBS News/*News* Journal Controversy
JOHN SWEENEY, PUBLIC EDITOR
Wilmington News Journal

To most people, Wilmington, Delaware, is a blurred traffic sign on Interstate 95—a non-destination between Baltimore and Philadelphia. Major sporting events are rare. For Delawareans, the annual McDonald's Classic is more than just another stop on the Ladies Professional Golf Association tour; it's a major spring social event. People wrangle to get tickets. It's a place to meet friends and make a day of it. It's also a place to see and be seen. The golfers are treated like celebrities. The natives proudly enjoy the attention as television broadcasts Wilmington live to the world.

The local newspaper, the *News Journal,* treats the week-long event as more than just another sports show. In addition to actual golf coverage, the paper covers the fashions, the economic ripples, and the show-biz aura of a nationally televised event.

In May 1995, when the tournament was underway, the *News Journal* sent reporter Valerie Helmbreck to write a color story, just like other feature writers did every other day of the tournament.

Helmbreck, a former television writer for the paper, decided to talk with the CBS television staff. She knocked on the door of the CBS trailer, explained who she was, and climbed inside. The interview started with staff members and then Ben Wright, the CBS golf commentator, joined. The others soon left and Helmbreck and Wright continued their talk.

The interview became international news. Wright was quoted as saying, "Let's face facts here. Lesbians in the sport hurt women's golf." Among his comments was "They're going to a butch game and that furthers the bad image of the game. " He also said, "Women are handicapped by having boobs. It's not easy for them to keep their left arm straight, and that's one of the tenets of the game. Their boobs get in the way."

Before the article ran, the *News Journal*'s editors grilled Helmbreck. When they became convinced of what she had, they assigned other reporters to get reactions from the golfers and the network.

CBS officials were interested in knowing one thing: Did Helmbreck have the comments on tape? When they were told no, they issued a denial. Wright didn't say these things. The reporter made it up.

Wright was summoned to New York for a CBS interrogation and sent back to Wilmington where he issued his own denials, calling the article a pack of lies. Wright was in the broadcast booth for the final day of the tournament. His on-air colleagues expressed their sympathy for the shabby treatment he got. The athletes at first voiced their dismay at the comments but soon backed down. He didn't say it, they said in unison. It was all made up.

Many Delawareans attacked Helmbreck for embarrassing the state. "The tour won't come back" was a typical response. Meanwhile, the *News Journal* was deluged with interview requests. The reporter was ordered by her editors not to respond to questions from other reporters. Camera operators from tabloid television shows roamed the paper's parking lot and peered in the cafeteria window, hoping to sight Helmbreck. The editor of the story was besieged by radio talk-show hosts from around the country.

Soon, reporters at other newspapers and radio and television stations said they were beginning to hear from New York people that Helmbreck was a lesbian, the paper's primary writer on gay topics, a well-known male hater, and that she had written extensively about lesbians.

None of this was true, but the tenor of the questions had changed. It was no longer "What did he say?" It was now "What's her lifestyle?"

One golf writer told the *News Journal*'s sports editor he had heard Wright say similar things. But Helmbreck was outside the club. Her article was bad for golf, the writer said. CBS continued to issue its denials; she has no proof, its officials said.

Essentially, the issue became "Who do you believe? CBS or a reporter from a nowhere paper?"

Eventually, the controversy subsided. Ben Wright went on broadcasting. Valerie Helmbreck went on reporting in Wilmington. Wright's contract was renewed. But Helmbreck still had to answer questions and accusations.

Then in December of the same year, *Sports Illustrated* printed an article claiming that Wright had changed his story. He told friends he had made the remarks, but they were supposed to be off the record. *Sports Illustrated* also produced a witness to the original interview, a tour caddie who had overheard the conversation. He told *Sports Illustrated* that Helmbreck was accurate. Helmbreck had written what Wright said, the witness told the magazine.

In his defense, Wright told *Sports Illustrated* that at the time of the interview Helmbreck was going through a divorce and had lost custody of her children. He characterized her as a lesbian. None of the charges were true.

The firestorm erupted again. This time CBS fired Wright.

Micro Issues:

1. Should the original story have been published? Why was it news?
2. If you were the editor, would you automatically believe the reporter if an interview subject cries foul?
3. Was the newspaper right to let the attacks go unanswered?

Mid-range Issues:

1. Was this story news outside Wilmington?
2. Should reporters always use a tape recorder?
3. How can a news organization ethically withhold its own people from being interviewed when they are newsworthy?

Macro Issues:

1. Would the newspaper's response have differed if it affected circulation or advertising?
2. How many stories go unreported because only reporters "inside the club" witness them? Should a reporter remain "outside the club?" If so, what steps can a reporter take to make sure he or she stays outside the club?
3. Should reporters rethink their behavior in media feeding frenzies?

CHAPTER V

Public Relations: Advocate or Adversary?

By the end of this chapter, you should be familiar with:

• why the relationship between the media and public relations is both
  symbiotic and strained.
• how the concept of advocacy can provide an ethical justification for public
  relations.
• how public relations practitioners help news journalists function.

Journalism and Public Relations: The Quintessential Struggle

Any controversy surrounding public relations as a profession must be viewed in light of the alternative. If the more than 200,000 public relations professionals in the United States did not exist, many stories would go unreported. Indeed, public relations began as a profession when many newsmakers found it difficult to get past journalism's gatekeepers to get their stories told. PR practitioners offered a way to unlock the gate and get stories into the newspapers for their clients. At the same time they offered "free" news to publishers.

Despite the occasional animosity between journalists and public relations practitioners, the relationship is truly symbiotic—they simply could not live without each other. No news organization is large enough to gather all the day's news without several public relations sources. Business pages are full of press releases on earnings, new product lines and personnel changes, all supplied by writers not paid by the media. Travel, entertainment and food sections of newspapers would be virtually nonexistent if not for press releases. On the other hand, the media provide the all-important audience for an institution that wants the publicity.

With this common need, why are the two professions sometimes at odds? Editors point their fingers at public relations practitioners who perceive their jobs in terms of the quantity (much) and the quality (favorable) of exposure they can get for their clients or causes. These practitioners, in turn, point to editors and reporters who come to each story with an agenda (a polite word for bias) that influences the outcome of the final story, usually in a manner unfavorable to the public relations professional's client.

Much of the problem stems from how each of the two professions defines news. To the public relations professional, the lack of breaking news is newsworthy. Plants that operate safely and are not laying off any employees, nonprofit organizations that operate within budget and provide needed services, companies that pay a dividend for the fiftieth consecutive quarter are all signs that things are operating smoothly and make for a story that the public should hear.

However, to the journalist, news is a change in the status quo: a plant that pollutes, employees who embezzle, firms that go bankrupt—all are worthwhile news stories. Caught in the middle, the news consumer probably prefers a choice of both stories. However, shrinking newsholes and static amounts of airtime won't allow both, and the editorial bias is toward disruption more often than efficiency.

As the journalistic gap has grown between the two professions, public relations professionals have found it necessary to resort to staging events to get their good news on air or in newspapers. Such events—ribbon cuttings, press conferences, open houses, and the like—are a phenomenon Daniel Boorstin (1962) calls the "pseudo-event." The timing, the staging, and the location of a pseudo-event are set with the cameras in mind. Media owners, sensing a cost-efficient story with good visuals that fosters community goodwill, have historically been willing to attend (Epstein 1974).

A story from Minneapolis illustrates the quintessential pseudo-event. The story announced that former University of Oklahoma law professor Anita Hill, who in 1991 publicly charged then Supreme Court Justice-elect Clarence Thomas with sexual harassment, would *not* be coming to Minneapolis. Advance publicity about her visit had generated so many donations for an endowed professorship in her name that Hill did not need to appear in person, said the promoters. In short, the publicity had made the event moot. While pseudo-events are normally "news" staged solely for the benefit of the media, in this Alice-in-Wonderland-type case, the media actually kept the news event from occurring by giving coverage to the announcement of the upcoming event.

Boorstin claims that as much as one-fourth of all news fits the pseudo-event scenario—events that would not have occurred or would have occurred differently if not for the presence of a camera, including such examples as bill and treaty signings, official send-offs, most press conferences, photo opportunities, and most demonstrations, sit-ins and strikes. Reporters and photographers don't always share their publisher's enthusiasm for these events for two reasons. First, they feel used. Second, reporters prefer stories that they research themselves to stories handed to them.

While the Minneapolis case is an extreme example, many nonjournalists attempt to trade on the credibility of the news to advance their cause. A news story carries more clout with readers or viewers than does an advertisement. Although readers and viewers may not know the terminology, they have a sense that a media gatekeeper is at work screening stories of dubious reliability. When the public relations professional successfully places a story in the media, it has the credibility of having passed through the gate, a benefit of the doubt paid advertising does not receive.

Add to that the serendipity that the story is free and an ad is not, and the motivation is great for the public relations professional to attempt to influence the editorial content. This is done either by hyping an unimportant story or by putting the company's "spin" on a legitimate story, making sure that only the company line gets heard. With the stakes high—promotions, for instance, hang in the balance for those who continuously get favorable coverage for their institutions—the chance for abuse is high as well.

Public relations professionals place a strain on news desks with their constant flow of news releases to the print and electronic media. As many as 90 percent of all press releases received are dumped by editors after a quick glance. Yet the flow of news releases continues virtually unchecked, since many organizations measure the effectiveness of a PR office by output, not publication. This system creates resentment on the part of the public relations professional whose articles never seem to be printed, and resentment from the editor who must sift through the mass of releases against the possibility of overlooking a usable one.

History of the Profession

Public relations as a profession is a modern development based on a rationale as old as the ancient proverb affirming that "a good name is more desirable than great riches" (Proverbs 22:1). And good names, just like useful symbols, are essential in politics.

Samuel John Adams recognized the value of using events or symbols to arouse emotion during the American Revolution. He used slogans like "Taxation without representation is tyranny," and he staged the Boston Tea Party. In the 1820s, Andrew Jackson's presidential campaign attempted to reach beyond the rich to the common folk, using techniques that foreshadowed many public relations practices. Amos Kendall, a member of the famous "Kitchen Cabinet," was Jackson's pollster, counselor, ghostwriter, and publicist. Though Kendall did not hold the title, he also served as the first presidential press secretary and congressional liaison. Matthew St. Clarke, a publicist for the Bank of the United States, opposed Kendall's efforts, through press releases, reports and pamphlets. Clarke's efforts to develop a candidate helped create the myths surrounding the historical figure Davie Crockett.

After decades of use in the political arena, attempts to influence public opinion moved to the private sector. This new wave of public relations was originally called "press agentry." One of its earliest and best practitioners was P. T. Barnum, who also exemplified the early philosophy of press agentry in his statement "There's a sucker born every minute."

The building of great businesses empires in the nineteenth century—sometimes referred to as "industrial trusts" run by robber barons—often angered the public and the press. Workers were beginning to organize themselves into unions and management, and the trusts were criticized by many. Journalists who reported on their often unsavory practices were called "muckrakers," a term coined by President Theodore Roosevelt. Their stories helped to spur public opinion to support trust-busting legislation, the Sherman Antitrust Act being the best known.

Beleaguered businesspeople also turned to public relations to counteract what they viewed as negative news and, more importantly, impending government regulation. In 1889, George Westinghouse established the first corporate public relations department. He hired Pittsburgh newspaperman E. H. Heinrichs to wage a fierce struggle in the media with Thomas A. Edison over the relative merits of AC and DC electric current. Westinghouse won, and today we use alternating current in our homes. Other businesses followed Westinghouse's lead.

Ivy Lee, considered one of the founders of modern public relations, became publicity adviser to a group of U.S. coal mine operators beset by labor problems early in the twentieth century. As a Pennsylvania Railroad employee, Lee pioneered the practice of giving the press full information about railroad accidents, bringing about new thinking in public relations as a source of complete rather than one-sided information. Lee's efforts foreshadowed one of the dominant contemporary theories of public relations, the notion that public relations practitioners, their corporate employers and the public need to have an equal—or symmetrical—relationship (Grunig and Hunt, 1984).

World War I forced the government into the public relations business. In 1917 Woodrow Wilson authorized the creation of the Committee on Public Information, headed by George Creel. The committee conducted a national campaign to mobilize public support for the war, to encourage enlistment in the armed forces and to promote the sale of Liberty Bonds. The committee conducted public rallies in major cities, using such film celebrities as Charlie Chaplin and Mary Pickford to inspire patriotism. The industry grew rapidly after the war, and in 1923 Edward L. Bernays, considered the other contemporary founder of the field, published *Crystallizing Public Opinion.*

World War II again brought the federal government into the public relations business. The Office of War Information (OWI) was founded in 1942 to once again act as a catalyst to recruit U.S. soldiers and factory workers and to find funding for the war. After the war the OWI became the United States Information Agency, a powerful tool for U.S. propaganda. One of the agency's responsibilities was and is the Voice of America radio broadcasts, sending news and features about the United States to the rest of the world.

The founding of the Public Relations Society of America (PRSA) in 1948 through the merger of the National Association of Public Relations Council and the American Council on Public Relations was a major step in the professionalization of the field. Today, its ethics code is the professional standard.

By the end of the twentieth century, more than 2,000 PR firms operated in the United States, with many more around the world. The scope of public relations today is hard if not impossible to define, with no uniformly accepted simple definition of the craft or art of public relations. What is known is that thousands today work in a profession designed to "spin" or otherwise manipulate the news in favor of their clients. At the individual level, the goal of the profession is information acquisition, opinion change, and often behavioral change. At the system level, public relations provides the media and the public with necessary assistance in the information and news gathering process.

Advocacy in an Adversarial Society

Hegel argued that thesis and antithesis should produce synthesis—a coming together of ideas. And if democracy has a central philosophy it could be that society benefits when people of different thoughts arrive at collective judgments about public issues through public debate. It is perhaps illuminating to note that the partisan press was the predominant medium when the Constitution was written. And in the midst of this cacophony of one-sided and often virulent broadsides, the states ratified what we now call the First Amendment, which states that "Congress shall make no law respecting . . . freedom of speech." According to the Founders, speech need not be neutral or two-sided to be protected.

As the United States grew and diversified into a country of labor and management, urban and rural, rich and poor, and people of all races, inevitable conflicts grew. Because it was a land where every individual enjoys a right to "life, liberty, and the pursuit of happiness," and where the courts settled important disputes by the rule of law, many individuals and institutions decided they could function more effectively if they paid someone to "advocate" for their point of view.

The justice system has long recognized the need for each side to have an advocate to navigate the adversarial system of the courts. Landsman says the system requires a "zealous advocate." According to adversary theory, "when each actor performs only a single function the dispute before the court will be resolved in the fairest and most efficient way" (1984, 45–46). In the system, each advocate must find and present the most persuasive evidence and downplay that evidence that might be harmful to the client.

The original practitioners of public relations—Edward L. Bernays and Ivy Lee—both claimed to act as "lawyers in the court of public opinion." Their role, as they saw it and as most in the profession understand it today, was to win the battle for public opinion through targeted media messages. Often these messages presented a one-sided or highly selective point of view, but in a country where multiple opinions found a voice, such messages were viewed as ethical.

Does the claim to be similar to a lawyer in a court of law make the public relations professional an advocate for a client's truth or an adversary to media professionals who must find the truth about a client? Does a public relations professional, whose output might end up in the media and therefore influence public opinion, have any more right to be selective in that truth telling than journalists? Does the fact that the rules of the marketplace, or the legislature, differ from those of a courtroom mean that advocacy may be a good, but incomplete, guide to ethical behavior?

Those who support the advocacy model argue that any misleading information put out by public relations professionals will be somehow "self-corrected" by the gatekeepers of the media or by the self-righting "marketplace of ideas." Those who reject the advocacy model do so on two grounds: first, they assert that advocacy too easily morphs into distortion and lies; second, that the long-term health of many enterprises, from business to government programs, is ill-served by "spin" and better served by honest, timely communication—even at the expense of short-term losses.

This concept of telling the truth in times of crisis, or becoming an advocate for the long-term health of a particular client, has become one of the foremost professional principles for public relations practitioners engaged in crisis communication. The history of the field would suggest that businesses and agencies whose actions demonstrate that public health and safety are more important than short-term profits—in sum, telling the truth even when it hurts—are quite likely to profit substantially in the long term.

That was the lesson that public relations practitioners learned a generation ago from Johnson & Johnson's handling of the "Tylenol scare," when seven people in the Chicago area died as a result taking Tylenol capsules laced with cyanide. Johnson & Johnson voluntarily pulled the product off the shelves, reimbursed consumers who had purchased it but could no longer use it, and cooperated completely and openly with both government investigators and the media. Less than two years after the incident, the result was that Tylenol's market share had increased and the corporation itself was trusted by the public. Contrast this set of actions with those of Firestone/Bridgestone's stonewalling over the recall of faulty tires on sport utility vehicles—and the long-term impact of those actions on corporate health. Public relations practitioners who advocate telling the truth in times of crisis can serve both their clients and the public without fear of compromising professional or personal ethics.

Deaver (1990) provides a useful tool (see Figure 5.1) in which he identifies four layers in a continuum of truth and the intent of those who practice it. At the top are those intending to inform, followed by those intending to persuade, followed by those who often intend to entertain, and finally by those who intend to deceive. It is interesting to note that Deaver distinguishes between "TRUTH," which is absolute and usually derived from an ultimate source of authority, and "truth," which is the documentable facts and information we deal with every day.

Deaver's configuration puts public relations and advertising safely within the realm of what society deems acceptable behavior. Their purposes are distinct from those of their journalistic peers, but well above the level of deceit.

Figure 5.1
The Continuum of Truth

Truth Continuum	Intent
TRUTH/truth Facts and information Journalistic news	to inform accurately and fully with no apparent bias
p.r. copy editorials/columns advertising copy propaganda	an intent to persuade by using selective information; the truth but not the whole truth
parables and allegories fiction honest error	non-truths told with no intent to deceive
deceit "white lies" BLATANT LIES	intent to deceive, even if for a purpose claimed to be justifiable

Hodges (1986) says that the notion of professional responsibility can be summed up in a single question: For what am I prepared to respond ably? In other words, what have my education and my experience equipped me to do and to assume responsibility for?

Ask a public relations practitioner "To what are you ably equipped to respond?" and they might answer "To respond to a crisis for a client" or "To generate favorable media attention for a client." However, there are greater responsibilities.

Hodges further states that responsibilities come from three sources. First there are those that are *assigned,* such as employee to employer. Second there are those that are *contracted,* where each party agrees to assume responsibilities and fulfill them. Third there are the *self-imposed* responsibilities, where the individual moral actor takes on responsibilities for reasons indigenous to each individual.

It is our contention that public relations, practiced ethically, will not only fulfill the assigned or contracted responsibilities with the employer or the paying client but also will take on the greater calling of self-imposed responsibilities. These self-imposed responsibilities could include such constructs as duty to the truth and fidelity to the public's good. The more self-imposed responsibilities the PR professional assumes, the more ethical the profession will become as practitioners see their personal good as being synonymous with the public's good.

When Seeing Isn't Believing: News Releases on Video

In the 1990s, the press release has gone high-tech, produced on video, and distributed via satellites to television stations. For instance, when television news showed "smart bombs" hitting their targets during the Persian Gulf War, the footage was produced by the military and the public relations firm of Hill and Knowlton, not by news organizations (Safer 1992). Much of the video coverage of the Gulf War came courtesy of these military video news releases, commonly referred to as VNRs.

Medialink, a firm involved in the distribution of VNRs, says that health and medical subjects are "the most useful" (read: most aired) VNRs. Business, political and lifestyle/fashion, or sports follow as good VNR topics, in that order. The 106 news directors responding to the survey preferred a timely ninety-second story to an "evergreen" release ("news" that could be aired at any time). They were likely to use a VNR in whole or in part when it could be incorporated into a local interest story. Nearly 75 percent of the news directors also indicated they would consider airing "issue-oriented" VNRs. More than half said VNRs should be clearly identified as public relations releases, including naming the source; 25 percent said they identify a company only if it is clearly relevant to the story. Some 18 percent said they do not identify the sponsor behind an aired release at all.

The general public probably didn't notice the growing VNR industry until a *TV Guide* cover story in February 1992 carried the headline "Fake News." Suddenly the VNR industry found itself under media scrutiny. The article, which focused on the Hill and Knowlton packaging of Operation Desert Storm for the media, warned viewers they were being tricked into assuming that sponsored messages were real news.

In response, the public relations industry retrenched and surfaced with a "Code of Good VNR Practice for Video News Releases." Operating within the guidelines of the code would give the VNR packager a "seal of approval" to be affixed to the video. The code also recommended that an opening slate—seen by the newsroom, not by the viewers at home—include clear identification of a VNR as such, the name of the sponsoring company or organization, the name of a contact person and full information about anyone seen on the video. This provides the needed information should anyone in the television newsroom choose to follow up on the release. The code requires that all information contained in a VNR be accurate and verifiable "to the extent possible." Yet except for the seal, the code calls for no signal to the viewer that the material comes from an outside source.

According to a 1994 article in the *Public Relations Journal,* institutional resistance to VNRs has decreased for one simple reason—lack of resources (Greenberg 1994). TV news and programming directors are often understaffed and lack the budget to cover many newsworthy stories. Larry Pintak, president of Pintak Communications International in Washington, D.C., claims that "VNRs are now seen as a much more serious tool for conveying information. The industry has weeded out the people who want to produce VNRs that don't stand a snowball's chance of getting aired."

Conclusion

While the proliferation of news releases is a source of mild irritation between the professions of journalism and public relations, it is a minor nuisance compared to the differences in how the two sides approach "hard" news stories. Unfortunately, some public relations practitioners see their jobs not only as telling the good news about their company, but also as keeping the bad news from being told. This standoff results in the perpetuation of a vicious cycle. Business executives perceive that the press is out to "get" them, so they refuse to speak, while the press perceives that a corporation has something to hide by its silence.

Public relations began as a profession when certain newsmakers wanted more media coverage. Today because of what business perceives as a negative bias, many public relations professionals are used as dissemblers of legitimate stories. Some businesses have found it expedient to refuse to cooperate with the media, and some have extended the policy to all employees. For instance, one major retailer does not even allow its managers to grant interviews about the expected best-selling toys for the upcoming Christmas season. Though this policy seems a bit extreme in a Christmas feature story, it is based on the assumption that most of the time the media will want information that will harm a business.

The average news consumer rarely observes this constant struggle for control over the content of the news, yet he or she is affected by it. How should we evaluate a profession with the goal of persuading in a manner that does not look like traditional persuasion or the goal of preventing the dissemination of information that might harm the illusion that has been created?

Practitioners in the field justify their profession with the following arguments: First, the stories they attempt to tell are the unreported or the underreported stories of products that work, employees who are honest, and corporations that are good community citizens. Second, the rules are set by the other players in the game—the media. Finally, if the media would ever agree that good news *is* news, the animosity and duplicity might diminish.

Suggested Readings

Boorstin, Daniel. 1962. *The image.* New York: Atheneum.
Cutlip, Scott. 1994. *The Unseen Power: Public Relations—A History.* Hillsdale, N.J.: Lawrence Erlbaum Assoc.
Vonnegut, Kurt. 1952. *Player Piano.* New York: Dell Publishing Co.

CHAPTER V CASES

CASE V-A
Quit, Blow the Whistle, or Go with the Flow?
ROBERT D. WAKEFIELD
Wakefield Communications

Anyone who spends sufficient years in public relations will face a crisis of conscience. Practitioners are trained for the tenuous task of balancing institutional advocacy with the "public interest" (Newsom, Turk and Kruckeberg 1996). Yet this role can lead to personal conflict, as it did in my case.

The setting was an urban school district with about forty schools and more than 350,000 students. Its superintendent was nationally reputed for innovative community outreach, and he was a media favorite. I worked with him for five years before he accepted a statewide position. His replacement was a quiet man with conservative views who, along with the administrative team he brought with him, believed that educators were trained to run the schools and could do so best with minimal interference.

Like most inner-city school districts, the system was losing students as people moved to the suburbs. In the previous decade, a student population that once filled four high schools could now fill only three.

The seven-member school board had approached—and then abandoned—the question of closing one of the schools because the proposal aroused such strong feelings among students, faculty, and parents. However, the new administration, trying to balance those responses against the financial drain of supporting an additional high school on taxpayer dollars, decided to broach the question again.

Promised a tumultuous situation, the new administrators aggravated the problem by how they handled it. Rather than sharing the issue with the community or with school faculties to seek a mutually agreeable solution, they tried to resolve the entire problem behind closed doors.

I first learned about the closed-door approach at a "study meeting" with the school board. The new superintendent held these informal meetings during his earliest days in the district; they tended to be so boring and ambiguous that journalists seldom attended.

Before the meeting in question, the superintendent asked me whether any media would be present. I told him one reporter might come late. As the meeting began, I was surprised to hear him tell the board and the few staff members, "If any reporter shows up, I will change the subject—but today we're going to take about closing a high school." He then outlined the results of meetings he had already held on the issue, discussed a proposal from a local community college to buy the building so it would not be abandoned and sought the support of the four high school principals.

Thus began my ethical conundrum. I agreed that the enrollment problem was serious and that closing a school was probably the best alternative, but I opposed the administration's method of resolving the issue. As public relations officer, I believed that public institutions must be open and that involving those affected by the closure in the actual decision-making process would eventually generate long-term support for whatever decision was made. I was appalled at the attempts to exclude the public; but I said nothing.

Closed doors can quickly swing ajar, and it took less than one day for news of the decision to leak. The school targeted for closure was one of the oldest in the state. It had recently received a U.S. Department of Education award as an exemplary inner-city school, but its community was the least affluent and arguably the least politically powerful.

The day after the "study session," and with a regular board meeting scheduled for the same evening, reporters called to verify what they were hearing. (Chief executives often forget that supervisors of individual units within the system have their own allegiances. In this case, one of the high school principals left the "study meeting" and informed his teaching staff that they would be receiving transfer students "from that inner-city school." The rumors began.)

After the phone calls, I asked the superintendent what he planned to say at the board meeting and was told, "We will discuss space utilization needs." I told him about the calls and that our jobs would be threatened if we were not truthful with the community. To his credit, he responded quickly and openly.

The evening meeting unfolded as expected. The room was jammed with district patrons and with the media. The expected lines were drawn. Underlying the fervor was a common these: closing a traditional high school was awful enough, but the secretive way in which the administration had reached its conclusions was unforgivable.

The next several weeks were an intense period of work for a young public relations officer. I did media interviews, talk shows, and forums to explain the situation. I also met with dozens of teachers, parents and citizens, both to hear their comments and to take their suggestions. I had to be careful that my words represented the district instead of myself. I had worked with some local reporters for several years and felt comfortable giving them background so they could seek additional materials without revealing me as the original source. It was a personal risk, but the reporters never betrayed my trust.

Two additional incidents epitomized my ethical struggles. The first occurred after the initial board meeting, when a top administrator said the community misunderstood why decisions were made behind closed doors. I lobbied for openness. The administrator admonished me to remember who paid my salary, a rebuke that confirmed the new administration did not share my own values.

The second incident occurred when I was asked to meet with a man who had been chosen to speak on behalf of the community. I had taken only a few steps into his office when he said to me, "You don't agree with your administration, do you?" My response was silence while he explained his position.

For some reason, it was this encounter that forced my crisis of conscience. Do I quit, blow the whistle, or keep quiet? I had a wife and child to support; the employment picture at the time was not robust. Right or wrong, I surmised that the various relationships I had developed could appease many angry feelings. I also believed in the importance of education. So, I decided to stay through the crisis, then seek new employment.

About one month into the crisis, the board retained a consultant who, like me, believed in open communication.

Two weeks later, four board members came to my office and requested a meeting. Because this constituted a majority of the board, such an assembly violated the law requiring the meeting be made public. I violated the law and invited them to stay. They said they were worn down by the constant tension and asked what I, as a public relations practitioner, thought they should do.

To me, the answer was straightforward. Relying on basic public relations formulas and common sense, I suggested that they could diffuse the tension by reverting to what should have been done in the first place: announce that selected representatives from throughout the city would form a committee to help review the situation and come to a decision that would then be discussed by the board. To my surprise, the board members took this advice to the administration, and much of what I recommended was done.

A few months later, the school was closed in a tearful farewell. And, five weeks after the school closed, I accepted a job with a local public relations firm.

Micro Issues:

1. What sort of press releases or other talking points should Wakefield have prepared once the rumors began?
2. Should Wakefield have gone off the record with reporters he trusted?
3. Are there some sorts of decisions governmental bodies make that really should be kept from the media and hence the public? Is this one of them?
4. How should Wakefield have responded to the racial subtext of some of the protests about the closing of the school?

Mid-range Issues:

1. Should Wakefield have "blown the whistle" on the board members who requested an illegal meeting?
2. Was it appropriate for Wakefield to advise the board to take an approach different from that suggested by the superintendent?
3. How much does Wakefield's previous experience with a different superintendent influence his understanding of how the district works? How did this "workplace" socialization influence his ethical thinking?
4. How does the fact that Wakefield was not in on the initial decision making— what scholars have called an "asymmetrical public relations relationship"— appear to have influenced the events or the ethical response to them?

Macro Issues:

1. To whom should Wakefield be loyal?
2. Should he ever have told members of the community of his own personal views?

3. How does Wakefield's job compare with that of a press secretary for a political figure?
4. Is it ever appropriate to keep journalists in the dark about how political decisions are made?
5. Is a symmetrical public relations relationship a realistic goal in contemporary public or corporate life? If your response is "no," what does that mean for the ethics of the profession?

CASE V-B
Role of Public Relations in the Alar Scare
PHILIP PATTERSON
Oklahoma Christian University

David Fenton was given a difficult task in October 1988: to get the public interested in yet another study by an activist group with a small budget. The group was the 100,000-member Natural Resources Defense Council (NRDC) and the study was entitled "Intolerable Risk: Pesticides in Our Children's Food." At issue was the effect of the pesticide Alar on cancer rates in young children. For a fee of $25,000 (Anthan 1990), Fenton attacked the challenge with vigor, and met with huge, but controversial, success.

Fenton's work began when he agreed to promote the group's announcement that children were being exposed to the pesticide Alar beyond recommended levels, according to NRDC calculations. Alar, the trade name of the chemical daminozide, acts as a growth retardant to keep apples on the tree longer and preserve them on the way to market, producing redder fruit with a longer shelf life (1989).

However, exposure to an excess amount of Alar is linked with cancer, and the EPA has established strict levels acceptable for human consumption. Unlike pesticides, Alar is absorbed into the fruit, making it impossible to wash off. NRDC contended that children were at risk of receiving too much Alar for two reasons: the disproportionate number of apples they eat and their smaller body size.

Fenton's goal was to create a story "to achieve a life of its own" (1989, 9). Obtaining this goal required deal making not unlike that of a Hollywood press agent. An agreement was made with *60 Minutes* to allow breaking the story on February 26, 1989. Interviews with monthly magazines, which operate on the industry's longest lead times, were booked months in advance to ensure publication at the peak of the talk-show appearances by recruited celebrities.

Media exposure of the Alar announcement included the covers of *Time* (Toufexis 1989), *Newsweek* (Beck 1989; Begley and Hagar 1989) and *Consumer Reports* (1989). Fenton also claimed credit for placing the story on *Good Morning America, Today, CBS This Morning, Donahue,* and the network newscasts. Additional coverage came on the cover of *USA Today* and in other newspapers, as well as in *U.S. News & World Report* (Siberner 1989), *People, Redbook, Family Circle, Woman's Day,* and *New Woman* magazines.

Other methods were used to spread the message. A 900 phone number was installed to give consumers up-to-the-minute information on the Alar situation. Meryl Streep and cast members from the television shows *thirtysomething* and *L.A. Law* joined news conferences. Streep conducted sixteen interviews by satellite with local anchors in major television markets and testified before a U.S. Senate subcommittee on Alar's use.

Controversy over the message came almost immediately, while controversy over the method soon followed. The initial *60 Minutes* report opened with Ed Bradley making an assertion called a "flat-out lie" by the Washington Apple Commission. He began:

> The most potent cancer-causing agent in our food supply is a substance sprayed on apples to keep them on trees longer and make them look better. That's the conclusion of a number of scientific experts. And who is most at risk? Children who may someday develop cancer from this one chemical called daminozide." (Warren 1989, 1)

The *60 Minutes* segment was viewed by approximately 30 million viewers. This report and the resulting intense coverage led to a scare in the marketplace. Actions taken included the banning of apples by several school systems, including New York City, Chicago, and Los Angeles, and the opening of pesticide-free produce sections in grocery stores, actions that Fenton claims occurred as a result of his publicity.

"Our goal was to create so many repetitions of NRDC's message that average American consumers (not just the policy elite in Washington) could not avoid hearing it—from many different outlets within a short period of time. The idea was for the story to achieve a life of its own and continue for weeks and months to affect policy and consumer habits." (1989, 9)

Evidently the strategy succeeded in that respect. The spokesperson for the Chicago Board of Education, Bob Saigh, blamed a "media stampede" on the Chicago school system's decision to ban apples in its cafeterias.

Why the intense media publicity and the massive public reaction surrounding the findings? The effect of Alar was not a recent discovery. In fact, in 1973 tests on animals showed its carcinogenic qualities, and the EPA had earlier tried to ban it.

Theories of the media's fascination with the Alar announcement abound. *Newsweek's* environmental reporter suggested that perhaps the attraction to the media was what Hitchcock played out in his movie *The Birds:* one of our deepest-seated fears is that the benign will suddenly turn menacing (Carlson 1989). Forensic psychiatrist Park Dietz suggested that "part of what happened here is something characteristic of all mass hysteria incidents, a perceived threat to children or childbearing. Then there is the element of invisible hazards. Here you have the issues of children and invisibility. They were very powerful" (Warren 1989, 1).

Peter Sandman, former director of the Environmental Communication Research Program at Rutgers University, thinks it was the made-for-media symbolism of the apple. "Apples are a symbol of innocence and innocence betrayed. Kids eat them. There's the Adam and Eve story and Snow White" (Haddix 1990, 44).

When a well-orchestrated media campaign threatened to challenge the ages-old assumption that "An apple a day keeps the doctor away," the media appeal was irresistible.

The media rarely, if ever, revealed that the information they were airing came from the NRDC's point of view. Chemical industry spokesperson Elizabeth Whelan was, by her own count, quoted in or interviewed on the Alar issue by the two U.S. wire services, several newspapers including the *Chicago Tribune* and the *Washington Post,* two news services, and talk shows such as *Larry King Live,* without the media once mentioning that she was funded by industry sources, including Uniroyal Chemical Company, the manufacturer of Alar (Kurtz 1990). In an interview for *Columbia Journalism Review,* Whelan said that to worry about such matters is "chilling the discussion," adding that "Everyone is funded by someone" (Kurtz 1990, 44).

Eventually, however, the strategy backfired. In October, 1989, the *Wall Street Journal* (1989) used a leaked memorandum between Fenton and the NRDC in an unattributed editorial that ran under the headline "How a PR Firm Executed the Alar Scare." The confidential memo obtained by the *Wall Street Journal* outlined the strategies used by Fenton, but taken out of context it looked less like strategy than manipulation. Media watchdog groups, such as Accuracy in Media, jumped on the issue, spending thousands of dollars getting the "real" Alar story out to their constituencies, and trying to force CBS chairman Laurence Tisch to retract the original *60 Minutes* story.

The result was an unwanted type of publicity for the NRDC. Its executive director, John Adams, later told a reporter for the *Washington Post,* "We wanted to get a maximum amount of coverage. What we did instead was that we blew it. We got everybody angry at us. I'll never let myself get in this situation again" (Haddix 1990, 45).

Predictably, the apple industry struck back with a $2 million campaign launched by the apple growers. Full-page ads appeared on Friday, March 10 in the *New York Times, Washington Post, USA Today,* and *Los Angeles Times,* asserting that a person would have to eat 28,000 pounds of Alar-treated apples a day for seventy years to obtain a dose of the chemical comparable to that given the laboratory mice in the NRDC study. By March 14, the ad had run in several dozen other newspapers (Warren 1989).

Other countermeasures were tried as well. The public relations firm of Hill and Knowlton was hired to counter the negative publicity. Both the EPA and the FDA publicly disputed the report. But even while working with a bigger budget, the apple growers' efforts lacked the media impact of the campaign designed by Fenton. "We got rolled," explains Hill and Knowlton's Frank Mankiewicz. "When you're dealing with a nutritionist named Meryl Streep, you haven't got a chance."

Many consumers were not convinced by the rebuttals. By the fall of 1989, the effect of the first apple crop without Alar was being felt, particularly in the Northeast, where the McIntosh apple, a variety particularly susceptible to early dropping, was down more than a million bushels, forcing some growers out of the apple business. Two years later, one Colorado legislator would introduce a bill in the Colorado House of Representatives that would make it a crime to disseminate "false information . . . which casts doubts on the safety of any perishable agricultural food product" (Goodman 1991). Years later in the fall 1996 issues of *Columbia Journalism Review,* the controversy still brewed with claims that the scare was for real, and a long letter to the editor from Whelan in the following issue stated the industry's position once again.

When questioned in 1989 about his tactics, Fenton says that the methods differed only slightly from the marketing campaigns of the corporations that are polluting the environment with their products. "These corporations spend millions on their campaigns and when a small group attempts to use the same methods, they get criticized" (Fenton 1989). Clayton Yeutter, agriculture secretary at the time of the incident, is among those who disagree, calling Fenton's methods "environmental terrorism" (Anthan 1990).

As for the leaked document, Fenton says that the biases of the *Wall Street Journal* are well-known and that "they do this type of thing all the time" (Fenton 1989). He refused to share any of the rest of the information in the memo, saying that it was proprietary information belonging to the NRDC. Lorraine Voles, national coordinator of Mothers and Others for Pesticide Limits, the group that secured the services of Streep, echoed the sentiments of Fenton: "I think those tactics (used by Fenton) have to be used. It's like handicapping yourself if you don't do it" (Haddix 1990, 45).

Micro Issues:

1. Did the techniques used by Fenton appear to be overly aggressive? If so, in what way? From what you know, were the tactics justified by the evidence?
2. Is there an alternate approach that would go beyond the frequently ignored press release yet stop short of creating the widespread consumer concern caused by this campaign?
3. Was the *Wall Street Journal* justified in exposing the confidential memo?
4. Is a representative such as Whelan obligated to inform interviewers of the funding for her organization even if she is not asked?

Mid-range Issues:

1. The headline of the *Wall Street Journal* op-ed piece claimed that Fenton's organization executed the scare. From what you have read in this case study, is that correct or is that an overstatement? What statements, if any, in the case lead you to believe that the scare was executed by Fenton?
2. Fenton's organization managed the Alar story, including timing the breaking of the story, making spokespersons available for interviews, staging press conferences, and the like. Does that amount of management affect the truthfulness of the story?
3. You are a journalist seeking to write a story about Alar. Of what use are celebrities like Streep and the casts of *L.A. Law* and *thirtysomething* to the story? Do you interview them? Do you accept their expertise on the issue? Is the fact that celebrities are being used to spread the message a story in itself?
4. Of the media that ran the story, is there a difference in the amount of fact checking that should be done by the staff of *60 Minutes* and the staff of *Oprah* before airing a story about the apples? Are the editorial expectations in a story such as this different for *Redbook* than for *Newsweek?*
5. Were the media guilty of hyping the Alar story since it contained the pathos and good visuals required for airing or publication?

Macro Issues:

1. If you were in the position of helping to publicize an issue like the Alar issue, how important would it be to you to be on the side you perceive to be correct? Could you, for instance, take the apple growers' money in this case? Could you take the NRDC's money? If the issue were abortion, could you help either side? Gun control? Toxic-waste disposal?
2. Before issuing a news release, should the public relations practitioner weigh the consequences, such as the farmers going bankrupt? In light of the government's assurances that the apples were safe, was the action of Fenton Communications morally justifiable?
3. What should be the relationship between public relations and the news? Should public relations press releases be identified as such? Should they always be rewritten if they are used? Should the facts be checked by the media?
4. Should news be labeled as originating from a point of view? Could the average reader or viewer have known the individual biases of the NRDC? Of Whelan? Of Streep?

CASE V-C
A Case of Need
DENI ELLIOTT
University of Montana

The call came to Portland, Maine, newsrooms on a snowy, quiet day in early February. Norma Lynn Peterson, a seven-year-old from the neighboring town of Windham, had end-stage liver disease. A candidate for a liver transplant at the well-respected Pittsburgh transplant center, Norma, her family, and supporters had little to do but wait and hope that a suitable donor organ would become available in the year that doctors said Norma otherwise had to live.

It soon became obvious that while they waited and hoped, the family would also need to raise money: the associated costs of Norma's illness were a tremendously hard burden for the working-class Peterson family, even with health insurance that would cover 80 percent of the $200,000 surgery. That's what the phone call was all about. A Valentine's Day potluck dinner had been planned to raise money for Norma Lynn. The volunteer fund-raiser who contacted news media did so because he thought that the community's willingness to help Norma Lynn might make a good news story.

Fund-raising activities on behalf of Norma Lynn continued throughout the spring. In mid-July, the long-anticipated call from Pittsburgh came. A liver had been found. Norma and her parents flew from Portland to Pittsburgh in a private ambulance airplane, paid for by donations.

By this time, thanks to local news coverage, almost everybody in the state knew about Norma Lynn. The Petersons' willingness to cooperate with news media allowed readers and viewers an inside look at the medical crisis and how one family coped. Norma Lynn's dark eyes, long hair, delicate ivory skin, and sweet, shy nature quickly won the hearts of reporters and opened the pocketbooks of those who got to know of her plight.

More than $100,000 in cash donations had been placed in the Norma Lynn Fund. Local merchants had donated items to the Peterson family, including a video camera and a puppy. Well-wishers showered the little girl with cards, gifts, and testimonies to her bravery.

Norma Lynn's transplant surgery was successful. Two serious complications arose in the first few weeks after surgery: she required a second operation to repair a leaking bile duct and then developed a liver virus from which she recovered.

It was a surprise to the Petersons when the doctors announced a month after the transplant that Norma was ready to return home. The air-ambulance company that had transported Norma to Pittsburgh for her surgery was caught by surprise. The costs of the trip home had not yet been covered: a local business had donated a private jet and pilot, the wages of a nurse to accompany Norma on the flight had been donated as well, but the jet's fuel costs would run about nine hundred dollars.

The manager of the air-ambulance company had an idea. Local television news had certainly been getting a lot out of the Norma Lynn story; they should be willing to give something back. He called the first of the three network affiliates, picking the one that he thought had done the best job for Norma Lynn, and asked for three hundred dollars, one-third of the amount he needed. The news director was willing to make the donation, but only if the station could send a reporter and photographer on the plane in exchange. It turned out that there were two empty seats on the plane. The station could have them, the manager decided, but only if they donated the full nine hundred dollars.

Micro Issues:

1. Was this story newsworthy?
2. Without media coverage, the Petersons would not have raised more than a few thousand dollars. Is there a problem with the Petersons' using local news coverage as a fund-raising tool?
3. How much and what kind of news coverage was appropriate? Pre-surgery? During her hospitalization? Afterward?
4. Was it acceptable for the address of the Norma Lynn Fund to appear in nightly news stories?
5. Should the news stories have made clear that 80 percent of Norma Lynn's medical costs were covered by insurance? Was it deceptive not to tell the audience how much money her family actually needed to complement insurance coverage?

Mid-range Issues:

1. How should the news organizations have responded to the air-ambulance company's request for donation? Did the local media owe something to Norma Lynn?
2. The news organization that came up with the nine hundred dollars effectively shut out its competition from riding home from Pittsburgh with Norma Lynn. The competitors complained that the station had bought exclusive news coverage. Did their action constitute buying the news?

Macro Issues:

1. What criteria should news organizations use in determining whether an individual with medical or financial need is newsworthy?
2. Some doctors complain that media coverage of one individual's wait for an organ donation can result in that individual's getting an organ more quickly than other, sicker patients. Should medical need influence coverage decisions?
3. Should news organizations be concerned about issues of fairness to other families in financial need? Should they provide equal coverage for the next child? And what about the next?
4. When news organizations publicize an individual's financial need, do they owe the audience any reassurances about the worth of the cause or about how the donations will be used?

5. Should news organizations give an accounting of how much money is actually used for the medical crisis and what happens to the remainder?
6. Does it matter if excess funds raised go into a trust fund to offset future expenses? Go to help other sick children in financial need? Go toward other non-related expenses, like the purchase of a new car or house?
7. Do news organizations incur a responsibility to tell the audience where their donations are going?
8. Is there a story in the fact that some children die because their families cannot raise the money for catastrophic health care?

CASE V-D
The Gym Shoe Phenomenon: Social Values vs. Marketability
GAIL BAKER
University of Florida

Sprinkled between the abandoned burned-out buildings and the glass-covered vacant lots of Chicago's South Side are bigger-than-life billboards featuring famous athletes wearing expensive Nike gym shoes. Basketball superstar Michael Jordan claims he can jump higher while wearing the shoes; former football great Bo Jackson boasts he can run faster in Nike athletic shoes. Controversial movie director Spike Lee says people of different backgrounds would get along better wearing good athletic shoes.

The company is excited about the "Air Jordan" and "Bo Knows" athletic shoe campaigns it developed for the African-American market. And to ensure that the campaigns are sensitive to African-American consumers, Nike hired legendary Georgetown University basketball coach John Thompson as a $200,000-a-year consultant.

In addition, Nike is careful to select only athletes with "squeaky clean" reputations. Neither Jordan nor Jackson has ever been involved in drugs. Both are family men who are active in their communities. The company believes these two men can clearly be considered role models for the African-American youths who see, hear and read the advertisements. It is thought that these celebrities add credibility to the product and enhance the image of the expensive shoes, which cost between $50 and $125 a pair.

Back in the Chicago ghetto, a sixteen-year-old black youth is shot and killed on his way to school. Police surmise that he is murdered for his $125 gym shoes, the only clothing missing from his bloody body when the authorities arrive. Unfortunately, this is not the first case of assault or murder provoked by a pair of expensive shoes. Because they have become so fashionable and because they are so expensive, inner-city children are robbing and killing each other to look more like the athletic celebrities they wish to emulate.

Some gangs name themselves after the shoes and shave the name into their haircuts. Parents sometimes sacrifice necessities to purchase the shoes for their children.

The popularity of the shoes and the violence that is sometimes associated with them is noticed by leaders in the African-American community. Nike is criticized in the media for selecting black athletes as spokespersons.

Eric Perkins of the Educational Testing Service calls the use of black athletes "exploitative, because advertisers are playing into the subliminal fascination with black superiority in the white collective psyche." Others criticize Nike for what they believe to be a lack of minority hiring and black community support. Nike is also accused of promoting athletics over academics. Only 1 in 10,000 high school athletes ever becomes a professional, and only 20 percent of all black college athletes ever finish college.

Jesse Jackson and other religious and civil rights leaders call for a national boycott of Nike to protest the company's business practices. Rev. Jackson is particularly critical of the African-Americans who endorse athletic shoes, saying "They are exploiting an ethos of mindless materialism."

Operation PUSH (People United to Save Humanity), a civil rights organization founded by Rev. Jackson, joins the boycott effort. PUSH officials complain that sales of Nike shoes to blacks total $200 million annually, while the company has no high-ranking black executives and does not do business with black-owned advertising agencies. The company responds by saying that sales to non-whites account for only 14 percent of its sales. Nike also states that 7.5 percent of its 4,200 U.S. employees are black.

Fourteen weeks into the boycott, the Rev. Tyrone Crider, executive director of Operation PUSH, says the boycott would continue "until Nike decides to put money in black-owned banks, advertise with black-owned media, do business with black-owned businesses, and put a black on its board of directors."

On the other side of the issue, Nike spokespersons say it is just good marketing to use Bo Jackson and Michael Jordan in their advertisements. "He (Jackson) is a person kids can look up to. He's crazy about his kids and his wife and family. He's somebody who has applied himself and came from a really humble background," says Melinda Gable, public relations executive for Nike.

Jordan, Lee and Thompson meet with Jackson in an effort to stop the boycott. The meeting is unsuccessful and the boycott continues.

Nike announces during the boycott that it will hire a minority vice president and name a minority to its board of directors by 1992. The company also hires a minority advertising agency, Muse Codero and Chen, out of Los Angeles, to handle a portion of its account.

Nike shoe sales, unaffected by the boycott, increase 58 percent over the same period the previous year. After several months and a number of news articles and television stories, the Nike boycott fades from the national headlines and Nike continues its use of black athletes in its advertising campaigns. Inner-city crime continues, but few news reports link the violence to clothing or shoes.

Following the boycott, the company develops a "Bo Knows School" campaign featuring Jackson and distributes thousands of book jackets to inner-city schools. On it Jackson appears in a graduation cap and gown, a band uniform, a scientist's white lab coat, and a Greek philosopher's toga. The book jacket reads, "Bo knows all this stuff because he stayed in school."

Although the company now receives applause for its interest in education, critics still question the tie-in with African-American athletes.

Micro Issues:

1. Is Nike advertising responsible for the inner-city violence that occurred after its campaign?
2. Did Nike's decision to hire an ethnic advertising agency relieve the company of its social responsibility or was it just a public relations ploy?

Mid-range Issues:

1. Is Nike guilty of stereotyping African-Americans by using athletes in their ads?
2. If Nike didn't use athletes to promote athletic shoes, whom should it select?
3. Should athletes be used as role models in advertising aimed at black youths since such a small percentage of African-Americans ever play professional sports?
4. Do product manufacturers need to be sensitive to the social and economic conditions of their potential clients, or should they be able to market any product that sells, as long as it's legal?

Macro Issues:

1. Should advertisers respond to pressure placed upon them by community activists?
2. Can advertising be held accountable for social problems that stem from poverty and lack of opportunity?

CHAPTER VI

Privacy: Looking for Solitude in the Global Village

By the end of this chapter, you should be able to:

• appreciate the difference between the right to privacy and a need for privacy.
• distinguish between the law and ethics of privacy.
• understand the concepts of discretion, right to know, need to know, want to know, and circles of intimacy.
• understand and apply Rawls's veil of ignorance as a tool for ethical decision making.

Why Privacy in the New Millennium?

If there was one area in media ethics that was stretched almost beyond recognition in the latter part of the twentieth century, it was privacy. And the assault involved no less a person than the president of the United States. What the world got to see was a public discussion of sex—and what constitutes sex—played out before the U. S. Congress, the national television audience, and newspaper readers across the country. Americans learned that an intern who brought former President Bill Clinton pizza late one night had become his partner in oral sex for many months. She retained a semen-stained dress from the affair; the nation learned of it and of the results of the DNA tests.

However, Congress learned of the affair because a "friend" of Monica Lewinsky's had taped her telephone conversations, which included hours of distraught discussion about her relationship with the president. We watched thunderstruck as Hillary Clinton, now a U.S. Senator, denied knowing of the affair. We also watched her public stoicism when her husband admitted that he had lied to her as well as the rest of the American people.

We watched the impeachment proceedings, and read newspaper accounts of independent counsel Kenneth Starr's sexually explicit report. Many U.S. newspapers printed the report verbatim. Just in case they did not, the U.S. House of Representatives made it available on the Internet without benefit of editing or warning to subject matter and content. Shortly after that Larry Flynt, who publishes *Penthouse* magazine, promised a $1 million reward for accurate information about Republican Congressional figures who engaged in behavior similar to that of President Clinton, but without the benefit of an independent counsel inquiry.

The Clinton-Lewinsky affair came to symbolize the media's apparent inability to make distinctions between news and what one scholar has characterized as mediated voyeurism, "the consumption of revealing images of and information about others' apparently real and unguarded lives, often yet not always for purposes of entertainment but frequently at the expense of privacy and discourse, through the means of the mass media and the Internet" (Calvert 2000, 23). Calvert lists such diverse activities as hidden camera reports, the paparazzi phenomenon, video surveillance in businesses as well as private homes, and suggests that such technology-based media content has forever changed journalism. "Our notions of news and human interest stories have shifted over time. Today, voyeurism passes as news." (Calvert 2000, 29).

Yet even Calvert admits that news some might consider voyeuristic can have an important purpose. In early 2000, NBC *Today Show* host Katie Couric, whose husband had died about two years earlier from colon cancer, had her own colonoscopy broadcast on national television. Several months before that, talk-show host Oprah Winfrey videotaped women having mammograms—although visual images of the women's breasts never aired due to carefully selected camera angles. The goal in both cases was a worthy one: protecting the public health by demonstrating that routine medical screening exams don't hurt and can save a life. In these instances, Couric and women in Winfrey's report gave up some element of privacy that most Americans continue to cherish.

Not everyone is so open. After the 2000 presidential election, NBC's well-regarded political correspondent Tim Russert noted in an interview with Vice President-elect Richard Cheney that for months he had asked for specific information regarding the health of Cheney's heart only to be stonewalled with generalities. It was only after Cheney had a mild heart attack that the public got an accurate and detailed response to Russert's questions and learned that Russert had asked them in the first place.

Domestic politics are not the only place where the lines between what is private and what is public seem to have disappeared. Reality television treats us to *Survivor* and *Temptation Island*, the Internet brings us images of women giving birth and teens losing their virginity. We watch in horror as the victims of Kosovo emerge, only to flip the channel to *Real World* and *Road Rules*. Through it all we remain confused about whether we are responding as normally curious human beings, citizens who need information, or journalists doing important work in a democratic society.

The Need for Privacy

Much has been written on the "right to privacy," a right made problematic by the fact that the term never appears in the U.S. Constitution. Relatively little, however, has been written about the "need for privacy." Philosopher Louis W. Hodges has attempted to focus attention on the need for privacy. He says that "without some degree of privacy, civilized life would be impossible" (Hodges 1983). Both a personal and societal need for privacy exists, Hodges claims.

First, we personally need privacy to develop a sense of self. Constance T. Fischer (1980) states that people need privacy to "try out" new poses, future selves, etc., without fear of ridicule by outsiders. If we are to become the person we wish to be, a certain degree of privacy is needed to develop that person apart from observation. Religious cults that seek cognitive control over their members do so in part by depriving the members of any real degree of privacy, restricting both growth and reflection.

Second, society needs privacy as a shield against the power of the state. As the state gains more information about its citizens, it is increasingly easy to influence, manipulate, or control each one.

Precisely because the state is seen as the agency of the citizens' own authority, its independent power is feared, and limitations on the power of the state, such as the Bill of Rights, were established in order to protect private life (Neville 1980). Throughout history, totalitarian regimes have used extensive government surveillance—the near absence of privacy—as a major component of any attempt to create a uniformly subservient citizenry. George Orwell's *1984* is an example of one author's image of government in the absence of privacy.

Therefore, while much of the debate focuses on the *right* to privacy, an equally compelling argument must be made for the *need* for privacy. Privacy is not to be viewed as a luxury or as an option; it is a necessary component of a democracy upon which many of its values such as freedom, individual dignity, and autonomy rest.

Perhaps no issue in contemporary journalistic ethics has been as troubling as invasions of privacy. That trouble exists for at least two specific reasons. First, community and national standards are changing. What was once strictly private, for instance the mention of breast surgery in the newspaper or on television, is not only common but also is credited with saving lives. Second, privacy is both a legal concept in the domain of the courts and an ethical concept debated by philosophers. Confusion over which analysis is appropriate confounds our thinking.

The result is that journalists have been caught between what the law allows and what their consciences will permit. This confusion has led to ethical bungling on a scale that has probably undermined the entire profession's credibility and fed two stereotypical notions: one, that journalists will do anything to get a story, and two, that audiences will willingly consume anything the journalist delivers. These images are not only at odds with reality, but they also make getting and understanding legitimate stories even more difficult.

Legal and Ethical Definitions

The legal notion of privacy began in 1890 with a *Harvard Law Review* article, written by lawyers Samuel Warren and Louis D. Brandeis (who eventually became a U.S. Supreme Court justice), calling for a constitutional right to privacy. Today privacy is guarded legally in four distinct ways:

1. Intrusion upon a person's seclusion or solitude, or into private affairs, such as invading one's home or personal papers to get a story.
2. Public disclosure of embarrassing private facts, such as revealing someone's notorious past when it has no bearing on that person's present status.

3. Publicity that places a person in a false light, such as enhancing a subject's biography to sell additional books.
4. Misappropriation of a person's name or likeness for personal advantage, such as using Michael Jackson's likeness to sell Pepsi without his permission.

While this four-part list is straightforward, the court's interpretation of it is not, placing privacy among the least satisfactory areas of Constitutional law. Not only are decisions themselves contradictory, but also some of the concepts themselves are open to question or change. What once might have been an embarrassing, private fact—for example, that an unmarried woman is pregnant—is now commonplace knowledge and, some would argue, fashionable. Information once available for the asking, such as a student's telephone number, is now closed by a maze of privacy legislation enacted in the 1970s and 1980s.

To further cloud the issue, the claim to privacy is different for different categories of people. Public figures, for example, are subject to a different standard than are others, as are "limited" public figures and even "accidental" public figures thrown into the spotlight by chance. Just exactly who the courts will consider a public figure fluctuates. When the media invade privacy, the legal remedies occur after the fact. A huge monetary award can make a plaintiff rich, but it cannot return that sense of control the initial invasion takes away. For this reason alone, the law provides an unsatisfactory solution. Ethical thinking prior to broadcast or publication is preferable to a court battle.

The ethical basis for privacy is much older than the legal one and appears throughout literature. The bulk of this work asserts that privacy is something we all possess by being human. Modern philosophical interpretations make the assumption that privacy is considered a right, a way of protecting oneself against the actions of other people and institutions. Privacy carries with it the connotation of control and limited access. The individual should be allowed to control who may have certain sorts of information and, sometimes, the context within which that information is presented.

Part of what is confusing to us about the concept of privacy is that, as a concept, it cannot stand apart from community. Responsibility for keeping things private is shared: individuals have to learn when to withhold information, the community has to learn when to avert its eyes completely or to narrow its gaze. Legal scholar Jeffrey Rosen notes that this attention to the role of the community in avoiding the unwanted gaze stems from Talmudic law. "Jewish law, for example, has developed a remarkable body of doctrine around the concept of *hezzek re'iyyah,* which means 'the injury caused by seeing' or 'the injury caused by being seen.' This doctrine expands the right of privacy to protect individuals not only from physical intrusions into the home but also from surveillance by a neighbor who is outside the home, peering through a window in a common courtyard. Jewish law protect neighbors not only from unwanted observation, but also from the possibility of being observed" (Rosen 2000, 18-19).

Medieval law, too, recognized the possibility of injury due to the unwanted gaze, a deep foreshadowing of telephoto lenses or hidden cameras and microphones that have become an almost reflexive part of some forms of investigative/entertainment journalism. Like the philosophical approach developed by the Greeks, in both these instances privacy is linked to our ability to "become" human and retain some element of dignity while doing it. "Only citizens who respect one another's privacy are themselves dignified with divine respect," (Rosen 2000, 19).

The Continuing Conflicts

Most would agree with Grcic (1986) that while privacy is a prima facie right, it sometimes can be negated by other, more compelling rights. In simpler times, the right to invade privacy belonged almost exclusively to the government. The government can demand, for example, that an individual relinquish control of a substantial amount of private information to complete federal and state income tax forms. Further, failure to provide such information makes one legally liable. For the survival of the entire political community, the government demands that its citizens provide it with certain information that is otherwise private. However, specific rules govern such disclosure. The government cannot legally give your tax return information to other interested parties. Such a check on government power theoretically allows the maintenance of some level of individual privacy.

However, the government is not the only institution today that can demand and receive private information. Banks, credit companies, doctors and attorneys, all can request (and usually receive) a variety of highly private information, the bulk it willingly disclosed. Inevitably, such disclosure is one-directional. While you are required to provide your physician with your medical history to ensure proper treatment, your physician might be surprised if you inquired about his or her success rate with a particular surgical procedure, and she certainly is not required to give it to you. Doctors in Massachusetts were uncomfortable and protested when the state passed a law requiring such information be made available to patients.

Computers and databases have become tools for gathering and repositories for storing private information. Huge industries have cropped up selling a single commodity: private information. When you buy a house or apply for a job, you will watch as the information industry disgorges huge amounts of legal and financial information about you with about a 40 percent chance of some error, according to industry figures. The tensions over what should or should not remain private are not resolved; they are merely accounted for and debated in today's complex society.

However, Warren and Brandeis had the press, not the government or financial institutions, in mind when they wrote their precedent-inspiring article. The pair developed their novel legal argument after a breakfast in celebration of Mr. Warren's wedding was covered by the press, an article that would be a benign social mention today if it made the press at all. Offended by this "outrage," Warren and Brandeis could not have anticipated trash television, "kiss-and-tell" books, computerized databases, or the myriad other ways the mass media disseminate private information about people who are more or less willing to disclose it. The issue is not more complex today than it was during the country's formative years, but the ways privacy is violated are substantially different, and perhaps more threatening.

Distinguishing Between Secrecy and Privacy

People tend to think of private information as something they would like to keep secret, but such thinking confounds these two related but separable concepts.

Secrecy can be defined as blocking information intentionally to prevent others from learning, possessing, using, or revealing it (Bok 1983). Secrecy ensures that information is kept from *any* public view. Privacy, however, is concerned with determining who will obtain access to the information. Privacy does not imply that information will never reach public view, but rather that an individual has control over what information becomes public and to whom.

Secrecy often carries a negative connotation. However, we agree with Bok in asserting that secrecy itself is neither morally good nor bad. Privacy and secrecy can overlap but are not identical. "Privacy need not hide; and secrecy hides far more than what is private. A private garden need not be a secret garden, a private life is rarely a secret life" (Bok 1983, 11). Privacy can and should be balanced against other considerations; secrets are something an individual decides to keep.

In *Dietemann v. Time,* jurist Alan F. Westin viewed privacy as the ability to control one's own "circles of intimacy." In the case, two reporters lied to Dietemann to enter his home and later expose him as a medical quack practicing medicine without a license, at home. While the courts saw some social utility in exposing such behavior, Dietemann, they ruled, had a reasonable expectation of privacy in his own home.

Philosopher Louis W. Hodges has used the concept of circles of intimacy to develop a working concept of privacy for journalists and other professionals. If you conceive of privacy as a series of concentric circles, as Figure 6.1 illustrates, in the innermost circle you are alone with your secrets, fantasies, hopes, reconstructed memories, and the rest of the unique psychological "furniture" we bring to our lives. The second circle you probably occupy with one other person, perhaps a spouse, a parent, roommate, or loved one. In that circle, you share private information. In order for that relationship to work well, it needs to be reciprocal, and it should be based primarily on trust. The third circle contains others to whom you are very close—probably family or friends, perhaps a lawyer or clergy member. Here, the basis of relationships is still one of trust, but some communications can be primarily one way—and you do not expect to have complete control over them. As the ripples in the pond of intimacy continue to spread, what you reveal about yourself becomes progressively more public and less intimate, and you lose progressively more control over information about you.

Using this model of expanding circles, privacy can be considered individual control over who has access to your various circles of intimacy. Invasion of privacy occurs when your control over your own circles of intimacy is wrestled from you by people or institutions. Rape victims who unwillingly see their names in print or their pictures broadcast frequently speak of the loss of control they felt during the experience as being similar to the loss of control during the rape itself.

Journalists, both as individuals and as representatives of powerful institutions, can and sometimes do invade circles of intimacy. Awareness of the concept will allow you to consider the rights of others as well as balance the needs of society in crit-

Figure 6.1
The Concept of Circles of Intimacy

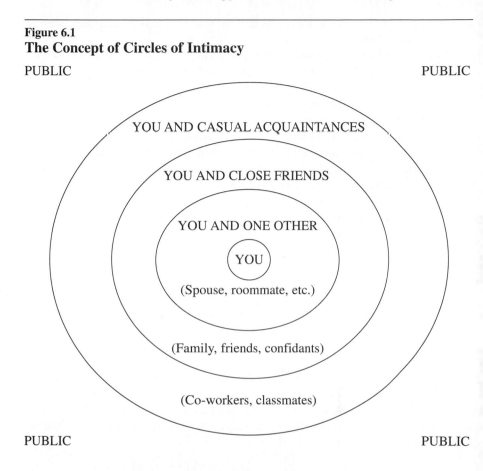

PUBLIC   PUBLIC

YOU AND CASUAL ACQUAINTANCES

YOU AND CLOSE FRIENDS

YOU AND ONE OTHER

YOU

(Spouse, roommate, etc.)

(Family, friends, confidants)

(Co-workers, classmates)

PUBLIC   PUBLIC

ical ways, particularly when the issue is newsworthy. Under at least some circumstances, invasion can be justified, but under other circumstances invading privacy constitutes usurping an individual's control and stripping him or her of individuality and human dignity.

Discretion: Whether to Reveal Private Information

With the distinction between privacy and secrecy in mind, the next problem confronting the ethical journalist is "discretion"—a word not usually associated with journalism. Bok (1983, 41) defines discretion as "the intuitive ability to discern what is and is not intrusive and injurious."

We all decide at times to reveal private information, and doing so wisely is a mark of moral growth. Discretion demands moral reasoning where the interests of more than one party are balanced. Once a source decides to reveal private information, a reporter's discretion remains the sole gatekeeper between that information and a public that might need the information or might merely want the information. The journalist is forced to rely on moral reasoning to decide if he is feeding the voyeur or the citizen in each of us.

What is a journalist to do with information resulting from another's indiscretion? Kantian theory would suggest that the journalist treat even the indiscreet source as the journalist herself would wish to be treated, making publication of the indiscretion less likely. Yet many journalists claim that, in practice, everything is "on-the-record" unless otherwise specified. In situations like these, a return to Ross's list of prima facie duties could be helpful. What is my duty to an often vulnerable and sometimes unwitting source? To a curious readership or viewership? To a media owner who wants (and pays for) my story? Which duties emerge as foremost to the journalist who should make such decisions more consistent.

Perhaps no new medium is more "on-the-record" than the Internet. We speak of information as "being posted" without examining the assumptions or the motives of those doing the posting. The courts are unclear on whether posting on the Internet constitutes actual publication.

However, considering media behavior, it appears that not everyone is willing to wait for ethical thinking to take hold. In the last few years of the twentieth century, the courts, the U.S. Congress, and state legislatures, particularly in California, are imposing a form of discretion—at least on journalists. California law now provides that a person may be held liable for a "constructive invasion of privacy" even if no physical trespass occurs. This statute was aimed primarily at the paparazzi who stalk Hollywood celebrities, but according to some it would have impact on journalists as well. "Paul Tash, executive editor of the *St. Petersburg Times* and chair of the Freedom of Information Committee of the American Society of Newspaper Editors, told Congress when it was considering similar legislation that it 'would protect villains, frauds and scoundrels against diligent photojournalists who would bring them and their activities to light,' " (quoted in Calvert 2000).

When Right to Know Is Not Enough

Just as the distinction between secrecy and privacy is easily confused, there is also a misconception both on the part of journalists and the public among the concepts of "right to know," "need to know," and "want to know." However, the three concepts are distinct and not interchangeable.

Right to know is a legal term often associated with open-meeting statutes and based on the philosophy that government runs more honestly in the open. Right to know is a form of counterbalancing government power. In recent years both federal and state governments have passed right to know laws. These laws are a legal, not ethical, construct. Journalists have a legal right to the same information that other members of the public may obtain—for example, the transportation of hazardous materials through their communities.

Ethical problems can emerge from right to know information. Is it ethical to print everything a journalist has a legal right to know? For instance, police reports routinely carry the names of suspects, victims, and witnesses to a variety of crimes. Does the journalist publish such information, even though it has been legally obtained? Clearly, even right to know carries with it ethical considerations.

Need to know originates in the realm of philosophy. Media ethicists such as Deni Elliott (1986) have argued that one of the functions of the mass media is to provide information to citizens that will allow them to go about their daily lives in society, regardless of political outlook. Citizens may have a legal right to much of this information, but perhaps not all of it. In this view, providing information the public needs to know includes within it the concept of journalistic tenacity and responsibility.

Too often, when journalists assert that the public has the "right to know" a fact, what they mean is that citizens "need" such information to get along in their daily lives. For example, the average citizen cannot examine bank records. That duty is left to auditors and the government. But with the recent turmoil in the financial sector, journalists could reasonably argue that at least some information about the health of financial institutions and the character of those who run them is needed by the public to make informed economic decisions. Need to know often requires a tenacious journalist, as the law is not a tool to access information for such stories.

Need to know is the most ethically compelling argument of the three. Need to know demands that an ethical case be constructed for making known information that others wish to keep private. Need to know also demands that journalists present the information in a manner that will make its importance evident to a sometimes lazy citizenry.

When an argument is framed in terms of right to know, it reduces the journalist to ethical legalism: I will do precisely what the law allows. When an argument is framed in terms of need to know, however, it means that counterbalancing forces have been weighed and that bringing the information to light is still the most ethical act. Asserting your right to know may be the best way to get the facts regarding a crime, but only by weighing the public's need to know will you be satisfied with the decisions you make in airing the story.

Finally, there is the issue of want to know, which speaks to the curious human being in all of us. Want to know is the least ethically compelling rationale for acquiring information and disseminating it. We all want to know a lot of things—what our neighbors do in the evening hours, how much money other people earn, and who in Hollywood is sleeping with whom. While we may want that information, however, we don't really need it and most certainly have no right to it. It serves the function of gossip, providing us with small talk or a smile.

By nature of their occupation, journalists often become repositories for much "want to know" information. A number of media outlets have been founded on the public's desire to know about celebrities, criminals, and even common folk. More than half a century ago, *Police Gazette* titillated its readers with information they wanted to know that no other media outlet provided. The *Police Gazette* today has been replaced with reality-based television, some of it even focusing on the work of police but all of it designed to garner ratings and hence profits. Reality television, and its Internet permutations, provide evidence that U.S. culture itself is shifting the concept of privacy more toward want to know. That shift raises an important professional issue: when "want to know" becomes enmeshed in the profit motive, is the long-term result a loss of public understanding of the distinctions between journalism and entertainment that will make it more difficult for journalists to do their important work in the coming decades?

John Rawls and the Veil of Ignorance

Preserving human dignity in times of crisis is a difficult task. Political philosopher John Rawls, considered this century's most articulate proponent of the social contract theory of government, has provided a helpful exercise to help make decisions about particularly thorny privacy issues (Rawls, 1971).

Rawls's theory of "distributive justice" is designed to take the best from utilitarian theory while avoiding some of its more fundamental problems. It begins with the premise that justice should be equated with fairness. In order to achieve "justice as fairness," Rawls suggests an exercise he calls the "veil of ignorance." In the exercise, before any member of a community can make an ethical decision affecting others, he or she must take an "original position" behind a veil of ignorance.

Behind the "veil," everyone starts out in the original position as equals who do not know whether they will be powerful or powerless when they emerge into the community from behind the veil. Rawls suggests that rational people would be willing to make and to follow those decisions when individual distinctions made on the basis of gender or socioeconomic status are cast aside.

For example, if the issue is whether to photograph or interview survivors at the scene of an airline crash, one could gather many people with diverse views behind the veil. Among them could be a reporter, a photographer, a survivor, a victim's family, an average reader or viewer, the management or owner of the media outlet, the owner of the airline, paramedics at the scene, the flying public, and others. Behind the veil, in the original position, none of the participants would know what their status would be when they emerged. Their arguments would then be free of bias that comes from points of view. The participants would argue the pros and cons of the public's need to know and the victim's right to privacy without knowing whether they would emerge as a reporter, a reader, or a victim.

Rawls's veil of ignorance provides journalists with an important tool to use when they begin an ethical dialogue much like the one Bok recommends (see chapter I). Behind the veil of ignorance it is possible to walk in the shoes of the stakeholders, to air various views, and then to make a reasoned choice.

When people begin their deliberations behind such a veil, Rawls suggests that two values emerge: *we will act so that individual liberty is maximized, and weaker parties are protected.* We will look at each concept separately.

First, Rawls suggests the liberty of all will be valued equally. Behind the veil, freedom of the press (a liberty journalists cherish) becomes equal to freedom from unwarranted intrusion into private life (a liberty readers cherish). How one retains both becomes a debate to be argued from all points of view without the bias of status since each participant is in the original position, ignorant of personal position or status.

Second, under the framework the weaker party is usually protected. Few participants would make an ethical decision that might not be in the interest of the weaker party unless the evidence was overwhelming that it would better the lot of the entire group. Behind the veil participants would be forced to weigh the actual and potential harm that journalists, as powerful people representing powerful institutions, could inflict on people who are less powerful.

It is important to note that consensus is not required, and maybe even not expected, behind the veil. The veil of ignorance is designed to facilitate ethical discussions, not stymie them from lack of unanimity. By going behind the veil, the ethical decision maker arrives at what Rawls calls "reflective equilibrium." In the state of reflective equilibrium some inequalities are allowed. However, they will be the inequalities that contribute in some significant way to the betterment of most individuals in the social situation. For instance, the consensus of the group behind the veil might be to run a photo of a victim of tragedy if it might prevent a similar tragedy from occurring.

Reflective equilibrium summons what Rawls calls our "considered moral judgment." Decisions would be based on the principles we would be most unwilling to give up because we believe doing so would result in a grave wrongdoing for all. Balancing the liberties of various stakeholders, while protecting the weaker party, allows for a thorough exploration of all of the issues involved, which utilitarianism sometimes fails to address.

Using the concepts of right to know, need to know, discretion, and circles of intimacy, along with Rawls's concept of distributive justice, will provide you with the ethical tools to begin the work of balancing conflicting claims. These tools will enable you to better justify your choices, to make decisions systematically and to understand what went wrong when mistakes occur.

Selected Readings

Alderman, Ellen, and Caroline Kennedy. 1995. *The right to privacy.* New York: Alfred A. Knopf, Inc.

Bok, Sissela. 1983. *Secrets: On the ethics of concealment and revelation.* New York: Vintage.

Grcic, Joseph M. 1986. "The right to privacy: Behavior as property." *Journal of Values Inquiry* 20, 137–44.

Hixson, Richard F. 1987. *Privacy in a public society.* New York: Oxford University Press.

Hodges, Louis W. 1983. "The journalist and privacy." *Social Responsibility: Journalism, Law, Medicine* 9, 5–19.

Orwell, George. 1949. *1984.* San Diego: Harcourt, Brace, Jovanovich.

Rawls, John. 1971. *A theory of justice.* Cambridge, Mass.: Harvard University Press.

Rosen, Jeffrey. 2000. *The Unwanted Gaze: The Destruction of Privacy in America.* New York: Random House.

Schoeman, Ferdinand D., ed. 1984. *Philosophical dimensions of privacy: An anthology.* New York: Cambridge University Press.

CHAPTER VI CASES

CASE VI-A
Public Grief and the Right to Be Left Alone
PHILIP PATTERSON
Oklahoma Christian University

One early spring morning, *Riverside Press–Enterprise* photographer Fred Bauman rushed to the scene of an accident. A twenty-two-month-old boy had been hit by a car in front of his home. The driver of the vehicle was entering the driveway to drop off another child with the babysitter.

The mother of the boy, Dawna Read, rushed to the site and sank to her knees in prayer, covered by the blood of her son, as paramedics attempted to save him. It was at this moment that Bauman shot the photo.

According to Bauman, who was also the photo editor at the time the photograph ran, a lengthy discussion was held in the newsroom before the decision to publish was made. Bauman said the determining factor in the decision was the possibility that the stark reality of the picture might prevent future accidents through safer drivers or more watchful parents.

"We decided that even if one life was saved, it was worth it," Bauman said.

In the days to follow, reader response poured in, largely against running the picture. Bauman said that no other picture in his three decades with the *Press–Enterprise* created the outpouring of emotion that this one did. Among the callers were some who threatened Bauman.

Micro Issues:

1. If you had been dispatched to the scene of the accident, would you have photographed the grieving mother? With a telephoto lens?
2. If other media (e.g., a competing newspaper, the television stations) were photographing the woman, would that fact enter into your decision?
3. Could the drama of the moment have been told equally well in some other manner?

Mid-range Issues:

1. Is the decision to take the photo a different ethical decision than the decision to run the photo? In other words, what do you think about a shoot first, decide later policy?
2. If a local television station obtained videotape of the incident, would you run it? Is there a distinction between a still photograph and a video? Would a color photograph be more objectionable?

Photo by Fred Bauman. Riverside Press–Enterprise. *Used by permission.*

Macro Issues:

1. The rationale used by the editors of the *Press–Enterprise* to run the controversial photo in hopes of preventing future accidents is a utilitarian one. In this case do you think the greatest good to society outweighs the emotional damage done to the woman by running the photo?
2. Is utilitarian ethics a good rationale to apply to these situations? If yes, defend it; if no, what moral philosophy would you put in its place?
3. How might the concept of discretion have helped the photographer and his editors explain their choices?

CASE VI-B
Arthur Ashe and the Right to Privacy
CAROL OUKROP
Kansas State University

"Tennis great Arthur Ashe has AIDS," began the dispatch fed by *USA Today* to its overseas edition and the Gannett News Service on April 8, 1992.

Ashe, a disciplined athlete who overcame racial barriers, was forty-eight. He was the first African-American to win the U.S. Open and Wimbledon tennis championships. He was reluctant to go public with his disease, but was given little choice.

On April 7 he had been contacted by *USA Today* reporter Doug Smith about a rumor telephoned in to the newspaper that Ashe had AIDS. After speaking with Smith, Ashe talked with *USA Today's* executive editor for sports, Gene Policinski. Policinski asked Ashe if he was HIV-positive, and the response was "could be." Ashe asked Policinski to delay the story for thirty-six hours. Policinski would not promise Ashe the delay. Ashe called a press conference for April 8.

The call from *USA Today*, Ashe said at the press conference, put him in the unenviable position of having to lie if he wanted to protect his family's privacy.

"I am sorry that I have been forced to make this revelation at this time. After all, I am not running for some office of public trust, nor do I have stockholders to account to. It is only that I fall in the dubious umbrella of, quote, public figure, end of quote."

Later Ashe wrote in the *Washington Post* that going public with a disease such as AIDS was "akin to telling the world in 1900 that you had leprosy."

Ashe was married and was the father of a five-year-old daughter, Camera, thought to have been protected from knowledge of his disease prior to the call from *USA Today*. Ashe had known since 1988 that he had AIDS, apparently contracted from a blood transfusion required during heart surgery in 1983. Blood was not routinely checked for the virus before 1985.

It is clear in articles appearing since Ashe's press conference that a number of journalists knew about Ashe's disease, but chose to protect "Arthur Ashe's Secret" (Frank Deford, *Newsweek*, April 20, 1992).

"Keeping my AIDS status private," Ashe wrote in the *Washington Post*, "enabled me to control my life."

Was *USA Today* right or wrong? An editorial in *The Christian Century* (April 22, 1992) called this a "tale of media irresponsibility and corporate greed," an example of "entertainment posing as information."

In the editorial in *The Christian Century*, Peter Prichard, editor of *USA Today*, claims that "When the press has kept secrets . . . that conspiracy of silence has not served the public. . . . Journalists serve the public by reporting news, not hiding it. By sharing his story, Arthur Ashe and his family are free of a great weight. In the days ahead, they will help us better understand AIDS and how to defeat it."

Public-figure privacy decisions are often difficult, this one perhaps particularly so. Ashe had, over the years, earned much respect. In addition to his accomplishments

©1992 Gary Markstein. Used by permission.

in tennis, he had participated in human rights struggles in the United States and was a leading critic of apartheid in South Africa. He was the author of a lauded history of African-American athletes in the United States.

Arthur Ashe died from AIDS-related complications in February 1993.

Micro Issues:

1. Should Policinski have promised Ashe the requested thirty-six hours during which to prepare a statement?
2. Were Deford, Roy Johnson, and others who knew about Ashe's disease months before the press conference right to keep Ashe's secret?

Mid-range Issues:

1. What if Ashe's ailment were an inoperable lung cancer or Lou Gehrig's disease? Would the media decision have been justifiable then?
2. If Ashe had contracted AIDS through a homosexual encounter, should that have been part of the story? Would it change the decision-making process?

Macro Issues:

1. Does the Ashe case really differ significantly from, say, the rape of a celebrity? Both are public figures, but according to the policy of many news media only the rape victim would be afforded anonymity.
2. What is the public's stake in knowing Ashe had AIDS? Does that stake override his right to privacy?

CASE VI-C
Culture, Law, and Privacy: Should Ethics Change in a Cultural Context?
LEE WILKINS
University of Missouri–Columbia

On May 27, 1998, the head of Jun Hase, 11, was found outside a middle school in Kobe, Japan, with a note stuffed in the victim's mouth saying, "Stop me if you can." The rest of the boy's corpse was found later the same day at a television relay station on a wooded hill not far from where his head was discovered.

A milkman and an employee told reporters that they saw a middle-aged man carrying a black garbage bag near the front gate of the school where Hase's severed head had been found. Other journalists interviewing local residents printed and broadcast stories that those living nearby had spotted an unfamiliar black sedan or a white station wagon near the school, and that the driver was a man who appeared to be in his early thirties or forties.

One month later, on June 28, a fourteen-year-old boy was arrested in connection with the murder. He also was charged with assaults on four other children, one of whom also had died. Prior to his arrest, he was detained at a police station for thirteen days, then twenty-eight days as other charges were added to the original ones. He confessed to the murders and was sentenced to a juvenile facility.

Potential criminal activity involving juveniles in Japan falls under what is called the Juvenile Law, first instituted in 1949. Under that statute, minors under sixteen cannot be punished. They are instead sent to a reformatory or put on probation. This decision is made by a family court, not a criminal one, and a prosecutor is not present. Before the trial begins, police investigators send the judge all the evidence they have collected during their investigation, including the results of questioning a suspect. According to another section of the law, information on children suspected of crimes should not be made public; trials under the Juvenile Law are closed to the public, including the news media.

The law was introduced to help children who have committed a crime rebuild their lives. In fact, from 1950 to the year of the murder, the number of crimes committed by Japanese juveniles had declined steadily.

Soon after the suspect was arrested, the magazine *Focus,* owned by publishing house Shinchosha, posted on its Web site a photo—but not the name—of the middle school student suspect. The posting prompted other users to disclose the boy's name and family background on bulletin boards. The paper version of the 600,000-circulation periodical also carried a black-and-white picture of the suspect wearing a blazer and tie. A second magazine owned by the same publishing house also ran a photograph of the boy. Both publications sold out.

Other news organizations, including many major newspapers, refused to run an advertisement for *Focus* that included the suspect's picture. Many convenience stores and kiosks also refused to sell the magazines.

Two days after publication of the photo, the Justice Ministry admonished Shinchosha to recall the magazines in which the photo appeared. It was the first-ever appeal for a recall of the publication and the tenth time the ministry had responded to a media violation. However, the ministry's request was non-binding and the publishing firm refused.

Others, including writer Kenjiro Haitani, asked the publication to acknowledge it had made a mistake. "It is a grave violation of the boy's human rights as guaranteed by the Juvenile Law," Haitani said in an essay that also was printed in *Focus*.

The chairman of Japan's Federation of Bar Associations issued a statement saying that the publication of the photo "tramples on the spirit of the Juvenile Law and is inexcusable."

"I have observed a number of cases in which irreparable damage has been done to people's lives and reputations by an overzealous press convinced that law enforcement is one of its duties," wrote Kenichi Asano, a former reporter for Kyodo News Service and now a director of Japan's Liaison Committee on Human Rights and Mass Media Conduct. "In fact, historically, the Japanese news media have tended to function as a support, rather than a counterbalance, to official authority."

Shinchosha dismissed the criticisms, saying the crime was so heinous that the boy did not deserve the law's protection and that seeing his face would help people understand the nature of the crime. "This unilateral decision to withdraw the magazines interferes with freedom of (the) press and expression, and we will not accept this recommendation," said Teruo Kosuge, deputy editor of *Shukan Shincho*.

News accounts of the murder also generated coverage of other issues, among them the efficacy of Japan's Juvenile Law and whether the increasingly serious nature of some juvenile offenses merited its protection. News articles also explored the nature of Japanese culture and its historic tradition of ritual suicide. Other groups in Japan called for a crackdown on violent videos and video games, asserting that they had influenced the young murderer.

About one year after the murder took place, the parents of the elementary school child who had been killed sued the murderer and his parents for damages, arguing that the killer's parents knew that their son showed abnormal behavior but failed to address it.

Micro Issues:

1. Should the journalists have published the "eyewitness" accounts, which turned out to be grossly inaccurate, before an arrest was made?
2. Does the publication of the photo, without further identification, protect the privacy of the accused?
3. Should the fact that the accused murderer, and his victim, are both juveniles influence news decisions about when and how they should be identified?
4. Should the juvenile's family become part of the news story? If so, in what way?

Mid-range Issues:

1. About the same time this case was occurring, U.S.-based media outlets were printing and broadcasting the name of the fourteen-year-old who murdered schoolmates in West Paducah, Kentucky. Which decision is appropriate? Why?
2. Japanese journalists function without an American-style First Amendment. Assume you are a Japanese journalist. How would you criticize or commend the actions taken by the Japanese media?
3. Should the sales of the two magazines in question be considered an indication of public sentiment on the Juvenile Law? How would you respond to a reader if you refused to publish such a photo? To a stockholder in the publishing house?

Macro Issues:

1. Should the United States consider adopting either informal guidelines or mandatory legal requirements governing the news media that are similar to those of Japan's Juvenile Law? Why or why not?
2. Your text discusses the notion that privacy is an essential element of our humanity, and as such does not vary from culture to culture. If you accept this argument, how do you explain the cultural variation in interpretation of this ethical concept?
3. The Japanese Juvenile Law assigns responsibility for the nurture of children to many groups in society, including the news media. What ethical theory supports such a view? Could this view be transferred from Japanese culture to other cultures? Why or why not?

CASE VI-D
Computers and the News: A Complicated Challenge
KARON REINBOTH SPECKMAN
Truman State University

Reporter Paula Baldwin has a ten-year-old son who regularly rides the school bus. One day her son tells her he doesn't want to ride the bus anymore because he thinks the bus driver "isn't safe." He tells Paula he has smelled alcohol on the driver's breath and that the bus has almost been involved in an accident several times.

Baldwin regularly covers the education beat, but she is aware that several newspapers have won awards for matching the names of school bus drivers with a variety of computerized law enforcement databases, all of which are public records.

Baldwin approaches her paper's crime reporter, Marty Tharp, and pitches the story: Baldwin will obtain a list of the district's bus drivers, the paper will purchase the state's list of motor vehicle traffic violations and the National Crime Information Center database. The two reporters will then load the databases into the paper's computer system.

The computer will match the names of the bus drivers with driver's license records. Then, using the driver's license numbers, they will match individual records with the state violations and the national crime center database.

The two reporters estimate that acquiring the databases would cost the paper about $2,000 and that it will take a month to analyze the information and write the story. However, they tell their city editor that using such methods, other reporters have found school bus drivers with suspended licenses, a history of bad driving, and even records of criminal activity, including child sexual abuse. They tell the editor that they believe the financial investment is worth the gamble, particularly where the safety of children is involved.

The editor reluctantly authorizes the purchase and allows the reporters to begin work on the story, although he will not free them completely from their daily duties.

The acquisition and downloading of the information goes well. However, Baldwin and Tharp discover that the national crime database lists only the arrest and charge, not the final disposition of the case. Further, the state records are updated only every six months, and some of the names of bus drivers Baldwin has acquired cannot be matched with certainty with driver's license records.

However, of those records that can be matched, the team has learned that at least six of the district's drivers are driving on suspended licenses and that several others have moving violations on their records, including driving under the influence. The national database indicates that two of the drivers had been arrested on felony charges.

They are convinced they have a story, but that all the details aren't yet nailed down. The reporters ask their editor for advice on how to proceed.

The editor, meanwhile, has developed a dilemma of his own. His tennis partner is the paper's circulation manager, and in the process of informally discussing the story, both realize that the state's driver's license database could provide them with information about potential subscribers.

Using the database, they can determine current addresses, ages and social security numbers of many living in the paper's circulation area. Then, using the social security numbers from the driver's license records, they can perform credit checks on potential subscribers, learn what magazines and other services many of them receive, discover what property they own, and then conduct a target marketing circulation campaign geared to different demographic groups with different needs.

The circulation manager adds that she believes the paper's advertising director would love to have some of the same information. She wants to know when the news side will be done with the database so circulation can have it.

Micro Issues:

1. What steps should the reporters take to check out the facts in the databases?
2. At what point, if ever, should the paper notify the individual drivers of its investigation? Its findings? Should the school district be notified? When?
3. Whose interests are more important—those of the children or the bus drivers?

Mid-range Issues:

1. How much reliance should the paper place on the overall accuracy of the databases?
2. Does the paper have a responsibility to report inaccuracies to the agencies in charge of the databases? To its readers?

Macro Issues:

1. Design a policy for your news organization outlining what it will and will not do with databases it acquires after the "news side" has used them.
2. Do computer databases raise new privacy issues? Does the use of computer databases reframe existing privacy concerns? Which ones?

CASE VI-E
Competition, Deadlines, and the Mistreatment of Richard Jewell
GREG LISBY
Georgia State University

On July 27, 1996, around 12:45 A.M., Richard Jewell, a security guard employed to protect AT&T's interests and property in Atlanta's Centennial Olympic Park during the Summer Olympic Games, showed an agent with the Georgia Bureau of Investigation an unattended green knapsack lying beneath a bench outside a sound and light tower that was being used for a performance at the AT&T Global Olympic Village stage. Federal agents called to the scene determined that the knapsack contained a bomb, and Jewell and other law enforcement officers quietly began evacuating the area.

At 12:58 A.M., a bomb threat was called in to law enforcement officials from a pay phone three blocks from the scene. The tower and most of the immediate area surrounding the bomb had been cleared by the time it exploded at approximately 1:20 A.M., killing one visitor, leading to a fatal heart attack for a foreign journalist on the scene, and injuring 111 others.

For the next two days, the thirty-three-year-old Jewell was hailed as a "hero." He was interviewed by several major newspapers and television networks, including NBC's *Today* show, about his role in spotting the knapsack, alerting authorities, evacuating the area, and helping the injured.

On Tuesday, July 30, however, FBI agents interviewed Jewell about the bombing while telling him he was participating in a training film on how to investigate suspicious packages. When agents asked Jewell to "pretend" to waive his right to an attorney, he called his lawyer and ended the meeting.

That same day, *The Atlanta Journal & Constitution* learned of police suspicions and revamped the front page of its special afternoon Olympics "Extra" supplement to spotlight Richard Jewell as "the focus of the federal investigation." Although the story was not attributed to any source, the paper has since said that three of its employees independently confirmed the investigation. The newspaper was distributed around 4:30 that afternoon, and a CNN anchor read the story verbatim on the air shortly afterward.

That night each of the three major networks' newscasts picked up the story, and the next day virtually every one of the country's major newspapers gave the story front-page billing. An exception was the *New York Times,* which ran a piece inside its "B" section, focusing more on the media than on Richard Jewell.

Many news organizations later cited not wanting to "appear foolish" by not running a story or the suspect's name when so many other organizations were. Many were also careful to point out that Jewell had not been charged, or even officially named as a suspect. Investigators had been discovered staking out Jewell's apartment, and by late afternoon the media, led by CNN and local Atlanta television stations, joined them. By midday Wednesday, an estimated 200 national and international journalists were on the scene as federal investigators, including agents from the FBI and the Bureau of Alcohol, Tobacco and Firearms, searched the apartment Jewell shared with his mother, and took away boxes of belongings and Jewell's pickup truck. In one of the few statements he made to the media at the time, Jewell "categorically" denied being the Centennial Olympic Park bomber in response to a reporter's question, an exchange that was also shown on CNN and NBC.

NBC also reported on July 31 that agents that day had searched the shed near a cabin Jewell had rented in northeast Georgia before he had moved to Atlanta in May. ABC and CBS, however, reported that the FBI's suspicions of Jewell might be diminishing, with ABC citing the lack of evidence—of fingerprints at the phone from which the 911 call originated, of a voice match, and of the short time span between the 911 call and the explosion.

On Thursday, August 1, the front page of The *Atlanta Constitution* detailed the search in an article that included the name and location of Richard Jewell's apartment complex. The apartment number, its address, and a map detailing its location were included in an inside story.

According to the *Constitution*, Jewell became a suspect after the president of Piedmont College, a small campus in north Georgia, contacted authorities after seeing Jewell interviewed on television. He said that Jewell, who had once worked as a security guard for the college, had been "overzealous" in the pursuit of his duties there, harassing students and asking to work undercover.

Prior to his job at the college, Jewell had been a deputy for the Habersham County Sheriff's Department until he wrecked his patrol car, was demoted to jailer, and subsequently resigned. His 1990 arrest for impersonating a police officer in DeKalb County in metropolitan Atlanta was also widely reported. Media organizations stated that the FBI was looking at whether Jewell fit the "profile" of a loner who might have planted the bomb in order to draw attention to his heroism; indeed, some said he had sought out interviews after the bombing. (It was later revealed that an AT&T spokesperson, not Jewell, had solicited interviews on his behalf.)

On Friday, August 2, two of the bombing victims filed suit against Richard Jewell. They alleged that he failed to clear the area around the bomb before it exploded.

On August 3, the FBI returned to Jewell's apartment with a subpoena for hair samples and fingerprints. Jewell and his lawyer, G. Watson Bryant Jr., refused to allow more voice samples or a polygraph test. About two weeks later, Jewell passed a lie detector test administered by an expert his legal team hired because they "didn't trust" the FBI to conduct the exam. In an article detailing the results, The *Atlanta Journal–Constitution* quoted several people extolling the expert's integrity, but the next day reported that the expert had also "cleared" two other men subsequently convicted as felons.

Richard Jewell left his apartment for the first time in five days on Sunday, August 4, when Bryant spirited him past law enforcement officers and the media still keeping vigil in the parking lot. He met with criminal lawyer Jack Martin, who with Bryant on Monday tried without success to unseal the affidavits filed by the FBI to obtain its search warrants.

During the next week the *Journal–Constitution* reported on Bryant's assertion that a piece of bomb shrapnel recovered by the FBI from the apartment was a "souvenir" given Jewell by other guards at the park, and on Martin's demonstration, by walking the route involved with a reporter, that Jewell didn't have the time to make the 911 call.

The role and behavior of the media during the investigation were examined on ABC's *Viewpoint* on August 22. Discussing "The Bizarre Case of Richard Jewell" were Martin and Bryant, along with representatives from CNN, ABC, CBS, NBC, and NBC's Atlanta affiliate. The FBI, the Georgia Bureau of Investigation, and the *Journal–Constitution* declined to attend.

Four days later, at a news conference called by Jewell's lawyers, Richard Jewell's mother made an emotional appeal to President Bill Clinton, asking him to direct the Justice Department and the FBI to state whether or not they intended to charge her son. She also asked the media to leave them alone, stating that their life was a "nightmare." The White House did not comment, but a few days later Attorney General Janet Reno declined to exonerate Jewell, saying that she understood the Jewells' feelings but that the investigation had to be pursued. The *Journal–Constitution* commented that the exchange was part of a public relations campaign mounted by Jewell's lawyers—by then four in number—to get the FBI and the Justice Department to clear and apologize to their client.

A federal magistrate ruled on September 14 that the lawyers would be permitted to see portions of the FBI affidavits submitted to justify the search warrants. On September 22, Richard Jewell gave his first public interview since coming under investigation, by appearing on CBS's *60 Minutes*. The discussion with correspondent Mike Wallace focused on whom he would sue if he were not charged.

By the end of September, the FBI agreed to "less obtrusive" surveillance of the Jewell apartment, and on Saturday, October 5, returned most of the property it had seized from the apartment and the north Georgia sites, including Mrs. Jewell's collection of Tupperware. The following day, in lieu of taking an FBI polygraph, Jewell submitted to a six-hour interview in what the *New York Times* called a deal approved by the Justice Department in which Jewell would receive within six weeks of the interview a letter clearing him if no damaging information was revealed during the questioning. Attorney Lin Wood later told the *Journal–Constitution* there was no guarantee of such a letter.

In a court hearing on October 8, U.S. District Judge J. Owen Forrester rebuked the media for "the worst example of media coverage I've ever seen since watching *La Dolce Vita*" (Federico Fellini's 1960 film depicting journalists as vultures). Forrester cited published reports of material in the sealed affidavits for search warrants as evidence of a probable leak by law enforcement officials, and was assured by U.S. Attorney Kent Alexander that a Justice Department and FBI investigation into the leaks was underway.

Fourteen guns were returned to Richard Jewell that day. Two days later, the *Journal–Constitution* published a "letter to the editor" from Alexander that defended the FBI's conduct in the investigation.

On Saturday, October 12, the *Journal–Constitution* reported "little progress" in the bombing investigation "as the FBI turns its attention away from Richard Jewell." The next day, it reprinted an *American Journalism Review* article critical of the media coverage the Jewell story had received.

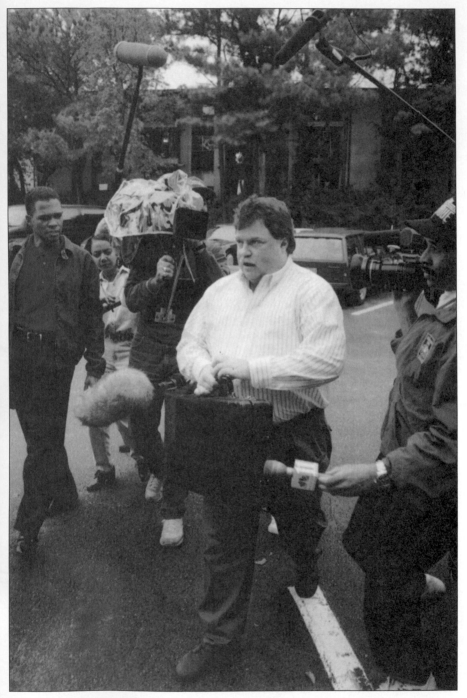

AP/WIDE WORLD PHOTOS.

Less than two weeks later, on October 24, Judge Forrester ordered public disclosure of the affidavits in response to a motion filed by the *Journal–Constitution* and the Atlanta ABC affiliate, WSB-TV, saying he believed Jewell was no longer the focus of the investigation.

Although the affidavits had already been released to Jewell's legal team, and the disclosure of such documents during a criminal investigation was unusual, Forrester called the situation "unique."

On Saturday, October 26, Alexander issued a letter to Richard Jewell's lawyers notifying them that Jewell was no longer considered by the Justice Department to be a target of the investigation. The letter expressed regret that "the Jewells have . . . endured highly unusual and intense publicity that was neither designed nor desired by the FBI." The absolution received front-page treatment in the *Journal–Constitution* and the *New York Times* the next day.

Richard Jewell held a news conference on Monday, October 28, which was carried live by CNN and all three network affiliates in Atlanta. Introduced by his lawyer as the "114th victim" of the Olympic bombing, Jewell characterized press coverage of him as "all lies," said he had never asked for media attention before that day, and declared the day the start of "the other part of my nightmare—trying to restore my reputation and good name."

Micro Issues:

1. In the days following Jewell's press conference, media organizations defended the manner in which they had reported the story, saying they were following "common procedures." Identify the "common procedures" of reporting a news story such as the one described here. Discuss the ethics of each procedure.
2. Richard Jewell's attorneys indicated that he was planning to sue several news organizations, including the *Journal–Constitution,* NBC News, and NBC anchorman Tom Brokaw. However, many people don't sue to win; instead they win by suing. What are the ethical issues involved in Richard Jewell's attempt to restore his reputation by threatening a lawsuit for libel, when—as a public figure—he would have an extremely difficult time establishing the necessary legal standard of fault required to collect monetary damages?

Mid-range Issues:

1. The results of an ABC News poll conducted at the time of Jewell's exoneration revealed that 69 percent of Americans thought Jewell had been unfairly treated by the media; 82 percent said it was not acceptable for the media to identify a suspect before he or she was charged. Under what circumstances, if any, is it ethically permissible for the media to identify a suspect before he or she is charged with a criminal offense?
2. Justify your answer to the previous question using ethical reasoning and principles.

3. In late 1996, NBC agreed to pay Jewell more than $500,000 to avert a lawsuit over comments made by Tom Brokaw. In your opinion will the threat of lawsuits "chill" the media from reporting on suspects in the future?

Macro Issues:

1. Deadline pressure, the competition for news, and "pack journalism"—the individual assignments of a number of reporters to follow a single person or issue for weeks or months at a time "like a pack of hounds sicked on a fox" (Crouse 1974, 7) all contributed to the media's coverage of Richard Jewell's heroics at the Olympics. How might deadline pressure have been handled differently yet within an ethical framework? How might the journalists have competed,for news differently in this situation?
2. How is the journalistic standard of objectivity twisted by "pack journalism"?
3. How did the concept of authority as an accepted source of information affect the media's attitude toward Richard Jewell? Under what circumstances, if any, is it ethically permissible for the media to allow themselves to be used as either an investigative or surveillance arm of the police? Do they have any different ethical obligations than do ordinary citizens witnessing a similar situation?

CHAPTER VII

The Mass Media in a Democratic Society: Keeping a Promise

By the end of this chapter, you should be familiar with:

• how a society's media are shaped by the form of its government.
• many of the criticisms leveled at the way the U.S. media cover government and elections.
• why the media should be concerned with social justice for the powerful and the powerless alike.

Introduction

Americans view the written word as essential to political society. The First Amendment to the U.S. Constitution states:

Congress shall make no law respecting an establishment of religion, or prohibiting the free exercise thereof; or abridging the freedom of speech, or of the press; or the right of the people peaceably to assemble, and to petition the government for a redress of grievances.

In academe, scholars such as John C. Merrill (1974) assert that the First Amendment should be interpreted purely as a restriction on government. This view emphasizes the role of freedom of expression and downplays assertions of journalistic responsibility.

Some journalists concur. *Washington Post* managing editor Leonard Downie, speaking to a 1989 meeting of journalism educators, said he expects his reporters to act "as if they live on an island." "I know that makes me unpopular," he said, "but my interpretation of the First Amendment is that it means strictly that government should not interfere with the press."

We prefer a different view. Madison, Hamilton, and Jay, in the *Federalist Papers*, asserted that communication among the citizens serves an important political purpose. The founders expected citizens to be informed and then to participate in politics. They expected that political debate, including what was printed in the press of the day, would be partisan and biased rather than objective, but they also believed that from this cacophony of information the rational being would be able to discern the truth.

As the authors made clear by circulating those documents as a series of newspaper articles, one way to enhance political learning was publication in the media of the time. Citizens had an obligation to read such information; the press had an obligation to provide it.

Tucked within all of this, we believe, is a promise that the mass media, both in 1791 and two hundred years later, will provide citizens with what they need to know to get along in political society. Scholars have labeled this analysis of the media's role in a democratic society the "social responsibility theory" of the press. However, assuming such a responsibility is becoming progressively more difficult. Some of the difficulties emanate from the structure of the contemporary American political system and, hence, are appropriately the subject for political reform. Others reflect the ethical choices contemporary journalists are making. After providing some historic context, it is to those issues we will turn.

A Democracy Without Mass Communication

In ancient Greece, the highest form of human existence was the *polis*—literally "community." But the polis was special, for as Aristotle noted, it was "an association of free men." The polis governed itself; the ruled were the rulers.

In the ancient myth, the art of politics was a gift from the gods, who provided men with *adios,* a sense of concern for the good opinion of others, and *dike,* a sense of justice, or that which makes civic peace possible through the adjudication of disputes. In the ancient myth, these gifts were bestowed on everyone, not only on some ruling economic or social elite. All men were able to exercise the art of politics through rhetoric and argument in the assembly, a form of direct democracy that survived for only a few years in Athens. Certain Native-American tribes exercised a similar form of democratic decision making, but in Europe, ancient Greece was the first—and last—place it was seriously attempted.

Socratic teaching took issue with the myth. Not everyone, according to Plato and Socrates, was capable of knowing *adios* and *dike*. Democracy was the refuge of the herd; it took a philosopher king to rule. Indeed, in his book *The Trial of Socrates,* I. F. Stone maintains that the Athenians condemned Socrates to death not because he insisted on teaching philosophy but because the philosophy he taught was profoundly anti-democratic.

The Greeks, of course, had no media system; their political interaction was face to face, at least among the men who ruled. But their democracy, founded as it was on conceptions of knowing and rhetoric, never assumed an uninformed or lackadaisical citizenry. The Greeks didn't need newspapers or television to govern themselves, but they did demand political and cultural literacy. Without knowing it, their highly developed vision of democratic theory, one which viewed political information as a citizen's fundamental right (not the commodity that contemporary news organizations consider it), anticipated the core of modern problems in twenty-first century democracies (Encabo 1995).

Modern Mediated Problems: Learning About Leaders

Athens was small enough that "pure" democracy was possible. By the late 1700s when the framers were crafting the U.S. Constitution—on which almost all other modern democracies have been modeled—the architects of government knew it was not possible for each citizen to be involved in every political decision. They established a representative democracy in which certain members would be elected by their fellows to speak for them—to represent their views—in the legislature. (In ancient Athens, leaders were named by drawing lots.) This concept of representative government drew heavily from the ancient Greek tradition of *adios,* a concern for the good opinion of others.

In the twenty-first century, the issue has been reframed: Can people become acquainted well enough with any candidate to acquire an opinion? Except for a small group of government and corporate insiders, the mass media have become the primary mode of receiving political discourse. In addition to providing voters with facts, something that is generally assumed to be the role of news, the media also provide citizens with a framework to understand those facts, the realm of culture and myth that is the role not only of news but also of entertainment and advertising.

Study of media coverage of political campaigns has uncovered some disturbing trends. Journalists function as a pack; there is seldom any really distinctive political reporting during elections (Crouse 1974; Sabato 1992). However, campaign assignments remain sought after by members of the national press corps for reasons of personal prestige. The person who covers the winning candidate for the network will almost assuredly become the White House correspondent for the next four years, a guarantee of celebrity status, increased income, and, many would argue, real political power. The journalists covering a national election have almost as much at stake as the candidates they cover.

Further, journalists treat front-runners differently than they do the remainder of the candidate pack (Robinson and Sheehan 1984). Front-runners are the subject of closer scrutiny, but those examinations are seldom about issues, even though it is issue-oriented reporting that tends to provoke political interest and public participation (Patterson 1980). Instead, electoral reporting focuses on personality, a key component of political leadership, but certainly not the only one.

Candidates and their paid consultants seem to have intuitively understood what academic research has shown. They've developed strategies that will allow them either to capitalize on front-runner status and image or to compensate for a lack of it. Free media—synonymous with a positive story on the 5:00 P.M. news—has become the watchword of most state and national political campaigns. The candidates have created the "photo opportunity" and the "Rose Garden strategy." Both seem designed to thwart anything but the most carefully scripted candidate contact with the voting public.

At the same time, the media has the right, and some would say even the responsibility, to get "behind the curtain" (Molotch and Lester 1974) to the real candidate. What happens then often makes news in ways the candidates could not have foreseen, as the following three illustrations show.

In 1972, going into the New Hampshire primary, Senator Edwin Muskie of Maine was considered the Democratic front-runner. Just days before the primary, Muskie, reacting to media criticism of his wife, broke down in tears according to reports in the *Washington Post* that were disputed even by some on the scene, including Muskie. But the damage was done. Muskie was finished as a political contender.

During the 1980 primary season, CBS correspondent Roger Mudd concluded an interview with Democratic challenger Edward Kennedy with this question: "Mr. Senator, why do you want to be president?" The rambling answer that resulted clearly revealed that Kennedy had no scripted answer for why he was challenging incumbent Jimmy Carter of his own party and led many of his critics to continue to claim he was running only on the family name.

In the 2000 presidential race, future President George W. Bush refused to provide details of what he characterized as "youthful mistakes" to the press corps, many of whom were asking questions about previous cocaine use. Several months later, a novice television reporter at a Fox affiliate in Maine broke the story that Bush had been arrested for drunk driving when he was forty. Neither revelation had an impact on the result of the presidential contest.

Journalists face a number of questions in cases such as these. Just because the information is available and even accurate does not automatically mean that it is relevant. While political character is definitely a bona fide issue in an election of national importance, where is the threshold for what counts as a mark of character or the lack thereof? Voters must winnow the field of candidates in some way. The question is whether this sort of journalism is adequate for making that political decision.

These changes in the electoral process take place in a cultural backdrop where the word "politician" has become synonymous with "crook" and "liar." Instead of being perceived as the honorable calling it was in ancient Greece, politics for many Americans is viewed as an unsavory activity. Such images come to us not only through the news but also through entertainment. Frank Capra's film *Mr. Smith Goes to Washington* paints the exceptional politician as common man and hero, against a backdrop of crooked politics as usual. A similar vision is manifest in the 1993 film *Dave.* Our current views are equally skewed. Whether it's *The Candidate, Bulworth,* or *Primary Colors,* the entertainment media portray politicians at best as absent or weak, at worst as downright sleazy.

Modern Mediated Problems: Getting Elected

Political scientists agree that the mass-mediated election has redefined electoral politics. It's also changed our understanding of mass communication, blurring the distinctions between advertising and news from the voters' point of view. As many researchers have noted, all politics—and hence all political communication—is symbolic.

Let's begin with some research findings. Voters sometimes learn more about candidates' stands on issues from advertising than they do from news (Patterson 1980). Factual accuracy, therefore, must be the starting point for ethical political advertising. As philosopher Hannah Arendt has noted, "Freedom of information is a farce unless factual information is guaranteed and the facts themselves are not in dispute" (Arendt 1970). Other scholarly studies have found that news stories about elections emphasize strategy and tactics, rather than stands on issues (Sheehan and Robinson 1984).

The media system is interactive—voters who want to become informed about the candidate's policy choices get the information from ads, some of them labeled "negative" or "attack" ads, in part because policy information is missing from news stories. Negative political ads are literally as old as the republic. One early patriot, Yale President Rev. Timothy Dwight, claimed that if Thomas Jefferson were elected, the Bible would be burned, the French national anthem sung in Christian churches, and women dishonored in the most biblical of senses. The majority of voters obviously didn't believe him.

Ed Stein. Reprinted with permission of the Rocky Mountain News.

Contemporary voters are providing scholars with evidence that they, too, can discern among the various types of political ads. Comparative ads, ones that contrast candidate positions on specific issues, are viewed as information rich, and voters view them as an appropriate part of political discourse. Attack ads, ones that are personal and negative, that contain no "positive" or "issue-oriented" information, are disliked and distrusted. Voters appear to be able to distinguish between negative, comparative, and positive or biographical ads (Jamieson 2000). Furthermore, recent analysis indicates that the majority of political ads fall into the positive or contrast categories (Benoit 2000), providing ample evidence that it is possible to create ethical political advertising on the local, state, and national levels.

Journalists are deciding that covering the advertising a campaign produces can result in legitmate news stories focused on policy issues. These news stories, often called "ad watches," appear in both broadcast and print and have the goal of putting the claims in political ads to the tests of truthfulness and context. While the scholarly findings are not conclusive, anecdotal evidence from states as diverse as Colorado, California, and North Carolina suggests that aggressive news journalism focusing on attack ads and negative campaigning can have an impact on the voters' knowledge of particular candidates and their evaluation of those candidates. In addition, we would suggest that it is the responsibility of journalists to evaluate political advertising as legitimate news and to hold candidates publicly accountable for the advertising sponsored by a campaign, or in the grayer areas, advertising paid for by political action groups in favor of a particular candidate that same candidate refuses to disavow.

For example, we would suggest that an important, but largely unreported, news story of the 2000 election would be the hundreds of political radio ads paid for by the National Rifle Association and its assorted state political action committees in favor of specific candidates, but which included the tag line "the [insert name of candidate here] campaign is not responsible for this ad." Journalists should be willing to ask who is responsible for the public statements of political action committees.

Everyone seems to agree on a single starting point: political advertising is unique (Kaid 1992). However, we suggest that the same ethical principles that apply to advertising (outlined in chapter III) can be applied to political advertising as well. Further, many philosophers link facts with rationality, particularly in the area of political debate. The use of emotional arguments designed to stir listeners or viewers "to set aside reason" has been characterized as a "violation of democratic ethics" (Haiman 1958, 388). There may, however, be times when valid issues have strong emotional content, such as the ongoing debate over abortion. At those times, the melding of emotion with issue content in such cases is not prima facie unethical.

Students of history will realize that many totalitarian regimes have used emotional appeals to either gain or retain power. However, such ads usually lack any public revelation of evidence to support the claims. Making the evidence behind political assertions public—what Kant called the "transcendental principle of publicness"—has historically been the role of the news media. We believe such reporting stands on firm ethical ground. The lack of this sort of journalism was foreseen by Lippmann: "In the absence of debate, restricted utterance leads to the degradation of opinion. By a kind of Gresham's law the more rational is overcome by the less rational, and the opinions that will prevail will be those which are held most ardently by those with the most passionate will" (Lippmann 1982, 196).

If political advertising is indeed a special case, then journalists and their audiences should demand higher standards, more regulations, or both. While some of the solutions to the current problems have First Amendment ramifications, they are worthy of discussion. They include the following:

* Allot limited amounts of free time to qualified candidates for major office to level the playing field for candidates without destroying the bottom line at already strapped broadcast outlets.
* Strengthen state regulations against corrupt campaign practices and find ways to enforce those regulations.
* Establish a federal campaign commission to hear complaints about ethical abuses in campaign communication, particularly in advertising.
* Encourage journalists to stop covering the "horse race" aspect of campaigns and focus on problem and policy solutions.
* Hold candidates accountable for their ads, not only in verbal terms but in visual and audio terms as well.
* Teach journalists to read and report on the visual imagery of a campaign, and to ask candidates questions about it.
* Allow attack ads only if they include the image of the candidate directing the attack.
* Reject unfair or inaccurate ads created by political action committees.
* Conduct ad watches as part of media coverage of a campaign, analyzing the ads for omissions, inconsistencies and inaccuracies.

We have one final point about money, politics, and getting elected. First, it takes money to buy ads, and in contemporary democratic societies that means the candidate with the most money often has the loudest voice. Many of those in public life, such as former New Jersey Senator Bill Bradley or Arizona Senator John McCain, argue that a surfeit of money in the political system is corrosive. How to deal with the money that finances political advertising is an important policy question, one with significant ethical overtones. We certainly cannot "solve" it in this brief chapter, but it is worth considering whether a highly profitable media system such as the one in the United States might not be able to find a way to "give back" access to political candidates who cannot raise enormous sums to purchase newspaper space and broadcast airtime.

Modern Mediated Problems: Covering Political Character

Conceptualizations of character have changed significantly since the founding of the republic, when character was defined in Aristotelian terms—an observable collection of habits, virtues and vices. Freudian psychology has altered that definition to include motivation, the subconscious, and relationships that help to form all of us as people. What journalists cover is "political character:" the intersection of personality and public performance within a cultural and historical context. Character is dynamic; it represents a synergistic interaction of a person within an environment (Davies 1963).

Journalists who explore character often do so for an ethical reason, despite apparent invasions of privacy. Privacy in Western culture is regarded as a right that can be negated by other more compelling rights (Grcic 1986, 141). Political figures are powerful people. Ethicist Sissela Bok (1978) has noted that when an unequal power relationship is involved, it is possible to justify what would otherwise be considered an unethical act. To paraphrase Bok, at the core of any serious investigation of the private character of public people is the notion that if the person one wishes to investigate is also in the position to do one harm, then invading privacy in an attempt to counter that threat is justified.

However, that invasion also needs to meet some tests (Schoeman 1984):

- The invasion must be placed in a larger context of facts and history. Since one of the definitions of invasion of privacy is the subject's loss of control over the context of information (Westin 1967), an effort to study character must include enough context to provide meaning.
- The revelation of private facts about political figures should meet the traditional tests of journalistic publicity and evidence. Further, these private facts need to be linked to public, political behaviors before publication or broadcast becomes ethically justifiable.
- The invasion of privacy must further the larger political discourse. Investigation of the character of political figures must meet the most demanding ethical test: the need to know.

Careful reporting on character can pass these tests. However, journalists must also be willing to weigh the harm done to others, particularly those who have not sought the public limelight. While public officials do have the capacity to do harm, that argument is much less compelling when applied to parents, spouses, children, friends and other family members. Journalistic investigation of character may often involve others, but publication or broadcast of what is learned should be considered only if public awareness of such facts furthers the political discourse.

Even reporting that passes these three tests must be filtered through discretion. Merely publishing private information without this tie to a more public role is a form of "tabloid journalism" that casts doubt on journalistic motives and credibility. More seriously, such publication denigrates politicians in such a way that every official becomes a "crook," "liar," or "philanderer" without some larger understanding of why those character traits may or may not be important in doing the public's business.

Reporters covering political character should be aware of some or all of the following building blocks of character:

- The politician's development of a sense of trust.
- A politician's own sense of self-worth and self-esteem.
- The development of a politician's relationship to power and authority.
- Early influences on adult policy outlook.
- How a politician establishes contact with people.

- The flexibility, adaptability, and purposefulness of mature adulthood.
- The historical moment.

The media's current emphasis on covering political character provides the best illustration of the need to balance the demands of governing with privacy considerations. No culture has ever expected its leaders to be saints; in fact, some cultures have prized leadership that is decidedly unsaintly. By emphasizing an almost inhuman standard of public behavior, the mass media may be setting a standard of public behavior that may be impossible to meet as well as politically inadvisable.

However, an in-depth and nonjudgmental explanation of character can spur and expand the political debate, particularly if journalists treat character as one political story among many and if they are willing to imbed character in a history and political context Americans share. A deep exploration of character may help Americans think deeply about what we as a political system mean by and need from leadership.

Modern Mediated Problems: Governing

One of the ironies of democratic politics is that, in order to accomplish something, you first have to get elected. But accomplishing something, not getting elected, is the major work of politics. Many inches of newspaper space are devoted to the process on the local level. Local television news provides much less attention to policy making. Regulatory agencies, the courts, and even Congress are not considered glamour beats by the national press corps.

Yet the national press corps, particularly, has changed how the policy process operates. No one is quite certain when the "media leak" originated, certainly back in the last century. Not only has a leak to a reporter become a fact of political life; it appears to alter how policy makers, and sometimes policy itself, work.

Political scientist Martin Linsky (1986) describes how leaks have become part of the Washington policy-making process. Government officials, both elected and appointed, use the mass media to help make policy in a variety of ways, he says. Sometimes they leak a story to find out how others will react to an idea, a practice known as floating a "trial balloon" in the press. Other times, policy makers will leak a story because they wish to mount either public or bureaucratic support for or opposition to a set of options.

Sometimes leaks take the form of whistle-blowing when a government employee honestly believes the public good is not being served by working through the system. Watergate's famed and unnamed source, "Deep Throat," apparently was motivated by such a belief when he leaked parts of the government investigation into the break-in to *Washington Post* reporters Bob Woodward and Carl Bernstein. Anti–Vietnam War activist Daniel Ellsberg admits a desire to fuel opposition to national policy was much of his motivation in leaking the Pentagon Papers to the *New York Times*.

Still other times, government officials leak a story to put a particular reporter or publication on notice about who really holds the power in a particular situation. Network news correspondent Bill Moyers was taught that lesson by Lyndon Johnson, who told him that he planned to fire J. Edgar Hoover, a scoop Moyers reported. The very next day Johnson appointed Hoover director of the FBI for life. Moyers was stuck with a story that was accurate but not true. Worse, he had become the subject of Johnson's well-known propensity for power plays. It was a lesson in trust and political power Moyers never forgot.

Linsky's work about the role of the media in the policy-making process raises at least two important points regarding ethical journalistic practice.

First, leaks are becoming a more acceptable way of doing government business and policy makers are using them skillfully. In the summer of 1989, when terrorist groups in the Middle East threatened to kill one or more of the Americans they held hostage, then-President George H. W. Bush allowed a staff member to leak a story to a trusted *New York Times* reporter that the United States would retaliate militarily if hostages were killed. Bush's message was sent to the terrorists not through diplomatic back channels but on the paper's front page.

Second, leaks can alter the outcome of the policy process itself. President Bill Clinton's 1993 trial balloon about the potential of freezing the Social Security cost-of-living allowance provoked immediate congressional opposition, yet it enlarged the range of politically acceptable options—including taxing a larger percentage of some Social Security benefits—to reduce the nation's deficit.

Of fundamental importance for journalists is the question of whether reporters, editors and their news organizations should become consciously involved in the process of governing, and in what manner? Such willing involvement runs counter to established notions of objectivity but not to the history of the media themselves. Leaks are so common that journalists can no longer plead ignorance of either their existence or of their impact. Instead they must decide if, and how, they are willing to be used—and for what political purposes. These are difficult questions, particularly when big stories, professional prestige, and the chance to influence world events hinges on the outcome of ethical decision making.

Modern Mediated Problems: Arrogance Without Authority

Although the evolving role of the mass media in a democratic society has been widely analyzed, most ethicists agree that the media's primary function is to provide citizens with information that will allow them to make informed political choices (Hodges 1986; Elliott 1986). As part of performing that job, the media are expected to act as a watchdog on government. This watchdog role arises from the founders' original skepticism of concentrated political power. The watchdog media enable citizens to learn about and then check inappropriate government activity.

While the Founders built many checks and balances into the original U.S. system, those checks and balances were designed to enable government to continue to function. The Founders tried to guard against any single check fundamentally undermining the American experiment. The watchdog media—examined from this perspective—also have a "guide dog" function. Their goal is to help citizens make their way through the political process, not to immobilize them with a series of false trails or a sense that all political activity is futile.

However, many contemporary media critics argue that a particular style of covering politics, one emphasizing conflict and wrongdoing, has soured both journalists and citizens on American democracy. Political reporter E. J. Dionne in *Why Americans Hate Politics* (1991) argues that definitions of news that emphasize conflict inevitably help to degenerate political debate into a shouting match between diametrically opposed factions that have no reason to compromise. He notes that contemporary debate about both abortion and race has taken on this "us vs. them" quality, one that fails to acknowledge an important series of majority agreements on both issues—namely that abortion is not a particularly good method of birth control and that a sizable majority of Americans accept that human beings are of equal value and that learning to get along with one another is crucial in daily, political life.

Dionne adds that politics without government, a concept that seems to have rhetorical support across the political continuum, is an oxymoron. While he does not blame the mass media for creating these sorts of false rhetorical divisions, he does hold those in his own profession accountable for failing to point out what they mean in the context of a democratic form of government. In this, Dionne agrees with Plato, who said that democratic politics, while a "degenerative" form of government, was probably the best available system considering that human beings were its primary components.

Media critic James Fallows goes one step further. He holds a journalism permeated by a cynical and conflict-laden view of politics directly responsible for voter apathy, Congressional gridlock, and government via opinion polls rather than political leadership:

> The harm actually goes much further than that, to threaten the long-term health of our political system. Step by step, mainstream journalism has fallen into the habit of portraying public life in America as a race to the bottom, in which one group of conniving, insincere politicians ceaselessly tries to outmaneuver another. The great problem for American democracy in the 1990s is that people barely trust elected leaders or the entire legislative system to accomplish anything of value. . . . Deep forces in America's political, social and economic structures account for most of the frustration of today's politics, but the media's attitudes have played a surprisingly important and destructive role." (Fallows 1996, 7)

In fact, media critic Katherine Hall Jamieson (1992) has suggested that, when it comes to politics, journalists should get themselves a new definition of news. Instead of emphasizing events and conflict, Jamieson believes news stories could equally revolve around issues and multiple policy perspectives. This suggestion even has some support in academic research; readers are more interested in coverage that emphasizes policy issues than fights and horse races (Sheehan and Robinson 1984).

Implicit in this and other criticism is a concept not only of journalistic rights but also of responsibilities. Fallows and others insist that journalists have a right to report on government. But implicit in that right is the sense that successful governing is a political outcome that matters and that the media themselves are a powerful institution within the democratic system and hence partially responsible for its continued well-being. The cynical assumption that government can never act for the public good, and the arrogant stance that journalists and the media organizations they represent are somehow outside the political system, are almost nihilistic in this view. We, like many journalists and scholars, believe there is real meat behind this critique of "mad dog" journalism. Conscientious ethical practice will allow journalists and media consumers alike to begin the work of carving out new understandings of our *responsibilities and rights* when the mass media become involved in the American democratic political system.

Mediated Modern Problems: Social Justice

Just as there are members of a power elite, there are also those who feel excluded from political society. While some scholars have argued that one interpretation of U.S. history has been the gradual extension of the franchise to ever more diverse publics, that extension of basic rights has been uneven and contentious. All of these minority groups seek access to the political process and, since the mass media have become major institutional forces in that process, they seek access to media as well.

Media ethicists suggest these political and social out-groups provide the mass media with a further set of responsibilities. They assert that the mass media, and individual journalists, need to become advocates for the politically homeless. Media ethicist Clifford Christians suggests that "justice for the powerless stands at the centerpiece of a socially responsible press. Or, in other terms, the litmus test of whether or not the news profession fulfills its mission over the long term is its advocacy for those outside the socioeconomic establishment" (Christians 1986, 110).

This socially responsible view of the media suggests that journalists have a duty both to promote community and to promote the individuals within it. Those who are in significant ways outside the community—economically, socially, or culturally different—need a voice.

By advocacy, Christians does not mean reporting that espouses only one sort of political or social agenda. Rather, he insists,

> Press portrayals feed into public discourse and play a portentous role in the shape our culture and the sociopolitical realm ultimately take. In its loftiest sense, the press ought to amplify public debate and reconstitute the argument so that it becomes an important public forum where significant issues of social justice are fruitfully raised and resolved. (Christians 1986, 123)

Christians's argument can be amplified beyond democracy's racial, ethnic, and economic out-groups. In contemporary democratic society, clearly some "things" also are without political voice. The environment, racial equality, and events beyond American shores all have difficulty finding a powerful domestic spokesperson. These issues cross traditional political boundaries. Those who will be affected by them also seem to be without a voice.

Communitarian thinking takes social responsibility to the next level. It urges that justice—rather than truth—become the ethical linchpin of journalistic decision making. If justice becomes the fundamental value of American journalism, than the media—functioning at institutional level—have the goal of transforming society, of empowering individual citizens to act in ways that promote political discussion, debate, and change (Christians et al. 1995).

What makes journalists uneasy about either the communitarian or social responsibility approaches is that they smack of a kind of benevolent paternalism. If individual human beings carry moral stature, then assigning one institution—in this case the mass media—the role of social and political arbiter diminishes the moral worth of the individual citizen. The mass media become a kind parent and the citizen a sort of wayward child in need of guidance. Such a relationship does not promote political maturity.

While the weight of recent scholarly opinion sides with Christians, such a view is not without risk. If accepted, it means a thoroughgoing change for the mass media in the U.S. political system. That change would bring about other changes, some of them not easy to anticipate. But whether change is what's needed, or merely a return to the strict libertarian view, both call for some sophisticated ethical reasoning. As Thomas Jefferson said, being a citizen of a democracy is not easy—to which journalists might well add, neither is covering one.

Suggested Readings

Dionne, E. J., Jr. 1992. *Why Americans hate politics.* New York: Touchtone.

Fallows, James. 1996. *Breaking the news: How the media undermine American democracy.* New York: Pantheon.

Fry, Don, ed. 1983. *The adversary press.* St. Petersburg, Fl.: The Modern Media Institute.

Jamieson, K. H. 2000. *Everything you think you know about politics. . .and why you're wrong.* New York: Basic Books.

Linsky, Martin. 1986. *Impact: How the press affects federal policymaking.* New York: W. W. Norton.

Madison, James S., Alexander Hamilton, and John Jay. *The Federalist papers.*

Merritt, Davis. 1995. *Public journalism and public life.* Hillsdale, N.J.: Lawrence Erlbaum Associates.

CHAPTER VII CASES

CASE VII-A
Channel One: Commercialism in Schools
ROZALYN OSBORN

Channel One is a twelve-minute newscast designed for teenagers—middle school through high school—broadcast via satellite into classrooms across the United States. It is viewed in more than 350,000 classrooms, in 12,000 schools, and by about 8 million students every day—about 40 percent of the nation's total students in this age group (Fox 1996; Bormly 1996; Bormly 1999; Hoynes 1998; Kennedy 2000; Walsh 2000). It was first developed by Chris Whittle of Whittle Communications in 1989 in Knoxville, Tennessee. The program was purchased in 1994 by K-III Communications, now known as Primedia Inc., the owner of the *Weekly Reader, New York* magazine, and *Soap Opera Digest.*

The *Channel One* offer is difficult for schools to resist, especially schools in poor districts or with little funding. The corporation provides schools with communication technology equipment, including a satellite dish, networked cable wiring, a VCR, and a nineteen-inch television for every classroom. The equipment, valued in the 1990s at about $50,000, is provided, installed and maintained at no cost to the school. In return, schools agree to air *Channel One* to a large majority of their students every day.

What lies at the center of the debate over *Channel One* and programs like it is advertising. As part of the twelve-minute program, students view two minutes of advertising. In one school year, that means students who view *Channel One* see about 700 commercials, the equivalent of about one day of class time (Dudley 1998, Fox 1997). In its first year of operation, *Channel One* sold $51 million of commercials, more than ESPN or CNN sold at similar times (Robertson 1999). The ads, with a cost of about $185,000 per thirty seconds, are the largest contributor to *Channel One's* annual $100 million in profit (Dudley 1998).

William Hoynes, a Vassar College sociology professor, says *Channel One* is a "promotional vehicle for itself and for youth culture and style. This approach. . .promotes a friendly environment for advertising" (Walsh 2000, 15).

Channel One supporters maintain the technology and information the outlet provides are invaluable, particularly in poorer schools. They contend that brief exposure to advertising is worth the gain in technology and materials. Most teachers and students approve of *Channel One* (Bormly 1999) and say they believe the acquisition of the technology in the schools is without risk and that the programming seems to combat chronic lack of knowledge of current events among teenagers. Though many are concerned with the impact of the commercials, most think the benefits outweighed those negative aspects. Teachers particularly said the programming promoted current events knowledge and that it presented hard-to-discuss subjects important to teens' lives.

Critics focus on the outlet's commercial aspect, maintaining that schools should be a protected environment. By accepting the commercialization that comes with *Channel One,* opponents argue that schools are targeting a captive audience (Fox 1997; Kennedy 2000; Robertson 1999). As consumer activist Ralph Nader said in hearings held before the U.S. Senate in 2000, *Channel One* harms "children, schools, taxpayers, and democracy by forcing students to view the ads. *Channel One* opponents maintain that money made from the selling of commercials is tantamount to selling out students and their minds to advertisers and corporations (Bell 1999; Fege & Hagelshaw 2000; Hoynes 1998; Robertson 1999; Walsh 2000).

Opponents also claim the programming does not result in a significantly better understanding of current affairs (Hoynes 1998). Moreover, *Channel One* promotes materialistic attitudes, say critics. According to Commercial Alert, a Washington, D.C., watchdog group, "*Channel One* doesn't belong in schools because it conveys materialism and harmful messages to children, corrupts the integrity of the schools, and degrades the moral authority of schools and teachers" (Kennedy 2000, 21). Based on academic studies of students exposed to the programming, scholars note, "Students who watch *Channel One* news evaluate advertised products more highly and express substantially more consumption-oriented, materialistic attitudes than do students who do not watch *Channel One*" (Hoynes, 1998, 340).

In 1999 Commercial Alert sent letters to all *Channel One's* major advertisers, asking them to discontinue advertising on the program. Only one company, Nabisco, replied, saying, "We do not believe evidence supports the charge that two minutes of daily advertising is putting our children's future at risk" (Walsh 2000, 16).

Micro Issues:

1. How is *Channel One* different from the student newspaper or yearbook that sells advertising? From the PTA fundraiser?
2. Are there certain sorts of ads that should be censored from *Channel One?*
3. A news service called ZapMe! installs and maintains computer labs for schools, providing they agree that schools log four hours per day per computer and allow ZapMe to place ads of marketers on its Internet connections. It also tracks student demographic information. The company asks your local school district for permission to sign a contract. Do you write an exposé of the practice or an editorial praising it?

Mid-range Issues:

1. Are there certain areas of U.S. life that should be protected from commercialization? Why?
2. How would you respond to the argument that *Channel One* helps students learn, particularly about difficult issues?

Macro Issues:

1. How do you respond to Nader's comments that commercialism in the schools is a threat to democracy?
2. What other sorts of commercialism appear in public schools? How is *Channel One* like or unlike those forms of commercialism?
3. How might John Rawls analyze the impact of *Channel One,* particularly in less affluent school districts?
4. Should other nations adopt this method of supporting public education? Why?

CASE VII-B
Singapore: Balancing Democracy, Globalization, and the Internet
SEOW TING LEE
University of Missouri

The tension between technology and censorship shows up most clearly in the Internet explosion in Singapore. Nestled in the heart of Southeast Asia, Singapore is a thriving city-state that has overcome a dearth of natural resources to become one of the juggernaut economies of Asia. Known as the "Asia Miracle," the tiny island has a population of nearly 4 million people in an area of 254 square miles—about one-fourth the size of Rhode Island. Modern and cosmopolitan with a skyline of glass and steel, it is no longer the exotic East so vividly documented by Kipling and Conrad. It is also here that the tension between technology and censorship—between Eastern values of community spirit, harmony and cooperation and Western ideals of individualism, competition and freedom of expression—is intensely played out.

One of four Singaporeans is an Internet user. The number of registered Web sites in Singapore increased from 900 in 1996 to more than 20,000 at the beginning of the millennium.

Singapore has come under intense global criticism for what many, especially Westerners, consider harsh Internet regulation. Among the allegations are that the Singapore government requires all dial-up Internet users to go through a proxy server that filters content. Web sites and newsgroup postings containing sexual, racial, religious, or provocative political views are said to be blocked and removed.

Singapore's dilemma seems like a simple one: it wants to harness new information technologies for developmental purposes and yet is keen to maintain strong control over information. It recognizes the potential of the Internet to offer opportunities for sharpening the country's competitive edge. Yet it also harbors deep-seated concerns about the impact of pornography, violence and the incitement of racial and religious hatred—materials easily accessible on the Internet—on social harmony.

In the past, censorship could be easily enforced by keeping out magazines, books, movies and music by banning their distribution, prohibiting home satellite dishes and revoking the licenses of publishers who overstep the line. The Internet, however, is a different ballgame altogether. Given its borderless and global nature, it defies censorship for several obvious reasons. First, the Internet represents a convergence of interpersonal communication, news media, non-news media information, commerce and computing software. The availability of E-mail and instant messaging services, among others, confounds any extensive censorship effort.

Second, because the Internet is a convergent medium, authorities would have to distinguish between personal and public consumption. It is clear that some of the materials on the Internet cannot be considered as mass media *per se* because many Web sites, electronic bulletin boards, and chat rooms cater only to members of particular groups of society. Third, the explosion of Web sites on the Internet deters any governmental action.

The government's jurisdiction over the Internet covers only materials for public consumption. Singapore has repeatedly denied vetting private E-mail or monitoring an individual's access to Web pages. Any attempt by the government to vet private E-mail for objectionable materials would be met with howls of protest.

The government, however, is not a lone voice. Censorship persists in Singapore because of widespread public support for control over pornographic material. There is less support for curbs on political expression, although Singapore politics often closely follows ethnic lines.

New forms of media spawned by the Internet are difficult to control, but that has not stopped Singapore from trying. A statement on the Web site of the Singapore Broadcasting Authority (SBA), the authority in charge of regulating the Internet, reads, "SBA has established a policy framework for the Internet with the view to promote and facilitate its growth while at the same time maintaining social values, and racial and religious harmony. These policies are also in place so that users are empowered to use the Internet for its benefits."

Beginning July 1996, Internet Service Providers (ISPs) had to abide by a code of what the community regarded as offensive or harmful to Singapore's racial and religious harmony. Prohibited material was defined as material that is objectionable on the grounds of public interest, public morality, public order, public security, national harmony, or is otherwise prohibited by applicable Singapore laws. Guidelines indicated what is considered offensive, and the following are considered:

1. whether the material depicts nudity or genitalia in a manner calculated to titillate;
2. whether the material promotes sexual violence or coercion;
3. whether the material depicts people clearly engaged in explicit sexual activity;
4. whether the material depicts someone under the age of sixteen engaged in any of the foregoing acts;
5. whether the material to vet private E-mail for objectionable materials would be met with howls of protest.

Enforcement results in censorship after publication because authorities must consider the context in which the material appears. A light-touch enforcement policy also has been adopted. And, given the multiracial and multireligious nature of Singapore society, Internet regulations are consistent with regulations covering print and broadcast media. All these regulations are rooted in sociohistorical ground. Before independence, the three major racial communities—Chinese, Malays, and Indians—had lived as distinct, isolated societies without a shared culture or past. As a result, the political loyalties of most Singaporeans were based on ethnicity and loosely associated with religion. The country's early experiences with racial riots and bloodshed have led the government and the public to tread carefully where racial or religious sensitivity are concerned. Irresponsible media reports were blamed for three riots, and the events were used as justification for Singapore's tight censorship. This stance was reinforced in the 1960s and 1970s when the threat of communism manifested itself. Nation building has been the dominant goal of the government since independence after World War II.

Censorship law dampens the spread of Internet use, but economic pragmatism sometimes rules. To attract foreign investment and expand electronic commerce, in

1998 Singapore decided that Internet Service Providers are no longer liable if their customers used their services to visit forbidden sites. This step marked a major relaxation in attempts to control Internet content.

Given the limit to what domestic legislation can achieve, the country has turned to a softer strategy emphasizing public education and industry self-regulation, in addition to government regulation. The three-pronged approach involves the following:

1. promoting public awareness, through public education, of the positive and negative aspects of the Internet;
2. encouraging the industry to take the initiative to self-regulate and set its own standards;
3. implementing a light-touch policy framework in regulation of Internet content based on consultation with the industry and the public.

Micro Issues:

1. How is what Singapore is doing different from requiring U.S. libraries or other public places to filter Internet content?
2. Would the same approach of public education and self-regulation function in another democracy, say the United States or the United Kingdom?
3. How does a journalist function under these circumstances? Which is more problematic under these conditions, government censorship or self-censorship?

Mid-range Issues:

1. In 1995 when Microsoft founder Bill Gates visited Singapore, he had this to say about the attitude of the country's officials toward the Internet: "They are going to try to have their cake and eat it too." Given your reading of the situation what did Gates mean by this? Is he correct? How do the country's history and culture inform your analysis?
2. Do you foresee any problems in asking the industry to help regulate itself?
3. Do emerging democracies, in general, face different sets of issues regarding the Internet?

Macro Issues:

1. Which philosophical theory best supports Singapore's approach to the Internet?
2. Which philosophical theory best supports the U.S. approach?
3. Some scholars have suggested that the Internet is more a medium of commerce than information. If this is true, how does that change what a nation can hope to accomplish through public policy or legal regulation of the Internet?

CASE VII-C
Victims and the Press
ROBERT LOGAN
University of Missouri

Alice Waters's daughter, Julie, seven, has leukemia. Her illness was diagnosed in its early stages in March 2000. Julie's physicians believe her condition can be successfully treated.

Ms. Waters, thirty-seven, lives in a mobile home in an unincorporated area a few miles from Metroplex, a city of 1.5 million. Ms. Waters's street is the only residential section in the area. At the north end of the street—which has twelve mobile homes on each side facing one another—are four large gas stations that catch traffic off the interstate that runs a quarter-mile away to the west. At the south end of the street (about a quarter-mile away) are two large tanks that are a relatively small storage facility for Big Oil Inc. Next to this—starting almost in her backyard—is the boundary of a successful, 700-acre grapefruit orchard, which borders on a municipal landfill. About a quarter-mile away are large well fields that are the principal source of drinking water for Metroplex.

In July 1999, a six-year-old boy in the household two doors down from Ms. Waters was diagnosed as having leukemia. He was not as lucky as Julie; his diagnosis was late in the progression of his disease, and he died in December 2000. In 2001, an infant girl became the second baby born with birth defects in the neighborhood within seven years. Both families moved before Ms. Waters came to the neighborhood in 1999.

Internal medicine specialists Dr. Earnest and Dr. Sincere met Julie soon after she was admitted to the hospital in October 2000. They were instrumental in getting funding for Julie's care when her mother was unable to pay. They are members of Worried M.D.'s for Social Responsibility, a self-proclaimed liberal, national public-interest group that gets actively involved in national political issues.

The physicians told Ms. Waters that they were suspicious about the causes of Julie's illness. Three cancer and birth-defect incidents on the same street, the physicians said, were not a coincidence.

In November 2001, they began to collect water samples from the well head at Ms. Waters's house. They sent the samples to a well-regarded testing lab in another city. Since then, they have tested the water at a professional lab every four months. Every test revealed traces of more than ten human-made and natural chemicals often associated with oil storage tanks, pesticides, grapefruit orchards, gas-station leaks, lead from automobile emissions, and a large landfill.

However, each chemical occurs consistently at six to fifteen parts per billion, which is considered safe for drinking water via standards set by the U.S. Environmental Protection Agency (EPA). At higher levels these chemicals are associated with carcinogenic risks or increases in birth defects, but the levels found at Ms. Waters's well head are within safety thresholds set by the EPA. There is no evidence the chemicals are associated directly with the health problems found in Ms. Waters's neighborhood.

At a fund-raising party last night for mayoral candidate Sam Clean, Drs. Earnest and Sincere privately told Clean what they have found. Clean is a well-known public figure, has a reputation as an environmentalist, owns a successful health-food restaurant chain, is media wise, and looks good on television. He is a long shot to become mayor and needs fresh issues to draw attention to his candidacy.

At 11:00 A.M. today, KAOS news radio begins running as the top story in its twenty-minute news rotation "Clean Attacks City Lack of Cleanup." In the story, Clean gives a sound bite attacking city officials for "ignoring cancer-causing agents in water in a neighborhood where children have died, which is next door to the city's water supply." He describes the neighborhood's medical problems and describes (without naming) Julie and Alice Waters. The news report explains that water from the neighborhood has several "toxic agents believed to cause cancer at higher levels" and points out that the city's water wells are within a quarter-mile of oil tanks, gas stations, a grapefruit orchard, a landfill, and septic tanks. County officials are said to be unavailable for comment. The report runs throughout the day at twenty-minute intervals.

By 2:30 P.M., calls to the switchboard have jammed the newsroom. The callers who get through are frightened about their drinking water. City Hall's switchboards are jammed. The callers sound upset and ask whether their water is safe to drink.

By 4:00 P.M., reporters from the local ABC affiliate are already knocking on doors in the trailer park and sending live reports from the scene. Neighbors tell them where Alice and Julie Waters live.

At 4:15 P.M., your managing editor gives you the story. You are an ambitious reporter for *Metroplex Today,* the only morning newspaper in Metroplex. Both of you realize this is clearly page-one potential, but you have only a few hours before deadline for the next morning's edition. After a few phone calls, you discover that the mayor, the city council, and most city and county officials are all out of town at a retreat and are unavailable for comment. The regional EPA office is not answering the phone.

A trusted spokesperson for Regional Hospital tells you that Drs. Sincere and Earnest are furious at Clean for releasing the story and have no comment. She fills you in with all of the above information.

The same Regional Hospital spokesperson says Ms. Waters does not want to be interviewed. She suddenly realizes that her husband, whom she walked out on several years before, might see the story and return to town.

Sam Clean is more than happy to talk to you.

Micro Issues:

1. Is Clean a reliable enough source on whom KAOS radio could base its reports?
2. Should KAOS have broadcast the story?
3. Should you respect Ms. Waters's wishes and leave her and her daughter out of the story?
4. Are Dr. Earnest and Dr. Sincere reliable sources?
5. What do you tell the public about whether the water supply is safe?

Mid-range Issues:

1. Would you be working on the story if KAOS and ABC had ignored it?
2. Would you be working on the story if there was little public reaction after the KAOS broadcast?
3. If Ms. Waters decides to do an interview on ABC later today, do you then include her in your story?
4. If city and county officials remain unavailable, how do you handle their side of the story? Does that delay publication until you can get more information, or do you go with what is available?
5. Are there unbiased sources you can contact about risk assessment? Who?

Macro Issues:

1. How do you handle the discrepancy between the information from the EPA and the skeptical scientists and environmentalists?
2. What is the public's probable reaction to reporting this story? Should your newspaper take any precautions to prevent public panic? If so, what should they be?
3. How risky is the water compared to risks we take for granted, such as traveling by car? Can you think of a relevant comparison for your article comparing the relative risk of the water to a well-known risk?
4. Is it the media's role to speak for a society that is averse to many risks? How might the media accomplish this function?

CASE VII-D
The David Duke Candidacy: Fairness and the Klansman
KEITH WOODS
The Poynter Institute for Media Studies

In the fall of 1991 David Duke, a former Ku Klux Klan Grand Wizard, made a run for the Louisiana governor's mansion.

He had sat for the past year in the state legislature, an ineffective representative from a small Republican district in the New Orleans suburbs. He had not passed a single piece of legislation, was routinely heckled when he took the House floor, and found that many of his colleagues would avoid standing close to him lest they get captured in the same photograph or the same video frame.

The media had alternately ignored him and held him up to public scrutiny and criticism. Though he had repeatedly disavowed any recent connection to the Klan, Duke was discovered selling white supremacist materials from his legislative office.

The evidence was compelling that the only difference between the old Duke and the new Duke was minor cosmetic surgery, a haircut and the stamp of approval from voters in Metairie's District 81.

Then he ran for governor. His primary opponents were formidable: incumbent Gov. Buddy Roemer, a Democrat-turned-Republican held in generally high regard by the media because of his reformist ideals; former Gov. Edwin Edwards, a populist Democrat with enough charisma to withstand two federal indictments in his previous twelve years in office; and Republican Congressman Clyde Holloway, a conservative whose legitimacy with voters would surely siphon votes from Duke.

For most of the campaign, Duke was given very little chance of even making a runoff. When the votes were counted on October 19, he had come within three percentage points of finishing first in the primary.

He would face primary leader Edwards in the runoff, and Louisiana voters would face the unpleasant task of choosing between a former Klansman and a proven scoundrel.

The *New Orleans Times–Picayune* had underestimated Duke twice before: when he ran an impressive, though losing, campaign for the U.S. Senate against powerful incumbent J. Bennett Johnston and when he shocked the newspaper and many voters by capturing District 81. Having witnessed Duke's statewide popularity yet again, the newspaper took decisive and controversial steps to help defeat him.

Two days after the election, the newspaper's top editors and editorial writers gathered around a newsroom conference table for a meeting that would greatly influence everything from the paper's editorial direction to the focus of its daily coverage.

The unusual meeting, fruit of an election-night brainstorming session between editor Jim Amoss and then-metro editor Peter Kovacs, produced this plan: the newspaper would employ its best editors to research and write a series of five editorials—twice as long as the standard editorial—that would make a fact-based, methodical argument against Duke's candidacy. Each editorial would be promoted on the front page.

AP/WIDE WORLD PHOTOS.

The decision to use key newsroom editors to write the editorials, including the capitol bureau chief in charge of state government coverage, pushed the *Picayune* newsroom across the line of objectivity at the outset of its runoff coverage. Amoss characterized the four weeks that followed as no less than a battle for the soul of the electorate.

In those four weeks, the newspaper focused the attention of more than forty staffers on the election, with much of the focus falling upon the flaws and fallacies of Duke's candidacy. As themes developed in the campaign and in the newsroom—Duke's recent racist and anti-Semitic musings, his dubious religious conversion, his ties to bigots, his political immaturity—the newspaper hammered away on the front page and editorial page. Sometimes the editorials were on the front page.

Many readers howled with displeasure. Most were Duke supporters who blasted the newspaper's obvious bias. Some were Edwards supporters worried that the *Picayune* would provoke a groundswell of sympathy support for Duke. The newspaper began running full pages of letters to the editor, most opposing Duke, some praising the newspaper. It was a break from the *Picayune's* tradition of refusing letters that support political candidates, a break the newspaper explained to its readers in an editorial page blurb.

When the unprecedented editorial series "The Choice of Our Lives" had run its course, the *Picayune* mailed out reprints of the series to newspapers across the state, encouraging them to quote the editorials at will.

Several staffers wrote op-ed pieces before the election, giving readers a glimpse into an angst-torn newsroom where the prospect of Duke becoming governor brought some to tears and kept emotions on edge.

The angst found its most profound expression in an internal debate about the fate of a story dubbed "The Duke Voters." Aware that Duke's supporters were regarded as racist extremists, particularly by those in the newsroom, the newspaper sought to show the faces and hear the voices of the ordinary voters who supported such a controversial politician.

Once written, the story became the center of unusual attention. Several editors visited Amoss in his office in the days before the story was to run, pleading with him not to print it. Some said that by showing the Duke supporters in all their simple humanity so close to the election, the newspaper was giving comfort to racists and encouraging their votes. Amoss listened, but the story ran as written on the front page of the Sunday edition one week before the election.

Though Duke received 671,009 votes, he was soundly beaten in the runoff, with Edwards taking 60 percent of the vote. Duke blamed his defeat on a lot of negative press, the *Picayune* and its sources.

Micro Issues:

1. What is the reporter's responsibility to objectivity when covering a person so widely believed to be a social pariah?
2. Is it possible for the reporters to be fair to Duke without being objective?
3. Did the *Times–Picayune* owe equal loyalty to readers who supported Duke and to those who opposed him?

Mid-range Issues:

1. Should newsroom editors, who assign and help shape the bulk of the day's news stories, ever be allowed to write editorials related to those stories? If yes, under what circumstances?
2. What effect, if any, do you think the publication of staff op-ed pieces critical of Duke might have had on the newspaper's image and credibility in the community?
3. Is it possible for a newspaper in such a situation to be as aggressive with its editorial push—including publication and dissemination of the editorial series—without unduly influencing the news coverage?
4. What are the challenges to a reporter trying to reflect the views and wishes of a community so polarized, particularly when politics and prejudice are so enmeshed?

Macro Issues:

1. Are there circumstances under which a news organization can so clearly identify a harmful political choice that it is justified in campaigning against a candidate? If so, when?
2. Where would such a line be drawn in this case? At membership in the Klan? At associations with Klan members? What if the candidate held racist views but never disclosed them publicly?
3. How does a news organization fairly cover a candidate whose notoriety becomes such a huge part of the story?
4. Editor Jim Amoss said that if the paper had taken a less aggressive tack and Duke had won, he knew the paper would be held culpable to some extent. Is that a legitimate concern for a newspaper or its editor?

CASE VII-E
Military Censorship of Photographs
PAUL LESTER
California State University–Fullerton

The United States has been engaged in military conflicts both honorable and questionable. Inspired by the need to report each war to an anxious public, journalists have traveled to the front lines to produce stories and pictures both supportive and critical. As the informational and emotional power of visual images has become more understood, military strategists and politicians have instituted various forms of censorship of images in an attempt to protect their troops and to control public opinion.

Termed "Desert Storm" by the military and the "Gulf War" by the media, the clash with Iraq over Kuwait was an example of the often tenuous relationship between government officials and journalists. Hundreds of journalists throughout the world were in Saudi Arabia covering the fight, but only about a hundred made up the official military press pool. With more than 500,000 U.S. troops in the area and fighting erupting on several fronts, newspapers, for example, relied on only sixteen journalists to cover every ground unit in the country. Although most reporters accepted the fact that a pool was necessary, many were frustrated by the military's slowness in

AP/WIDE WORLD PHOTOS.

transporting the pool members to troubled areas. Once there, pool members were accompanied by an ever-present military escort.

U.S. Department of Defense ground rules signed by all journalists prohibited reporting that would in any way endanger the troops. A journalist had to get approval before attempting any story. Once the piece was completed, the story and pictures were subject to U.S. and allied military censorship. Although there was no stated prohibition against showing wounded or dead soldiers, some journalists were wondering halfway into the war why they had not "seen one picture of bloodshed (or) anyone who's dead yet." Charges of "news management" and a "credibility gap" between official and pool reporter accounts surfaced. Claiming that press pool restrictions were too harsh, several U.S. publications and a few individual authors asked for a federal court injunction against the Defense Department's pool procedures.

The Gulf War was difficult to cover. It was primarily an air campaign waged in the middle of the night using fast-moving aircraft carrying computer-guided missiles with video cameras in their nose cones to signal the results of their prearranged missions. The Iraqi government was extremely hostile to journalists, only allowing a handful of correspondents to report from its side of the conflict. The isolated nature of the terrain was a further barrier to full-access coverage. It was simply not possible to conveniently drive across the huge desert seeking frontline firefights as in previous wars.

Besides, it was quite dangerous to try such a mission, as Bob Simon and his crew from CBS discovered. Simon and his associates decided to drive to Iraq through the desert on their own because they were frustrated by the military's strict censorship controls over their actions. They were soon captured by Iraqi forces and detained until the end of the conflict. Despite these dangers and restrictions, CNN's coverage of the night bombing of Baghdad was particularly impressive, as was the subsequent damage to buildings in that ancient city reported by Peter Arnett—the only American correspondent able to report with his words and images from Baghdad.

As never before, technology played a significant part in fighting and reporting the war. Arnett and others were able to report from the far-off country because of the use of a portable satellite transmitter. Photographers were able to quickly send their images to their waiting editors because of digital cameras and transmitters. Nevertheless, most still photographers and videographers were frustrated by their lack of access to any real fighting scenes. They were left to cover noncombat scenes involving soldiers drilling. Once the ground war had commenced, a few journalists found themselves riding along with the tank units. But most of the fighting occurred at night, making it extremely difficult to record action scenes. Most of the pictures of the fighting areas in Iraq were of the long lines of Iraqi prisoners captured by military forces.

One highly emotional picture that did get through military censors was taken by *Detroit Free Press* photographer David Turnley. Turnley was riding with the 5th MASH medical unit inside Iraq. A fierce firefight had recently erupted between Saddam Hussein's Republican Guard and the 24th Mechanized Infantry Division.

A helicopter—filled with Turnley, medical personnel, and equipment—touched down about a hundred yards from a frantic scene. An American military vehicle had just taken a direct hit. Soldiers on the ground were upset as they said it had mistakenly been struck by a U.S. tank. The wounded were quickly retrieved from the vehicle and carried to the helicopter. Sgt. Ken Kozakiewicz, suffering from a fractured hand, slumped into the helicopter. The body of the driver of Kozakiewicz's vehicle was placed on the floor of the helicopter inside a zippered bag. A medical staff member, perhaps thoughtlessly, handed the dead driver's identification card to Kozakiewicz. Turnley, sitting across from the injured soldier, recorded the emotional moment with his camera when Kozakiewicz realized that his friend had been killed by the blast.

Later at the hospital, Turnley asked the soldiers their names. He also asked if they would mind if the pictures were published. They all told him to get the images published.

The rules of combat enforced by the military required that Turnley give his film to military officials for approval for publication. A day after the incident, Turnley learned that his editors had not yet received his negatives from the Defense Department officials. Military officials insisted that they were holding the film because the images were of a sensitive nature. They also said that they were concerned about whether the dead soldier's family had been informed of his death. Because of Turnley's argument that the family must have been informed by then, the officials released his film.

His photographs were eventually published in Detroit and throughout the world. The picture of Kozakiewicz crying over the loss of his friend was called the "Picture of the War" on the cover of *Parade* magazine. Several months after the war, Turnley spoke to Kozakiewicz's father, who had been in one of the first U.S. military units in Vietnam. Reacting to the censorship of images by military officials, David Kozakiewicz explained that the military was "trying to make us think this is antiseptic. But this is war. Where is the blood and the reality of what is happening over there? Finally we have a picture of what really happens in war." For David Kozakiewicz, showing his son grieving over the death of a fellow fighter gave added meaning to the soldier's death.

Micro Issues:

1. Should the photographer have taken the picture?
2. Should the photographer have asked permission of the injured soldier to take the picture?
3. Does a picture of a grieving soldier belong on page one?
4. Should photographers be allowed to travel along with military personnel to the fighting fronts?

Mid-range Issues:

1. Would criticism be lessened if the image were run small and on an inside page?
2. If the soldier is not from your newspaper's local area, why should the picture run?
3. How would you as an editor react to a reader's complaining that the picture demoralizes America's war effort?

Macro Issues:

1. What moral philosophies influence an editor who uses the picture and a reader who complains about its use?
2. Does the military during a war have the right to censor images produced by a photographer?
3. Does "pool" coverage during a war offer the best solution for informing the public back home?
4. Should an editor wait to publish a picture of a dead person until relatives are informed? Why or why not?
5. Should journalists avoid taking and publishing images that criticize a nation's war effort?

CHAPTER VIII

Media Economics: The Deadline Meets the Bottom Line

By the end of this chapter you should be familiar with:

• how advertisers gain influence in the media economic equation and the ramifications of that additional influence.
• the economic realities of the social responsibility theory of the press.
• the economic and legislative initiatives that have combined to place control of information in the hands of fewer and larger corporations.
• the problems of programming for diversity in a numbers-driven media.

Introduction

In the movie *Absence of Malice,* Paul Newman is asked if he has taken his complaint concerning an inaccurate article about him to the newspaper. He replies, "Have you ever tried to talk to a newspaper?" For most Americans, the point is well taken. A faceless, nameless, non-locally owned media is becoming a reality in all but a few communities. Today the media are predominantly corporate owned and publicly traded, with media conglomerates among the largest of the world's corporations. The corporate owners of the average news operation are more insulated from contact with news consumers than virtually any other business owner in America.

The pace and size of the mergers that created these media conglomerates in the last two decades of the twentieth century are staggering. In rapid succession, General Electric bought NBC, Westinghouse bought CBS and later sold it to Viacom, and the Disney Corporation purchased ABC, each deal worth billions. Westinghouse/CBS merged with Infinity Broadcasting to create the nation's largest radio chain. Time Warner, created by a billion-dollar merger earlier in the 1990s, acquired the Turner Broadcasting System—including such properties as WTBS, TNT, CNN, and Headline News—and then was itself acquired in 2000 by Internet Service Provider America Online in a deal estimated at $115 billion. Telephone giant MCI bought a 13.5 percent interest in the News Corporation, the parent company of Fox Television (bought earlier by Rupert Murdoch's New Corporation), while Microsoft and NBC combined to create MSNBC, a multimedia venture.

The CBS sale is illustrative of how intertwined all media have become. The Federal Communications Commission (FCC) gave its approval in May to the 2000

$46 billion merger between Viacom and CBS. Viacom's assets include MTV, VH1, Nickelodeon, Paramount, Blockbuster, Simon and Schuster, and Spelling Entertainment. At the time of the acquisition of CBS, Viacom also increased its holdings by acquiring television stations, syndicators King World and Eyemark, a radio and outdoor advertising empire, and several cable networks.

As they get bigger, the media must increasingly satisfy competing publics to survive. The desires of stockholders must be balanced with the mandate to keep the audience happy in programming and content decisions. At the same time, advertisers, who demand large numbers of readers and viewers for their messages, make claims on the media as well. The inherent tension created in trying to satisfy these competing publics creates many of the ethical problems discussed in this chapter.

The Penny Press Revolution

Financing the American media through advertising is so deeply ingrained in the system that it is hard to imagine any other way. Yet newspapers supported solely by their readers thrived in America for more than a century. As recently as 1920, then-Secretary of State Herbert Hoover argued in vain for a commercial-free broadcast industry to be funded by the sellers of the receivers. While the airways eventually became filled with commercials, Hoover and the Federal Radio Commission (now FCC) won one important battle: the public is the owner of the airwaves and the station is merely the "trustee" of that commodity.

Today each medium has found its own formula to economic security—from "free" network television on one end of the continuum to books, movies, and a handful of magazines such as *Ms.* and *Consumer Reports* on the other—that pass on virtually all of the production costs to the consumer. Most media organizations lie somewhere in between.

That formula for contemporary economic security began on September 3, 1883, when Benjamin Day, publisher of the *New York Sun,* started a revolution when he lowered the price of his newspaper to a penny at a time when his competition was selling newspapers for a nickel. He gambled that he could overcome the losses with additional advertising revenue—if circulation increased. When his gamble paid off, virtually every publisher in town followed his lead. Soon after, Frank Munsey lowered the cost of *Munsey's Magazine* from a quarter to a dime and watched as his circulation increased eightfold in two years to half a million readers.

What Day and Munsey did was farsighted. By pricing their products at or below the cost of printing, they cast their economic future with their advertisers. What was not foreseen, however, was the diminished role the consumer would play in the process.

Under the old pricing structure, subscribers were an end in themselves. Each represented a percentage of the profit, no matter how minuscule. Under this system, readers purchased news, entertainment and opinion content. Under the new system, advertisers purchased readers. The individual subscriber became a means to an end.

Content is now relegated to the status of "bait" to catch readers and viewers to be sold to advertisers, as Bill Moyers points out in an interview for PBS's *The Promise of Television*:

> Every manager or owner I know in commercial television now simply accepts television as a by-product of the merchandising process. That changes how you regard the people for whom you are producing or creating television. They are there to be seduced, to be sold something that somebody wants to sell. You are simply a transmission belt between someone trying to sell a product and the person who has the money to buy it, and it changes altogether your sense of your mission, your purpose, or your obligations to that viewer.

Casualties from the Revolution

Three problems emerged from the penny press revolution that shifted the profit center from consumers to advertisers. First, in an attempt to attract the largest audience possible, media outlets "homogenized" their content, dealing in topics guaranteed to offend few individuals while hoping to garner large audiences. The result is journalism that takes no risks unless research shows that the audience will follow. In fact, Gannett's *USA Today* was developed from a marketing plan, not as a news concept.

Network news presidents "know," for instance, that the public has an interest in only one foreign story at a time. So while the "pack" went first to the Persian Gulf and then Somalia in the early 1990s, the continuing horrors of Bosnia and the killing fields of El Salvador went unreported or at best underreported. Similarly, events are reported more than processes. Stories written for the masses focus on quick-onset disasters such as Hurricane Andrew but not on the slow-onset disaster of global warming that may be spawning ever larger hurricanes.

Second, the penny press revolution made it more difficult for diverse voices to find a mainstream forum. The late Randy Shilts of the *San Francisco Chronicle*, the first reporter in the United States assigned to the AIDS beat, claimed that AIDS coverage was stymied in its early stages as it was perceived to be a "gay plague" of interest only to the homosexual community (Shilts 1987). Only when celebrities such as Rock Hudson and "innocents" such as Ryan White contracted the disease did it get widespread mainstream media coverage (Rogers and Chang 1991).

Third, the penny press revolution hastened the inevitable conflicts between the interests of the now powerful advertisers and the interests of less powerful consumers over controversial content. Advertisers exert both obvious and subtle influence over a media content (also discussed in chapter III). For instance, scholars (Kessler 1989; Miller 1992) found that magazines receiving a great deal of revenue from the tobacco industry were significantly less likely to print articles about the health impact of tobacco. This omission was even more startling because many magazines, particularly women's magazines, claimed to focus on women's health issues. Kessler credits the indirect influence of the tobacco industry on these publications as a factor in the rise of tobacco-related cancers in women during the latter half of the twentieth century. Additionally, with three tobacco companies consistently ranking among the top ten spenders of all U.S. advertisers, the influence of that money on editorial content continues to be felt, a fact the *Seattle Times* acknowledged in June 1993 when it stopped accepting tobacco ads worth about $100,000 annually to the paper. The movie *The Insider* recounts the impact of the same lobby on CBS.

Just what role profit ought to play in the media depends in part on the view one takes of the media's role in society. In the section below, we will examine two important descriptive theories of the press that have dominated American thought and look at the role profit and economics play in each.

Libertarian and Social Responsibility Theories Revisited

Mass communication research has several descriptive theories. An underlying assumption of these theories is that any media system "takes on the form and coloration of the social and political structures within which it operates" (Siebert, Peterson, and Schramm 1956, 3). Eventually, theorists predict, the media will reflect the political and economic structure of a society. For instance, a capitalist society will eventually create a media system funded by the hope for economic gain, i.e., advertising.

Two of the best known descriptive theories of the press are the libertarian and social responsibility theories. Together they describe more than 200 years of thinking on the role of information in a society and how it should be delivered.

The *libertarian theory* of the press grew out of the changes that swept Europe from the Reformation to the Renaissance. In keeping with the basic tenets of the Enlightenment, libertarian theory assumes that people are rational and that truth is discoverable in a secular, empirical way. According to libertarian theory, political authority rests with the individual. Government's role is to ensure the domestic and foreign peace, but the individual is supreme in politics—a belief spelled out in the Preamble to the U.S. Constitution. Because the individual is rational, government should do the individual's bidding. People are viewed as having both the time and the inclination to become literate and involved in public affairs.

With these assumptions, the libertarian theory of the press reflects Milton's concept of the "marketplace of ideas." Anyone could operate a printing press, particularly anyone aligned with a political group. Those who ran the presses of the day, because they were partisan, would provide partisan versions of reality. The rational citizen would select the truth from among the partisan versions available.

Within this theory, the press's most potent antagonist would be government, which libertarians viewed as locked in a perpetual power struggle for political supremacy with the individual. The duty of the press was to support the individual in that fight. The result was a media system that supported a well-informed individual in a quest for well-being and happiness.

The ensuing five hundred years have done much to change our view of humanity and of society. Three intellectual changes were instrumental in this shift. First, Freud and modern psychology changed our view of rational humanity. We now believe that people are often illogical, sometimes irrational, and motivated by a variety of needs and drives (Davies 1963). People are not uniformly energetic or educated. For this reason, they will not always seek out and sometimes will not understand information to which they have access.

Second, knowledge, indeed reality itself, has been transformed. Societies have begun to realize that what we think of as a "fact" is subject both to perception and change, a philosophical view known as pragmatism. The "fact" that matter cannot become energy was successfully challenged by Einstein. Truth has become ephemeral.

Third, society has become more cosmopolitan. As people moved to cities and as waves of immigrants reached American shores, people discovered they were as different from one another in culture and language as they were alike in their quest for a better life. What was truth for one group was not truth for another. Literacy, at least literacy in English, was a cherished ideal, not a reality. Mass markets of many sorts emerged.

These shifts transformed the press of the 1800s into the mass media of the late twentieth century. Life today in the United States often seems comprised of a series of self-interested subgroups. A new media system was required. Today, the mass media are no longer the written word, but also television, public relations, advertising, entertainment and every conceivable hybrid, including the Internet. Few people, even in the age of the personal computer, can own a media outlet. Existing outlets are largely corporate owned and eschew partisanship in favor of objectivity. The marketplace of ideas became a monopoly supermarket, and the goods it carried were uniformly "vanilla."

With these changes came a new descriptive theory of the press. The theory was developed in the 1940s by a panel of scholars, the Hutchins Commission, with funding from Henry Luce, the conservative founder of *Time* magazine. No journalist sat on the commission. Despite this, the *social responsibility theory* of the press continues to fascinate both academics and practitioners because it attempts to compensate for changes in modern political, social, and cultural life.

Social responsibility theory acknowledged what was already a reality by the 1940s: the number of media outlets is limited; people are often self-interested and sometimes lazy. Because of these changes, the media have certain responsibilities in the political system. According to the Hutchins Commission, the media have the following five functions in society:

1. To provide a truthful, comprehensive, and intelligent account of the day's events in a context that gives them meaning.
2. To serve as a forum for exchange of comment and criticism.
3. To provide a representative picture of constituent groups in society.
4. To present and clarify the goals and values of society.
5. To provide citizens with full access to the day's intelligence.

The goals of social responsibility theory are troubling to journalists. While the theory acknowledges the world is intellectually and socially a different place from that of the libertarian view, it provides no clear guidelines for journalistic behavior in this new era.

Indeed, some of the guidelines the theory does provide are ambiguous. How should the forums operate? Whose values should be presented and clarified? Others appear to be mutually exclusive. For example, the media's role as mirror and critic may conflict with some interpretations of media objectivity. Other guidelines might simply be impossible to achieve—for example, providing intelligent discourse about the day's events in a nightly newscast of less than twenty-three minutes.

An even more fundamental problem hobbles social responsibility theory: it gives little attention to modern media economics. This omission occurred in part because the multinational corporations and chain ownership were still on the horizon when the Hutchins Commission codified the theory. Because the theory was developed early in the McCarthy period, there also was an unwillingness to link economic and political power for fear of being labeled Marxist. This central omission means that *the social responsibility theory, like libertarianism, does not deal with the realities of concentrated economic power,* particularly in an era when information has become an increasingly valuable commodity. Today some of the most troubling problems in media ethics stem from journalism's dual responsibilities to citizens and to stockholders, and the social responsibility and libertarian views of the press provide little guidance on these issues.

Media Economics in the Modern Era: Cutbacks and Consolidations

If the founders envisioned a marketplace of ideas where all views would be aired and the truth would emerge, by the late twentieth century the dream had died. Information in the United States had fallen into the hands of a very few well-financed corporations. In every key media format—radio, television, newspapers, magazines, cable television, and motion pictures—more than half of the gross revenues were concentrated in the hands of fewer than five corporations. The result is what media economics researcher Ben Bagdikian has called "a defacto ministry of information within a democracy" (Bagdikian 1990, 5).

The history of newspapers is indicative of the consolidation trend in all media. At the turn of the century, William Randolph Hearst, Joseph Pulitzer and the Scripps family sought to widen their influence and enlarge their bank accounts by building the first newspaper chains. For the first time, profits made by selling information and advertising within a community left that community destined for corporate accounts in distant banks. Gradually, the concept of what a newspaper owed a community changed as well. Newspapers were no longer a public trust, but a public utility akin to a power company. Newspapers were delivering to a community a necessary product—information—without any of the regulations of those companies that deliver electricity and gas, and most often without competition. Consequently, the profits of newspapers are three to five times higher than most corporations—today averaging between 20 to 30 percent annually. Some niche markets, for example, business publications, routinely expect 40 percent per year.

Today, corporate chains own nearly 90 percent of the nation's daily newspapers, compared to 20 percent at the end of World War II. One chain, Gannett, owns nearly one hundred newspapers in addition to the nationally circulated *USA Today*. Fewer than thirty cities are currently served by competing dailies. Recently, Dallas, Minneapolis, Cleveland and Los Angeles joined the growing list of cities served by a single newspaper. In 2000, Denver newspapers signed a joint operating agreement, consolidating advertising and circulation, but not news. Historically, such agreements have meant the death of one of the papers involved within a decade.

To many, the rise in corporate ownership marked a decline in the quality of journalism. In *The Media Monopoly,* Bagdikian quotes media acquisitions expert Christopher Shaw, telling clients that profits from a newspaper can be tripled in two years through a combination of staff reductions and increases in advertising and subscription rates. "No one will buy a 15 percent margin newspaper without a plan to create a 25 percent to 45 percent margin," Shaw said (Bagdikian 1987, 7). Former Gannett chairman Allen H. Neuharth told Bagdikian, "Wall Street didn't give a damn if we put out a good paper in Niagara Falls. They just wanted to know if the profits would be in the 15 to 20 percent range" (Bagdikian 1987, xxi). James Squires (1993), former editor of the *Chicago Tribune,* claims that the corporate takeover of U.S. newspapers has led to the "death of journalism."

The Gannett operation is an example of the direction of the newspaper industry. Founded in 1906 with $20,000 in capital, Gannett has grown to annual revenues approaching $10 billion, ranking in the middle of the Fortune 500 top companies in America. It operates newspapers in forty-five states, the District of Columbia, Guam, the United Kingdom, Germany, and Hong Kong, and it owns a number of television stations as well. At one point in its history, Gannett profits increased 87 quarters consecutively, a streak unheard of in most industries.

Broadcasting also has felt the impact of consolidation. In the mid-1980s in the first round of takeovers, each newsroom operation was downsized. ABC cut a total of 200 employees from its news operation; CBS axed 215. NBC virtually cut its *Nightly News* writing and production staff in half, in part because parent company GE saw nothing wrong with the on-air product during a seventeen-week writers' strike that caused the newsroom to operate shorthanded (Schoenbrun 1989).

This era of cutbacks and consolidations has been noted by media researcher Robert McChesney (1997) who makes this analogy:

> Imagine if the federal government demanded that newspaper and broadcast journalism staffs be cut in half, that foreign bureaus be closed, and that news be tailored to suit the government's self-interest. There would be an outcry that would make the Alien and Sedition Acts, the Red Scares and Watergate seem like child's play. Yet when corporate America aggressively pursues the exact same policies, scarcely a murmur of dissent can be detected in the political culture.

Not only did the financial environment change, but the legal context for media ownership changed too. The net effect of the Telecommunications Act of 1996 is to ensure that media ownership will become increasingly concentrated thanks to more relaxed multiple and cross-ownership rules. Here are a few of the changes brought by the 1996 legislation:

- Companies may now own as many radio and television stations as they wish, up from fourteen radio stations and seven television stations as recently as the early 1980s. The only restriction on ownership of broadcast stations is that the total reach of the stations can only be 35 percent of the nation's households.

- A single owner can own up to eight radio stations in the nation's largest markets and up to half of the stations in the nation's smaller markets. This is a radical change from long-time policies that prohibited any media "duopolies" in a single market.
- Television networks can now own and operate cable television systems, and telephone companies can now be cable television providers in their local service areas, a cross-ownership previously denied by the FCC.
- It is now legal for the phone company to provide programming content in addition to phone services. Conversely, it is now legal for cable television companies to compete for your phone business.

These new rules set the industry in a buying and selling whirl. More than one-third of all radio stations in the United States have changed hands since 1996. The Telecommunications Act raised station prices to incredible heights, putting them out of reach of the typical entrepreneur. In 1996 alone, 2,045 radio stations were sold, for a total of $13 billion. Major radio chains, such as Infinity and Clear Channel Communications, went on cross-country buying sprees for radio stations, driving the prices up as they went. Less than six months after the signing of the Telecommunications Act, both chains owned more than a hundred stations. In some cases, a single chain would own all of the talk radio stations—a major source of news and information—in a single market. In some cases, acquired stations were reformatted with automated programming meaning fewer jobs and higher profits for the new owners.

As the legal landscape was changing, the major media players also discovered the synergy that could be developed through "vertical integration." Under vertical integration, a media empire attempts to own a combination of media properties that take a project from development to distribution. Disney, which in the 1990s added ABC-TV to its ownings, is the industry leader in vertical integration. For instance, the film *Hunchback of Notre Dame* earned a "disappointing" $99 million at the box office but generated more than $500 million in revenues in other Disney ventures (McChesney, 1997).

Virtually every media company was suddenly and concurrently both for sale and in acquisition mode. As corporations expanded and diversified, so did profits. Typical of the returns are Disney and Time Warner. Early in the 1990s, each averaged returns of 15 percent annually; by the end of the decade the average was 30 percent.

And the legal landscape is likely to continue to shift. Michael Powell, the chairman of the Federal Communications Commission and George W. Bush appointee, said in the Spring of 2001 he favors abolition of the "cross ownership" rule, which prohibits a single entity from owning a newspaper and broadcast station in the same city. With more Republican appointees expected to the FCC, the rule likely will be abolished, allowing a single corporation to own most media properties in the same market—a defacto monopoly.

Becoming a player in the media game today is a far cry from the days of the single editor beginning a partisan newspaper, as envisioned by Milton. When Gannett wanted to launch a national newspaper, the corporation spent more than $800 million before *USA Today* turned a profit. When media mogul Rupert Murdoch wanted to create a fourth television network, he lost nearly $100 million in the first two prime-time seasons of his now healthy Fox network. At the same time that technology is making more media outlets available than ever before, these staggering start-up costs have closed the door to all but a few and changed the complexion of the media industry to an exclusive club where only the rich and powerful need apply for membership.

As the mass media have themselves become enormous, economically powerful institutions, they have joined what political scientist C. Wright Mills (1956) called the "power elite," a ruling class within a democratic society. Power is found not only in the halls of government but also on Wall Street. And power is found not only in money or armies; it is also found in information. Media organizations, precisely because they have become multinational corporations engaged in the information business, are deeply involved in this power shift.

This emergence of media as economic and political power brokers leads us to question how a powerful institution such as the mass media, which traditionally has had the political role of checking other powerful institutions, can be checked. Can the watchdog be trusted when it is inexorably entwined with the institutions it is watching? As media corporations expand exponentially in the pursuit of profit, who will watch the watchdog?

Government is probably the only institution capable of providing a counter to the massive economic power of the media. Yet government provides a variety of subsidies to the industry. In addition, government functions as a regulator of the broadcast and advertising industries, ensuring profits to both these groups by limiting access to the airwaves and legislating fair play in advertising. So, more often than not, the U.S. government supports big media rather than acting as a counterweight.

Economics and News

As media ownership becomes the privilege of the rich, an elite few control an important ingredient of democracy: news. When the few who own the media view it only as a business, the problem gets worse. Dan Rather, CBS's *Evening News* anchor, expressed the concerns of many journalists in a *New York Times* op-ed column he wrote:

> News is a business. It has always been. Journalists understand and accept that. But journalism is something else, too. Something more. It is a light on the horizon. A beacon that helps the citizens of a democracy find their way. News is an essential component of a free society. News is a business, but it is also a public trust. (Rather, 1987)

The lean years of the late 1980s and again in 2001 focused attention on the fact that good journalism is often expensive, and in an era of static subscriptions and smaller ad revenues, few newsrooms enjoy budgets as large as in past years. The three television networks have closed entire bureaus, and many newspapers have pulled back on overseas correspondents, leaving coverage of foreign news to the wires and CNN.

The effect of these cutbacks is lost news for the consumer. One photojournalist, Brad Clift, told us that he went to Somalia months before U.S. troops were dispatched, using his own money because he felt the starvation there was an underreported story. Only an occasional network crew and a handful of newspapers pursued the Somalia story until then-President Bush committed U.S. troops to the region in December 1992. Most news organizations, like the photojournalist's employer, declined to cover the emerging story, pleading that they had depleted their international budgets by covering Operation Desert Storm.

In reading the code of ethics of the Society of Professional Journalists, two of the "guiding principles" of journalism speak directly to the ethics of media economics: (1) seek truth and report it as fully as possible; and (2) act independently.

Seeking truth can be financially and personally expensive. Several media outlets that have been honored in the "Darts and Laurels" column written by *Columbia Journalism Review* managing editor Gloria Cooper demonstrate that many media organizations and professionals do seek truth at great personal and corporate cost.

Seeking the truth can be personally and financially expensive. And, the following anecdotes illustrate that truth doesn't always win the financial battle.

In April 2001 San Jose Mercury News Publisher, Jay Harris, resigned his job at the *Knight-Ridder* paper saying he could not acquiesce to corporate demands for increased profits that would have resulted in newsroom layoffs at a time when the area his paper served was hit by the dot.com recession in Silicon Valley. Several weeks later, Harris gave an impassioned speech to the American Society of Newspaper Editors in which he said that corporate demands for increased profits were undercutting the journalistic mission.

On the other hand, the *Seattle Times* was willing to stand by aviation reporter, Byron Acohido during most of the decade of the 1990's when Acohido began to write about design problems with Boeing's 737 tail section. His reporting culminated in a five-part series in October 1996 pegged to air crashes involving the plane—one of the most common in any airfleet around the world. Boeing is one of the largest employers in the Seattle area, and Acohido's efforts were met with years of corporate stonewalling and antagonism. However, in 1999 the federal government, in part in response to Acohido's work, began to pressure Boeing to redesign the tail section. The company agreed early in 2000. (Coleman 2000)

In 1997 *Los Angeles Times* reporter David Willman began an investigation into deaths associated with a new block-buster drug for diabetics called Rezulin. As editors of the paper noted, Willman's series "revealed truths that bear directly on a matter of profound importance to all Americans; the presumed safety of newly approved prescription drugs," (Coleman, 2000 p. 120). Over the next year, the *Times'* coverage sparked increased media attention. The drug was eventually withdrawn from the market in 2000, but not before journalists and members of Congress had questioned the Federal Drug Administration's approval process and considered whether the corporation should be criminally indited for its acts.

Acting independently, another of the Society of Professional Journalists guidelines, can also be expensive. For many media outlets, independence is as simple as buying tickets to the movies reviewed and sports events covered. However, it goes far beyond that for others, such as the journalists and photographers who were captured and held by Iraq soldiers when they ventured away from U.S. military pools to see the Persian Gulf War firsthand.

Both the *Lexington Herald–Leader* and the *Syracuse Post–Standard* faced reader boycotts and threats against individual reporters when they opened investigations of local, successful college basketball programs. Reporters for the *New York Daily News* exposed the numerous allegations of incompetence by a medical doctor who was spending more than $150,000 a year in advertising in the *News*.

Unfortunately, these uplifting stories of personal corporate enterprise are far too rare in an industry that demands more than 20 percent pretax profit from its holdings. This demand for profits generates subsidiary problems as well. Entry-level salaries for journalists in both print and broadcast are among the lowest starting salaries of any jobs requiring a college degree—under $26,000 in the year 2001. The all-consuming focus on ratings in the broadcast entertainment industries is often blamed for a variety of ills, among them programming more concerned with attracting masses than creating quality.

Finding Profit Through Service

Advertising revenue declines in the late 1980s and early 1990s hit virtually every medium. The economy forced U.S. media owners to rethink the methods that were once so profitable. What many found was that a return to treating the consumer as an end rather than a means was not only the right thing to do, it was profitable as well.

McKinsey and Company made "excellence" a buzzword in business circles with studies that formed the basis of the best-selling *In Search of Excellence*. In 1985, the firm was hired by the National Association of Broadcasters to study eleven of the nation's great radio stations, such as WGN in Chicago, and report to the group's annual convention about what made an excellent radio station. Their findings were (1) the great radio stations were audience-oriented in their programming, often breaking down the traditional walls that defined formats, and (2) the great radio stations were community-oriented in their promotions, becoming synonymous in their communities with charitable events and community festivities.

The attitude is summed up by WMMS (Cleveland) general manager Bill Smith (National Association of Broadcasters 1985):

> If you want a car to last forever, you've got to throw some money back into that car and make sure that it's serviced properly on a continual basis. Otherwise, it's going to break down and fall apart. We know that we're constantly rebuilding the station one way or another. We throw the profit to the listening audience . . . to charities, to several nonprofit organizations, to free concerts or anything to affect the listeners of Cleveland as a whole. If we can donate the money to light up Terminal Tower, if that's what it's going to take and nobody else is going to do it, we'll do it . . . and we get and hold our listeners, year-in and year-out, because they identify us as being community-minded.

Social Responsibility in the New Millennium

When the social responsibility theory was framed in the 1940s, the primary informational concern was scarcity: people might not get the information they needed for citizenship. Today, however, the primary informational concern is an overabundance of raw data: people might not filter out what they need through all the clutter. Media and their distribution systems changed, but the theory remained silent, especially about the role of profit in the development of systems for gathering and disseminating information. This meant that, until recently, government agencies such as the FCC were still basing policy decisions on the scarcity argument when any consumer with cable or a satellite dish knew otherwise.

The Newspaper Preservation Act of the 1970s, the AT&T antitrust suits of the 1980s, the Telecommunications Act of the 1990s, and other battles finally focused the attention of the U.S. government on the fact that delivery of entertainment and information is indeed big business and is currently in the hands of a very few—something the libertarian framers of the Constitution sought to avoid.

The clash of large, well-financed institutions for control of information is a modern phenomenon. Classical ethical theory, which speaks to individual acts, is of little help in sorting out the duties and responsibilities of corporations larger than most nations that control the currency of the day: information. Political theory, particularly Marxist theory, is of some help in identifying the problem, but communism has been rejected as a potential solution throughout most of the world.

Americans are equally unwilling to accept government as the solution to counter the concentrated economic power of the media, and government has been loathe to break up the large media conglomerates. During the lifetime of the readers of this book, the power and role of "big media," such as AT&T and Time Warner, should emerge as *the* most important issue in media ethics. Can an institution that began as a lone printer with a press "flourish" without a change in vision as a multinational with billions in assets?

History says "no." Adaptability is the key to institutional survival. The Roman Catholic Church lost much of its intellectual and political hold on Western Europe when devotion to dogma overruled commitment to parishioners. The Reformation resulted. Likewise, the Mandarin class lost political control in ancient China because it could not change with a country that was moving into the twentieth century. Social and political history has not been kind to big entities. Media conglomerates will thrive only to the extent that they can adapt both to serve the diverse communities into which their far-flung empires take them and to react quickly when they fail. The ones that do it well will survive.

Suggested Readings

Auletta, Ken. 1991. *Three blind mice: How the TV networks lost their way.* New York: Random House.
Bagdikian, Ben H. 2000. *The media monopoly.* 6th ed. Boston: Beacon Press.
Mills, C. Wright. 1956. *The power elite.* New York: Oxford University Press.

CHAPTER VIII CASES

CASE VIII-A
Ms. Magazine—No More Ads!
PHILIP PATTERSON
Oklahoma Christian University

Ms. magazine printed its last commercial issue in October 1989, and returned in June 1990 as one of the few mass circulation magazines in history to eschew advertising and rely entirely on its readers for support.

While vowing to continue in the tradition begun by the group of women activists who founded the magazine in 1972, one thing was now different: the price. Readers would be asked to pay $35 for six issues, a price that has since increased.

The new publisher, David Lang, who bought *Ms.* when it was struggling to make ends meet, at the prompting of the magazine's editors, decided to fund the magazine entirely on readers' subscriptions.

Gloria Steinem, a co-founder of *Ms.* said the magazine has always walked the line between unvarnished advocacy and the demands of the people who pay the bills. She authored an exposé for the premiere issue entitled "Sex, Lies and Advertising." In it, Steinem revealed the stories of advertisers who didn't want to be placed near articles dealing with abortion, gun control, illness, large-size fashion, anything depressing.

The new editor-in-chief, Robin Morgan, told the *Denver Post,* "Now we can say all the things we never got to say for 18 years. We have to keep reminding ourselves of that" (*Denver Post,* 1990).

Andrea Kaplan, spokesperson for Lang Communications, said *Ms.* would need 50,000 to 100,000 subscribers to show a profit, a standard achieved by its third issue. At the time of its suspension in 1989, *Ms.* had 550,000 subscribers but was losing money.

Ms. is not the only magazine to take action against the constraints of advertisers. Some magazines—for example, *Consumer Reports,*—refuse advertising altogether. Other publications such as *Modern Maturity, The New Yorker,* and *Mother Jones* have implemented strict advertising policies. *Modern Maturity* refuses all ads that depict aging in a negative light, said Robert E. Wood, publishing director of the magazine, claiming in interviews that advertising is as important as editorial in shaping the overall feel of the magazine.

At *The New Yorker* all proposed advertisements are sent to a committee that evaluates each ad's motives and relevance to the magazine's targeted audience. Only if the committee approves the ad will it be published. Similarly, the staff of *Mother Jones* magazine refuses to publish ads that are sexist, racist, or exploitive.

Ms. magazine's decision to eliminate advertising drew attention to the difficulties publishers face regarding ethics and advertising today. It raised questions about the role of the media as an information outlet and questioned the motives of advertisers and publishers alike.

Micro Issues:

1. Is *Ms.* infringing on the advertiser's right to freedom of speech?
2. Is *Ms.* courting financial ruin by shunning the advertising that supports it?
3. Is *Ms.* depriving its readers of an informative medium through its elimination of ads?
4. If a magazine edits an article to satisfy an important advertiser, does it have any obligation to inform readers of the decisions?

Mid-range Issues:

1. Are consumers able to distinguish between editorial content and advertisements? Does it matter?
2. How could *Ms.* magazine responsibly satisfy the desires of its advertisers and its readers simultaneously?
3. How would the particular advertiser problems of a liberal feminist magazine such as *Ms.* compare to another periodical such as *Newsweek?*

Macro Issues:

1. Is it the media's job to censor advertisements for the public?
2. By running an ad, is a publication endorsing the product being advertised? Should publications be held responsible for the claims of their advertisers?
3. Is a magazine ethically required to be an open forum for all advertisers who have the ability to pay? According to what standards?

CASE VIII-B
Crossing the Line? The *L.A. Times* and the Staples Affair
MEREDITH BRADFORD AND PHILIP PATTERSON
Oklahoma Christian University

The *Los Angeles Times,* in a "special report" on December 20, 1999, called attention to an event its editors perceived as a breach of journalism ethics. The multi-story report was entitled "Crossing the Line." What made this report extraordinary is that the *Times* itself had crossed the line that triggered this journalistic exposé.

A few weeks earlier, the Staples Center, a $400 million sports and entertainment arena in downtown Los Angeles had opened to great fanfare. Most observers shared the hope that the facility, which would house two basketball franchises and one hockey team, would spark a revitalization of downtown. Staples Inc. had won the naming rights to the arena by paying $116 million.

Tim Leiweke, president of the Staples Center, left with $284 million more to raise, had initiated talks with McDonald's, Anheuser-Busch, United Airlines, Bank of America, and others to become "founding partners." He was eager to have the *Los Angeles Times* as a founding partner because of previous joint successes and because he thought the paper could contribute value beyond cash.

The Staples arena already had a promotional arrangement with the *Los Angeles Times* in exchange for cash payments from the *Times* and free advertising in the paper. "The arrangement is similar to that many big-city papers have with their local professional sports teams," said David Shaw, the *L.A. Times* Pulitzer prize–winning media critic, in an investigative piece on the controversy (Shaw 1999). "But for the Staples Center, Lieweke wanted more. He wanted the *Times* as a founding partner."

Since the Staples Center could be a major contributor to the revitalization of downtown Los Angeles, *Times* executives were "eager to participate," Shaw said.

The price for founding partners ranged from $2 to $3 million per year for five years. Jeffrey S. Klein, then senior vice president of the *Times,* who supervised early negotiations on the Staples deal, "didn't think it was worth what they were asking." Negotiations stalled for several months in 1998 until a "Founding Partner Agreement" was accepted on December 17, 1998, between the L.A. Arena Company and the *Los Angeles Times.* Part of the language in the agreement stated the two companies "agree to cooperate in the development and implementation of joint revenue opportunities."

"Although all of the principals in the negotiations say that the precise terms of the Staples deal are confidential," Shaw reported, "information from a variety of sources shows that in effect the *Times* agreed to pay Staples Center about $1.6 million a year for five years—$800,000 of that in cash, $500,000 in profits and an estimated $300,000 in profits from what Leiweke had called 'ideas that would generate revenue for us.'"

This latter part of the deal was clarified in a clause of the final contract that said, in part, that the *Times* and the L.A. Arena Company would agree to cooperate in the development and implementation of joint revenue opportunities such as a special section

in the *Los Angeles Times* in connection with the opening of the arena, or a jointly published commemorative yearbook, Shaw said.

These "joint opportunities" were to create $300,000 of net revenue for each party
annually. According to the contract, these opportunities would be subject to the mutual agreement of both parties.

On October 10, 1999, the *Times* published a special 168-page issue of its Sunday magazine dedicated to the new Staples Center sports and entertainment arena.

Only after the section was published did most of the paper's journalists learn that
the *Times* had split the advertising profits from the magazine with the Staples Center.
Feeling that the arrangement constituted a conflict of interest and a violation of the
journalistic principle of editorial independence, more than 300 *Times* reporters and
editors signed a petition demanding that publisher Kathryn Downing apologize and
undertake a thorough review of all other financial relationships that may compromise
the *Times's* editorial heritage.

The petition, in part, stated "As journalists at the *L.A. Times,* we are appalled by
the paper entering into hidden financial partnerships with the subjects we are writing
about. The editorial credibility of the *Times* has been fundamentally undermined."

Less than two years before the episode, Downing had been named publisher by
Mark Willes, the new chief executive of Times Mirror Corporation, parent company
of the *Los Angeles Times* despite having no newsroom background. Her previous
experience had been as a legal publicist. Willes had moved from General Mills to
Times Mirror in 1995. Willes had made no secret of his desire to " 'blow up the wall'
between business and editorial" (Rieder 1999). He was also on record as telling
American Journalism Review in 1997 that "[the] notion that you have to be in journalism 30 years to understand what's important, I find rather quaint"(Rieder 1999).

Downing did apologize, calling it a "major, major mistake." After taking questions at a two-hour staff meeting on October 28, she admitted that she and her staff
"failed to understand the ethics involved" (Booth 1999). Downing meanwhile canceled all future revenue-sharing deals with Staples, promised to review all contracts
with advertisers, and ordered up awareness training for the ad side.

For his part, Willes seemed to reverse his earlier stance when he said, "This is
exactly the consequence of having people in the publisher's job who don't have experience in newspapers" (Reider 1999).

On the business side of the paper the arrangement was widely known and discussed openly for most of 1999. Downing says she deliberately withheld the information from Michael Parks, the paper's editor, but did not direct her subordinates on
the business side not to talk about it to him or to anyone else in editorial, according
to several reports.

Shaw reports that Willes argued that the absence of such discussion only shows
the need for "more communications, not less. . . . The profit-sharing deal happened
not because The Wall came down," Willes says, "but because people didn't talk to
one another when they should have."

In an interesting argument, Downing claimed if the editorial side of the paper did
not know about the profit-sharing deal with the Staples Center before printing, then

the Sunday magazine devoted to the Staples Center would be unbiased. The uninformed editorial staff would have no reason to be biased.

Many critics from inside and outside the newspaper agree with Shaw that "readers have no reason to trust anything the *Times* wrote about Staples Center, or any of its tenants or attractions, anywhere in the paper, now or in the future, if the *Times* and Staples Center were business partners." He adds that readers will wonder whether other improper arrangements, formal or informal, might also exist or be created in the future with other entities, agencies and individuals covered by the *Times*.

Whether connected to the Staples affair or not, massive changes were in store for Willes, Downing, Parks and the *Times*. The newspaper was bought by the Tribune Company, publisher of the *Chicago Tribune,* in March 2000. All three employees were gone within a year.

Micro Issues:

1. Critique Willes's early and late statements about journalistic experience in newspaper management positions.
2. Is the actual loss of credibility as disastrous as the reporters felt, or does the public really have the same sensibilities as those in the profession?
3. How does entering into the contract with the Staples Center differ from the sports department accepting press passes for the events held in the arena?

Mid-range Issues:

1. If one acknowledges that "the wall" is good and necessary, how does that affect media engaged in advocacy journalism?
2. Shaw entitled his article "Journalism Is a Very Different Business." In what ways do you think journalism differs from other businesses?

Macro Issues:

1. In the new information age, where so many competing views can be found on most issues, is the "wall" still relevant?
2. When a newspaper is a publicly traded company, do the loyalties of the paper shift from the public to the shareholders? If not, how can you justify a move that might be counterproductive to profits?

CASE VIII-C
"Bonding" Announcements in the News
JOANN BYRD
Seattle Post-Intelligencer

The "Wedding Book" in the Sunday "Northwest Life" section of *The Herald* in Everett, Washington, includes weddings, engagements, and twenty-fifth and fiftieth wedding anniversaries. Each event submitted is reported with a one-column picture and about two inches of copy. People who want a more detailed announcement or their own language can buy a reduced-rate display ad, for which they write the copy.

In the fall of 1990, a lesbian couple filled out the form used to collect information and submitted it for the "Wedding Book" page. The women wanted to announce they had made a lifetime commitment to each other in a bonding ceremony attended by family and friends in a local park.

The *Herald* serves an area combining the suburbs of Seattle and surrounding rural communities. Many in the core communities had made it clear over the years that they expected the paper to reflect and reinforce conservative family values. The county had grown 36 percent in the previous decade and showed an increasing diversity of races, cultures, and lifestyles. Other institutions, including the state's biggest bank, had adopted policies recognizing unmarried relationships, and the city of Seattle had recently been involved in a visible campaign to have domestic partners of city employees declared eligible for medical insurance.

The decision to accept the announcement was made almost instantly. Simultaneously, Stan Strick, the paper's then-managing editor, suggested expanding the page to include, as the in-paper announcement put it, "significant personal milestones in people's lives, everything from adoptions to retirements."

Readers were notified of the change Sunday morning, November 25, 1990, in a story alongside the jumps of section-front pieces about gay couples who had exchanged vows and ministers discussing church positions on gay commitment ceremonies. The paper, with its page renamed "Celebrations," would be "one of the first in the nation to accept bonding ceremonies other than weddings," said the announcement.

The decision was condemned from pulpits in the county that morning, and people in the community began to protest. The women's announcement ran on the revamped page December 2, under a standing head, "Bondings," that matched the labels for "Weddings," "Engagements," "Anniversaries," and "Birthdays."

The community reaction became intense. Hundreds of angry subscribers canceled their subscriptions (as did some people who didn't have subscriptions). Letters and phone calls flooded the newsroom; a local businessman organized a protest group and visited the *Herald* advertisers, urging, although unsuccessfully, a boycott of the paper. Delegations from the conservative Christian community came to the paper to demand that the policy be rescinded.

Seattle television covered the debate, and national media interviewed Strick. The storm continued for months. Letters to the editor and organized letter-writing and telephoning campaigns followed national news stories. As other newspapers across the country were approached to publish gay bonding ceremonies, editors phoned for details of the *Herald's* experience.

Most of the complaints centered on Biblical interpretations condemning homosexuality. Those callers and letter-writers felt the *Herald* was endorsing sin, and giving to homosexual relationships the sanction that should be reserved for heterosexual marriages, engagements, and wedding anniversaries.

The *Herald's* position was that sexual orientation was not a morally relevant basis for refusing to accept the announcements, that a page of reader-generated "significant personal milestones" simply had to give people equal access.

The policy has not been changed, but no other gay couple in the county submitted an announcement in the years following. One advertiser quit advertising for several weeks. Many of those who canceled subscriptions have not returned.

Micro Issues:

1. Should the paper have accepted the announcement?
2. What options could you imagine? (Should the paper, for instance, have treated it as a news story rather than institutionalizing gay commitments on its announcement page?)
3. Some critics thought the *Herald* was bragging about being "one of the first" to accept gay bonding announcements. Would it have been better to skip the advance notice and simply publish the bonding ceremony and the new publication procedures for the page?
4. Some defenders likened the paper's decision to publishing mixed-race marriages before such notions were thought "socially acceptable." Is that a legitimate parallel? Are there others?

Mid-range Issues:

1. Gay commitments are not recognized by most state laws. Should the paper publish any arrangements that do not have legal status?
2. This case arose on a page where "news" is defined by people who want to make the announcements, not by reporters working a beat. Does that raise different ethical questions in the newsroom?
3. How far should the newspaper go in giving people equal access to its pages? Is anything anybody wants to announce okay?

Macro Issues:

1. Offending people and their most deeply held beliefs is not morally justified unless there is an overriding moral obligation. How much should the paper weigh the probability of offending a large portion of its audience by doing what it considers morally correct in this case?

2. Chances are that there would have been less dispute if the change had occurred at a paper in a big city. Are the values at stake here different from community to community, and should all newspapers' decisions recognize that?
3. How much should a secular entity like a newspaper reflect religious beliefs?
4. The women involved in this case were harassed by conservative groups for months afterward. Does a newspaper have an obligation to censor news that may harm those submitting it? If so, what are the criteria?

CASE VIII-D
Calvin Klein's Kiddie Porn Ads Prick Our Tolerance
VALERIE LILLEY
Kansas City Business Journal

As if a pantyless Brook Shields cooing "Nothing comes between me and my Calvins" weren't enough. As if displaying a nipple to sell millions of dollars of Obsession perfume wasn't pushing tolerance to its edge, Calvin Klein pressed further. His 1996 television and magazine advertisements showing young people posed in provocative positions had some critics calling them common child pornography and prompted an FBI investigation.

"It was the portrayal of youth that was part of people's rage," said Katie Ford, chief executive of Ford Models Inc. in a *Wall Street Journal* article. "I think obviously a line was crossed because it created such an uproar. That's not a personal opinion, but it seems to be America's opinion."

The ads were shot in an environment right out of a cheap back room or basement. The print ads feature unknowns such as Delancey Berzin, a fourteen-year-old male, who was paid $1,000 to pose topless in Calvin Klein jeans, according to the *Philadelphia Inquirer.* One male model unbuttoned his pants to reveal his underwear, looking as if he were in the midst of undress. Another young man is stripping off his shirt while looking vulnerable, and yet another photograph shows a young woman, lying spread-eagled on a bench with her denim miniskirt yoked up and revealing her underwear-covered crotch. She wears an innocent expression while she teases a piece of hair.

The sleazy effect was intentional. The $6 million campaign was shot by Stephen Meisel, who built his career on photographing seductive greats, such as Madonna in her 1992 book *Sex.*

Klein did get one thing out of the campaign: free publicity. *Washington Post* columnist Bob Garfield described it best: Klein releases his ads and "lobs them into the firetrap of the media culture. The ladder trucks and pumpers of journalism race to the scene, bystanders run to see what the commotion is about and, as they stand in their nightclothes gawking, appalled but somehow also titillated by the conflagration, Klein strolls by and sells them $100 million worth of pants."

Klein said placing the kiddie porn stigma on his clothes was not his intention. In a full-page *New York Times* advertisement, Klein said the ads' message was intended to show "that young people of today, the most media savvy yet, have a real strength of character and independence. They have a strong defined line of what they will and will not do."

The campaign was withdrawn in August 1996 after a public outcry. The main force behind the dissent was the Rev. Donald Wildmon, founder of the conservative American Family Association (AFA). He urged retailers to boycott the ads and threatened to have AFA members picket stores if they didn't comply.

Perhaps one of the problems in pushing public taste is that Klein used young males in these exploitive roles. In the ads that ran on MTV, an older male voice asked

AP/WIDE WORLD PHOTOS.

youthful-looking men, "You got a real nice look. How old are you?" "You think you could rip that shirt off you?" and "That's a nice body . . . do you work out?"

Society has long accepted the use of young women in this role, but boys are still off-limits. "To get sexy little guys gazing moistly at the camera, that gives everyone a terrible shock because boys are not to be used in this way," said Anne Hollander, author of *Sex and Suits,* in a *Washington Post* article.

Yet minor-aged models who do seductive shoots do so willingly. Model Rainer Hammer, fifteen, who wants to pose for Klein and has already been photographed by Meisel, is typical of the would-be models. She built up a portfolio of pictures of her in shackles and underwear. She has posed with a boy in a bed for Replay jeans. Wearing jeans, he lay on top of her and slightly lifted up her white undershirt. "I know the models in the Calvin Klein ads, and they don't care," she told the *Wall Street Journal.* "To us it's acting."

Micro Issues:

1. Do the ads described meet your definition of kiddie porn?
2. Do the ads described meet your definition of bad taste?

Mid-range Issues:

1. Has Klein been able to manipulate the media with his shocking commercials? Is it possible that free publicity was the intent of this modest-budget ad campaign?

2. What should be the proper media response to those who use shock tactics to try to garner publicity?

Macro Issues:

1. How do you respond to the claim that the commercials were shocking because boys were placed in vulnerable positions? Would the commercial have generated as much publicity if all the models had been female?
2. These commercials were accepted by major media outlets. What duty does a medium have to reflect the mores of the culture in which it operates?

CASE VIII-E
Punishing the Messenger: The Tobacco Industry and the Press
STEVE WEINBERG, ASSOCIATE EDITOR, *COLUMBIA JOURNALISM REVIEW*
University of Missouri–Columbia

When ABC News, under the cloud of a $10 billion libel suit, apologized to Philip Morris in August 1995 for an award-winning investigation entitled "Smoke Screen," most journalists were stunned. The network's action damaged the credibility of a top-notch news organization, perhaps undermined investigative reporting as a journalistic genre, and encouraged lingering questions about the impact of the bottom line on corporate decision making regarding news stories.

The two-part investigative piece reported by Pulitzer prize winner Walt Bogdanich stated that tobacco companies, including Philip Morris and others, added nicotine to cigarette tobacco with the purpose of keeping smokers hooked on the drug. The story itself had been exhaustively researched for more than a year, and all of the sources but one—"Deep Cough"—had agreed to go on the record with their comments. In the process of researching the story, Bogdanich learned that, during the manufacturing process, nicotine is actually removed from tobacco at one point only to be added back into the tobacco later.

Less than a week before the show aired on the news magazine *Day One,* the U.S. Food and Drug Administration (FDA) issued a letter stating that it believed there was mounting evidence that nicotine is "a powerfully addictive agent" and that "cigarette vendors control the levels of nicotine that satisfy this addiction" (Weinberg 1995, 27).

Spokespersons for the tobacco industry were quoted in the segments, and Philip Morris, just days before the show was to air, sent ABC News a two-paragraph statement that said, in part, "Nothing done in the processing of tobacco or manufacture of cigarettes by Philip Morris increases the nicotine in the tobacco blend above what is naturally found in the tobacco." The investigative report never made the allegation that nicotine levels were increased beyond those that occur naturally; rather it suggested the tobacco companies had the ability to remove some of the drug from cigarettes and had chosen not to do so.

Controversy erupted after the first part of the story aired on February 28, 1994. A second segment, which aired one week later, focused on the list the tobacco companies had supplied to the federal government of 700 cigarette ingredients. Thirteen of those ingredients are banned in food. Philip Morris was not mentioned at all in the second segment.

Journalists applauded the work. The coverage won a George Polk award and a DuPont/Columbia University award. Congressional hearings into the tobacco industry were called as a result of the story. One day before those hearings were to begin, Philip Morris sued for libel, asking for $5 billion in compensatory damages and $5 billion in punitive damages, despite the fact that Virginia law capped punitive damage awards at $350,000. The story about the libel suit ran nationally, often without the notation about the award restriction. In addition, the tobacco giant gave every indication that it would pursue the suit vigorously, spending more than $1 million per month for more than a year on the litigation.

At ABC, newspeople saw what they perceived as an immediate chilling effect. The day Philip Morris filed the lawsuit, two independent producers were notified by a producer at ABC's program *Turning Point* that their documentary on the tobacco industry's advertising tactics and production transfers to overseas sites was being shelved, despite the outlay of about $500,000.

Legally, the going was equally difficult. Although the network gave every indication that it intended to fight and win the libel suit, discovery tactics by Philip Morris bedeviled the process. Documents that normally would have been public were marked as trade secrets, thus sealing them and making them impossible to report on. Worse yet, from the journalists' point of view, Philip Morris attempted to unearth Deep Cough's identity by subpoenaing records of reporters' phone bills, credit card purchases, and travel in an attempt to retrace the journalist's footsteps to Deep Cough's door. A judge initially approved of the subpoenas in the discovery process but later reversed himself after the network contested the decision.

As in many expensive lawsuits, talk about a settlement surfaced from time to time, starting in the summer of 1994, just three months into pretrial discovery—and just as rumors began that Disney might make ABC part of its entertainment empire. Insiders weren't surprised. But it wasn't until almost a year later, on June 30, 1995, that the *Wall Street Journal* reported that settlement talks had begun anew. By that time, and despite assurances from ABC's trial lawyers, other lawyers and some ABC managers had decided that portions of the investigative report would not withstand trial scrutiny.

It turned out that the trial lawyers had been kept away from the settlement negotiations. In-house lawyers, who were joined in the final days by renowned First Amendment lawyer Floyd Abrams, worked with Philip Morris's litigators on the language of an apology to the two tobacco companies. (Abrams had been involved in the case briefly, before the settlement talks began). The network's statement ultimately ran in more than 700 publications under the headline "Apology Accepted." Philip Morris dropped the suit.

The apology was clearly a victory for Philip Morris, but was it a sellout for ABC? If "Smoke Screen" contained one or more factual errors, it might be possible to consider the extremely limited language of the apology and the absence of any monetary awards (ABC did agree to pay the other side's legal fees, at least $15 million), a victory of sorts for the network. ABC's assertion in the apology letter that it stands behind the show's intended principal focus and the signing of the reporter and producer to new long-term contracts with substantial raises—even though both refused to sign the settlement agreement—are a vindication of sorts for the show.

ABC was purchased by Disney after the suit was settled.

Micro Issues:

1. Should Deep Cough have been allowed to remain off the record?

2. What standards of evidence should journalists doing investigative work demand from their sources and documents?
3. How should other news organizations that covered the libel suit have reported it?

Mid-range Issues:

1. Should journalists work out agreements about legal liability with their editors in advance of broadcast or publication?
2. Should the journalists have been willing to wait on the story and work with government regulators on the issue?
3. What professional values are served by stories such as "Smoke Screen."
4. Does reporting on undesirable products or issues—toxic waste or tobacco, for example—demand a different professional standard than reporting on city government?

Macro Issues:

1. What is the responsibility of "corporate ownership" to encourage and protect investigative reporting?
2. Do journalists, who increasingly work for large corporations, have a responsibility to the public to find mechanisms to counter the demands of the bottom line?
3. Do journalists have a watchdog role when it comes to covering corporations and economically powerful interests?
4. Compare "Smoke Screen" to Upton Sinclair's classic *The Jungle*. Would such a treatment of the tobacco industry be possible today?

CHAPTER IX

Picture This: The Ethics of Photo and Video Journalism

By the end of this chapter, you should be familiar with:

• the legal and ethical issues involved in photojournalism in the area of privacy.
• the technology available for altering photos and of the ethical and
  epistemological issues those possibilities raise.
• the definition of and to recognize eyewash.

Introduction

Perhaps the most instantaneous of all ethical decisions in the mass media is the one made by the photographer at the scene of a news story: Shoot or don't shoot? How a photographer prepares for such moments, and what decisions he makes when a questionable situation arises, is sometimes thought to be the only issue in photo and video ethics. However, a number of ethical issues surround the visual part of the business, many of them evolving rapidly with new technology. In this chapter we will discuss the following:

1. Balancing the right to privacy and newsworthiness.
2. Staging video and news photographs.
3. Changing images electronically.
4. Selective editing to support a point of view.
5. Using unrelated eyewash photography in news.

What do these issues have in common? Perhaps it is that they all seem to center on the twin themes of fairness and accuracy. However, once the problems are identified, the answers are not that simple. What is fair? What is accurate?

While each photographer and photo editor will have to answer these questions individually, perhaps some minimum standard can be established: No image used in the news, whether video or still photograph, is ethical unless it treats the subjects or topics fairly and attempts to present an accurate and unambiguous picture of reality.

We will examine the inherent problems of visual communication, then look at specific ethical issues.

Problems in the Process

Age-old axioms assure us that "The camera never lies" and that "Seeing is believing." Yet no photograph or videotape can be completely accurate, since the mechanics of photography demand that the lens and film make choices the eye is not required to make. These differences between the eye and the camera influence perception, as Arthur Berger points out in *Seeing Is Believing.* Because of the many variables in photography—camera angles, use of light, texture, and focus—Berger says a picture is always an *interpretation* of reality, not reality itself. He adds that a dozen photographers taking pictures of the same scene would produce different views of the reality of it. For instance, one photographer, Nat Fein, won the Pulitzer prize for photography while taking a picture of an event dozens of photographers were shooting—the retirement of Babe Ruth. By moving to the rear of his subject, Fein captured a different angle and told a different and more dramatic story with his photo.

Not only does the camera differ from the eye in its ability to manipulate angle, light, and focus; cameras also capture an isolated reality by presenting us with a slice of life, free from context. In *About Looking,* John Berger says:

> What the camera does, and what the eye can never do, is to fix the appearance of that event. The camera saves a set of appearances from the otherwise inevitable supersession of further appearances. It holds them unchanging. And before the invention of the camera nothing could do this, except in the mind's eye, the faculty of memory. (1980, 14)

Although the camera and the eye are vastly different in their functions and their abilities, most media consumers believe the photographs they see because most people assume their eyes don't deceive them. In this unguarded assumption lies the possibility for manipulation and deception.

Compounding the reality problem is the importance of visuals to both the electronic and print media. No major story is complete without a photo or footage. In this rush to shoot compelling visuals to accompany a story, photojournalists must juggle deadline and competitive pressures with other, less tangible qualities, such as privacy.

To Shoot or Not to Shoot?

Each day, before pictures are chosen, cropped, and placed in the paper by the appropriate editor, another important decision is made in the field by photographers. Arriving on the scene of newsworthy events, she must make several decisions. The most basic of these is whether or not to take the photo of a subject who is in no position to deny the photographer access to the photo. Often these vulnerable subjects are wounded, in shock, in grief. In that newsworthy moment, the subject of the photograph loses a measure of control over his or her circles of intimacy. That control passes to the photographer, who must make a decision.

Goffman (1959) claims people possess several "territories" they have a right to control. Included in Goffman's list are two territories that are problematic to the visual journalist: the right to a personal space free from intrusion (i.e., by a camera lens) and the right to preserve one's "information," such as a state of joy, grief, etc., from public view.

By its very nature, photojournalism is an intrusive and a revealing process—two violations of Goffman's sense of self. In many cases, it appears that someone else's misfortune is good fortune for the photojournalist. One study (Junas 1980) found that more than half of the winning images in top photography contests were pictures of violence and tragedy.

Inevitably, every photojournalist happens on an assignment that will intrude _on a subject's privacy. Garry Bryant (1987), a staff photographer with the *Deseret News* of Salt Lake City, offers this checklist he goes through "in hundredths of a second" when he reaches the scene of events such as the ones that were just described:

1. Should this moment be made public?
2. Will being photographed send the subjects into further trauma?
3. Am I at the least obtrusive distance possible?
4. Am I acting with compassion and sensitivity?

To this list, however, Bryant adds the following disclaimer (1987, 34): What society needs to understand is that photographers act and shoot instinctively. We are not journalists gathering facts. We are merely photographers snapping pictures. A general rule for most photojournalists is "Shoot. You can always edit later."

Many photojournalists have taken comfort in the "Shoot first, edit later" arrangement that they hope will shift the ethical decision to a later, less frenzied moment. However, sometimes it is the *act* of shooting the photograph (discussed in chapter VI) that offends the subject as much as the subsequent publication. One of the most memorable photos of the assassination of presidential candidate Robert Kennedy is a photo of Ethel Kennedy, his wife, attempting to block the lenses of photographers immediately after the shooting.

Many editors argue that decisions cannot be made concerning photos that do not exist. Not every picture of grief needs to be ruled out just because the subject is vulnerable. Newspaper readers and television viewers need to know that drugs kill and leave behind grieving parents and friends. Where to draw the line is a decision best made in the newsroom rather than at the scene. The photographer who attempts to perform a type of ethical triage at the scene of a tragedy might find his career in jeopardy if the assignment fails to capture the pathos of the event when all other photographers succeeded. In addition, the photographer who fails to capture some of the event, for whatever reason, fails to capture some of the truth for the audience.

However, the window of time for deciding later is closing. Today's microwave technology means that the media can be "Live at Five" on the scene of a tragedy, broadcasting footage even before the immediate family is alerted. Scenes that might once have been edited as the story was compiled now go straight on the air. An important stage in the ethical decision-making process is bypassed when such stories are aired live.

How can the victims of these tragedies come to life as vulnerable humans with feelings to a professional who sees the world most of the time through a lens? That question was asked at a conference held on the campus of Texas Christian University entitled "Crime Victims and the News Media." The conference brought together victims of violent crime and the journalists who covered their stories. One participant, Jeff Greenfield, who was ABC's media critic at the time, noted, "Once a journalist hears their simple, eloquent stories of what happened to them, he will never approach the story of a human tragedy in quite the same way."

Essentially, the photographer who is deciding whether and how to photograph a tragedy is wrestling with the dilemma of treating every subject as an end and not merely a means to an end. We can agree that powerful images of accident victims may cause some drivers to proceed more safely, but if that message often comes at the expense of an accident victim's privacy, is it a message that needs to be told? Bovée (1991), in an essay entitled "The Ends Can Justify the Means—But Rarely," offers this set of questions to help the photographer find the answer.

1. Are the means truly morally evil or merely distasteful, unpopular, etc.?
2. Is the end a *real* good or something that merely *appears* to be good?
3. Is it probable that the means will achieve the end?
4. Is the same good possible using other means? Is the bad means being used as a shortcut to a good end when other methods would do?
5. Is the good end clearly greater than any evil means used to attain it?
6. Will the means used to achieve the end withstand the test of publicity?

While application of this test might help the photographer make some decisions, the choices will always be tough. The line between newsworthiness and intrusiveness, between good pictures and bad taste, is often blurry. Donald Gormley, general manager of the *Spokane Spokesman–Review,* offers some insight into the difference between photos that are universally offensive and photos that are simply tough to view:

> Compassion is not the same as good taste. If a reader knows the person pictured in a very dramatic photograph, he may find it offensive. That's a sin against compassion. If he is offended whether he knows the person or not, the sin is probably one against good taste. (1984, 58)

Staging Photographs

Every photographer has had this feeling: you are about to capture that perfect moment on film, except _____. You can fill in the blank with any number of problems. For the photographer at a birthday party, the issue is inconsequential. You simply remove the offending child, relight the candles, or arrange the scene and try again. To the photojournalist attempting to convey the truth of a story, however, the issue is much more complex: to tamper with the subject is to rearrange reality.

The issue is not a new one. As early as 1876, an enterprising photographer staged a picture of his own death (Lester 1992). More than a hundred years later, the ethics of the issue of staging remain unresolved, even in major news organizations.

For instance, during the 1992 November sweeps period, NBC's magazine show *Dateline* aired an eighteen-minute segment on a faulty design of General Motors pickup trucks that concluded with video of a truck exploding into flame immediately after a side-impact collision. More than 300 people had died in such collisions since GM had introduced the trucks. The story included gripping still photographs of charred bodies pulled from accident scenes, court documents from the many suits

Calvin and Hobbes

by Bill Watterson

filed against GM over the truck's design, and videotaped testimony from independent auto safety experts and a former GM engineer, all saying that the corporation had known about the design flaw yet had chosen to do nothing.

However, NBC did not inform viewers that, in order to capture the closing video, "sparking devices" had been mounted on the test cars by the independent testing agency the network had hired as part of its investigation. Even with the addition of the sparking devices, only one of two test vehicles had exploded on cue and the fire had gone out almost immediately.

About two months after the story aired, a jury returned a $105 million damage judgment against the automaker in a wrongful death suit litigated around the truck's design flaws. The NBC story had not been introduced in the court case. A week after the jury returned the verdict, General Motors filed a libel suit against the network, charging—among other things—that the network had staged the concluding video. In an unprecedented move, anchors Jane Pauley and Stone Phillips read a three-minute retraction of the original *Dateline* story, admitting that the network had aired the concluding video even though it was staged. The NBC–General Motors confrontation proved to be the end for network news president Michael Gartner. He resigned less than a month later.

The NBC incident raises several questions. Is there a place for reenactment in the news? If so, when? How should such photos and video be labeled? The issues are not trivial, nor are they resolved. In a poll conducted by the National Press Photographers Association, the number-one ethical problem reported by photojournalists was set-up shots.

"Your work sounds interesting." Francesca said. She felt a need to keep neutral conversation going.

"It is. I like it a lot. I like the road, and I like making pictures."

She noticed he'd said "making" pictures. "You make pictures, not take them?"

"Yes. At least that's how I think of it. That's the difference between Sunday snapshooters and someone who does it for a living. When I'm finished with that bridge we saw today, it won't look quite like you expect. I'll have made it into something of my own, by lens choice, or camera angle, or general composition or all of those.

"I don't just take things as given; I try to make them into something that reflects my personal consciousness, my spirit. I try to find the poetry in the image."

The Bridges of Madison County
Robert James Waller

The questions surrounding fakery and staging speak to the purpose of news photography. Two possible purposes exist: the "mirror" and the "window" photograph (Szarkowski 1978).

The mirror photograph attempts to subjectively recreate the world in whatever image suits the photographer. Anything can be manipulated: light, proportion, setting, even subject. On the other hand, window photographs should be as objective a picture of reality as the medium will allow, untouched by the bias of the lens or the photographer.

Each type of photography has a function. A large percentage of the government-commissioned Dust Bowl–era photographs that have seared our memories of the Depression would fit into the mirror category. Photographers searched for settings, posed people, and shifted props to achieve the maximum effect.

On the other hand, the photos that show us the horrors of war and famine, and arouse public opinion, are windows, where the photographer captures the moment with no attempts to alter it. *The problem comes in the substitution of one for the other.* When a photograph mirrors a photographer's bias, yet is passed off as a window on reality, the viewer has been deceived.

Electronic Manipulation

Another major ethical issue in visual reporting is manipulation. Again, the history of photo manipulation is long. It has included such crude drawing-board techniques as scissors and paste, darkroom techniques such as "burning" and "dodging," and, more recently, airbrushing.

Today, technology allows increasingly sophisticated changes to be made to an image after it has been captured. In fact a recent study by the Rochester Institute of Technology found that one in ten color photographs in print have been altered (Brugioni 1999).

Technology has, in fact, made the word "photography"—literally "light writing"—obsolete, as a lighted reality no longer must exist in order for a "photograph" to be created. Photos and video are now what Reaves (1987) calls a "controlled liquid," capable of being manipulated into a seamless, yet totally unrealistic image. What this technology will ultimately lead to, Reaves claims, is an epistemological shift away from photography as irrefutable evidence of a story to photography as changeable story illustration. Eventually, she argues, as the public realizes that photographs can be—and frequently are—electronically altered, photos could lose their "moral authority." Tomlinson (1987) adds that technology could render photos nonadmissible as legal evidence once they lose the assumption of validity.

With an overwhelming amount of technology available for enhancing photos, editors must consider the ethical ramifications of their use. Once expensive technologies such as "morphing" one image into another, creating images directly from pixels with no real image required, or the digital insertion of existing images into new contexts are now common software applications on home computers. As a more sophisticated audience approaches the video or photography in the media, viewers will bring with them a skepticism not present in previous generations of consumers.

Most editors and photographers agree that manipulation or staging of news photos is generally more culpable than manipulation or staging of feature photos. The photo editors of a picture book such as *A Day in the Life of America* operate under a different set of audience expectations than the photo editors of the *New York Times.*

While the editors of *A Day in the Life of America* were criticized for a highly manipulated cover photo, their critics were misdirected. In the photo, a cowboy was moved closer to a tree, and the moon was moved and enlarged so the cowboy appeared as a silhouette against a full moon. The cover was not meant to be an accurate representation of reality. It was merely illustrative of the contents inside the book, which, according to its editors, contained no other manipulated photos. Similarly, advertising and entertainment operate under yet another set of imperatives.

The reasoning for this multiple standard is a presupposition that *while art may be manipulated, information may not* (Martin 1991). Such a flexible standard would be allowed under a categorical imperative as a permissible act, provided that:

• the photographer's intent is to merely make the photo more aesthetically pleasing and not to deceive; *and*
• the intended audience recognizes the difference; *or*
• the difference does not make audience members think or act in a manner in which they might not otherwise have thought or acted.

Selective Editing

Another ethical question centers on the video editing process: whether editing itself renders a story untrue or unfair. While this complaint is not new to television, the charges leveled against video editing are more vociferous, since editing for time considerations is a much more noticeable constraint than editing for space. Scenes aired out of sequence, answers dubbed behind questions that were not originally asked, and a preponderance of one view dominating the final cut at the expense of another view are some of the most frequently cited instances of "selective editing."

Actually, the term "selective editing" is redundant. *All* editing is selective. The issue is who does the selecting, and what predispositions they bring to the process. Some observers have noted that a dual standard is emerging between words and photos. A strange ethical dichotomy has long existed in the business of creating and processing print news and the photos that accompany it. The writer is allowed to reorder facts and rearrange details into an inverted-pyramid story on the rationale that the reader wants the most important facts taken out of sequence, and even out of context, and placed first in the story for more efficient reading. The result is praised as good writing and is taught in every journalism program.

However, should a photographer attempt to do the same thing with a camera—rearrange reality to make a more interesting photo or videotape—the result is called "staged." Our unwillingness to allow visual journalists the same conventions as print journalists says something fundamental about the role of visuals in the news. Media tradition says that while the truth in a print story about an explosion can contain only the highlights, the truth of a photo about the same explosion should be kept in context.

Such an analogy to print is important. When a writer edits, the result is called focusing, and it is applauded. When a photographer or video editor does the same thing, he or she is open to accusations of distortion. That is because we evaluate news photos according to print standards: linear and logical. Yet video and photographs are neither. They have a quality Marshall McLuhan called "allatonceness" that we are not quite comfortable with as a technology. Just what the photographer can do with the visual truth the camera uncovers is still a topic of debate.

Some photographers argue that to take away the possibilities that computer technology allows is to put them at a disadvantage in trying to tell a story visually. Should a photographer attempt to rearrange reality to make a more interesting photo or piece of film, the photograph is denigrated as "staged." And if a computer is used to correct focus or remove distractions, the photograph is derided as being "manipulated." In either case, the photographer could face sanctions.

However, as long as readers hold the view that "Seeing is believing," that view—whether based in reality or not—becomes a promise between the media and their audience that photographers and videographers should be hesitant to break. While many photojournalists argue that "Seeing is believing" should have never been a cultural truism (see Lester 1992), others argue that we must work within our readers' or viewers' predispositions about the truth of what they see. Steve Larson, director of photography for *U.S. News & World Report,* summarized this viewer-based rationale:

> The photo is a record of a moment in time. We're on shaky ground when we start changing that. We must maintain this pact. Catching a moment in time has history. When you look at a Matthew Brady photo there is that sense "this really happened." I believe strongly that's where photography draws its power. (Reaves 1991, 181)

Eyewash

Another ethical issue in photojournalism is the controversial use of stock photos or file footage to illustrate news stories. Such "eyewash" is used regardless of the context of the original photograph and sometimes without the consent of the subject (Tomlinson 1987).

For instance, an article on compulsive gamblers might show a woman enjoying herself on a sunny afternoon at the races. While her action is taking place in public view, she might or might not be a victim of the syndrome addressed in the article, although the casual reader might infer that she is, indeed, a compulsive gambler. In this context, the photo is serving the purpose of eyewash, decoration for a story that bears no genuine relationship to it.

Eyewash has had a brief history in the courts. A Washington, D.C., television station used a tight shot on a pedestrian facing the camera, chosen at random, to illustrate the "twenty million Americans who have herpes." The court ruled that the combination of the film and the commentary was sufficient to support an inference that the plaintiff was a victim of herpes, which she contended was not true.

However, not all plaintiffs are successful. One young couple photographed in a public embrace in the Los Angeles Farmer's Market later saw their private moment published in Harper's Bazaar illustrating an article entitled "Love Makes the World Go 'Round." The California Supreme Court noted that the couple had "waived their right of privacy" by their voluntary actions and said that publication of the photograph merely extended and increased the public who could view the plaintiffs in their romantic pose.

With the rulings of the courts ambiguous on the matter of eyewash, the media have created divergent policies to cover the issue. Some newspapers and television stations, for instance, will use no picture not directly related to the story. Others limit the use of file or stock footage to that which is clearly labeled. Others limit the shooting of eyewash only by insisting that it occur in public view.

The issue is exacerbated by the voracious appetite that both television and the print media have for visuals. Virtually all surveys have shown that the presence of a photo adds to the number of readers for a newspaper story, while television insists that viewers will watch "talking heads" for only a few seconds before diverting their attention elsewhere. The answer to the question "Have you got art?" often means the difference in running or killing a story. At other times, good visuals can get a story in the coveted first slot on the nightly news or the front page of the newspaper.

Given the importance of visuals to a story, it is not surprising that ethical lines blur. Coleman (1987) tells the story of his young son's falling off a horse and breaking his arm. A photographer friend took a picture of the boy "dirty, tear-stained, in great pain, slumped in a wheelchair with his arm in a makeshift sling" on his way to the operating room. About a year later, a textbook publisher ran across the photo and wanted it as an illustration for a book on child abuse. Coleman denied the request but added that the photo could have run with little or no repercussion if he had not been easily available for the publisher to ask. Had that happened, the public would have been deceived by a photograph of a boy who had been a victim of nothing more than a childhood accident.

Conclusion

Visual ethics is emotionally charged and constantly changing with new technology. *What this means is that the consumer of news photography is being presented with a product that is sometimes too raw to be palatable and sometimes too polished to be believable.*

The problem lies in the nature of the photojournalist's job. On a day-to-day basis, photography can be a mundane and poor-paying job. When an opportunity for a gripping photo does arise, like word that police are searching for a drowning victim, the desire to break out of the daily grind can lead to one of the extremes: a photo that is too raw with emotion or a photo that is worked over electronically until it bears little resemblance to reality.

Photojournalists should operate under this version of Kant's categorical imperative: *Don't deceive an audience that expects your pictures to be an accurate representation of a particular quality of reality.* Fortunately, only a small percentage of photos offend, and only a small percentage of photos are staged or electronically manipulated. However, photographers are dealing with a trust that readers and viewers have placed in them. If that trust is betrayed, it will be slow to return.

Suggested Readings

Berger, Arthur Asa. 1989. *Seeing is believing.* Mountain View, Cal.: Mayfield Publishing Co.

Berger, John. 1980. *About looking.* New York: Pantheon Books.

Journal of mass media ethics. 1987, Spring–Summer. Special issue on photojournalism.

Lester, Paul. 1991. *Photojournalism: An ethical approach.* Hillsdale, N.J.: Lawrence Erlbaum Associates.

_____. 1996. *Images that injure.* Westport, Conn.: Greenwoood Press.

CHAPTER IX CASES

CASE IX-A
Raid, Reunion, or Neutral Coverage? The Elián González Story

PAUL MARTIN LESTER
California State University–Fullerton

DENI ELLIOTT
University of Montana

Who can ever forget the saga of five-year-old Elián González snatched from certain death off the coast of Florida?

Certainly no one exposed to U.S. news media in the winter of 2000 could forget the story. From November 25, 1999, when Elián was rescued at sea until July 6, 2000, when his father was named a national hero in Cuba, the *Miami Herald* ran more than 600 stories that detailed Elián and the custody fight between estranged family members that ensued. The national news media were equally enthralled with the melodrama.

A pair of sports fishermen found Elián along with two adults in inner tubes off Fort Lauderdale. His mother, Elizabeth Brotons Rodriguez, took him on the dangerous journey without telling his father, Juan Miguel González. She and ten others drowned in the attempt to reach the United States.

Elián soon became a symbol in the minds of Miami relatives and others wanting to show the repression of the Castro government in Cuba. Rather than follow the usual U.S. custom of sending the boy home to his father, a public legal battle commenced pitting the U.S. Justice Department and Attorney General Janet Reno, the Cuban government, Elián's father, and Elián's family and supporters in Miami against one other with each step reported in detail to and by eager news media. Marisleysis González, twenty-one, Elián's second cousin, typified the zealous nature of the family members when she said, "God wanted him here for freedom. And he's here and he will get it."

While the legal actions took place in various venues, the public relations efforts of the Miami-based family proceeded in a consistent fashion. Less than a month after being rescued, Elián toured the Disneyworld amusement park in Orlando with reporters and photographers invited along for the outing. And whether playing with friends from the neighborhood, going to school, or eating an ice cream cone, photographers took pictures and reporters wrote stories as the family allowed access.

After all the legal avenues had been exhausted, the family still refused to return the boy to his father, who was by then waiting for him in the United States. Early Saturday morning on April 22, armed U.S. Immigration and Naturalization Service (INS) agents rushed into the Miami caretakers' house and forcibly removed Elián so that he could be reunited with his father. Newspapers across the world printed images and stories on their Easter Sunday front pages.

214

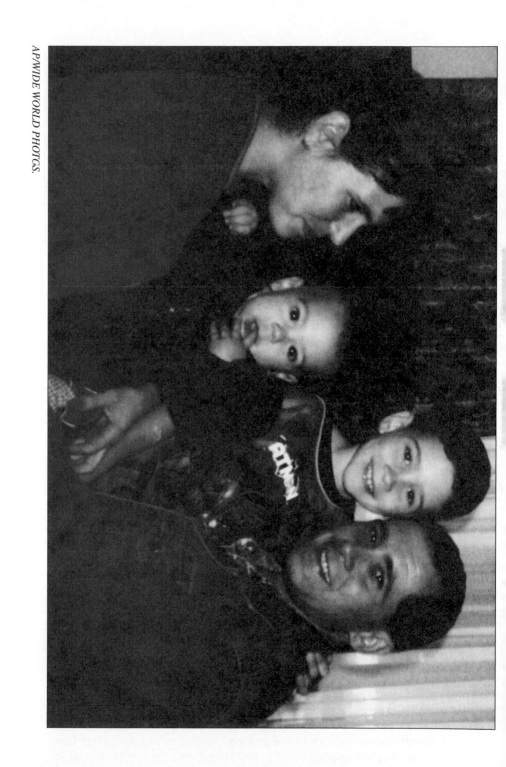

But the story didn't end there, for even though Elián was with his father and Cuban family outside Washington, D.C., what followed were more rounds of legal maneuvers by both sides to either keep Elián in the United States or allow him to return to Cuba. Meanwhile, Elián's father's lawyers started their own public relations campaign by allowing photographs of a happy Elián playing with his father or with schoolmates flown in especially from Cuba. Finally, at the end of June, all legal maneuvers were exhausted and Elián and his family returned to Cuba. Within a week, President Fidel Castro decorated Elián's father as a Cuban national hero.

What captivated and summed up the story for most newspaper readers was the early morning raid on the Little Havana house to take Elián from his Miami family. Although at least ten photographers were at the scene, Alan Diaz's striking series of images from inside the house were the most obvious pictures to be considered by editors. Diaz, a freelance photographer working for the Associated Press (AP) (he now works full-time for the AP) was born in New York City but lived in Cuba for many years and knew the Cuban culture and language. He befriended the family by covering the story every day from its beginning. When the early morning raid occurred, he was the only photographer let into the house to take the now famous pictures.

A look at twenty newspaper front pages revealed three basic editorial approaches that influenced picture, graphic design, and headline decisions. Editors either emphasized the drama of the early morning raid, focused on the emotional story of a father reunited with his son, or tried to show both stories. Which pictures were selected, how those images were displayed on a page, and what headlines accompanied the story all combined to give the impression to some readers that the publication was either anti-Castro, pro-Castro, or neutral.

All twenty newspapers used somewhere in that day's edition the striking image by Diaz of an INS agent holding an automatic rifle pointed toward a terrified Elián in the closet of his family's home. Another popular picture choice was a happy Elián reunited with his father. Other images included those taken outside the home as a woman agent ran with Elián to a waiting van, people protesting in the streets, distraught Miami family members, and government officials explaining their actions to the public.

Headlines also demonstrated three approaches by editors. A few newspapers emphasized the raid in their headlines (we use uppercase and lowercase to simulate the actual headlines): "Armed agents seize weeping Cuban boy in night-time raid." "Agents seize Elián by force." "QUE VERGUENZA! (HOW SHAMEFUL!)." Some papers featured the reunion: "Elián back in arms of Dad." "Raid Reunites Elián and Father." "REUNITED." Several newspapers tried to tell both sides of the story in their headlines: "CUBAN BOY SEIZED BY U.S. AGENTS AND REUNITED WITH HIS FATHER." "Raid Reunites Elián and Father." "RAID . . . REUNION."

An editor had to decide which pictures to use, how the pictures were presented on the front page, and what headlines to include for the emotionally driven and highly politicized story. The decision became a tricky balancing act with an editor knowing that someone on one side of the affair or the other would ultimately criticize any decision.

Note: To read more details about this case and to view twenty newspaper front-page layouts and the photographs taken by Alan Diaz during the raid (or rescue, depending on your point of view), see "Judging Elián from raid to reunion: Words and pictures combine to tell different stories," Paul Martin Lester, *News Photographer,* July 2000, pp. 28–35.

Micro Issues:

1. Is the Elián story one that warranted coverage on a daily basis?
2. As an editor, do you use only the famous picture of an anonymous INS agent pointing a 9 mm MP5 submachine gun toward Elián and a family friend? Do you feature only the image of a tranquil father and son reunited again? Does running either photo alone indicate a bias toward either Attorney General Janet Reno or Cuban President Castro?

Mid-range Issues:

1. Can too much coverage inflame already incensed readers and cause a further split among various cultural groups within a community?
2. What can news personnel do if they suspect that those involved with a story are manipulating the press in order to gain publicity?
3. What do you believe would be an ethical layout of the photos? Compare your decision to a copy of your nearest metropolitan newspaper, if the archived front page is available.

Macro Issues:

1. Should the news always be objective, or should an organization take a side in a controversial issue?
2. Can a reporter's credibility be legitimately questioned if she becomes personally involved with the subjects of a story?

CASE IX-B
Problem Photos and Public Outcry
JON ROOSENRAAD
University of Florida

Campus police at the University of Florida were called on a Saturday to a dorm to investigate "a large amount of blood on the floor of a women's bathroom," according to police reports. They determined that the blood "appeared to have been from a pregnancy miscarriage" and began searching the dorm area. Some time later a police investigator searching through a trash dumpster behind the dorm found bloody towels, plastic gloves, and a large plastic bag containing more towels and the body of a six- to seven-pound female infant.

Police discovered no pulse. Rigor mortis had set in. After removing the body from the bag, the police briefly placed the body on a towel on the ground next to the dumpster. The photographer for the student paper, the *Independent Florida Alligator,* arrived at this time and photographed the body and dumpster.

Later on Saturday, the eighteen-year-old mother was found in her dorm bed and taken to the university's hospital. The hospital exam revealed "placenta parts and the umbilical cord in her" and she was released later in good health. A local obstetrician contacted about the case said that judging by the size of the infant, it was likely a miscarriage and not an abortion. The infant was determined to be about seven months developed.

The story began on the front page of the Monday issue, across the bottom of the page, under the headline "UF police investigate baby's death at dorm." It jumped inside to page three and was accompanied by the photo.

It was a dramatic photo, contrasting two well-dressed detectives and one uniformed policeman with the naked body and contrasting the fragile human form with the harsh metal dumpster filled with pizza and liquor boxes. The photo was played seven by five inches.

The story was well-written and the photo dramatic but likely offensive to many—potentially so offensive that the newspaper's staff debated most of Sunday about how to use it. The editor decided to run it, but in an unusual move she wrote an editor's column explaining why that appeared on the opinion page of the same issue. It showed a scene one might visualize in a ghetto but not on a college campus. It showed that supposedly sexually educated and sophisticated college students still need help. The editor wrote:

> *"Even with these legitimate reasons we did not run the picture on the front page. This is partially in response to our concern that we do not appear to be exploiting this picture to attract readers. . . . We also examined the photographer's negatives to see if there were any less graphic prints. . . . Is the message perceived by the reader worth the shock he or she experiences? After pondering what we feel is a very profound photo, we decided there is. This was a desperate act in an area of society where it is not expected. The picture shows it."*

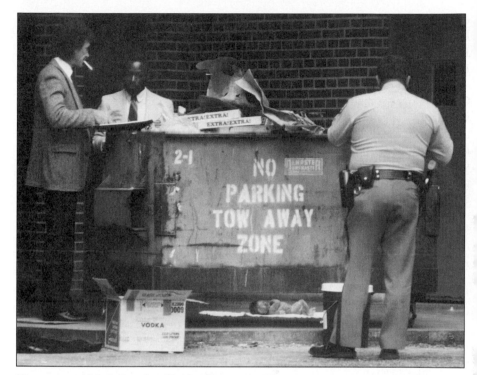

Photo courtesy of the Independent Florida Alligator. *Used by permission.*

The local daily covered the story Monday in a police brief. No photo ran.

It was determined that the body was from a miscarriage. The woman involved left school. The campus paper got several letters critiquing its coverage of the story. Many chose to criticize the editors for running the photo, while some praised the staff for pointing out the problem and for listing places on campus where sex and pregnancy counseling was available. Some letters did both.

An example of some of the outrage over the running of the photo by the *Alligator* came from a female student who called the coverage "the most unnecessary, tactless piece of journalism I've ever encountered." Another letter from a male student called the photo "in poor taste and extremely insensitive." The writer added, "There are times when good, sound judgment must override 'hot' copy."

Perhaps the most pointed comment came from a female writer who added twenty-four other names to her letter. The letter stated that "the incident *could* have been used to remind people that they need to take responsibility for their own sexuality. The story *could* have been used as a painful reminder that there are many uneducated, naïve people out there who need help. But, unfortunately, the *Alligator* chose to sensationalize the story with a picture, completely nullifying any lesson whatsoever that might have been learned."

Micro Issues:

1. Should the photographer have taken the picture?
2. Is this a legitimate story, and if so, does it belong on page one?
3. If this was the only photo available, did the paper then have to run it?
4. Various letters to the editor called the photo "unnecessary," "tactless," and "insensitive." What would you say to those charges if you were on the staff?

Mid-range Issues:

1. Does running the photo inside lessen any criticism of poor taste? Did its placement mitigate any ethical criticism?
2. If the staff was so unsure, was the editor correct in writing a same-day rationale for its publication?
3. Critique the reasoning stated by the editor in running the photo. What moral philosophy, if any, would lead one to agree with the action?

Macro Issues:

1. Should a paper play a story and photo like this to crusade about a problem?
2. Is the perceived social value of such a picture worth more than the shock and criticism?
3. Was the writer correct in her assessment that the shock of the photo negated any good that might have been done by the story?
4. Should a campus newspaper have a different standard—of taste, play, news value—than a "regular" daily?

ACADEMIC EVALUATION, AWARDS AND STUDENT STATUS

DEAN'S LIST

At the end of each academic year, students in good standing whose records demonstrate outstanding academic performance for that year are recommended for placement on the New College Dean's List.

In general, this honor is either on the basis of GPA or on the basis of judgment if the student has a substantial number of Pass/Fail credits or has "restrictions on registration." These are the criteria for placement on the Dean's List:

Grade-Point Average

Recommendation will be made for students with at least 50 percent, and at least 16, of the year's completed credits for letter grades; without "restrictions on registration"; and with a GPA of at least 3.3 for the Freshman Year and 3.4 thereafter. This University minimum required GPA is raised by an increment of .01 for each Pass/Fail credit a student has earned up to a maximum GPA of 3.45 for the Freshman Year and 3.56 thereafter. Unresolved Inc. grades may inhibit a student's placement on the Dean's List.

Judgmental Recommendation

Judgmental recommendation will be made for students with less than 50 percent, or fewer than 16, of the year's completed credits for letter grades, and for students with "re-..."

ACADEMIC EVALUATION, AWARDS AND STUDENT STATUS

5. Students will be on academic probation as long as their cumulative grade-point average remains below 2.0 and is above the University's minimum retention standards. They will continue to be subject to all the requirements of students on academic probation.

6. After completing 88 semester hours, students whose cumulative grade-point average is below 2.0 for two subsequent consecutive regular semesters will be dismissed from the University. Students who have been dropped may appeal to the Academic Records Committee only through the Office of University Advisement.

7. A full-time student on academic probation may carry no more than 15 semester hours (16 if the student is taking one or more four-credit courses). A part-time student on academic probation may carry no more than 6 semester hours (7 if the student is taking a 4-credit course, or 8 if the student is enrolled in New College).

8. Students on academic probation may not elect an optional Pass/D+/D/Fail grade.

9. When appropriate, students admitted to the University through a special academic program will be exempted from these probation criteria until they are released from the program.

Restrictions on Registration

Any student may be prevented by the Dean of New College from registering for more than a fixed amount of credits if two or more PR's (8 s.h.) are outstanding in a given Session; or if it is felt that the amount of the student's course work should be limited in the student's own interest; or if the student is not satisfying graduation requirements in a timely and orderly manner.

Timely and Orderly Satisfaction of College and Area Graduation Requirements

Students must satisfy both College and Area Graduation Requirements in a timely and orderly manner. Students failing to do so are subject to dismissal from the College and the University or to a change in student status from "good academic standing" to "academic probation" or "restrictions on registration."

Students placed on academic probation or subject to dismissal from the College and/or the University will be informed in writing of their status and of the procedure for appeal of that status.

23

nominated for judgmental recommendation by themselves, their instructors or their advisors. They may decline nomination or placement. Unresolved Inc. grades may inhibit a student's placement on the Dean's List.

CASE IX-C
Faking Photos: Is It Ever Justified?
JAMES VAN METER
Freelance Photographer, Bellingham, Washington

Chris Jones, a reporter with a large, metropolitan daily newspaper, is told by a source that a computer software corporation is considering his city as a plant site. Jones calls to confirm the tip, and the corporation's public relations representative reads him the following statement:

> *Our corporation is interested in purchasing the two-block area between Third and Maple Streets on Washington Avenue. The corporation believes the site would be to its advantage, with easy access from the interstate and the airport and adequate parking space. The plant would produce software material and offer jobs to trained applicants. We are preparing to make a more than substantial offer to the landowner, Joe Sullivan. The corporation hopes to begin production on the plant three months from now, in March.*

Jones notes in his story that the proposed site, commonly known as skid row, houses several run-down hotels, bars, and a homeless shelter.

One week later, Jones talks to Sullivan and the corporate representative again. He learns an offer was made to purchase the land, and although Sullivan is eager to accept, he will wait three days to give his response.

Jones's city editor makes a photo assignment, asking for shots of the homeless people who live in the two blocks. The city editor tells veteran photographer Steve Stone he needs strong, emotional pictures to run with a story about how the homeless shelter cannot afford to move to another location. The city editor also wants the photographs to run before Sullivan responds to the corporation's offer.

Stone spends an entire day walking up and down Washington Avenue, trying to get close enough to the people sleeping and eating on the streets. Yet they either cover their faces, walk away, or plead with him not to take their pictures.

During the morning of the second day, Stone manages to take some photographs, but after he develops them he discovers that his images did not capture the pain he felt when seeing firsthand how these people struggle to survive.

Under deadline pressure, Stone calls some of his friends and asks them to pose for him as homeless people. He takes his friends, dressed in torn clothes with black greasepaint smeared on their faces, into an alley near, but not on, skid row. Stone takes some created photographs and turns them into his editor minutes before deadline.

The city editor is so impressed with Stone's work that he decides to run one of the photographs on the front page the next day, with photo essays on two inside pages.

The day the photographs are printed, both the newspaper and the computer software corporation are flooded with phone calls protesting the plant site. Later that day, the corporate executives hold a press conference, saying they believe it would be best to look into other plant locations in the city.

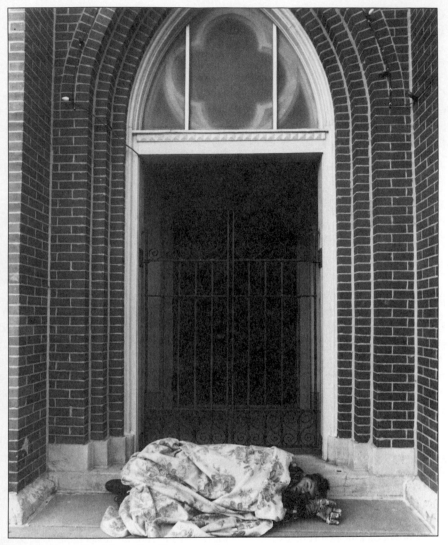

Photo by James Van Meter. Used by permission.

Is it likely that such deception would work? Examine closely the photo of the man sleeping in the doorway of the church building that accompanies this case. He is a college student who volunteered to pose for the photographer. He is neither poor nor homeless.

Micro Issues:

1. Should Stone have told his editor that he was having problems getting the right photographs before he set up the shots?

2. If you were Stone, would you have gone ahead and taken pictures of the homeless people despite their protests?
3. After letting the editors see the photographs, should Stone have told them how he took the photographs? Justify your answer.
4. What is the editor's obligation in framing the assignment?

Mid-range Issues:

1. Because the photographs were an obvious factor in the corporation's decision to find another location for the plant, did the end justify the means?
2. Do you think the photographer allowed his personal feelings about the issue of the homeless to interfere with his professional judgment?
3. Does the fact that the photos closely mirrored reality make a difference in whether the deception was ethically justified?
4. What do you see as the difference between asking a friend to help you fake the photo and directing a cooperative homeless person to pose for you? Is one any more truthful than the other?
5. What is the distinction between the faked photo and a print journalist who writes about a composite character?

Macro Issues:

1. Does a photographer create a pseudo-event just by showing up with his camera?
2. Should a news photographer voice his personal opinion through his photographs? Explain your answer.
3. In this case, the photographer recreated a likely news scenario—a homeless man lying in a church entry. In 1992, NBC's *Dateline* recreated a fiery truck collision on camera by rigging the truck with incendiary devices before it was rammed by another vehicle. It is a fact that some homeless people sleep in doorways and some trucks explode on impact. Is there a difference in NBC's efforts to ensure good video of a crash and this photographer's efforts to ensure good photos of the homeless? If so, what are the differences? Are both equally culpable activities?

CASE IX-D
"Above the Fold": Balancing Newsworthy Photos
with Community Standards
JIM GODBOLD, MANAGING EDITOR
JANNELLE HARTMAN, REPORTER
Eugene Register–Guard, Eugene, Oregon

Author's Note: On November 10, 1993, a nightmare unfolded in Springfield, Oregon, a quiet town adjoining the university community of Eugene, as Alan McGuire held his two-year-old daughter, Shelby, hostage in their house. By the end of the standoff both were dead and the media had captured some horrific photos.

Seven children had died as a result of child abuse in Lane County, Oregon, in the twenty months prior to that day and the media had just witnessed the eighth. Jim Godbold was the assistant managing editor of the Eugene Register–Guard at the time. The remarks below are from an interview with him months after the event.

Godbold: The call came over the police scanner shortly after noon. We responded to a hostage situation, a man holding someone at knife point in a Springfield neighborhood. We knew it was probably 20 minutes from the *Register–Guard* in the best of possible circumstances so we really scrambled. Photographer Andy Nelson and police reporter Jannelle Hartman went as fast as they could to the area.

We got there when the police were trying to set up a perimeter to get people away from the area. It was real pandemonium right when Andy arrived. The situation didn't unfold for more than a few minutes before there was a burst of flame inside the house that caught the attention of the police officers, and they immediately made the decision that they were going to have to go inside.

A group of officers ran at the door, and then all of a sudden Alan McGuire, the man who was in the house, came hurtling through the front window on fire. I am not even sure if police officers knew how many people were in the house at the time. His wife had escaped from the home. She had been held at knife point and bound, and she had somehow gotten out and she let police know that their two-year-old daughter, Shelby McGuire, was in the house.

Shelby was a hostage and being held at knife point. Police saw her and tried to set up a telephone line so they could negotiate with McGuire, but the events unfolded rapidly, and after Alan McGuire jumped through the front window police broke down the door. Two officers hauled McGuire's flaming body to the ground and tried to douse the flames with a garden hose. Inside the house one of the officers saw Shelby McGuire sitting upright on the couch. She had a plastic grocery produce bag over her head, and it apparently had been duct-taped in some fashion, maybe around the neck.

They immediately tore the bag away. A detective picked Shelby up and sprinted out of the house with her. It was at that moment that Andy Nelson snapped his picture of one of the officers with Shelby's body in his arms, running out, two other officers standing on the side of the doorstep, another officer with a hose near

Photo courtesy of the Eugene Register–Guard. *Used by permission.*

Alan McGuire, and Alan lying on the ground. The flame's now out, but the charred and still smoking body was present in the viewfinder as Andy snapped the picture.

At that moment the officer with Shelby McGuire, the two-year-old, began mouth-to-mouth resuscitation on the front lawn. Andy subsequently took a photograph of that. Then they rushed both Alan and Shelby McGuire to the hospital. We did not know Shelby's condition. The police didn't respond about whether she was able to be resuscitated.

We have a standing policy at the newspaper that as a general rule we don't run photographs of dead bodies of children. That immediately triggered the kind of review that we would go through to determine where this particular incident was going to stand up on our policy, whether or not anyone was going to argue for publication or against publication.

We began to talk about the policy and the potential community reaction that we might face. The discussion was pretty brief. The photo was so compelling and the

Photo courtesy of the Eugene Register–Guard. *Used by permission.*

situation that it sprang from so horrifying that we began looking at the photograph and saying, "Well, I don't know, but, look at what the photo has captured."

"People are going to be upset."

"This is potentially a photograph of a dead two-year-old child."

"Look at the concern and the expression on the police officers' faces. This is an example of what they deal with day in and day out. They are up against this kind of domestic violence hostage situation and people don't realize that."

So, the debate was intense, and yet pretty short. We prepared a selection of pictures, and we brought those to the then-managing editor Patrick Yak and made the case that this is going to be a tough photograph for us to run. This is going to be one that we are going to have to be prepared to defend. But we believe it's that kind of exception to the rule that we look for.

The public response to the publication of the Shelby McGuire photograph was unprecedented in my twenty-two years in journalism and unprecedented at this newspaper. I have not come across a case, having been shown a number of them subsequently, that is of the magnitude per capita of reader response to a single photographic image. We received on the order of 450 telephone calls that began the moment people got the newspaper, which started at 6:00 A.M. First they came into our circulation department. The circulation department switchboard became overloaded and gave them the main newsroom switchboard, which didn't open until 7:30. At 7:30 when they threw the switch, all 20 of our incoming phone lines lit up, and the calls began to roll over into a holding pattern that had never been utilized by our switchboard before.

I was called at home by Al Gimmell, the corporate controller, who said, "We are inundated with telephone calls. We need some help." So I immediately came in to try to handle telephone calls and I tried to find the time in between phone calls to call other editors in but the calls were coming so rapidly that every time I hung up it rang again. When I picked up my voice mail messages, I had thirty-one unanswered messages, and that was probably 7:45 in the morning.

The range of responses weren't monolithic, except in their anger. But the anger came from different places. For some people the anger came from a belief that we had simply stooped to a tremendously sensational graphic crime picture trying to sell newspapers. For others the anger came from the terrible sense of violation that the surviving mother and brother of Shelby McGuire would have to wake up to the morning after their ordeal and see this on the front page of the hometown newspaper.

Another component argued that this was wholly inappropriate for the kind of newspaper the *Register–Guard* has been and continues to be. That five-year-olds and six-year-olds were sharing the newspaper at the breakfast table and parents were finding themselves in a position of having to explain this horrifying incident and having the question "How is the little girl?" asked again. And there was also a range of response from people who were themselves victims of domestic violence or spouses of victims or had family members who were involved in it. For them it was a combination of anger and pain.

I spoke with literally dozens of people through tears. It was an emotional response that was overwhelming and people were extremely upset by the picture. Most asked the question "Why? I need to understand why the newspaper published this picture."

We were really, I think, at a loss initially to respond to that question. I think a lot of that had to do with being in a very real sense out of touch with a substantial number of readers. The kind of reaction that we had was not anticipated by anyone in the news department.

If we were presented with a similar situation and a similar photograph today, we would absolutely not do it the way that we did it in the Shelby McGuire case. Thousands of our readers have defined for us a boundary in this community and for this newspaper that I don't think until we began to see it materialize we had any sense of exactly where it was.

Micro Issues:

1. Look at the photos that accompany this text. The photo of the officer carrying out Shelby McGuire ran in full color above the fold, two-thirds of the page wide and six inches tall. Does a photo of that size oversensationalize the story?
2. The photo of Sgt. Swenson's attempts to resuscitate Shelby ran below the fold in a small two-column photo. Why do you think the decision was made to run this photo smaller and lower?

Mid-range Issues:

1. Does the fact that Shelby died influence your decision on whether to run the photos? If so, in what way?
2. Does the fact that at least one television station and the local Springfield newspaper were there with photographers influence your decision to run the photos? If so, in what way?
3. Does the fact that seven other children had died in Lane County in less than two years affect your decision to run the photos? If so, in what way?
4. The biweekly *Springfield News* chose to run a front-page photo of Alan McGuire falling out of the front window of his home, his badly burned flesh still in flames. However, they covered the front page with a wrapper that read "Caution to Readers" and explained the content of the stories and photos underneath the wrapper. Critique that approach to handling the story.
5. A local television station showed a few seconds of the scene described above after warning viewers of the violent nature of the video that followed. The station got fewer than twenty complaints. How do you explain the vast difference in the reaction to the broadcast and print photos?

Macro Issues:

1. What are the privacy rights of:
   a.   Shelby McGuire?
   b.   Shelby McGuire's mother and four-year-old brother?
   c.   Sgt. Swenson?
2. Critique the argument that these photos should be shown because they illustrate the type of tragedy that law enforcement officers are often called upon to handle.
3. Critique the argument that these photos should be shown because they illustrate the horror of domestic violence.
4. Critique the statement that "If we were presented with a similar situation and a similar photograph today, we would absolutely not do it the way that we did it in the Shelby McGuire case." In your opinion is that based on sensitivity to reader concern or caving in to reader pressure?

CASE IX-E
Horror in Soweto
SUE O'BRIEN
The Denver Post

On September 15, 1990, freelance photographer Gregory Marinovich documented the killing, by a mob of African National Congress supporters, of a man they believed to be a Zulu spy.

Marinovich and Associated Press reporter Tom Cohen spotted the man being led from a Soweto, South Africa, train-station platform by a group armed with machetes and crude spears. Marinovich and Cohen continued to witness and report as the man was stoned, bludgeoned, stabbed, doused with gasoline, and set afire.

It was one of 800 deaths in two months of black factional fighting as rival organizations vied for influence in the declining days of apartheid.

The graphic photos stirred intense debate among editors. In one, the victim, conscious but stoic, lies on his back as a grinning attacker poises to plunge a knife into his forehead. In the final photo of the series, the victim crouches, engulfed in fire.

As the series was transmitted, several member editors called up to question what the photographer was doing at the scene—could he in any way have stopped the attack? In response, an advisory went out on the photo wire, saying Marinovich had

AP/WIDE WORLD PHOTOS.

AP/WIDE WORLD PHOTOS.

tried to intervene and then, when told to stop taking pictures, had told mob leaders he would stop shooting only when they "stopped hurting that man."

Decisions on what to do with the photos varied across the country, according to a survey. If any pattern emerged, it was that newspapers in competitive markets such as Denver, Minneapolis–St. Paul, and New York were more likely to go with the harsh graphics.

The burning photo was the most widely used, the stabbing the least. Several editors said they specifically rejected the stabbing as too extreme. "It showed violence and animalistic hatred," said Roman Lyskowski, graphics editor for the *Miami Herald*. Another editor, who agreed that the stabbing was much more disturbing than the burning, said he recalled immolation pictures from the Vietnam era. "That's not as unusual an image as that knife sticking right out of the skull."

When the Soweto series cleared at the *Miami Herald,* the burning photo was sent to Executive Editor Janet Chusmir's home for her approval. At her direction, the immolation picture ran on the front page, but below the fold and in black and white. The detail revealed in color reproduction, Chusmir and her editors agreed, was too graphic.

At the *Los Angeles Times* and *Dallas Morning News,* however, the burning photo ran above the front-page fold—and in color.

The *St. Paul Pioneer Press* chose the stabbing for front-page color. "I look at the moment that the photo freezes on film," said News Editor Joe Sevick. "Rarely do you see a photo where a knife is about to go into somebody." The photo ran in color on the *Pioneer Press* front page, accompanied by the story Cohen had written on the attack and a longer story on the South African government's attempt, announced that day, to crack down on black-on-black violence.

In Denver, at the *Rocky Mountain News,* Managing Editor Mike Madigan wanted to run a comprehensive package on the Soweto story. The tabloid's only open page was deep in the paper, but a page-three box referred readers to the story with a warning the photos were "horrific and disturbing." Inside, stories on the attack and government crackdown and an editor's note on Marinovich's intervention accompanied three photos: the victim being led away from the train station, the stabbing, and the burning.

Most papers that ran the more challenging photos involved top management in the decision. Frequently, top editors were contacted by telephone, or came in from home, to give the photos a final go-ahead.

In most newsrooms, the burning or stabbing photos made it to the news desk for approval or rejection. But there, they sometimes were killed abruptly. "The editors at that point said no," one picture editor reported. "They would not take the heat."

Several editors deferred to the so-called "breakfast test." "The question is 'Which of those photos would help tell the story without ruining everyone's breakfast?'" asked Rod Deckert, managing editor of the *Albuquerque Journal.* One editor said his paper is especially likely to deemphasize disturbing material in the Sunday paper, which children often read with their parents.

But many editors who rejected the more brutal pictures said the "breakfast test" is irrelevant. "If you're putting out a paper in New York and don't have something that's going to cause some discomfort over breakfast, then you're probably not putting out the full paper you should," said Jeff Jarvis, Sunday editor at the *New York Daily News.* "I don't think the breakfast test works for the nineties."

Others cited distance tests. Some newspapers, in deference to victims' families, are less likely to use death photos from within their own circulation areas. Another editor, however, said his paper is *less* likely to run violent photos unless they are local and have a "more immediate impact on our readership."

Newspapers also differed widely on how they packaged the Soweto story. Some accompanied a photo series with the Cohen and crackdown stories, and a note on Marinovich's intervention. Some ran a single photo, often the burning, with only a cutline and a brief reference to the train-station incident in the "crackdown" story. Two respected big-city dailies, which omitted any reference to the Soweto attack in their accompanying stories, ran cursory cutlines such as "Violence continues: A boy runs away as an ANC supporter clubs a Zulu foe who was beaten, stabbed and set ablaze."

Although forty-one papers used at least one of the Marinovich photos, only four—the *Charlotte Observer, Akron Beacon–Journal, Rocky Mountain News* (Denver), and *USA Today*—told the story of Marinovich's attempt to halt the attack.

Among collateral considerations at many news desks was the coverage of South African troubles that had gone before. At least one editor said the Soweto photos, which followed several other beating and killing photographs from South Africa that had been used earlier in the week, were "just too, too much."

With only three exceptions, editors said race did not figure in their considerations. One white editor said the fact that both attackers and victim were black deprived the series of clarity: "You don't have a sense of one side against another. You don't have a sense of right or wrong." Two editors who identified themselves as African-American, however, argued for aggressive use of the photos. Both work in communities with significant black populations. "I think black readers should be more informed about this," one said. "Across the board, black Americans don't realize what's going on with the black-on-black violence."

Front-page placement and the use of color frequently triggered reader objections, but the adequacy of cutline information and accompanying copy also appear significant. The *Albany Times Union* was flooded by phone protests and subscription cancellations. Two other papers perceiving significant reader unrest—the *Dallas Morning News* and *Los Angeles Times*—ran the burning photo in color on their front pages. But each of the three papers also ran the front-page photos with only cutline accompaniment, referring readers inside to the stories that placed the images in context.

In retrospect, *Rocky Mountain News's* Madigan said he was very pleased with the final Soweto package and readers' reaction to it. "It wasn't so much the idea that, 'Yeah, we ran these really horrific pictures and, boy, it knocked people's socks off.' I don't think that was the point. I think it was more the way we handled it," he said. "Just one word or the other can make a terrific difference in whether the public starts screaming 'sensationalize, sensationalize,' or takes it as a thoughtful, important piece of work, which is what we were after."

Micro Issues:

1. In all but the most important stories, would you support a ban on dead-body photos in your newspaper or newscast?
2. Some editors believe it is their ethical duty to avoid violating readers' sense of taste or compassion. Others argue that it is their duty to force society to face unpleasant truths, even if it means risking reader anger and rejection. Whose side would you support?
3. Many readers suspect that sensational photos are chosen to sell newspapers, or capture rating points, by appealing to morbid tastes. Do you believe they're right?

Mid-range Issues:

1. Editors sometimes justify running graphic photos by saying they can provide a "warning bell," alerting people to preventable dangers in society. What values might the Soweto photographs offer readers?
2. Is the desire to avoid offending readers an ethical consideration or a marketing consideration?
3. Is it appropriate to base editorial decisions on what readers are likely to be doing at home: to edit newspapers differently, for instance, if they are likely to

be read at the breakfast table, or present newscasts differently if they are to air during the dinner hour rather than later in the evening?

4. As an editor, would you be more likely to run a photograph of someone being murdered if the event happened in your own community, or if it happened thousands of miles away and none of your readers would be likely to know the victim or his family?

5. Is there ethical significance in:
   a. whether a violent photo is run in color or black and white, or
   b. whether it is run on the front page or on an inside page?

Macro Issues:

1. Is aesthetic, dramatic, or photographic value ever reason enough to run a picture, regardless of how intrusive it may be or how it may violate readers' sensitivities?

2. Is it your responsibility as an editor to find out if a photographer could have saved a life by intervening in a situation, rather than taking pictures of it? Is that information you need to share with your readers?

3. Is it your responsibility as an editor to find out if the presence of the camera at the scene in any way helped incite or distort an event? Is that information you need to share with your readers?

4. When dramatic photographs are printed, how important is it for readers or viewers to be told all the background of the story or situation?

CASE IX-F
Looking at Race and Sex: When Do Photographs Go Too Far?
BEVERLY HORVIT
University of Texas, Arlington

How much should newspaper editors worry about disturbing their readers with provocative or possibly shocking photographs? Photographs of lynchings or photographs of gay men on the verge of a kiss? Some argue that editors have a responsibility to present realities that some readers would rather ignore. Others say a photograph can be so offensive to some readers that it turns them away rather than drawing their interest.

Editors at the *Charlotte Observer* in North Carolina dealt with these issues twice in 2000. In both cases, top editors chose to replate the cover of the paper's Arts section because they felt—as did some pressmen—that the designers' use of photographs and other elements had gone too far. In both cases, editors felt the need to explain their decisions to their colleagues and the public.

The Arts section of the January 30, 2000, Sunday edition featured a story on a horrific collection of postcards gathered by James Allen of Atlanta. The postcards show painful images of lynchings, primarily in the South and primarily of young blacks between 1870 and 1960. The collection, based at Emory University in Atlanta, was the focus of the new book *Without Sanctuary: Lynching Photography in America* (Twin Palm Publishers, 2000). Some of the postcards had been found in family scrapbooks as some Caucasians had saved the postcards as mementos of the events. Realizing that one person would send another a postcard depicting a lynching he or she had witnessed is sobering. Reading the eloquent report of Roberta Smith of the *New York Times* on the exhibit is enlightening. Seeing the postcards is profoundly disturbing.

Smith's report was published in the *New York Times* on January 13, 2000, and the *Observer* republished it about two weeks later. The article was accompanied by a small photograph of a postcard showing the lynching of a sixteen-year-old African-American. The section's design had been changed. That same day, *Observer* editor Jennie Buckner told readers in a column that three of her editors had approved running the photograph of the 1920 lynching as the dominant image on the Arts cover. Arts and Entertainment Editor Vinny Kuntz called the collection photos revelatory. "My hope is that the photo and story provoke each of us to look at ourselves, our past, our present, our future," Kuntz told readers.

Mary C. Curtis, features editor and columnist, noted that some of the lynchings shown in the postcards occurred in North Carolina. Her justification for running the photos: "Every day there are letters to the editor about the history and heritage of the South. What is the meaning of the Confederate flag? Is the past ever past? Was slavery really that bad? Why are blacks and whites so upset? One look at the picture, and you get some answers. You also get a warning. This is what human beings are capable of doing to one another. This cannot ever happen again."

The third editor, then-Deputy Features Editor Jean Marie Brown, now at the *Fort Worth Star–Telegram,* viewed the photographs as part of her history both as an

American and as an African-American. "In many ways, the era of lynchings was an American holocaust. I felt and still believe those images need to be seen so the nation can begin to comprehend the horrors and terror that one group of citizens inflicted on another," Brown told readers.

An image was seen by *Charlotte Observer* readers, but the image they saw was not nearly as dominant as that initially approved by Brown, Kuntz, and Curtis. As the Arts section rolled off the press as part of the *Observer's* preprint for its Sunday edition, some pressmen were stunned by the photograph and offended. Buckner told readers that she then showed *Observer* Publisher Peter Ridder one of those early copies. "He felt that the large photo on the front was so shocking that readers would never get past their revulsion to consider the picture's message—or even read the story," Buckner said in her column.

Ridder did agree with the journalists, though, that the photograph should be published. Ultimately, an editor's note warned readers that a graphic photograph accompanied the article's jump and the photograph of the postcard ran inside at less than two columns wide and about four inches deep. "With a magnifying glass, see the look on the littlest white boy's face in the photo on 2F as 16-year-old Lige Daniels dangles in 1920," Kuntz told readers. "What was the little white boy thinking? What kind of man did he grow to be? What are his kids like? And think, too, about what kind of world we want our children to inherit."

Buckner acknowledged in her column that not everyone, not even everyone in the newsroom, agrees the photograph should have been published at all. "Some argue that pictures of dead bodies simply don't belong in newspapers. Some think pictures like this further divide people," she said.

Just as the *Charlotte Observer* began the year 2000 with a dispute over the use of photography, so did the newspaper end the year. In December, the issue was not racism and the ugly history of lynchings, but rather homosexuality. How intimate a photograph would the *Observer's* largely conservative, Southern readership be comfortable, or even tolerate, seeing? The subject was Showtime's new series, *Queer as Folk*, which the *New York Times* described as an attempt to "jolt a mainstream audience," never mind a Southern one. The original image that appeared on the Arts section was of two young gay men leaning toward one another, apparently just a second away from kissing. The original art headline said, "Tongues Untied."

This time, the Arts section cover did not make it off the press. As had been the case with the lynching photo, some of the pressmen protested. They delayed the press start and asked the newsroom to reconsider the propriety of what soon would become known as the gay kiss photo," *Observer* Arts Editor Dean Smith told readers in a column.

Ultimately, Managing Editor Frank Barrows decided to replace the photograph. He told staffers in a memo, "I thought it was too erotically charged for a general-readership newspaper, especially when combined with display type that read 'Tongues Untied' directly over the mouths of the two people as they leaned so closely together that their foreheads touched."

In his memo, which was posted on the Poynter Institute's Web site on December 8, Barrows referred to an eloquent description of the incident written by Smith. In that memo, Smith indicated Barrows concern as follows: "If we repelled readers with that image, would they bother to read the story? Wasn't the play of the package and subject matter itself provocative enough? Did the image go a step too far?"

Barrows thought it did, and the photograph was changed to one showing two men standing next to each other, one with a drink in hand. That actor was Peter Paige, formerly of North Carolina and the focus of the article.

Although the lynching photograph stirred a modest debate among the letters to the editor in the *Observer,* the treatment of the gay kiss photo was debated nationwide and was even covered in the *New York Times.* Once word of the incident spread outside Charlotte, it was vetted from every perspective, on journalism Web sites like poynter.org and gay-theme sites like gay.com, Smith told readers. Discussion largely hinged on the question of prudence vs. censorship. The hate E-mail rolled in from Charlotte to Berkeley, California.

Had the *Observer* gone too far in making a controversial Showtime series the cover story for a Sunday Arts section? Or had the *Observer* editors done too little to confront the attitudes of some Southern conservatives? Smith received E-mail from readers covering the spectrum. One, for example, accused Smith, who's gay, of being an Uncle Tom, and another asked if the paper would be safe for his children to read.

Micro Issues:

1. If a photo offends readers who then won't read the attached story, is that an appropriate justification for deciding not to run a picture?
2. Do you believe such a decision would have been made in Los Angeles? Would a different decision be appropriate in a different geographic area?

Mid-range Issues:

1. Some journalists have suggested it's important for the newsroom to understand how "real people" react to photographs. The *Observer* took such reactions seriously. Was it appropriate? Was it ethical?
2. Both these photos are, in some sense shocking. Does the fact that they address different prejudices in mainstream society matter? Would it matter if the issue were invasion of privacy rather than shock?

Macro Issues:

1. Can visual images be a form of hate speech? Does that matter in this case?
2. Journalists are sometimes said to write "for the lowest common denominator." Other suggest that journalism has the power to transform. Evaluate both of these outlooks in terms of the editorial decisions surrounding these photographs. Which is more ethically persuasive?

CHAPTER X

Ethics in Cyberspace: New Questions and New Roles

By the end of this chapter, you should be able to:

• spot "old" ethical issues in their Internet incarnations.
• understand the role of copyright law in ethical decision making about Internet content.
• develop professional strategies for using the Internet as a reporting tool.
• delineate important policy issues the Internet raises for journalists.

Introduction

Cookies . . . and the Right to Read Unmolested

Academic philosophers sometimes debate whether any really new ethical issues emerge over time, or whether old issues merely resurface. Students of applied ethics (and by virtue of reading this book you are one) have a tentative answer to that question. The core ethical issue may remain the same, but its real-world manifestation, and the morally relevant facts, often call for original thinking.

In no field of media ethics is this truer than when thinking, talking and working with the Internet. The technology itself has so transformed the culture of the developed world—and has a promise through globalization of transforming the remainder of the planet—that ethical issues that might have bothered only a very few editors or advertising copywriters in previous generations now wind up on everyone's desktop work station.

Take cookies. A cookie, for those of you who haven't received one lately, is an electronic "marker" that particular Web sites are programmed to attach to your computer when you access them. Those advertising on the Web want to know who is looking at their site and whether they will purchase the advertised product. In rough parallel, cookies might be thought of as a sophisticated version of eye tracking—a research technique used by marketers to literally trace how the human eye moves across the page. The results of eye tracking studies, for example, have taught us that the upper right-hand corner of the newspaper page is where the human eye most often focuses and that a single dominant picture can encourage the eye to move around the page in the way the designer intended. Advertisers also use eye tracking research to determine what part of a particular design catches and holds consumer attention. Media researchers have used eye tracking for decades, and no one has claimed that it presented an ethical problem. Cookies, the electronic equivalent, should be treated the same way, right?

Not exactly.

Because the cookie is a marker that's attached to your computer hard drive, and in the earliest days of "cookies" you did not know when you had received one, it's capable of providing its originator with a great deal of information about you. What kind of computer do you own? What sorts of websites do you visit? For how long? What do you purchase? Did you use a credit card? The cookie gives marketers this kind of information without asking your permission and sometimes, for the web neophyte, without your knowledge. In short, a cookie on your computer hard drive can mean that you lose control of a great deal of information about you. Furthermore, the marketers can use the information they gain about you to find better, more effective, ways to sell you things. Law enforcement, or even the spouse you are divorcing, can subpoena such information. Marketers can, and do, sell the same information to other marketers. And, the United States, unlike the European Union, does not make such action illegal.

If phrases in the preceding paragraph sound familiar, they should. Recall that part of the definition of privacy (see Chapter VI) is the ability to control information about you and how that information is interpreted and used. What seemed like a great idea to marketers—to track consumer Web use through the novel approach of a "cookie"—raises important privacy questions. Those questions seem more urgent because of the nature and amount of information one can collect and connect by accessing the multiple consumer databases of which we are all a part. The privacy issue raised by cookies, in fact, is so significant that some suggest consumers have a legal right to access the World Wide Web without fear of their every movement being tracked, analyzed, and potentially resold. You have the right to read anonymously (Cohen 2000); information about you is your private property. Your computer constitutes your private space in much the same way your home does. Those who enter your home must do so, except in very rare circumstances, with your permission.

It is our contention that the Internet, using cookies as a good example, doesn't raise unique ethical questions so much as it asks us to rethink our standard answers to similar questions. The Internet brings into play distinctive morally relevant facts. And, because the Internet is a system, it also asks us to broadly consider the systemwide implications of ethically informed choices.

Ownership of Information: Legal Hints but Not Help

In October 1995, the *New York Times* found itself under siege from a distinguished group of authors, all of whom contributed occasionally to the paper. More than 300 writers and scholars—among them Norman Mailer, Alice Walker, Garry Trudeau, Kurt Vonnegut, Barbara Raskin, Roger Rosenblatt, Ben Bagdikian, and Carolyn Bird—signed a petition protesting the *Times's* newly implemented policy requiring writers to surrender syndication, electronic and other secondary rights to their work after articles were published in hard copy in the *Times.*

In an internal memorandum that became public in August 1995, the *Times* had announced it would require its freelancers to sign "work-made-for-hire" contracts. "The position on this is unambiguous: if someone does not sign an agreement, he or she will no longer be published in the newspaper." The writers responded that the memorandum was a historic break with publishing tradition where freelancers had been allowed to retain copyright to their own work.

What was really at issue, of course, was money. The freelancers wanted to be paid for the original publication of their efforts and for all subsequent publication of their work—regardless of medium. The *Times,* which was struggling to develop an Internet presence and to make money from that effort, was attempting to cut both costs and subsequent legal problems by demanding copyright ownership of its organizational contribution to the Information Superhighway. Since the *Times,* like all other news organizations, had been unable to turn the Internet into a profit center, it sought to reduce some expenses by curtailing its payments to freelancers. The writers, in turn, wanted the Internet to be governed by the same professional norms that had governed the print media—in other words, the writer retains the copyright and each user must pay for the privilege of reproduction.

United States copyright law, as it has evolved over the past 200 years, can be boiled down to two succinct concepts. The first is that the courts have repeatedly ruled "You can't copyright an idea." As Justice Louis Brandeis observed, "The general rule of law is that the noblest of human productions—knowledge, truths ascertained, conceptions and ideas—become voluntary communication to others, free as the air to common use" (*International News Service v. Associated Press,* 248 U.S. 215, 250 (1918) is the case quoted).

What can be copyrighted, however, is the particular execution of an idea. Mozart could not copyright the order of the keys on the harpsichord, but he could copyright the particular order of notes played on that instrument—the execution of an idea—in *The Magic Flute.*

The second basic concept of copyright law is that an idea that is sufficiently novel and concrete enough does warrant protection. This "novel and concrete" approach to ideas is rooted in the seventeenth- and eighteenth-century notion that ideas are like private property and, like private property, are worthy of protection. An entire line of cases involving television and radio formats has developed essentially through regarding particular formats and plot lines as concrete expressions of ideas that can be copyrighted. One legal scholar has noted that the essential feature of this branch of copyright law is "the right to determine what shall be done with an idea."

The courts currently protect ideas that are bound through contracts—what is called "expressed contract theory." This means that copyright is related not so much to ownership as to sales. In fact, some scholars assert that copyright doesn't protect ownership so much as it protects the right to copy (Halbert 1999). A contract may be expressed through money changing hands or a promise to disclose the idea to a third party (for instance, a publisher's promise to publish a novel). Even if an idea is obtained fraudulently, the courts have been willing to protect its originator. The courts also protect ideas under what is called "implied contracts." A freelancer submitting an article to a magazine in the hopes that it will be published is functioning under an implied contract that the publisher will consider the article but not steal it. Finally, the courts have developed a doctrine designed to impede unjust enrichment. Under this view, ideas should be protected because, to fail to do so, would allow one person or organization to enrich themselves while failing to compensate the original developer of the idea. For instance, in 1990 humorist Art Buchwald was awarded $900,000 when the courts found that his idea for the movie *Coming to America* had been developed into a successful film without any compensation to him.

However, Internet-based technologies have allowed those who create information to bypass industry delivery systems and deliver their products directly to the consumer (Halbert 1999). Popular author Stephen King in 1999 bypassed his own publisher and agreed to market a new novel on the Web, providing those who accessed the book chapters would directly pay King $1 for every chapter they downloaded. King curtailed his experiment after about six months, but not before he had sent a message to the publishing world that the Internet—at least for popular and well-known artists—could replace some of the marketing support the publishing industry normally provides. King's book, however, remains incomplete.

Legal theories and case rulings have not kept pace with the technology. The courts would normally consider a photograph a concrete expression of an idea. But what happens when the photograph has been cut into pixels, the individual pixels' colors changed, the shape of the pixels reorganized—say, from a camel to an elephant—and then the resulting image, which now looks a great deal like an elephant and lacks a negative to indicate that it was once a camel, is downloaded onto a Web site that belongs to your news organization?

Is the execution of the idea that the photograph represents the property of the photographer who shot the original image, the property of the multimedia author who took the photograph of the camel and changed it to an elephant, or the property of the news organization that ultimately distributed it in the form of electrons on a Web site? Is there an express or implied contract in any of these actions? Does the creator of the elephant image owe royalties or acknowledgement to the creator of the camel? Is putting something on a Web site the same thing as publication? Do these issues persist after death? For example, who gets paid for, and who holds the copyright to, an image of television star Lucille Ball who, years after her death, is electronically reproduced and inserted into a 1996 television ad for Service Merchandise? Furthermore, what if the creator of the ad could prove that the image of Ms. Ball was created out of a group of uncopyrighted pixels? Who then would own the Ball image? On such complex issues, the courts have been silent.

Historically, when one medium—for example, radio—has surpassed another—say, newspapers—in an important dimension such as timeliness, both mediums have evolved to take advantage of their unique strengths. Thus, as broadcasting developed, that medium tended to emphasize immediacy while print emphasized depth. Right now, it is unclear how the use and development of the Internet will influence these trends. Common ownership muddies the professional waters even further. Thinking

Ed Stein. Reprinted courtesy of the Rocky Mountain News.

about copyright has always included an element of "this came first," but that issue was defined in terms of weeks or years rather than nanoseconds.

The ability to digitize information challenges our intuitive assumptions about a variety of things—everything from the "reality" that a picture represents to the external symbol systems that words and images together create. Digitization enables media designers to confound the external referent as never before. Students at the turn of the century will recognize that John Wayne's image has been digitized and electronically inserted into a Coors ad. But students twenty years from now may not recognize the original John Wayne, may not know that he was a film star, and may not be aware that he has been dead for decades. They will have "lost" the external referent to the image. One consequence of that loss is that the Coors commercial may not be as meaningful, or seem as clever, to students of the next generation. But, there are other, more sinister possibilities, such as the twisting and destruction of meaning that Orwell raised in *1984.*

In addition to what may be copyrighted, the Internet emphasizes questions of when. We now work in a twenty-four-hour news cycle. Stories must be updated almost constantly. The 1990s phrase "All news all the time" has been narrowed in focus to "All election all the time," "All stock market all the time," or "All presidential scandal all the time" by cable and the Internet. Many professionals insist that the twenty-four-hour news cycle has resulted in the trivialization of news and a sensationalistic approach to news. Rumor can pass for information on the Web, further confounding traditional efforts at fact checking and decreasing the time for thoughtful decision making.

Ethical thinking combined with sound professional practice can provide some paths out of this virtual swamp. The first, and probably the most basic, maxim arises from the habits of sound professional performance. Cite the source of your information—or your electronic bytes. After all, journalists are required to note the originators of their information when reporting on documents or interviews. Multimedia designers should be subject to the same standard, just as music arrangers (as opposed to composers) or screenwriters currently are.

If noting the originators of your information creates problems, as it did for the *New York Times* in 1995, then be willing to accept those problems as the price of using the information. Many newspapers, for example, now sign contracts with freelancers that give the publication the rights to the first printing of the story and then return the copyright to the original author. In an ethical sense, such a professional standard allows news organizations and those who work for them to achieve two results. In the Judeo-Christian tradition, you have avoided theft, an ethically culpable act. Such arrangements also fulfill the ethical duty of beneficence, sharing credit with the originator of your information, whether that is a particular author or the source of a quote in a feature story. In our experience in this world of bits and bytes, application of a maxim of "Cite the source of your bytes" will prejudice you to the development of original and creative work. And, using your own stuff, and not someone else's, improves performance.

The second maxim that emerges from a discussion of deception is this: information that has the capacity to deceive the rational audience member as to its origin, original referent, or source must be regarded as suspect. While journalistic discussion of deception has generally focused on practices used to obtain stories, we believe the concept also applies to the relationship between the journalist and his audience. The issue is whether using digitized information is intended to mislead the audience. Thus, an October 1996 cover of *Life* magazine that combined more than 400 previous covers into an image of Marilyn Monroe does not intend to deceive the audience because the editors clearly explained what they did. But lifting an image from one Web site, downloading sentences from another, and combining them for your own news story without citing your original sources is an attempt to deceive both your editors and your audience.

While both plagiarism and forgery are clearly deceptive practices (Bok 1983, 218), the Web, with its nearly infinite possibilities as a source of information, has highlighted the need for journalists to take care. Even in a new era of pixels and bytes, journalists must maintain old-fashioned credibility with our audiences about the sources of our information and the means and methods of gathering that information.

Sources: New Technology but Continuing Issues

New technology often raises old ethical issues with additional permutations. Because the computer substitutes virtual interaction for the face-to-face variety, journalists using the Internet as a medium to conduct interviews or obtain data must take additional precautions to authenticate not just information but also sources. Sourcing via the Internet grafts new questions onto older ones.

Contemporary journalistic thinking about the role of news sources assumes an active audience. The notion is that readers and viewers may better understand and evaluate journalistic accounts if those stories identify journalists' information sources. Identification often goes beyond a mere name and address: journalists may provide background so audience members understand why a person or document is cited. The professional standard is that sources should be named and that journalists must have compelling reasons for withholding a source's identity.

Furthermore, granting anonymity is a mutual agreement between reporter and source, not a unilateral understanding imposed on one party by the other. Anonymous sources are expected to be the exception rather than the journalistic rule. Professional mores dictate that, should a reporter decide to grant anonymity, she does not have to divulge the source's identity to editors, other supervisors, or, in rare instances, the courts.

Like many contemporary professional practices, sourcing is not firmly rooted in journalistic history. In the era of the partisan press, story sources were most often the printers who controlled the presses. Further, printers were paid for their efforts by political partisans. Historians suggest that reader understanding of sources in the Revolutionary Era parallels contemporary understanding of a signed editorial.

Even the traditional practice of interviewing, now considered commonplace, was controversial at its inception. The critics claimed that interviewing would destroy reporting. Critics argued that if journalists adapted this reporting technique, they would slip into a moral morass, fall prey to aggressive exploitation and manipulation and would no longer serve the public. One *New York World* correspondent referred to the practice as a "modern American inquisition." In 1869, the *London Daily News* castigated those journalists who were practicing this new form of reporting, saying they brought the profession of journalism "into contempt." Editors and publishers feared then that reporters' use of the interview would lessen the control of the editor over the reporter.

Reporters' power grew with the use of the interview because they could select which quotations to use and determine which comments to include. As the journalistic practice of the interview developed concurrently with the rise of the professional ideal of objectivity, identifying news sources became accepted professional practice (Schudson 1995; 1978).

The role that sourcing plays with readers and viewers also has been questioned in mass communication research. One of the most widely accepted findings in the field is that audience members tend to disassociate the source from the message, what is known as the "sleeper" effect (Lowery and DeFleur 1988). Studies confirm that most people tend to retain the fact of what is said while forgetting the context in which they "heard" it. Practitioners, from Nazi master propodandist Joseph Goebbels through contemporary political consultants, have intuitively understood this human tendency to disassociate the source from the message. But readers and viewers are morally autonomous actors. Identifying news sources allows audiences to evaluate reports in terms of both content and a source's motives for divulging information.

The motives for providing and withholding information are sometimes central to political coverage, and political reporters have added an element of elasticity to the practice of anonymous sourcing.

The phrase "not for attribution" means journalists may quote what is said but agree to veil the source. Thus, the attribution "a high-level White House source" may mean anyone from the president himself to cabinet officers to other, well-connected administrative appointees. The phrase "on background" means journalists should consider the information given as an aid in placing facts in context. Background information also may be used as part of a sourcing trail: journalists in possession of background information may use their knowledge to try to get other sources to provide them with the same information on the record.

Journalists continue to debate allowing sources to go "off the record" or "on deep background." A strict interpretation of these synonymous phrases means that the journalist who accepts such information may not quote the specific source and, in addition, may not use his knowledge to pry the same information from other sources. This stringent interpretation has meant that editors have instructed reporters to literally leave the room when a source asks for such anonymity. Journalists have spent time in jail rather than reveal a source's identity. Less stringent interpretations suggest that journalists who accept information off the record may not name or in any way reveal the identity of the source but may use the information itself to leverage similar or related information from other sources.

Until quite recently such agreements were arrived at through face-to-face conversation and negotiation. However, the advent of the Internet and the ability of journalists to lurk at many places on the Information Superhighway have stripped many interviews of their context and nonverbal cues that have traditionally signalled whether information is on or off the record. Such agreements most often focused on the willingness of the source to be identified, but the Internet can alter this view. Journalists surfing for story sources or leads must be careful to identify themselves professionally on the Internet when they begin "conversing" with another Internet user. Some publications, for example the *Wall Street Journal,* maintain an informal policy that requires reporters to identify themselves as reporters when they begin their Internet conversations so there is less confusion about the role the journalist plays. The reasoning behind such requirements is that people, in this instance people who are "telepresent" through the Internet, need to know that they are dealing with a journalist working in a professional capacity when they respond to questions either about story ideas or Internet content.

Such professional identification—the Internet version of identifying yourself at the beginning of a telephone conversation—also raises additional professional issues. For example, it is possible for competitors, who also may be surfing the Net, to learn about the direction of a story or even of its specific content during the reporting process. This increases the chance that other news organizations will learn about stories or angles they have missed some time before actual publication. While this sort of competitive consideration has always influenced journalism, the Internet makes it easier and faster to learn what other news organizations are doing. However, most professionals agree that identifying yourself as a journalist is just as important when working on the Net as it is in face-to-face situations. Since journalists are well aware of the pitfalls of being deceived by a source, "wired" reporters should be more than sensitive to these problems when they become the party to the conversation with the power to deceive.

Whether in person or through fiber optics, journalists who cover police, the courts and other areas of public life often develop informal agreements with frequent sources about when and how information may be attributed. Such relationships are necessary but risky. Many journalists have had to decide whether they will "burn a source"—reveal the identity of a source who has been allowed to remain veiled in earlier stories—for a particularly important story. Burning a source means terminating a relationship that worked well for both parties. It is considered a form of promise breaking.

Keeping the trust between reporter and source intact is one reason that larger news organizations often will send an investigative reporter to cover a particularly sensitive story that arises on another reporter's beat. Sending an investigative reporter allows the beat reporter's sourcing agreements to remain undisturbed, ensuring a continuing flow of routine information while the investigation continues.

There are significant ethical justifications for using anonymous sources. They are:

- Preventing either physical or emotional harm to a source.
- Protecting the privacy of a source, particularly children and crime victims.
- Encouraging coverage of institutions, such as the U.S. Supreme Court or the military, which might otherwise remain closed to journalistic and hence public scrutiny.

It is this final justification that is used most frequently by journalists who cover institutions that have historically functioned in secret, such as the Supreme Court or the military. Reporters maintain that only when sources are allowed to remain anonymous will they provide newsworthy information that would otherwise place their careers or their physical safety at risk.

Policy Options: The Role of the Profession

The Information Superhighway, unlike some media technologies such as the printing press, was initially developed by the government for political reasons. The original Internet was a computer network designed first to support the military and then, in the 1960s, reorganized to allow scientists working primarily at universities and government laboratories worldwide to communicate quickly and easily among each other. This system remained confined to the intellectual and military elite until the early 1980s when the Internet, as we now know it, began to take shape.

This unusual history—a mass medium that was "invented" to support government policy—has made the Internet a difficult fit both for academic study and journalistic necessity. Unlike the printing press, which began as a private invention and remained private property, the Internet has historically owed a great deal to the government both in conceptual and financial terms. Because journalists never were part of the early history of Internet development, the notion of using the Internet as a profit-oriented mass medium is a very recent invention. Grafting a concept of mass communication onto a system designed for government-supported communication is fraught with the potential to raise some difficult questions.

The contemporary conceptualization of the Internet has government supporting a system that will wire and link all schools, libraries, and hospitals. This proposal, which has been partially funded but will cost billions, is rooted in both practical politics and ethical theory.

The political aspects are fairly straightforward: by linking schools, hospitals and libraries, the government is supporting an infrastructure that will promote education and learning and thus strengthen the economy through providing a better educated workforce. A better educated workforce is also generally considered a more efficient one, thus making U.S. workers more competitive worldwide as well as driving down production costs domestically. A better educated populace, of course, also has military implications: it enables the military to draw from a more qualified pool of recruits who are being asked to operate increasingly more complicated weapons. Thus, the reasoning goes, the federal government fulfills its constitutional responsibility to protect Americans from international as well as domestic threats by supporting a system that will promote the country's growth and development in many obvious and subtle ways.

Linking hospitals, of course, is also viewed as one way to simultaneously improve the quality of health care for many Americans while holding down medical costs. Again, the reasoning is that private, for-profit medicine would not be as likely to connect all hospitals; through government support the projected benefit can be distributed throughout American society.

This conceptualization of the Internet is also founded in ethical theory. As you may remember from the discussion of utilitarianism in chapter I, the notion of the greatest good for the greatest number has profoundly democratic implications. Wiring schools and libraries should, in theory, provide access to the Internet for every American. Indeed, some libraries in California have experimented with "Internet addresses" for the homeless. Universal access to the Internet through education also would follow Rawls's theory—it would allow the maximization of freedom (access) while protecting weaker parties (people of color, the poor) who might not have access to many other goods in U.S. society but can use the Internet as a way to better their individual and potentially collective lots in life.

Of course, journalists and journalism have not been included in this conceptualization. Yet many journalists have argued that access is only part of the picture—it does people little good to access information if they can't make sense of it. Some scholars have suggested that, as the Internet develops, journalism itself will change from a profession that primarily gathers facts—something anyone can now do on the Internet—to a profession that places those facts within a context and makes them meaningful. If the development of the Internet does indeed encourage professional development along these lines, then ethical thinking would demand that access to news coverage be distributed as widely as possible among the population and that it remain economically affordable.

That stance, of course, puts journalists at odds with all those segments of U.S. society that view the Internet as another potential profit center, including the multinational corporations for which increasing numbers of journalists now work. Insisting that affordable news become part of the policy making that is currently swirling around the Information Superhighway would challenge the long-standing U.S. tradition of regarding journalism and government as irreconcilable adversaries. Yet ethical (and in some ways political) thinking would seem to suggest that making news coverage accessible to every American via the Internet has significant potential benefits for the individual and society at large. It also would make journalists and the government partners, a true philosophical shift in the conceptualization of a "free" press. Finally, such a partnership would demand that journalists themselves take an active part in developing and implementing legislation that will affect their working lives. Such a change in attitude also would require a philosophical shift, one that places journalistic responsibility to political society on an even plane with worker responsibility to profitable media industries.

The Fragmentation of Political Culture

In the 1980s, Nicholas Negroponte, the head of MIT's Media Lab and an Internet guru of some note, created a unique publication, the *Daily Me.* Negroponte programmed his MIT computer to develop a daily newspaper based on his information needs and desires as well as past information preferences. The *Daily Me,* for example, carried a great deal of news about computers and universities and relatively less news about sports, U.S. politics, and the environment, for example. Negroponte, acknowledging that he had a good chance of missing stories that he either should know about or would be interested in that would fall outside his desired categories, programmed his computer to select 10 percent of the *Daily Me*'s content literally at random.

Today, all of us now have the capacity to develop a *Daily Me* from the vast collection of information now on the World Wide Web. Of course, reader and viewer selectivity is nothing new. How many people do you know who always read the sports page and never anything else? If most contemporary newspaper readership surveys are correct, about 35 percent of regular newspaper readers fit this profile. Or take the reverse problem. What if something new—say the emergence of a potentially deadly virus—is noted by doctors but given little media attention? How will you know to tell your *Daily Me* that, instead of looking at the *New York Times,* the better sources are the alternative press in the gay community in San Francisco and New York? This was exactly the case from 1981 through 1986, when many major publications, including the *New York Times,* refused to carry front-page stories about the AIDS virus at the same time the gay press was covering the epidemic.

Journalists acknowledge that newspapers and magazines produced in such a customized fashion as the *Daily Me* will give the reader more editorial control, but worry not only for their financial future but also about the impact of such enhanced selectivity on the larger political culture. The Internet, by placing responsibility squarely on the shoulders (or at least in the computers) of users, has the potential to fragment U.S. culture even more deeply than is the current case. For instance, political conservatives could read only certain points of view; many others would choose to read nothing about politics altogether. At some point, Americans may lose the shared political vocabulary and experience that is the foundation for representative, democratic government.

It is even more unclear what journalists themselves can do to alter this potential trend. News organizations are experimenting with interactive stories and individual editions tailored to particular groups of subscribers. Cable channels, newspaper sections, and magazine titles continue to search for select "niche" audiences, a fact that was true before the Internet, but absolutely necessary for survival today. No one yet knows what will work, what readers and viewers will accept, and what the impact of these changes will be on the larger political culture. What is clear is that journalists need to develop a better sense of how their work helps people make sense of their political, economic and social lives. The Internet has pointed out as never before the need for journalists to connect themselves to readers and viewers or face the consequences of being considered irrelevant and annoying. If there was ever a goad to improved professional performance, the Internet may be providing it.

Suggested Readings

Godwin, Mike. 1998. *Defending Free Speech in the Digital Age.* New York: Times Books.
Halbert, Debora J. 1999. *Intellectual Property in the Information Age.* Westport, Conn.: Quorum Books.
Negroponte, Nicholas. 1995. *Being digital.* New York: Alfred A. Knopf.

CHAPTER X CASES

CASE X-A
Ethics on the Internet: Abiding by the Rules of the Road on the Information Superhighway
BRUCE LEWENSTEIN
Cornell University

ComNet is a commercial online service with a wide range of options available to its subscribers. These include databases, E-mail capabilities, and forums for discussion of many topics. Some of these forums are available to all subscribers, while others require a separate sign-up system and are available only to registered users. In the case of JourForum, a discussion group for journalists, only working journalists may post or read messages to the group. Working journalists are defined as those employed by newspapers, magazines, or other legitimate publications; those whose names appear on the masthead of a regularly published magazine; those who belong to one of several professional organizations (such as the Society of Professional Journalists or the American Society of Newspaper Editors); or those who prove their legitimacy by presenting clips of their published work. ComNet is available both through direct modem connection and through the World Wide Web.

Subscribers to ComNet agree to abide by the service's "Rules of Behavior," which include prohibitions against objectionable or lewd language, illegal activity and "abuse of the service." Journalists signing up for JourForum are reminded of these rules and requested to use only their true names, as well as limiting their discussion to issues directly related to journalism. No specific statements are made about whether JourForum (or other parts of ComNet) are on or off the record. Mark Morceau is the "moderator" of JourForum—as well as its creator—and, through contractual arrangements with ComNet, the person responsible for ensuring that uses of JourForum abide by ComNet's rules.

In a new message to the JourForum, Miriam Zablonsky identifies herself as the editor of a newsletter about "alternative" (nontraditional) medical treatments. She presents many details about a new drug treatment for AIDS, including information about the research leading to the treatment. She wonders why the media has failed to cover the story, she says.

In a response, Harry Lee, a reporter for an online magazine about medicine, suggests that the media usually cover medical stories only after they appear in medical publications such as *The New England Journal of Medicine.*

Zablonsky goes ballistic. In a long, biting, bitter message, she complains about a major medical journal that, she says, refuses to publish information about the new treatment. She calls the editor of the journal, Katherine Kelly, "a fat, sexist, lying slob." Kelly is a well-known commentator on the excesses of tabloid journalism (especially its coverage of medical topics); her columns are often accompanied by her photo, showing a slim, stylish beautiful woman of forty-two.

A flood of messages appears, condemning Zablonsky's comments. To each one, Zablonsky responds with long, rambling diatribes about conspiracies of "them" (unspecified) to control the world, about the deep distrust that a journalist should have toward all major institutions, and about her own unwillingness to change or even compromise her positions, no matter what information is presented to her.

At this point (less than a day after the original message from Zablonsky), Mark Morceau posts a message reminding Zablonsky of ComNet and JourForum's rules about objectionable language and abuse of the service (including posting long messages on topics that aren't germane to journalism). In addition, he asks her to apologize to Kelly and to avoid libelous statements in the future.

Zablonsky refuses, citing (among other arguments in another long, rambling message) her rights to free speech and freedom of the press.

Morceau tells Zablonsky that JourForum is not a publication, so it is not subject to rules of free press. It is, he says, more akin to a private club, which can enforce rules on its members. He points to the requirement that contributors belong to professional journalism organizations as one of the ways that JourForum maintains its limited membership. (Zablonsky once worked for a daily paper, and she maintains her membership in SPJ).

If JourForum is a private club, responds Zablonsky, what she said isn't libelous, because the club isn't a public place or publication. (All of these messages, as with all JourForum messages, are publicly posted so any subscriber to JourForum can view them.)

The next day, Katherine Kelly joins the online discussion. She threatens to sue Zablonsky, claiming that she has been libeled in a public forum. The international community of journalists with access to JourForum is so large that it cannot be considered a "private" club, she argues. Any one of those subscribers can read this forum, she reminds Zablonsky, making it equivalent to a trade paper or magazine. It is as public as any traditional publication, Kelly argues. Moreover, she says, in a landmark decision in June 1996, a federal appeals court described online forums as one of the most important contributions to free exchange of ideas since the development of the printing press. Clearly, Kelly says, the canons of a free press—including the responsibility of avoiding libel—apply to online forums.

Cynthia Smith has been following the online discussion. She finds the issues of potential censorship, free press, and free speech fascinating. She writes an article about the fracas for her own newspaper's weekly "News from Cyberspace" page. That page appears on Thursdays in the business section of the paper; it is also available in the newspaper's online edition. In her story, Smith includes quotes from Morceau, Zablonsky, Kelly, and other members of the forum; the quotes are taken not from interviews but from the messages those people had posted online.

When Smith's story appears, she is accused (in another round of postings in JourForum) of violating the expectation many journalists had that their words in the online forum were "off the record" and would not be quoted.

Micro Issues:

1. Can Zablonsky be sued for libel? Should she be sued for libel?
2. Should Smith have asked for permission to quote?
3. Does Morceau have the right to control what material appears in JourForum?

Mid-range Issues:

1. Does it matter if Smith's article appeared only in the traditional paper format, only in an online supplement to the newspaper, or in a separate online magazine that does not have ties to a traditional-format publication?
2. Is there a moral difference between Zablonsky's potentially libelous statements and Smith's potential violation of the standards of on and off the record?

Macro Issues:

1. Is JourForum a public or private place? What difference would it make if any ComNet subscriber could read messages in JourForum, though only registered members could post messages there? (Compare JourForum to the floor of a convention, where members of the press are often identified with badges so that speakers know they are talking to a reporter.)
2. Under what circumstances does a reporter need to identify himself or herself? At what point do "private" conversations become open to reporting by others?
3. Are online publications subject to different rules than are traditional publications? If so, how do you distinguish between the rules that apply to publications that appear only online and those that appear in both online and offline versions? Does it matter if the online and offline versions are different or edited differently?

CASE X-B
The Witch and the Woods Mystery: Fact or Fiction?
KARON REINBOTH SPECKMAN
Truman State University

Maryland's Black Hills is home to a frightening witch who has remained in the area since Colonial times. Three young student filmmakers venture into the hills near Burkittsville searching for answers. However, the filmmakers do not return. Local officials are uncooperative about their disappearance, much to the dismay of relatives.

News flash: Although the students have not returned, their video has survived to tell the story about the mystery of the witch and the woods. Log on to the Web and see actual footage, read newspaper articles and police reports, and, finally, watch their surviving footage of this frightening apparition. And, if you dare, catch the documentary *The Blair Witch Project* in a theater near you.

Burkittsville was for real. The witch and three student filmmakers' story was not. However, fans debated the truthfulness of the stories on the Web and eventually crowded theaters to view a movie that many said was the scariest movie they had ever seen. *The Blair Witch Project* earned nearly $50 million in its first week of wide release and almost $150 million total in the United States alone. Two real independent filmmakers from the University of Central Florida, Daniel Myrick and Eduardo Sanchez, began their faux documentary in 1996 by auditioning for three actors to play filmmakers searching for the Blair Witch. Myrick and Sanchez decided the actors would improvise and film the menacing witch story themselves while the actors camped in the Maryland woods for six days and nights. They gave the actors a basic story line about the mythical witch and provided daily individual notes to each actor during the filming. The actors filmed themselves in black and white, using two hand-held cameras with 16 mm and Hi-8. Although the filmmakers left them individual notes and food, they induced terror by reducing food supplies, playing tricks on the actors, making strange noises and rustling their tent, and leaving a creepy stick figure hung in trees. The result was a grainy, shaky movie with a sense of reality and fear that eventually made many moviegoers afraid to walk to their cars after leaving the theater.

After Myrick and Sanchez edited the film to two-and-a-half hours, they marketed the film with a Web site that included "real" footage, fake newspaper clippings, and one of the actor's diaries, without telling readers the information was bogus. Their independent-filmmaker dreams came true when Artisan Entertainment purchased the film that originally cost $30,000 to 35,000 for $1.1 million at the Sundance Film Festival in January 1999. When Artisan bought the film, it took over the Web site and added more material, including outtakes, faked police reports, the history of the Blair Witch dating to the eighteenth century, and the story of one supposed filmmaker's mother and her squabble with police over the disappearance. Fans or believers from the original site launched new sites with links to occult and film sites.

Haxan Films, the marketing team of Artisan, placed the movie's clips onto John Pierson's *Split Screen* cable show, premiered its trailer on the insider Ain't it Cool

News Web site in April, and launched its own site for an initial investment of $15,000, which racked up varying estimates of 22 million to 75 million hits before the film's opening in July 1999. The mock documentary also ran repeatedly on USA Network in the weeks before the movie was released.

The filmmakers purposely blurred the fiction and reality line. Myrick said in *Entertainment Weekly,* "It's all fiction, but people are getting confused. We kind of count on that." And, as hoped, many fans were confused whether they were seeing a real documentary or a clever marketing tool. One parent, Disney Films Chairman Joe Roth, said in a *Los Angeles Times* interview, "It took all of my resources, as a parent and a studio head, to convince my fifteen-year-old son and his friends that Blair Witch wasn't a documentary. After what they saw on TV and the Internet, they felt like they were on the inside of the experience, not being told by a studio to see a movie."

Some movie-industry observers thought the critical *Blair Witch* lesson was that major film studios needed to adopt new "viral"marketing techniques to attract film-goers because the film was one of the most successful ever, comparing revenue to production costs. Other observers, however, believed the project and its use of faked material on the Internet raised more serious questions about what we believe on the Internet and how fans may be unaware they are not seeing actual events. Fiachra O Marcaigh, in an *Irish Times* article, said *The Blair Witch Project* was one of the most successful hoaxes ever to emerge from the Internet. He added, "The public is perfectly willing to suspend disbelief in the pursuit of entertainment. But as fiction encroaches further and further into reality, is there a danger that people will have trouble separating truth from untruth?"

To be fair, filmmaker Myrick said in another *Entertainment Weekly* interview that they were not trying to pull a hoax: "You go to our website or look at any of our other marketing and it looks and feels real, but every interview we've done we've told the process of how we made the movie. We walk the line because a lot of people really want to go in not knowing for sure one way or another."

Micro Issues:

1. Should the filmmakers—and then Haxan Films—have been more truthful with fans on the Web site?
2. Has the blurring of fact and fiction on the Internet happened in any news stories?

Mid-range Issues:

1. When do marketing tools influence events in a negative way?
2. What is the societal understanding of truth when marketers purposely blur fact and fiction?
3. Would this website pass the TARES test?

Macro Issues:

1. What special properties of the Internet make this medium more of a problem than other media when discerning between fact and fiction? How has the role of editors changed with the Internet?
2. What is the role of the news media in aiding the public in knowing that a "historical" event is fiction?
3. What are the ethical issues of "viral" marketing where media messages, true and untrue, are planted like a virus in the population which then spreads the message via word of mouth, e-mail, etc.

CASE X-C
The Napster Debate: When Does Sharing Become Thievery?
LAURA RIETHMILLER
University of Missouri–Columbia

In 1999, nineteen-year-old Shawn Fanning wrote a computer code that allowed visitors to his Web site (Napster) to search the hard drives of other connected users via the Internet and transfer music files in a compressed format known as MP3. This "peer-to-peer" sharing bypassed any central system, but with more than 250,000 users connected nightly to the Napster Web site, the selection of free music to share among peers was almost limitless. Once online, users could listen to music, "share" (read: copy) recordings, send instant messages to other users and learn about new artists using the site's new-artist feature.

Although the sharing was taking place between individual computer owners, Napster drew immediate criticism as the site that drew users together for an activity that skirted copyright law. Absent any bona fide reason for existence besides the questionable swapping of music files, the recording industry almost immediately mobilized to shut the service down.

By December 1999, the Recording Industry of America and assorted record labels sued Napster for contributory and vicarious copyright infringement in *A&M Records et al v. Napster*. Another lawsuit represented music composers. According to the plaintiffs, the alleged infringement by Napster amounted to an assault on the recording industry in the form of loss of sales (Greenfeld 2000). The industry contention was that Napster allowed users to steal intellectual property from musicians, diminishing their revenues, and ultimately their incentive to create new songs.

Although the Napster lawsuit may well be decided before you read this case, the peer-to-peer technology that allowed Napster to thrive will transfer to other media ranging from needlepoint patterns to feature films (Cohen 2000). The technology could be used for the transfer of books, magazines, newspapers, blueprints, photographs or any other form of intellectual product.

Sharing music did not begin with the Internet. Since the advent of reel-to-reel audio tape, music has been shared, mostly on a noncommercial basis, among friends. The invention of the home video recorder created a wave of controversy settled in 1984 when the courts ruled in *Sony v. Universal City Studios* that home taping for personal use was not an infringement of copyright.

Media innovations have often been greeted with dire predictions of their consequences. After the invention of radio, record companies were concerned that because people could listen to the radio for free, they would no longer buy recorded music. However, as radio proved to be a boon to the recording industry, the industry's stance changed from fear to embracing the medium so wholeheartedly that deejays were commonly bribed to provide more airplay for certain artists in the hopes of boosting sales (Mullaney and Ante 2000).

The same is true of the movie industry in its adaptation to the VCR. After a decade of fighting the small-screen versions of their product, producers began to see the importance of video in the "aftermarket" of a film—a portion of the market that now accounts for more than half of all film profits. With DVD technology, Hollywood has wholly embraced the rental and sale market, releasing versions of the movie with additional scenes and often director's commentary.

Is it possible that the Internet could simply become one more evolution in the life of the recording (and ultimately film and publishing) industry or will it be the end of the media as we know it? The answer seems to depend on whom you ask.

Micro Issues:

1. Is sharing music using any transfer device an infringement of copyright?
2. Does that fact that Napster merely facilitates copying among "peers" absolve those who created the program of any moral responsibility? How about the culpability of those who are sharing?
3. Does that fact that some artists request Napster to distribute their music freely give it a viable reason to continue operations in spite of the illegal uses to which the program is put?

Mid-range Issues:

1. Pick an analogy below for what the Napster Web site is most like. Defend your answer.
   a.   A lending library that loans books, movies, and sound recordings.
   b.   A friend's CD collection she is willing to share.
   c.   A radio station announcing the time an entire CD is to be played on the radio, facilitating both enjoyment and potential copying.
   d.   A wide-scale piracy operation such as those frequently found in foreign countries and which the U.S. government has protested against.
   e.   An opium den where drugs are consumed but not sold, a legal meeting place that facilitates illegal activity.
2. If the courts rule in favor of peer-to-peer file sharing as they did in personal copying for VCRs, does that end the ethical question? Why or why not?
3. The newspaper for which you work has a Web site and charges Internet users when they download specific articles. However, the fees for those articles are not shared with the employees. Is this different from Napster?

Macro Issues:

1. Should anyone "own" information? Does the fact that the composer frequently gives ownership of the song to a large corporation change the ethical considerations in Napster?
2. What ethical theory helps to solve the tension between artists and their recording companies and the users of Napster?

CASE X-D
What Were You Linking?

PAUL VOAKES
Indiana University

One of the oldest controversies in Southern politics helped to create one of the newest controversies in media ethics.

In May 2000, the South Carolina legislature voted to remove the Confederate flag from the Capitol dome in Columbia and to have it placed behind the nearby Confederate Soldiers Monument, but the issue had far broader appeal than just to South Carolinians. Activists on both sides in Alabama, Arkansas, Florida, Georgia and Mississippi were carefully monitoring the debate, expecting it would influence debates in their states over various displays of Confederate symbols. The National Association for the Advancement of Colored People (NAACP) was organizing a national boycott of South Carolina even after the compromise that put the "Rebel" flag behind the monument. The NAACP action included boycotting the products of several manufacturers that had recently built facilities in South Carolina. The national media were paying close attention to the story.

A few months earlier, the Associated Press had begun routinely adding URLs (Uniform Resource Locators, or Internet addresses) to its stories, which would link readers to related sources of information on the World Wide Web. This practice had by now become fairly common on the Web sites of many national news organizations, but the AP's handling of its links on this particular story illustrated the ethical pitfalls that can await online journalists.

For several weeks, at the bottom of every story involving the Confederate flag controversy in South Carolina, the AP listed the Web addresses of three prominent stakeholders in the story: the NAACP, the South Carolina Heritage Coalition, and the Sons of Confederate Veterans. Surfers to the Heritage Coalition's site found the group's position on the flag issue, and more: calls for "the confederate curriculum to be taught in all South Carolina public schools;" for "recognition of South Carolinians as Confederate/Southern Americans for National Origin status" on government forms; for state holidays commemorating the birthdays of Confederate leaders Robert E. Lee and Jefferson Davis; and for "civil rights protection for Confederate/Southern Americans in the workplace." By providing the link to this organization, the AP had given it unprecedented access to the U.S. public.

When a news organization offers a hypertext link to another site, is it responsible in any way for the content of that site?

This wasn't the first time the question had surfaced. In 1997 the *New York Times* published a story about efforts to establish the innocence of convicted killer Charles Manson, complete with links to "Access Manson" and other sites that suggest Manson's innocence.

In the early days of online journalism—way back in the mid-1990s—few editors thought to provide links to external Web sites as part of a news or feature story. Once editors became more enchanted by the ways in which a Web site "added value" to the printed version, links became frequently embedded in stories. By the end of the decade, however, a modest backlash had occurred as editors realized that (1) readers using the links were leaving the news site and quite often not returning and (2) readers may be associating the tone and views of the linked site with the provider of the original site.

In many cases, the linked Web sites simply add more detailed information or opinions to what was presented in the original story. This is often "unmediated" material that can pass directly from a source or advocate to the reader, without passing through the filters of journalists. Many Web observers and editors celebrate this capability, especially when the link goes to a site produced by a widely known, reliable organization. "I don't see that as a danger to democracy or the public interest," Jonathan Wolman of the Associated Press told the *American Journalism Review.*

But what if the journalist links readers to sites that publish more propaganda than fact, or that advocate racism, violence or pornography?

News organizations have taken different approaches to the "linking" debate. Some don't link at all, except to other pages within the same site. CNN.com tries to make sure its external links are balanced to represent the major positions of a controversy. The *New York Times* says it will link to no sites that "celebrate violence," present sexual content or advocate bigotry or racism. Other online newspapers, such as the *Chicago Tribune,* warn readers generally that by clicking on the hypertext, readers will be leaving the *Tribune's* site. Other sites warn readers that not only are they leaving the site but that external sites "are not endorsed" by the original site. Other sites warn readers that the information in external sites has not been checked for accuracy by the staff of the original site. Still others offer more specific warnings, such as the *Los Angeles Times's* warning to readers that if they linked to the site of the rock band Rage Against the Machine, they would encounter "adult language."

The AP has instructed its editors to use their "best news judgment" to determine which external sites to include.

As with most ethical controversies raised by fast-changing online technologies, there is no consensus at this time. Most online news providers do agree, however, on this much: linked sites do reflect, at least to some extent, on the journalistic decisions being made by the link provider.

Micro Issues:

1. Does each reporter have a responsibility at least to "check out" every Web site his or her story links to, if only to make sure the linked site still exists?
2. Should each reporter be able to vouch for the accuracy and reliability of each linked site?

Mid-range Issues:

1. Should news organizations provide any disclaimers about links before taking readers to the linked sites? If yes, what should those disclaimers say?

2. Should mainstream news organizations link only to Web sites of established, "respectable" organizations, in order not to be associated with fringe or extremist positions?
3. Who makes the call on what is respectable? Is this decision-making process a form of censorship or is it gatekeeping or something else entirely?
4. Should a news organization be able to vouch for the accuracy of every Web site to which it links?

Macro Issues:

1. What is the media's responsibility to society in terms of expanding the "marketplace of ideas" via the Web?
2. Will the free exchange of ideas and democratic debate be enhanced, or is widespread, unchecked linking more likely to distort and discourage honest debate?

CHAPTER XI

The Ethical Dimensions of Art and Entertainment

By the end of this chapter you should be able to:

• understand the link between aesthetics and excellent professional
    performance.
• explain Tolstoy's rationale for art and apply it to issues such as stereotyping.
• understand the debate over the role of truth in popular art.
• explain the prosocial effects of the entertainment media.

Introduction

During the twentieth century, the predominant use of the media shifted from the distribution of information to entertainment and the popularization of culture. In this chapter we will examine the ethical issues that arise from the field of aesthetics. We will apply these principles, plus some findings from social science, to the art and entertainment components of media industries, focusing on the responsibilities of the public as well as the creators of mediated messages.

An Ancient Misunderstanding

Plato did not like poets. The ancient Greek's reasoning was straightforward. Poets, the people who dream, were the potential undoing of the philosopher king. They were rebels of the first order, insurrectionists on the hoof. He banned them from the Republic.

But Plato's skepticism about the role of art is alive in contemporary culture. Few weeks elapse without a news story about an artist or entertainment program that has offended. You are probably familiar with at least some of the following:

• Attempts to ban books such as *Catcher in the Rye* or *Lady Chatterley's Lover* from public and/or school libraries for being too sexually explicit.
• The controversy over government funding of art that some claim is obscene.
• The furor over rappers such as Eminem (Martin Mathers) whose homophobic, misogynistic and sometimes clever lyrics offend many while earning nominations for the industry's top awards.

Such a response to works of art, whether it is by public officials or individuals, is essentially Platonic. Like Plato, those who would restrict the arts do so because they mistrust the power of the artist to link emotion and logic in a way that stimulates a new vision of society, culture, or individuals.

Of Tolstoy and Television

Tolstoy was the sort of artist Plato would have feared. In his famous essay *"What Is Art?"* Tolstoy argued that good art had one dominant characteristic: it communicated the feelings of the artist to the masses in the way in which the artist intended.

> To evoke in oneself a feeling one has once experienced and having evoked it in oneself then by means of movements, lines, colors, sounds or forms expressed in words, so to transmit that feeling that others experience the same feeling—that is the activity of art. . . . Art is a human activity consisting in this, that one may consciously by means of certain external signs, hand on to others feelings he has lived through, and that others are infected by these feelings and also experience them.

Tolstoy's application of his own standard—one that sounds remarkably like artistic social responsibility—was so demanding that he rejected the works of both Shakespeare and Beethoven as being incapable of being understood by the masses. While you may not agree with all of Tolstoy's specific applications, we believe his philosophical rationale has much to recommend it.

Tolstoy's rationale is particularly pertinent to photographers and videographers who, through their visual images, seek to arouse emotion as well as inform. The haunting pictures from Bosnia and Ethiopia have provided a spur for international concerns. Dramas, the AIDS quilt, and obituaries of famous artists who have succumbed to the disease have all aroused both our intellects and our emotions regarding AIDS. They invite action. Television and film documentaries have made viewers more aware of the plight of the mentally ill and homeless, raised important public policy questions, and occasionally made us laugh, through a unity of purpose and craft.

Such work reminds readers and viewers of the moral impetus of art by putting us in touch with characters and situations more complex than our own lives. By thinking about these fictional characters, we enlarge our moral imaginations. Both artists and journalists can provide such a stimulus, although it will not be reflected in every song, story, or film.

Unfortunately, Tolstoy's assertion that great art is defined by how it is understood by an audience also includes a genuine dilemma. There are those who, given even Tolstoy's life experiences, could not articulate the deep truths about human nature Tolstoy wrote about in *War and Peace*. Worse yet, we might not be able to sell those insights to a sometimes lukewarm public, or to produce them on demand for an hour a week, thirty-six weeks a year. The result might be popular art that loses its critical edge and takes shortcuts to commonplace insight. In fact, some

Calvin and Hobbes

by Bill Watterson

mass communication scholars have argued that the unstated goal of popular art is to reinforce the status quo; popular culture, they say, blunts the individual's critical thinking abilities.

Storytellers have a history as popular artists, and the mass media have become the primary cultural storytellers of the era. In *Propaganda,* Jacques Ellul (1965) argues that in a modern society storytelling is an inevitable and even desirable tool to stabilize the culture. To Ellul, this "propaganda of integration" is not the deliberate lie commonly associated with propaganda but the dissemination of widely held mores to the culture at large. This is precisely where the entertainment media get their power—not in the overt programming messages but in the underlying assumptions that (if unchallenged) will become widely held societal values.

Philosophers, sociologists, and artists have debated the meaning of art for the past 150 years. Prior to the Industrial Revolution, art was something only the well educated paid for, produced, and understood. Mozart had to capture the ear of the Emperor of Austria to get a subsidy to write opera. Such "high" or "elite art" provided society with a new way to look at itself. Picasso's drawings of people with three eyes or rearranged body parts literally provided Western culture with a new way of seeing. Michelangelo's paintings and sculpture did the same thing in the Renaissance.

But patronage had disadvantages. The patron could restrict both subject matter and form. Gradually artists discovered that if they could find a way to get more than one person to "pay" for the creation of art, artistic control returned to the artist. The concept of "popular art" was born.

Scholars disagree about many of the qualities of elite and popular art; some even assert that popular art cannot truly be considered art. While both kinds of art are difficult to define, the following list outlines the major differences between popular and elite art and culture:

1. Popular art is consciously adjusted to the median taste by the artist; elite art reflects the individual artist's vision.
2. Popular art is neither abstruse, complicated, nor profound; elite art has these characteristics.
3. Popular art conforms to majority experience; elite art explores the new.
4. Popular art conforms to less clearly defined standards of excellence, and its standards are linked to commercial success; elite art is much less commercially oriented, and its standards of excellence are consistent and integrated.
5. Popular artists know that the audience expects entertainment and instruction; elite artists seek an aesthetic experience.
6. The popular artist cannot afford to offend a significant part of the public; the elite artist functions as a critic of society, and his or her work challenges and sometimes offends the status quo.
7. Popular art often arises from folk art; elite art more often emerges from a culture's dominant intellectual tradition.

Many observers complain that the media reinforce the status quo by constantly depicting certain groups of society in an unflattering and unrepresentative way, presenting a distorted picture of reality to the reader or viewer. For example, when was the last time you saw an Arab on television as anything other than a terrorist or religious fanatic? Or a beautiful, blonde woman who also happened to be an engineer? Depictions and omissions such as the ones above reinforce cultural stereotypes and offend the groups involved. They also leave the media in the position of constantly having to explain why the media world is so different from the real world.

At least some such distortion is the natural outcome of compression. Just as substances such as rubber change form when compressed, so do media messages. Given only thirty seconds to register a message in a commercial, an advertising copywriter will resort to showing us the stereotype of a librarian, a mechanic, or a pharmacist. Using stereotypes as a form of mental shorthand is a natural way media work and was noted as early as 1922 by Walter Lippmann in his classic work *Public Opinion*. Lippmann said that for economy of time and maintenance of the status quo, we hold to stereotypes by defining first and seeing second. Soon, we expect reality to imitate art.

Mass communicators know the power of stereotypes and deeply held notions and use them. According to advertising guru Tony Schwartz (1973), advertising messages are often constructed backward. The communicator actually starts with what the receiver knows—or believes he knows—and then constructs a message that fits within that reality. Schwartz calls it hitting a "responsive chord." It works the same in entertainment. If you need a pimp to further the plot and time is tight, dress an African-American male appropriately and let the audience fill in the details. If you need a terrorist, anyone of Arab descent will usually do. The audience gets the idea of a pimp or a terrorist, but another idea has been planted as well—the racist notion that most pimps are minorities or that all Arabs are terrorists. While these images suit the artist's purposes, they are problematic.

Some scholars have made a more universal argument. Meyrowitz (1985) argues that television has become a "secret-revelation machine," bringing behaviors once confined to the "backstage" to the screen. The result is a loss of faith in institutions such as government, religion, and parenthood, with a resulting loss of stability. This loss of stability, Postman (1986) claims, can happen in one of two ways. In the Orwellian concept (found in *1984*) culture becomes a prison; in the Huxleyan concept (found in *Brave New World*) culture becomes a burlesque. Postman believes we are in more danger of the latter. Television is a threat to society precisely because most of its messages are so common yet people take them so seriously. Fore (1987) argues that every culture reveals itself through its underlying assumptions—the decisions it makes about what to value, how to solve problems, who is powerful, and what is taboo. In earlier cultures, these values were transmitted around the campfire; in our society, they are transmitted via television to a viewer who is separate from feedback and outside points of reference. These conditions, Fore argues, make the viewer subject to "a tunnel vision that encourages unquestioning acceptance of the world view he or she sees on the screen" (Fore 1987, 4).

The unquestioning acceptance of an unchanging reality is the antithesis of the effect Tolstoy intended art to produce. In Tolstoy's vision, art introduces the reader or viewer to the novel with such power and depth that what is novel can become known and what is known can become understood.

Truth in Art and Entertainment

No question in the field of aesthetics is more thoroughly debated with less resolution than the role of truth in art. Most philosophers seem to agree that artists are not restricted to telling the literal truth. Often artistic vision can reveal a previously undiscerned truth, a new way of looking at the world or understanding human nature that rings deeply true.

But just how much truth should the audience expect from entertainment? And how entertaining should the audience expect truth to be? There are several opinions. At one point on the continuum is the argument that there is no truth requirement at all in art. At another point on the continuum is the belief that one person's truth should be established as the accepted truth for all. This imposition of a specific moral, as opposed to ethical, "truth" is common to all cultures and political systems. In *The Republic* Plato had Socrates argue against allowing children to hear "casual tales . . . devised by casual persons." Its result, when applied to the mass media, is usually some form of licensing or censorship. In U.S. society, that battle historically has raged over library books.

Classics such as *Huckleberry Finn, Of Mice and Men, The Grapes of Wrath,* and *The Merchant of Venice* are but some of the long-revered and award-winning works that now face censorship by various school systems. The American Library Association reports that incidents of book banning rise each year and now reach more than one thousand instances annually, with little or no impedance from the courts. In 1982, the U.S. Supreme Court allowed a lower court ruling to stand that forced the Island Trees, New York, school district to reexamine a list of books considered objectionable (most of them by minority writers or about minority experiences) and to justify the censor's motives, but since that time the high court has not heard another book-banning case.

While books are important because they form the most permanent part of our cultural and intellectual web, television has been the medium that has been the most frequent contemporary target of censorship and protest. The protests began early in the medium's history. The 1951 airing of the show *Amos 'n' Andy* was condemned by the National Association for the Advancement of Colored People for depicting "Negroes in a stereotyped and derogatory manner." In 1964 the United Church of Christ set a legal precedent when it successfully challenged the license renewal of WLBT in Jackson, Mississippi, on the grounds that the owners had blatantly discriminated against African-Americans.

In the sixties, seventies, and eighties a variety of special-interest groups used more subtle methods to influence entertainment programming. Some, such as the Hispanic advocacy group *Nosotros*, worked closely with network bureaucracies, previewing potentially problematic episodes of entertainment programs, often altering program content before it reached the airwaves. Other advocacy groups employed strategic campaigns with advertisers and affiliates to influence the airing of certain episodes of popular shows or to make certain that some characters certain segments of society might find objectionable remained scripted in prime time.

The networks opted for a policy of balance, believing that co-option was superior to confrontation and that muting criticism in advance would have a positive impact on the networks' image and the bottom line. Yet, *New York Times* television critic Jack Gould framed the problem of artistic accountability in the early days of the ascendancy of advocacy groups: Such agreements "hold[s] latent dangers for the well-being of television as a whole. An outside group not professionally engaged in theatre production has succeeded in imposing its will with respect to naming of fictional characters, altering the importance of a leading characterization and in other particulars changing the story line" (Montgomery 1989, 21). For the artist, network attempts to "balance" competing advocacy-group interests had come close to recreating the patronage system, albeit a far more sophisticated one.

The struggle over censorship, which some label as disagreement over taste, becomes even more acute when governmental sponsorship is at stake. Some argue that because tax dollars are extracted from all, the programs they fund should be acceptable to all. Federal support for programs such as the National Endowment for the Arts (NEA) has been repeatedly questioned in Congress for the last decade, the latest in a series of Congressional initiatives. Conservatives objected to funding artists such as photographer Robert Mapplethorpe, whose blend of homoerotic photos and traditional Judeo-Christian symbols offended many. Eventually, the criticism was a factor in the resignation of one of the NEA's directors, Robert Frohnmayer.

The government also censors in other ways. Infinity Broadcasting has been fined several hundred thousand dollars for disc jockey Howard Stern's on-air profanity and offensive racial slurs. Stern himself became offended, saying that the FCC's action amounted to an enforcement of political correctness in a country that values free speech. Those who supported the FCC's action noted that Stern most often castigated people and groups who were already among society's most disadvantaged and who were among the least likely to be able to produce alternative programming.

The debates over freedom and censorship continue. Perhaps the only solution is found in the words of U.S. Supreme Court Justice William O. Douglas when he said, "If we are to have freedom of mind in America, we must produce a generation of men and women who will make tolerance for all ideas a symbol of virtue."

Entertainment, News, or Reality?

In his ingenious satire, *Network,* the late writer-director Paddy Chayefsky envisioned a time when the lines would be blurred between entertainment and news, rendering them indistinguishable. By the late 1980s, television was proving him right. However, Chayefsky was wrong in one detail. News did begin to take on the look of entertainment as he predicted it would; however, he did not predict that entertainment would also begin to look increasingly like news. Consider these television shows: *America's Most Wanted,* reenactments of crimes with photos or line drawings of the suspects, in which the audience is encouraged to help by calling in tips for police; another in the genre is *Unsolved Mysteries; Inside Edition,* a voyeuristic look at stories dubbed "too hot to handle" for traditional network news; others of the breed, including *A Current Affair,* and *Hard Copy, COPS,* and *Rescue 911.*

At the millennium, one of the hottest forms of television was "reality programming" where producers gambled that we would enjoy being voyeurs of other "normal" people placed in extraordinary circumstances. *Survivor,* the first megahit of the genre, vaulted CBS into the ratings lead and captured phenomenal audiences during the summer rerun season as viewers tuned in to see who would be the last individual left on the island. As the contestants left their island existence one at a time, they were hailed in the media as heroes, none more so than the eventual winner. Other attempts at reality-based programming, such as *Big Brother,* have met with less success.

Currently, dozens of such shows are in production simultaneously. From arrests to court trials to public confrontations, very little escapes our fascination. Whether called "trash television," "tabloid TV," or "infotainment" by critics, these shows are hot with local television programming executives. Such programming provides relief from returns of situation comedies and the sameness of game shows, draw large rat ings, and often come prepackaged with ads embedded in them, making them attractive to station owners. Another benefit to reality television—from the owners' point of view—is that it's cheap. Producers don't have to pay writers, worry whether writers will strike, sign multimillion-dollar contracts with stars, or pay for expensive sets and locations. Grit and greed go hand in hand.

Much attention was focused on the genre in the late 1990s when one guest on the *Jenny Jones Show* later murdered another guest when it was revealed on the air that the victim (a male) had a crush on the perpetrator (also a male). The revelation came as a total surprise to the man who later admitted to committing the murder. The family of the victim sued the show for its part in the murder. After a highly publicized trial, the television show won in court, but public opinion was clearly divided on the show's culpability.

Networks were not alone in reality-based programs. A teenage girl became a national celebrity when she put her life on the Web for all to view from a camera mounted on a computer in her bedroom that she called "Jennicam." A man in Dallas changed his legal name to "dotcomguy" and let the nation watch as he moved into a vacant house in 2000 with only a computer and lived an online life for 365 days before emerging in early 2001. In his exit interviews, he refused to reveal his real name, claiming that he wanted to retain his privacy.

Do such shows or Web sites do any harm, or are they simply diversions? You will recall from chapter VI the thinking based on the Talmud regarding the responsibility of the community to avert its eyes to prevent the "unwanted gaze" or "the injury caused by seeing." Perhaps the harm in these shows is that as I gaze on these admittedly willing individuals whether struggling on *Survivor* or arguing on *Jerry Springer* or *Judge Judy,* perhaps what is at stake is my dignity. According to Greek philosophy, privacy is linked to our ability to "become" human and retain some element of dignity while doing it. "Only citizens who respect one another's privacy are themselves dignified with divine respect" (Rosen 2000, 19).

The blending of facts and entertainment is not restricted to the small screen. Films such as *Nixon, Hoffa,* and *Thirteen Days* reflect a particular artistic vision based on fact. *Hoffa* director Danny DeVito sought to make an entertaining film that, while it actually portrayed the major facts of the teamster leaders's life, took symbolic liberties with many events and people. DeVito told the *Today* show audience in early 1993 that what he sought was entertainment—"not sitting down and reading a book."

Though these films and the reality-based television shows differ in format and content, they are alike in invoking the license allowed entertainment programming while retaining the authority of fact—a risky combination. By blending information and entertainment into an internally coherent package, the possibility for abuse of an unsuspecting audience exists. To understand how this can happen, we must look to the mass-communication theory of "uses and gratifications." Phrased simply, the theory says audience members will use the media to gratify certain wants and needs. People bring something to the message, and what they bring affects what they take away.

For example, seeking news and information is a common use of the media, with an expected gratification of getting information necessary for citizenship. Entertainment is another common media use, with its own expected gratification. Reality television, in keeping the look of news yet airing the content of lowbrow entertainment, may be produced to entertain but often has had the unintended "use" of informing. The problem arises when the information such entertainment programming provides about important institutions in U.S. culture, such as the court system or medical practice, or important political figures, such as Malcolm X, is fundamentally flawed.

This confounding of unexpected and unintended uses and gratifications is important. As *New York Times* columnist A. M. Rosenthal (1989) states, tabloid television shows are tantamount to buying news programming "off the shelf." He adds that stations buying such programs should add the disclaimer, "We did not put this stuff in the bottle, whatever it is."

With a look of authority (an anchor's desk, a courtroom, a police precinct) and the hype of their importance (e.g., "200 lives saved so far!"), these shows appear to be useful for acquiring information, thus gratifying the human need to know. However, by invoking their license as entertainment, such shows are free to bypass accuracy, fairness, balance, and other standards normally associated with news and to focus on more sensational elements to gather larger ratings.

In these shows, what is now being gratified is not the *need* to know, but the *want* to know in a way that some viewers might not even recognize it. In a *Times Mirror* poll, about half of the respondents said they believed *America's Most Wanted* was a news show, while only 28 percent said that it was entertainment (Thomas 1990). The result could be a population that gets its news from a program like *A Current Affair*. In the words of one woman interviewed by the *Dallas Morning News* (Wicker 1990) about marital relationships, "I only believe what I see on *Oprah*."

Aesthetics Is an Attitude

Artists see the world differently. While most people perceive only what is needful for a particular purpose, the artist works with what some philosophers call an "enriched perceptual experience." This aesthetic attitude is one that values close and complete concentration of all the senses. An aesthetic attitude is a frankly sensual one, and one that summons both emotion and logic to a particular end.

For example, the theatre audience knows that Eugene O'Neill's plays are "merely" drama. But they also provide us with an intense examination of the role of family in human society—an experience that is both real and personal to every audience member. Such intense examination is what gives the plays their power to move.

We believe that the makers of mediated messages, whether they are the executive producers of a television sitcom or the designers of a newspaper page, share this aesthetic impetus. These mass communicators are much like architects. An architect can design a perfectly serviceable building, one that withstands the elements and may be used for particular purposes. But great buildings—St. Paul's Cathedral in London or Jefferson's home at Monticello—do more. They are tributes to the human intellect's capacity to harmoniously harness form and function.

In fact, philosophers have argued that what separates the commonplace from the excellent is the addition of an aesthetic quality to what would otherwise be a routine, serviceable work. These qualities of excellence have been described as:

• An appreciation of the function realized in the product.
• An appreciation of the resulting quality or form.
• An appreciation of the technique or skill in the performance.

These three characteristics of aesthetic excellence characterize excellence in mass communication as well.

Take the newspaper weather page. Before USA Today literally recalibrated the standard, weather pages were generally restricted to the upper right-hand quadrant of the second page of a newspaper section. They were printed in black and white, in columns of tiny type. Newspaper editors believed that most people weren't interested in the weather—unless it was weird—and designed their pages accordingly.

USA Today editors, on the other hand, understood that their readers agreed with the observations of political columnist Molly Ivins: when people aren't talking about football, they talk about the weather. The editors devoted more space to it and printed it in color. They added more information in a more legible style and form. In short, they gave newspaper weather information an aesthetic quality. While much about USA Today has been criticized, its excellent weather page has been copied.

Although mass-communication professionals are infrequently accused of being artists, we believe they intuitively accept an aesthetic standard as a component of professional excellence. As philosopher G. E. Moore noted in his book Principia Ethica:

"Let us imagine one world exceedingly beautiful. Image it as beautiful as you can; put into it whatever on this earth you most admire: mountains, rivers, the sea, suns and sunsets, stars and moon. Imagine these all combined in the most exquisite proportion so that no one thing jars against another, but each contributes to increase the beauty of the whole. And then imagine the ugliest world you can possibly conceive. Imagine it just one heap of filth, containing everything that is most disgusting to you for whatever reason, and the whole, as far as may be, without one redeeming factor. . . . Supposing (all) that quite apart from the contemplation of human beings; still it is irrational to hold that it is better that the ugly world exist than the one which is beautiful." (Moore 1903, 83)

Substitute film, compact disc, poem, news story, photograph, or advertising copy for Moore's word "world" and we believe that you will continue to intuitively agree with the statement. While we may disagree on what specifically constitutes beauty in form and content, the aesthetic standard of excellence still applies.

The Prosocial Effects of Media Entertainment

Philosopher John Dewey noted, "Aesthetic experience is a manifestation, a record and celebration of the life of a civilization, a means of promoting its development, and is also the ultimate judgment upon the quality of a civilization." If such is the case, then the entertainment media have much to contribute to the healthy side of the ledger. Some are detailed here:

One of the biggest entertainment events of the 1980s was the "Live Aid" concert held on two continents simultaneously to benefit those starving in the Ethiopian famine. Engineered by English singer Bob Geldof, the concert and its subsequent album sales raised more than $100 million in relief funds and an untold amount of awareness of the extent of the sub-Saharan famine.

Other entertainers picked up on the concept and in quick succession, though with more modest success, came:

- USA for Africa, a group of American superstars who joined together to record *We Are the World,* with proceeds donated to African relief.
- Farm Aid, a concert of country-and-western singers, with profits going to America's drought-stricken farmers.
- Comic Relief, a comedy marathon by top-name comedians, with the profits helping the homeless.
- The Amnesty International worldwide rock tour in 1988 featuring Bruce Springsteen, Sting, Peter Gabriel, Tracy Chapman, and others, with proceeds funding human rights causes around the world.
- *For the Children,* a CD recorded in 1991 and featuring such artists as Paul McCartney, Bruce Springsteen, Sting, Barbra Streisand, and James Taylor raised more than $3 million for the Pediatric AIDS Foundation in its first twenty-four months.

Other entertainers have maintained a lifelong association with a single cause, lending credibility and recognition to worthy organizations such as UNICEF (Danny Kaye), the Muscular Dystrophy Association (Jerry Lewis), animal rights (Betty White), and world hunger (Harry Chapin).

Not every effort is quite so elaborate, yet many are equally effective. Paul Simon's *Graceland* album sold millions of copies and won a Grammy award in 1986, while focusing the world's attention on apartheid in South Africa and the plight of African-Americans. The HBO movie *The Tuskegee Airmen* showed the nation that America had once been guilty of many of the same attitudes, and the work of Spike Lee in the 2000 film *Bamboozled* showed us those attitudes persist. MTV, often criticized for the sex and violence content of its programming, sponsored the Rock Against Drugs (RAD) program in the late 1980s, and Rock the Vote in 1992, 1996, and 2000. The latter included news programming about the election aimed at young people as well as mobilizing messages urging the MTV generation to get involved in the political process.

Television entertainment programming is worthy of praise in several areas. *The Burning Bed* addressed the problem of violent relationships, while *Something*

About Amelia frankly discussed the tragedy of incest. Critically acclaimed programs in recent years have examined the possibility of nuclear holocaust and the plight of abused children, rape victims, the adult mentally handicapped, and other vulnerable segments of society. In addition, phenomena such as teenage suicide and Alzheimer's disease have been made more real to millions of Americans through docudramas. Media activist Elizabeth Thoman has called such prime-time television the major "continuing education" available to many adult Americans to help them learn to cope with contemporary crises (Thoman 1987).

Television helps kids, too. Shows such as *Sesame Street* and *Barney* have helped kids to acquire reading skills and learn how to get along. PBS's *Ghost Writer* and *Wishbone* promote literacy for older children.

Norman Cousins, former editor of the *Saturday Review,* even claims entertainment heals. He claims to have cured a collagen disease that had paralyzed most of his body through a self-prescribed routine of massive injections of vitamin C and laughter, in part induced by old film comedies (Cousins 1974). While it might be stretching the prosocial benefits of media entertainment to claim that the media can have medicinal power, entertainment can be meritorious. And meritorious programming need not be dull or commercially unsuccessful. The popular *Friends* provides television's most realistic look yet at the complex role of relationships in our lives.

Perhaps the most important positive effect is the media's ability to pull people away from the routine of everyday life and provide an outlet for escape. In an interview on the PBS series *The Promise of Television,* former CBS news commentator Bill Moyers said:

> The root word of television is vision from afar, and that's its chief value. It has brought me in my stationary moments visions of ideas and dreams and imaginations and geography that I would never personally experience. So, it has put me in touch with the larger world. Television can be a force for dignifying life, not debasing it. (Moyers 1988)

Though Moyers's comments were made specifically about television, the same argument can be made for a good book, a favorite magazine, music, or a film. And whether the media are a force for dignifying humanity or debasing it is largely in the hands of those who own it and work in it.

Suggested Readings

Calvert, Clay. 2000. *Voyeur Nation: Media, privacy and peering in modern culture.* Boulder, Colo.: Westview Press.

Leibert, Robert M., Joyce N. Sprafkin, and Emily S. Davidson. 1982. *The early window: Effects of television on children and youth.* New York: Pergamon Press.

Medved, Michael. 1992. *Hollywood vs. America.* New York: HarperCollins Publishers.

Montgomery, Kathryn C. 1989. *Target: Prime time. Advocacy groups and the struggle over entertainment television.* New York: Oxford University Press.

Postman, Neil. 1986. *Amusing ourselves to death: Public discourse in the age of television.* New York: Penguin Books.

CHAPTER XI CASES

CASE XI-A
Bamboozled: Truth (or Prophecy) in Satire of Popular Culture
LEE WILKINS
University of Missouri

Network television executive Pierre Delacroix, possessor of a Harvard education and the only African-American at an unnamed but fledgling cable network, is frustrated. He wants to make television shows about people who are like him—and all his good ideas have been rejected. Finally, in an attempt to rebuke his boss Dunwitty, a man who is unprejudiced by virtue of who he married and nothing else, he invents the most racist, stereotypical show he can imagine, culled from America's cultural past. *Mantan—The New Millennium Minstrel Show* features two African-Americans (dancer Savion Glover and comedian Tommy Davidson) who are forced to don black-face and repeat everything from watermelon-patch humor to a kind of shuck-and-jive repartee that was the foundation of vaudeville.

Delacroix miscalculates in only one way: his show is a hit. The largely Caucasian audience starts showing up at the studio in blackface, the performers become instant celebrities who slowly comprehend the deep irony of what they are being asked to do, and his assistant, an NYU-educated media grad who is so eager to please she slept with her boss, remains aghast not only at the idea but at its success. Meanwhile her rapper brother compromises his principles for a chance to audition.

Even though Spike Lee created the screenplay as well as directed this film, he had trouble finding money to support making and distributing this in-your-face satire of popular culture. Lee took the film's title from a speech by Malcolm X (the subject of one of Lee's earlier film efforts) where the leader of the Nation of Islam tells his supporters, "You've been hoodwinked. You've been had. You've been took. You've been led astray, led amok. You've been bamboozled." He took inspiration from at least one other film about the media—*Network*—a satirical look at the television news business in the late 1970s. Unfortunately for media consumers, several of *Network's* seemingly outrageous claims about the evolution of the medium have come true in the last few years, particularly with the advent of reality-based television. Knowing this, there is a deep uneasiness about many of the scenes and plot twists in *Bamboozled.* Does the satire here only incompletely veil where the culture is and where it might be going?

As is typical for Lee he spares no one, and many film critics said the film paints with a brush so broad that nuance becomes impossible. "I think his fundamental miscalculation was to use blackface itself. He overshoots the mark. Blackface is so blatant, so wounding, so highly charged, that it obscures any point being made by the person wearing it," wrote Roger Ebert, in his October 6, 2000 review.

Lee's cinematic statement that rap—which has become part of the larger American popular culture—is really just a contemporary minstrel show angered rappers who believe their art form is a true reflection of the modern African-American experience. "The sad part—they don't know it," Lee told a Denver audience in 2000. "One could make the argument that certain parts of rap, you might say gangster rap, those videos could be construed as a contemporary minstrel act. You could possibly say some shows on television are borderline minstrel shows. This film does a great thing; it poses questions."

Lee makes other points along the way. If you are a person of color, in order to be successful in the majority community you have to speak, write, dance, sing or embark on a career path in a stereotypical way. True? Also, the stereotypes in this film function in precisely the way suggested by another folk tale that has passed into the realm of politically incorrect. They are like "Brer Rabbit and de Tar Baby"—once stuck, you simply cannot get out.

To prove this point Lee closes his film with a montage of historic feature film footage of African-Americans singing and dancing just the way they do in *Mantan— The New Millennium Minstrel Show.* The audience is left to wonder whether U.S. culture has moved very far at all.

But other critics viewed the film, including its violent ending, differently. *"Bamboozled,* made by an older filmmaker at the peak of his craft, shows similar daring, politically and technically. Here, Lee is taking on the whole swamp of mangled media stereotyping, while at the same time savagely and justly satirizing modern TV industry practices. Yet, on another level, he's playing tribute to the resilience of art and defining the dilemma of artists . . . who, like those past entertainers, have to slant their talents to the clichés of their time." (Wilmington, 2000).

Micro Issues:

1. Is Roger Ebert correct in asserting that the use of blackface is so offensive that it should not have become a part of the film?
2. Some critics suggested that while Caucasian Americans need to see this film, African-Americans do not. Do you agree? Why?
3. After seeing this film, how would you construct a review? Would you use the racial slurs in the dialogue? What should a review for a film like this accomplish for readers or viewers?

Mid-range Issues:

1. Several newspapers opened chat rooms about the film and asked readers to comment. Some of those comments were reprinted as part of reviews. Is this practice good journalism? Why?
2. Scholars have found that audiences often don't understand that what they are reading or viewing is satirical. Instead, they take it as literal truth. What is the role of satire in the contemporary media marketplace? Do "mockumentaries" fulfill this role?

3. Considering what you know of contemporary U.S. society, could a Caucasian director have made or marketed this film?
4. Many young people may not be familiar with some of the verbal and visual stereotypes Lee inserts in the film. By repeating them, is Lee providing an inadvertent education in racism?

Macro Issues:

1. Lee's satire, among other things, takes on the notion of popular art when it involves minority communities and points of view. Do you believe Lee is correct—that all art is a compromise with culture?
2. Can something be both elite and popular art? Does *Bamboozled* reside in both categories? Is this distinction any longer appropriate in U.S. culture?

CASE XI-B
Playing Hardball: The Pete Rose–Jim Gray Controversy
BEN SCOTT
The Daily Oklahoman

Shortly before game two of the 1999 World Series, the All-Century baseball team was introduced to a sellout crowd in Atlanta and a nationwide television audience. Pete Rose received the longest ovation. But unlike his fellow honorees, most of whom were in the Baseball Hall of Fame, Pete Rose was not—he'd been banished from Major League Baseball for life for gambling on baseball while the manager of the Cincinnati Reds.

Known as "Charlie Hustle" during his lengthy major league career, Rose collected more base hits than any player in history. In the decade since his banishment by Bart Giamatti, the former Ivy League university president turned commissioner of baseball, fans on both sides have debated his banishment. Rose has always adamantly denied that he bet on baseball. The appearance at the World Series game was Rose's first appearance at a baseball game in more than ten years.

After the on-field ceremony, Jim Gray, an Emmy Award–winning reporter for NBC, caught up with Rose and asked him for an interview before the live television audience. But instead of lauding Rose and welcoming him back to the game, Gray immediately grilled the legend about his refusal to admit any guilt regarding the gambling allegations.

Gray had earned acclaim for confronting Mike Tyson about his actions immediately after a 1997 fight where Tyson bit off a chunk of his opponent's ear. He has a reputation for standing up to star athletes and asking the tough questions.

"Are you willing to show contrition, admit that you bet on baseball and make some sort of apology?" Gray asked Rose.

"Not at all," Rose replied. "I'm not going to admit something that didn't happen."

Gray, who had interviewed Rose more than fifty times in the past, didn't let the subject drop. He continued to badger Rose, stating the evidence against him was overwhelming and added, "Some people say you are your own worst enemy."

Finally, Rose said, "Jim, I'm surprised you're bombarding me like this on such a festive occasion."

NBC switchboards across the country were immediately deluged with calls complaining about Gray's interview, including two hours nonstop in Cincinnati where Rose had played and coached. The majority of the callers felt that Rose had paid the price for his past troubles and should have been allowed to enjoy his moment of recognition as one of the game's greatest.

New York Yankee outfielder Darryl Strawberry, a player in the World Series game and a man who was no stranger to bad press and bad choices, said, "It was a night of celebration for Pete Rose. Every player who has ever played cares about Pete Rose. It was embarrassing."

Yankee manager Joe Torre agreed. "For some reason, we've lost sight of the word 'respect.' We deal too much in shock value."

Yankee players decided to boycott Gray for the remainder of the Series. When Yankee outfielder Chad Curtis hit a game-winning home run in the next game, he made his feelings about Gray evident in a live post-game interview. "Because of what happened with Pete, we decided not to say anything," Curtis told a live audience, leaving Gray to shout questions after him as he walked away. "It's not a personal thing between me and Jim Gray," Curtis said later. "It's a thing the team decided."

NBC was forced to move another reporter into Gray's slot for the remainder of the series. Despite the animosity of the fans and players, NBC still supported Gray and his interview. Dick Ebersol, chairman of NBC Sports, called Gray "the best sports reporter of his generation."

Despite the public sentiment, Gray refused to apologize. "I stand by it and think it was a proper line of questioning," he said. He added that reporters had asked Rose the same questions at a press conference before the ceremony.

In a later interview with *Sports Illustrated,* Gray said he believed the forum for the questions was appropriate. "It was not overdone. Rose has put himself in a position to be pressed like that. Pete knew what was coming. I was trying to give him a window of opportunity to take his case to the public."

Media reaction to Gray's interview was mixed. The *Boston Globe's* Bob Ryan represents one side when he contends that "After two questions he should have realized it was going nowhere, that Rose would cling to the fiction that he did not bet on baseball as manager of the Cincinnati Reds" (Ryan, 1999). On the other side were journalists such as Bob Raissman (1999) of the *New York Daily News* when he wrote, "It was just another case of a guy on TV, who is supposed to supplement the moment, trying to make himself bigger than the game." More than fifty sports editorials were written nationwide on the controversy and the reaction to Gray's conduct was evenly split among his print peers.

Micro Issues:

1. Given the manner and context of the Rose interview, was Jim Gray out of line?
2. Does Rose's celebrity status have an impact on how much latitude a reporter like Gray has in the questioning?
3. Given what Gray knew would be Rose's response, was the interview necessary?
4. Should Gray have apologized? Justify your answer.

Mid-range Issues:

1. Was NBC correct in standing behind its reporter. If not, why? If so, then how can the network justify moving Gray out of the Yankee's dugout after the player boycott?
2. Did Gray do his employer a disservice by making himself less useful during the several games left in the Series?
3. Is the public's reaction a factor in determining if a journalistic action was ethical?

Macro Issues:

1. Sports reporters need athletes, and athletes, to maximize their earnings potential, need coverage. Given this symbiotic relationship, is objectivity possible? Desirable?
2. Critique the two quotes by Ryan and Raissman. Who do you think was right? Is there any way to reconcile the two opinions?

CASE XI-C
Hate Radio: The Outer Limits of Tasteful Broadcasting
BRIAN SIMMONS
Cascade College, Portland, Oregon

Trevor Van Lansing has what some would call the greatest job in the world. He is employed by KRFP-AM, an all-talk–format radio station in a large city in the West. His program airs weekdays from 3:00 P.M. to 7:00 P.M., and he is currently rated number one in his afternoon drive-time slot. Van Lansing is, quite simply, the most popular radio personality in the market. He is also the most controversial.

Each afternoon Van Lansing introduces a general topic for discussion and then fields calls from listeners about the topic. However, Lansing's topics (and the calls from his listeners) revolve around a recurring theme: the world as viewed by a Caucasian, Anglo-Saxon Protestant who also happens to be vocal, uncompromising, and close-minded.

A sampling of his recent programs typifies his show. On Monday, Van Lansing discusses a woman in a small Indiana town who quits her job in a convenience store to go on welfare because there is more money to be made on the federal dole than in the private sector. Says Van Lansing, "All these irresponsible whores are the same. They get knocked up by some construction worker, then expect the taxpayers to pay for them to sit around the house all day and watch Oprah Winfrey."

Callers flood the airwaves with equally combative remarks in support of and opposition to Van Lansing's comments. On Tuesday, the topic of racial discrimination (always a Van Lansing favorite) comes up. According to Van Lansing, "Those Africans expect us Americans to make up for two hundred years of past mistakes. Forget it. It can't be done. If they are so keen on America, let them compete against Caucasians on an equal basis without the 'civil rights crutch.' "

When one African-American caller challenges Van Lansing's thinking, the host responds, "Why don't you tell your buddies to work for what they get like us Caucasians? All you do anyway is steal from the guys you don't like and then take their women."

Wednesday finds Van Lansing lashing out against education: "The problem with today's schools is that our kinds are exposed to weird thinking. I mean, we tell our kids that homosexuality is okay, that we evolved from a chimp, and that the Ruskies are our friends. It all started when we elected women to school boards and started letting fags into the classroom. It's disgusting."

Thursday features an exchange between Van Lansing and an abortion-rights activist. At one point they are both shouting at the same time, and the airwaves are peppered with obscenities and personal attacks. By comparison, Friday is calm, as only a few irate Jews, women, and Mormons bother to call in.

Critics have called Van Lansing's program offensive, tasteless, rude, racist, obscene, and insensitive. Supporters refer to the program as enlightening, refreshing, educational, and provocative. The only thing everyone can agree on is that the show is a bona fide moneymaker. Van Lansing's general manager notes that the station's ratings jumped radically when he was hired, and that advertising revenues have tripled.

In fact, Van Lansing's popularity has spawned promotional appearances, T-shirts, bumper stickers, and other paraphernalia, all designed to hawk the station. "Sure, Trevor is controversial, but in this business that's good," says KRFP's general manager. "Van Lansing is so good that he will make more money this year than the president of the United States. Besides, it's just a gimmick."

Does Van Lansing see a problem with the content and style of his program? "Look," he says, "radio is a business. You have to give the audience what they want. All I do is give them what they want. If they wanted a kinder, gentler attitude, I would give it to them." He continues, "Don't get mad at me. Thank God we live in a country where guys like me can express an opinion. The people who listen to me like to hear it straight sometimes, and that's what the First Amendment is about, right?"

Finally, Van Lansing points out that if people are really offended by him, they can always turn the dial. "I don't force these people to listen," he pleads. "If they don't like it, let them go somewhere else."

Others disagree. The National Coalition for the Understanding of Alternative Lifestyles, a gay- and lesbian-rights group, calls Van Lansing's show "reprehensible." "Trevor Van Lansing is hiding behind the First Amendment. What he says on the air isn't speech; it's hate, pure and simple," says the group's director. "His program goes well beyond what our founders intended."

Adds a representative of the National Organization for Women, "Van Lansing is perpetuating several dangerous stereotypes that are destructive, sick, and offensive. Entertainment must have some boundaries."

Micro Issues:

1. Would you be offended by Van Lansing's program? If so, why?
2. Would Van Lansing's program be less offensive if the station aired another talk show immediately after his which featured a host holding opposite views?
3. How are the lyrics of rapper Eminem (Martin Mathers) like or unlike Van Lansing's rants? Is an artist subject to different restrictions?

Mid-range Issues:

1. Who should accept responsibility for monitoring this type of program? Van Lansing? The radio station, KRFP? The FCC? The courts? The audience?
2. What, if any, are the differences between Van Lansing's *legal* right to do what he does and the *ethical* implications of what he does?
3. Legal scholar Mari Matsuda (1989) has called for a narrow legal restriction of racist speech. She notes, "The places where the law does not go to redress harm have tended to be the places where women, children, people of color, and poor people live" (Matsuda 1989, 11). She argues that a content-based restriction of racist speech is more protective of civil liberties than other tests that have been traditionally applied. Could such an argument be applied to entertainment programming?

Macro Issues:

1. Are entertainers relieved of ethical responsibilities if they are "just giving the audience what they want?" Do Van Lansing's high ratings validate his behavior, since many people are obviously in agreement with him?
2. How does Van Lansing's narrow view of the world differ from a television situation comedy that stereotypes blondes as dumb, blue-collar workers as bigoted, etc.?
3. Van Lansing says that it's great that a guy like him can have a radio show. Is tolerance one of the measures of a democracy? If so, are there limits to tolerance, and who draws those lines?
4. How should democratic societies cope with unpopular points of view, particularly as expressed through the mass media? Does a social critic still have an important role, even if that criticism is unpopular?

CASE XI-D
Beavis and Butthead: The Case for Standards in Entertainment
PHILIP PATTERSON
Oklahoma Christian University

In October 1993, five-year-old Aaron Messner set fire to his family's trailer in Moraine, Ohio, killing his two-year-old sister. According to press reports and the local fire chief, the boy had been influenced by the pyromaniacal antics of MTV's *Beavis and Butthead.*

The Messner tragedy made headlines across the nation and brought *Beavis and Butthead* into the national limelight. However, the controversy over MTV's most popular show surfaced much earlier.

Beavis and Butthead is the creation of a self-professed former "awkward, miserable" adolescent, Mike Judge. Judge served as producer, animator, and voice for the show in its early days. He says that the two losers depicted on the show were modeled after kids he knew in junior high, and not unlike the ones he sees today.

Judge told an interviewer for *Texas Monthly* magazine that he considers *Beavis and Butthead* to be "lowest common denominator humor." He thought of the concept after noticing "Everything I saw on TV was so politically correct. I just had this urge to be offensive and juvenile."

From its debut in March 1993, the show hit a national nerve. Soon words such as "butt-munch" and "fartknocker" had made the popular culture lexicon. The annoying heh-heh-heh laugh was everywhere. The show garnered ratings four times higher than the typical MTV music video.

Beavis and Butthead focused on typical adolescent talk and humor. Girls were "chicks" to be scored on, though neither Beavis nor Butthead seemed capable. Bathroom humor abounded. A study by one *Rolling Stone* writer found that an anal reference was scripted every sixteen words.

The show had both critics and fans. *Time* magazine called it possibly "the bravest show ever run on television." *U.S. News & World Report* likened it to the "death knell of civilization." Psychologist and media figure Joyce Brothers praised it; South Carolina Senator Ernest Hollings condemned it. On the subject of Aaron Messner, Pulitzer prize–winning columnist Anna Quindlen wondered in her column why a five-year-old was watching MTV alone.

Some advertisers avoided the program, but parent corporation Viacom stuck with MTV's highest rated show. Just prior to the debut of *Beavis and Butthead,* MTV accounted for 22 percent of Viacom's revenues. Now the new show was the hottest item in Viacom's most profitable subsidiary.

The show that could get away with ridiculing the explosion of the Space Shuttle *Challenger* found itself in deeper trouble when first one real-life tragedy then another were blamed on the antics of its characters. Within a few months, four fires, a cat killing, and the throwing of a bowling ball off a highway overpass onto a car, which killed an eight-month-old girl, were blamed on *Beavis and Butthead* and reported nationally. A causal link was denied by MTV in all the cases, and indeed the evidence in the bowling ball incident was particularly weak, but *Beavis and Butthead* was now vulnerable to criticism from the mainstream press.

MTV responded by eliminating the 7:00 P.M. (EST) airing of *Beavis and Butthead,* moving the show to 10:30 and 11:00 P.M., at the same time arguing that less than 10 percent of the audience was under the age of twelve. The recurring motif of fire was also eliminated from the program, and a disclaimer warning viewers not to model the characters Beavis and Butthead's behavior was added. MTV issued a statement about the changes:

> While we do not believe the "Beavis and Butthead" cartoon was responsible [for the Messner tragedy], we feel the steps we are taking are the proper ones. "Beavis and Butthead" is made for the teenagers and young adults who make up the overwhelming majority of its audience. These viewers see the cartoon for what it is—an exaggerated parody of two teenaged misfits whose antics take place in a cartoon world . . . antics [the viewers] know are unacceptable and not to be emulated in real life. Nevertheless, we have decided to bend over backward as responsible programmers.

Micro Issues:

1. Part of the behaviors of the two characters in *Beavis and Butthead* included sniffing paint thinner and using an aerosol can and lighter to create a blowtorch. Should one assume that in an audience of millions that at least a few will try to emulate this behavior? Should that matter?
2. Can an advertiser reasonably expect to convince a *Beavis and Butthead* viewer to consume a certain beverage or buy a certain item? If so, what does that say about whether the show can alter a child's behavior in other areas of life?
3. Did MTV do the right thing by shifting the time the show aired?
4. Is the presence of a disclaimer urging viewers not to imitate the acts seen on the screen sufficient?

Mid-range Issues:

1. Satire has been around for centuries. Jonathan Swift once wrote "A Modest Proposal" suggesting that Irish Catholics should fatten their babies for consumption by the English. Some readers thought he was serious. Would that classic work pass the political correctness test today? Should satire be exempt from the traditional standards of what is acceptable in a society?
2. To what extent are the media responsible for the level of violence in our society?

Macro Issues:

1. One of the functions of media is to hold a mirror up to society. Is part of the criticism of *Beavis and Butthead* that the adults who see it don't like the reality that it reveals?

2. Who is ultimately responsible for what children should see on television:
   a. The media?
   b. The government?
   c. Parents?
3. If a product is defective, the manufacturer can be held liable under the doctrine of "strict liability" for the damage it causes. Should the media be held to the same standard as, for instance, pharmaceutical manufacturers, as some argue, since both produce a product to be "ingested"? Is it possible for a media message to be "defective"? If so, what should be the remedy?

CASE XI-E
Schindler's List: The Role of Memory
LEE WILKINS
University of Missouri–Columbia

In 1982 director Steven Spielberg purchased the rights to Australian novelist Thomas Keneally's retelling of the story of the "Schindler Jews," a group of about 1,100 Krakow, Poland, residents who survived the Holocaust because Czech businessman Oskar Schindler was willing to cajole, bribe, and bully the Nazis for their lives. Today, Schindler, a Roman Catholic by birth, is known in Israel as a "righteous person"; he is the only Nazi buried in Jerusalem's Mount Zion cemetery.

By 1992 when Spielberg began work on the film, both he and the world had changed. Bosnia was in the midst of "ethnic cleansing," as were nations in Africa and in the Far East, such as Nepal. Some polls indicated that more than half of the U.S. teenagers living in that decade had never heard of the Holocaust; about 23 percent of the U.S. public at the time maintained the gassing of 6 million Jews plus 5 million other "undesirables" in Germany and its occupied territories never happened.

"I think the main reason I wanted to make this film was as an act of remembrance," Spielberg told the film editor of the *Atlanta Journal and Constitution.* "An act of remembrance for the public record. Maybe it won't be seen by gallons of people who see my other movies, but it might be the kind of movie shown one day in high schools. I also wanted to leave this story for my children. I wanted to leave them a legacy of their Jewish culture."

What Americans, as well as Spielberg's children will see is a three-hour-and-15-minute examination of the conscience of Oskar Schindler, who entered World War II on the side of the Nazis, intending to make a profit. He hires Jews to work in his enamelware factory because they work for less than slave wages. Initially, he befriends the Nazis and the SS to help expedite his purchase and takeover of the plant. Later, after the Nazis have first ghettoized and then attempted to exterminate the Jewish population of Krakow, Schindler uses his personal charm, his connections, and most of his war-amassed wealth to have "his" Jewish workers first labeled as essential to the German war machine and later moved from Germany and into Czechoslovakia for safekeeping. None of the bombs manufactured at Schindler's plant ever exploded.

Spielberg shot the film in black and white on location in Poland. Much of the movie has a documentary feel; cinematography is at eye level. It was often Spielberg himself who focused the handheld camera. Hitler appears only once—in a photograph on someone's desk. And, by centering on Schindler, Spielberg captured the conscience of an uneasy hero.

As Keneally's book indicates, Oskar Schindler was a complex man. He managed to maintain outward friendships with many Nazis whom he despised. He was a sensualist who enjoyed good food, expensive possessions and carnal knowledge of women who were not his wife. Spielberg's film, which was rated R, depicted all of this, including scenes of lovemaking that involved full, frontal nudity and more distant shots of concentration camp existence in which Jewish inmates were required to run naked in front of their guards to determine who remained well enough to work and who was sick enough to be murdered.

Perhaps the most disturbing element of the film was Spielberg's portrait of the violence embedded in Hitler's "final solution" and of the banality of evil (Hannah Arendt's phrase used to describe convicted war criminal Adolph Eichmann) that individual human beings can come to represent. That sundered humanity is symbolized by Amon Goeth (played by Ralph Fiennes), the amoral, and some have suggested, sociopathic commandant of the labor camp from which many of the people who worked for Schindler survived. Whether it is the Nazis hunting the Jews who remain in hiding in the Krakow ghetto or Goeth's randomized murder of the men and women who lived in his camp as before-breakfast sport, the violence in the film is devastating not just for its brutality but also for its casualness.

When Spielberg's mother told him making *"Schindler's List* would be good for the Jews," Spielberg responded that "It would be good for all of us."

Critics, who had a difficult time accepting that the same man who directed *Jurassic Park* could also produce *Schindler's List* in the same year, praised the film for its aesthetic qualities and for its retelling of the story of the Holocaust in such a powerful fashion. The film also brought Spielberg multiple Oscars, an award that had eluded him despite his enormous popular success. After the film's release, President Bill Clinton said that every American should see it.

Writing in the *Washington Post,* Rita Kempley saw more than a superficial resemblance between Schindler and Spielberg. "And Schindler, played with élan by (Liam) Neeson, is really a lot like Spielberg himself," she wrote, "A man who manages to use his commercial clout to achieve a moral end."

Micro Issues:

1. Should a film like *Schindler's List* receive the same R rating as films such as *Road Trip?*
2. What is the appropriate role of a film critic for films such as *Schindler's List?* Should different standards be used to evaluate this film than some other Spielberg successes, such as *E.T.* or *Jaws?*
3. Would you allow a child under seventeen to see this film?

Mid-range Issues:

1. Should news accounts focus on events such as the ethnic cleansing in Bosnia with the goal of changing public opinion?
2. Are docudramas that focus on social issues such as spouse abuse or child molestation the appropriate mechanism to engage the public in debate or discussion about such serious questions?
3. Some people have argued that certain historical events, such as the Holocaust or the recent genocide in Rwanda, should never be the subject of entertainment

programming because entertainment can never capture the true horror of what has happened. How would you evaluate such an assertion?

Macro Issues:

1. Compare the moral development of Oskar Schindler in the film *Schindler's List* with that of the main characters in a film such as *Gandhi*.
2. John Dewey wrote about "funded memory," by which he meant how a culture remembers and reconstructs its own history. What is the role of entertainment programming in funded memory? What should be the role of news programming in such cultural constructions?
3. Tolstoy argues that good art communicates the feelings of the artist to the masses in such a way that others may experience the same feeling as the artist. How does this film accomplish that purpose?

CHAPTER XII
Becoming a Moral Adult

By the end of this chapter you should:

• know the stages of moral development as described by Piaget and Kohlberg.
• understand the ethics of care.
• understand the stages of adult moral development.

Introduction

Most college undergraduates think of graduation as the completion of an educational process. They view it as an end to a sixteen-year effort, and the beginning of that scary time in life when their preliminary commitments to work, other people, and lifestyle will be tested in the "real" world.

We suggest an alternate view, at least for ethical development. We'd like to suggest that your personal process of becoming an ethical person has now begun. Whether it has been through reading this book, taking a class in ethics, or making ethical choices in your life, what you understand about ethics now—and the choices you make—are a reflection of the person you are at this moment. The person you will be when you are thirty or forty will have added insight. Growth may change your decisions. This process is not only inevitable but also desirable.

This chapter is designed to provide you with an overview of some psychological theories of moral development. It attempts to allow you to plot your own development not only in terms of where you are but also in terms of where you would like to be.

Basic Assumptions About Moral Development: The Rights-Based Tradition

People can learn to develop morality just as they can learn to think critically (Clouse 1985). Scholars base this assertion on the following premises.

First, *moral development occurs within the individual.* Real moral development cannot be produced by outside factors, nor can it be produced merely by engaging in moral acts. People develop morally when they are aware of their reasons for acting a certain way.

Second, *moral development parallels intellectual development.* Although the two may proceed at a slightly different pace, there can be little moral development until a person has attained a certain intellectual capacity. For this reason, we exempt children and people of limited mental ability from some laws and societal expectations. While one can be intelligent without being moral, the converse is not as likely.

Third, *moral development occurs in a series of universal, unvarying and hierarchical stages.* Each level builds on the lower levels, and there is no skipping of intermediate stages. Just as a baby crawls before walking and babbles before speaking, a child must pass through the earlier stages of moral development before advancing to the later stages.

Fourth, *moral development comes through conflict.* As moral development theorist Lawrence Kohlberg notes (1973, 13), "A fundamental reason why an individual moves from one stage to the next is because the latter stages solve problems and inconsistencies unsolvable at the present developmental stage."

The two developmental psychologists who are the most cited experts in the field did their work decades and continents apart yet came to remarkably similar conclusions. Jean Piaget conducted his research in Switzerland in the 1930s by watching little boys play marbles, and in the 1960s Lawrence Kohlberg studied Harvard students. Together they have produced many of the most provocative insights in the rights-based tradition. They are often called "stage theorists" for their work in identifying and describing the stages of moral development.

CALVIN AND HOBBES copyright Watterson. Dist. by UNIVERSAL PRESS SYNDICATE. Reprinted with permission. All rights reserved.

The Work of Piaget

Swiss psychologist Jean Piaget turned his attention to children's moral development in the 1930s. He watched as boys between the ages of three and twelve played marbles, and he later tested his assumptions about their playground behavior in interviews. The box below presents the basics of Piaget's theory.

The children under age seven didn't really play a game of marbles at all. They made up their own rules, varied them by playmate and game, and delighted in exploring the marbles as tactile objects. Their view of the game-playing universe was centered exclusively on what each individual child wanted.

Piaget's Stages of Moral Development

EARLY DEVELOPMENT (before age 2)

• Interest in marbles is purely motor, e.g., put the marbles in your mouth.

FIRST STAGE—egocentrism (years 3–7)

• Children engage in "parallel play"; there is no coherent set of rules accepted by all.
• The moral reasoning is "I do it because it feels right."

SECOND STAGE—heteronomy (years 7–8)

• Children recognize only individual responsibility; obedience is enforced through punishment.
• Each player tries to win.
• Rules are regarded as inviolate, unbreakable, handed down from outside authority figures, usually older children.
• The children do not understand the reason behind the rules.

THIRD STAGE—autonomy (begins about age 11)

• Children internalize the rules; they understand the reasons behind them.
• They develop an ideal of justice and are able to distinguish between individual and collective responsibility.
• They ensure fair play among children.
• Children can change the rules in responses to a larger set of obligations.
• Authority is internal.
• Children understand universal ethical principles that transcend specific times and situations.

Piaget found that younger boys (ages seven and eight) played marbles as if the rules had been taught to them by their parents or other authority figures and as if violations of those rules would result in punishment. The boys believed the rules were timeless and that "goodness" came from respecting the rules. Boys in this stage of moral development believed "Right is to obey the will of the adult. Wrong is to have a will of one's own" (Piaget 1965, 193).

Children progressed to the next stage of moral development when the boys began to develop notions of autonomy. As they became more autonomous, the children began to understand that there was a reason behind the rules, and that the reasons (i.e., fair play and reciprocity) were the foundation of the rules themselves. Children in this stage of moral development understood that the rules did not originate from some outside authority figure but rather received their power from the group consensus because the rule itself promoted fair play and equality.

These children had internalized the rules and the reasons behind them. Understanding the rules allowed the boys to rationally justify violating them. For example, children in this stage of moral development allowed much younger children to place their thumbs inside the marble circles, a clear violation of the rules. But the younger boys' hands were smaller and weaker, and by allowing them a positional advantage, the older ones had—in contemporary language—leveled the playing field. They had ensured fairness where literally following the rules would have made it impossible.

Although Piaget worked with children, it is possible to see that adults often demonstrate these stages of moral development.

Take the videographer whose primary motivation is to obtain a great shot, regardless of the views of those he works with or his story subjects. This journalist operates within an egocentric moral framework that places the primary emphasis on what "I" think, "my" judgment, and what's good for "me."

Beginning journalists, the ones who find themselves concerned with the literal following of codes of ethics, may often be concerned with the heteronomy stage of development. This journalist knows the rules and follows them. She would never accept a freebie or consider running the name of a rape victim. It's against organizational policy, and heteronomous individuals are motivated largely by outside influences.

Just as the boys at the seasoned stage of moral development were more willing to bend the rules to ensure a fair game for all, journalists at the final stage of moral development are more willing to violate professional norms if it results in better journalism. The journalist at this stage of moral development has so internalized and universalized the rules of ethical professional behavior that he or she can violate some of them for sound ethical reasons.

Proceeding with a story that is unpopular, expensive, or out of the norm could be considered an example of journalism at the highest level of Piaget's schema. For instance, the Pulitzer prize–winning series by the *Des Moines Register* regarding the rape, recovery, and trial ordeal of a rape victim who volunteered to have her story told is an example of journalism that breaks the mold and goes far beyond the norm of stories of its type. Also indicative of this level of journalism is the painstakingly detailed series of articles written by two enterprising *Detroit Free Press* reporters who read volumes of the federal tax code and found it to be loaded with one-of-a-kind tax loopholes for individuals and businesses with political connections.

However, people seldom remain exclusively in a single stage of moral development. New situations often mean that people, including journalists and their sources, regress temporarily to a previous stage of moral development until enough learning can take place so that the new situation is well understood. But, such regression would not include behaviors that would be considered morally culpable under most circumstances, for example, lying or killing, despite the new context.

The Work of Kohlberg

Harvard psychologist Lawrence Kohlberg mapped six stages of moral development in his college-student subjects. The box below outlines Kohlberg's stages of moral development, divided into three levels.

Kohlberg developed a lengthy set of interview questions to allow him to establish which stage of moral development individual students had achieved. He asserted

---

The Six Moral Stages of Kohlberg

Level 1: Pre-conventional
Stage 1: Heteronomous morality is the display of simple obedience.
Stage 2: Individualism is the emergence of self-interest. Rules are followed only when they are deemed to be in one's self-interest and others are allowed the same freedom. Reciprocity and fairness begin to emerge, but only in a pragmatic way.

Level II: Conventional
Stage 3: Interpersonal conformity is living up to what others expect, given one's role, e.g., "brother," "daughter," "neighbor," etc. "Being good" is important, and treating others as you would have them treat you becomes the norm.
Stage 4: Social systems is the recognition that one must fulfill the duties to which one has agreed. Doing one's duty, respect for authority, and maintaining the social order are all goals in this level. Laws are to be upheld unilaterally except in extreme cases where they conflict with other fixed social duties.

Level III: Post-conventional
Stage 5: Social contract and individual rights is becoming aware that one is obligated by whatever laws are agreed to by due process. The social contract demands that we uphold the laws even if they are contrary to our best interests because they exist to provide the greatest good for the greatest number. However, some values such as life and liberty stand above any majority opinion.
Stage 6: Universal ethical principles self-selected by each individual guide this person. These principles are to be followed even if laws violate those principles. The principles that guide this individual include the equality of human rights and respect for the dignity of humans as individual beings regardless of race, age, socioeconomic status, or even contribution to society.

that only a handful of people—for example, Socrates, Gandhi, Martin Luther King, or Mother Teresa—ever achieved the sixth stage of moral development. Most adults, he believed, spend the greater portion of their lives in the two conventional stages. They are motivated by society's expectations.

Doing right, fulfilling one's duties, and abiding by the social contract are the pillars upon which the stages of Kohlberg's work rest. Under Kohlberg's arrangement, justice—and therefore morality—is a function of perception; as you develop, more activities fall under the realm of duty than before. For instance, reciprocity is not even a goal for students in the earliest stage, yet it is an essential characteristic of people in upper stages of moral development. Conversely, acting to avoid punishment is laudable for those in the first stages yet might not be as praiseworthy for someone who is operating on universal ethical principles. The further up Kohlberg's stages students progressed, the more they asserted that moral principles are subject to interpretation by individuals and subject to contextual factors.

Kohlberg's stages are descriptive and not predictive. They do not anticipate how any one individual will develop, but suggest how most will develop. In addition, there is a difference in moral reasoning and moral behavior. They are correlated but not totally overlapping phenomena. Kohlberg focused not on the goodness of moral decisions but on the adequacy of the cognitive structures underlying them.

Kohlberg's formulation has much to recommend it to journalists, concerned as they are with concepts such as free speech, the professional duty to tell the truth, and their obligations to the public and the public trust. However, Kohlberg's work was not without its problems. At least two aspects of his research troubled other moral development theorists.

Many scholars have argued that any generalizable theory of moral development should allow people who are not saints or religious leaders to attain the highest stages of moral development. While it has been argued that only saints can be expected to act in a saintly manner most of the time, history is replete with examples of ordinary people taking extraordinary personal or professional risk for some larger ethical principles. Many scholars felt that Kohlberg's conception—unlike Piaget's—was too restrictive.

Still more troubling was how those students who were tested on Kohlberg's scale performed. In study after study, men consistently scored higher than women on stages of moral development. This gender bias in Kohlberg's work—coupled with other findings from development psychology—prompted discussion about a different concept of moral development, founded on notions of community rather than in the rights-based tradition. It is called the ethics of care.

Parallel Assumptions About Moral Development: The Ethics of Care

The psychologists who are developing the ethics of care disagree with at least two of the fundamental assumptions underlying Piaget and Kohlberg.

First, while moral development occurs within the individual and parallels intellectual development, moral development does not always occur in a series of universal, unvarying, and hierarchical stages. Second, moral growth emerges through understanding the concept of community, not merely through conflict.

The rights-based scholars believe that moral development emerges from a proper understanding of the concept "I." Proponents of the ethics of care say that moral development arises from understanding the concept of "we."

Carol Gilligan's (1982) work provides the clearest explanation of the ethics of care. Gilligan studied women who were deciding whether to have abortions. As she listened to them, she learned that they based their ethical choices on relationships. The first thing these women considered was how to maintain a connection. Gilligan argued that the moral adult is the person who sees a connection between the "I" and the "other." The women spoke in a "different voice" about their ethical decision making.

For example, Gilligan presented the women with Kohlberg's classic ethical dilemma: the case of the desperate man and the greedy pharmacist. In this scenario, a man with a terminally ill spouse doesn't have enough money to purchase an expensive and lifesaving drug. When he explains the situation to the pharmacist, the pharmacist refuses to give him the medication.

Under Kohlberg's system, it would be ethically allowable for the man to steal the drug. However, women made this particular choice less often. Instead, they reasoned that the most ethical thing to do was to build a relationship with the pharmacist, to form a community in which the pharmacist viewed him/herself as an active part. In that situation, the women reasoned, the pharmacist ultimately would give the man the drug in order to maintain the connection.

Gilligan proposed that the women's rationale was no more or less ethically sophisticated than that expected under Kohlberg's outline. However, it was different, for it weighed different ethical values. Whether those values emerged as the result of how women are socialized in Western culture (an assertion that has often been made about Gilligan's work) or whether they merely reflected a different kind of thinking still remains the focus of heated academic debate. For our purposes, the origin of the distinction—and whether it is truly gender-linked—is not as important as the content of the thought itself.

Gilligan's notion of moral development is not neatly tied into stages and does not borrow as heavily from the tradition of logic and rights-based inquiry. Her closest theoretical counterpart is probably communitarianism with its emphasis on connection to community and its mandate for social justice.

If one were to carve stages from Gilligan's work, they would resemble:

- First—an ethic of care where the moral responsibility is for care of others before self.
- Second—an acknowledgement of the ethic of rights, including the rights of self to be considered in ethical decision making.
- Third—a movement from concerns about goodness (women are taught to believe that care for others is "good" while men are taught that "taking care of oneself" is good) to concerns about truth. It is at this stage of moral

development where commitment to a universal ethical principle begins, with truth at the core of that universal principle.

A complete sense of moral development, Gilligan observed, requires the ability "to (use) two different moral languages, the language of rights that protects separations and the language of responsibilities that sustains connection" (Gilligan 1982, 210). Contemporary journalists have struggled with the issues of connection. Since much of our profession is based on an understanding of rights as outlined in various legal documents, ethical reasoning for journalists almost always assumes a rights-based approach. This historically well-founded bias, however, has led journalists into some of their more systematic and profound errors in decisions about privacy, attitudes of arrogance toward sources and readers, and an unwillingness to be genuinely accountable to anyone.

News organizations can work to sustain community. If journalism as a profession is to mature ethically, it must see itself as the vehicle to help people become the citizens they can be and to help reconnect and sustain communities that have become increasingly fragmented, often by the very media that should have brought us together. In an essay entitled "Whose Values," written in the wake of the L.A. riots following the Rodney King verdict, *Newsweek* author Joe Klein wrote:

> Television brought the nation together in the '50s; there were evenings when all of America seemed glued to the same show—Milton Berle, "I Love Lucy" and yes, "Ozzie and Harriet." But cable television has quite the opposite effect, dividing the audience into demographic slivers. . . . Indeed, if you are a member of any identifiable subgroup—black, Korean, fundamentalist, sports fan, political junkie—it's now possible to be massaged by your very own television and radio stations and to read your own magazines without having to venture out into the American mainstream. The choices are exhilarating, but also alienating. The basic principle is centrifugal: market segmentation targets those qualities that distinguish people from each other rather than emphasizing the things we have in common. It is the developed world's equivalent of the retribalization taking place in Eastern Europe, Africa and Asia. (Klein 1992, 21–22)

If there was one common denominator from the vast variety of projects that claimed to fall under the "civic journalism" umbrella in the late 1990s, it was the fact that almost all of them had as a goal to bring people back together and foster a sense of community using the media as a primary tool in the process. To that end, the movement was a laudable one.

Where Do You Go from Here?

Perry (1970) postulates that one of the major accomplishments of college students is to progress from a simple, dualistic (right vs. wrong) view of life to a more complex, mature, and relativistic view. Perry states that students must not only acknowledge that diversity and uncertainty exist in a world of relativism but must also make a commitment to their choices (i.e., career, values, beliefs, etc.) out of the multiplicity of "right" choices available. And ethical choices abound in mass media careers. For instance, even the daily routine of setting the news agenda is an ethical issue since those decisions are often made by Caucasian males for others who are unlike them in significant ways. Even word choice is an ethical issue. Why do we see stories about "working mothers," yet none about "working fathers"?

Unlike physical development, moral development is not subject to the quirks of heredity. Each individual is free to develop as keen a sense of equity as any other individual, yet few reach their full potential. About your attempts to "grow" ethically, Kohlberg (1970) has offered one observation: we tend to understand messages one stage higher than our own moral judgment stage. Through "aspirational listening"— that is, picking an ethical role model on a higher level and observing that person— you can progress to a higher stage of moral development. This observation is not a new one. In fact, it dates to Aristotle, who suggested that virtues could be learned by observing those who possess them.

This book uses the case study method so that you may see ethical decisions that were made at higher and lower levels of moral reasoning and aspire to the former. Often in case studies, it is the reasoning behind the answer rather than the answer itself that is the best determiner of moral growth (Clouse 1985). *An important part of moral development is the recognition that motive, not consequence, is the critical factor in deciding whether an act is ethical.*

Elliott (1991) illustrates the difference in the following scenario. Imagine a situation where you are able to interview and choose your next-door neighbor. When you ask Jones how she feels about murder, she replies she doesn't kill because if she got caught she would go to jail. When you interview Smith, he says he doesn't kill people because he believes in the sanctity of life. It takes little reflection to decide which neighbor you would prefer. Elliott concludes:

"Ethics involves the judging of actions as right or wrong, but motivations count as well. Some reasons for actions seem better or worse than others" (1991, 19).

Suggested Readings

Belenky, Mary F., et al. 1988. *Women's ways of knowing: The development of self, voice and mind.* New York: Basic Books.

Coles, Robert. 1986. *The moral life of children.* New York: Atlantic Monthly Press.

Gilligan, Carol. 1982. *In a different voice: Psychological theory and women's development.* Cambridge, Mass.: Harvard University Press.

Levinson, Daniel J. 1978. *Seasons of a man's life.* New York: Alfred A. Knopf, Inc.

BIBLIOGRAPHY

Alderman, E., & Kennedy, C. (1995). *The right to privacy.* New York: Alfred A. Knopf, Inc.

Allossery, P. (2000, January 21). Benetton sparks controversy again: Series of magazine ads attack death penalty. *Financial Post,* p. C3.

Anthan, G. (1990, February 25.) Farm column. *The Gannett News Service.*

Arant, M. D., & Meyer, P. (1998). Public journalism and traditional journalism: A shift in values? *Journal of Mass Media Ethics, 13* (4), pp. 205–218.

Arendt, H. (1970). *The human condition.* Chicago: University of Chicago Press.

Aristotle. *The Nicomachean ethics.*

Ascher-Walsh, R. (2000, September 29). Rhymes with rich. *Entertainment Weekly.*

Axelrod, R. (1984). *The evolution of cooperation.* New York: Basic Books.

Bad Apple. (1989, May). *Consumer Reports,* pp. 288–291.

Bagdikian, B. H. (1987). *The media monopoly.* (2d ed.). Boston: Beacon Press.

———. (1990). *The media monopoly.* (3d ed.). Boston: Beacon Press.

Barsam, R. M. (1975). *Film guide to triumph of the will.* Bloomington, IN: Indiana University Press.

Beasley, M. H., & Harlow, R. R. (1988). *The new majority: A look at what the preponderance of women in journalism education means to the schools and to the professions.* Lanham, MD: University Press of America.

Beck, M. (1989, March 27). Warning! Your food, nutritious and delicious, may be hazardous to your health. *Newsweek,* pp. 16–19.

Becker, L., et al. (2000). Undergrad enrollments level off; graduate enrollment declines. *Journalism and Mass Communication Educator, 55: 3,* p. 68–80.

Begley, S., & Hagar, M., (1989, January 30). Dangers in the vegetable patch. *Newsweek,* pp. 74–75.

Bennett, L. (1988). *News: The politics of illusion.* Longman: New York.

Bentley, R. (1986, August 4). Lessons sought from tragic events. *Bakersfield Californian,* p. 15.

Berger, J. (1980). *About looking.* New York: Pantheon Books.

Black, J., Steele, B., & Barney, R. (1993). *Doing ethics in journalism.* Greencastle, IN: The Sigma Delta Chi Foundation and The Society of Professional Journalists.

Bok, S. (1978). *Lying: Moral choice in public and private life.* New York: Random House.

———. (1983). *Secrets: On the ethics of concealment and revelation.* New York: Vintage.

Boorstin, D. (1962). *The image.* New York: Antheneum.

Booth, C. (1999, November 15). Worst of Times. *Time,* pp. 79–80.

Bovée, W. (1991). The end can justify the means—but rarely. *Journal of Mass Media Ethics, 6,* pp. 135–145.

Braun, S. (1994, November 2). Tuning out the hype and gore. *Los Angeles Times,* p. 1.

Brooks, D. E. (1992). In their own words: Advertisers and the origins of the African-American consumer market. (A paper submitted to the Association for Education in Journalism and Mass Communications), Montreal, Canada, August 5–8.

Brotman, S. N. (1986, March 31). Keeping the public involved in broadcast licensing. *The National Law Journal,* p. 13.

Brugioni, D. (1999). *Photo fakery: The history and technique of photographic deception and manipulation.* Virginia: Brasseys.

Bryant, G. (1987, Spring-Summer). Ten-fifty P.I.: Emotion and the photographer's role. *Journal of Mass Media Ethics,* pp. 32–39.

Buckner, J. (2000, Jan. 30). Horrific photo forces us to face a painful past. *Charlotte Observer,* p. 3C.

Calvert, C. (2000). *Voyeur Nation: Media, privacy and peering in modern culture.* Boulder, CO: Westview Press.

Carey, J. W. (1989, Autumn). Review of Charles J. Sykes' "Profscam." *Journalism Educator,* p. 48.

Carlson, M. (1989, March 27). Do you dare to eat a peach? *Time,* pp. 24–27.

Cassier, E. (1944). *An essay on man.* New Haven, CN: Yale University Press.

Christians, C. (1986). Reporting and the oppressed. In D. Elliott (ed.),*Responsible journalism* (pp. 109–130) Newbury Park, CA: Sage Publications, Inc.

Christians, C. G., Ferré, J. P., & Fackler, M. (1995). *Good news: Social ethics and the press.* New York: Longman.

Christians, C., Ferré, J., & Fackler, M. (1992). *A social ethics of news.* New York: Oxford University Press.

Christians, C., Rotzoll, K., & Fackler, M. (1987). *Media ethics: Cases and moral reasoning.* (2d ed.). New York: Longman.

Clouse, B. (1985). *Moral development.* Grand Rapids, MI: Baker Book House.

Cohen, A. (2000, Oct. 2). A crisis of content. *Time,* pp. 68–73.

Coleman, A. D. (1987, Spring/Summer). Private lives, public places: Street photography ethics. *Journal of Mass Media Ethics,* pp. 60–66.

Coleman, P. A. (2000). "Fighting a fair war or tilting at windmills?" An unpublished master's thesis. University of Missouri. Columbia, Missouri.

Commission on Civil Disorders. (1989). The role of the mass media in reporting of news about minorities. In T. Goldstein (ed.), *Killing the messenger:100 years of media criticism.* New York:Columbia University.

Committee on the Judiciary—Tash Statement. (May 21, 2000). Available: http://www.house.gov/judiciary/10148.htm.

Conley, C. (2000, May 12). Students to create Benetton ads in post-Toscani era. *Campaign,* p. 30.

Conti, S. (2000, October 6). Benetton's think tank. *Women's Wear Daily,* v. 180, n. 67, p. 20.

Corliss, R. (1999, August 16). Blair Witch Craft. *Time,* p. 58–64.

Cousins, N. (1974). *The celebration of life: A dialogue on immortality and infinity.* New York: Harper and Row.

Crouse, T. (1974). *The boys on the bus: Riding with the campaign press corps.* New York: Ballantine.

Daniel, C. (1989). National security and the Bay of Pigs invasion. In T. Goldstein (ed.). *Killing the messenger:100 years of media criticism.* New York: Columbia University.

Daniels, J. (1965). *They will be heard: America's crusading newspaper editors.* New York: McGraw-Hill.

Dates, J. L. (1990). Advertising. In J. L. Dates and W. Barlow (eds.), *Split image: African Americans in the mass media.* Washington, D.C.: Howard University Press.

Davies, J. C. (1963). *Human nature in politics.* New York: John Wiley & Sons.

Day, L. A. (1991). *Ethics in media communications: Cases and controversies.* Belmont, CA: Wadsworth, Inc.

Deaver, F. (1990). On defining truth. *Journal of Mass Media Ethics, 5* (3), 168–177.

Deford, F. (1992, April 20). Arthur Ashe's secret. *Newsweek,* pp. 31–32.

Dionne, E. J. (1991). *Why Americans hate politics.* New York: Simon & Schuster.

Eisenberg, E. M. (1984, September). Ambiguity as strategy in organizational communication. *Communication Monographs, 51,* pp. 227–242.

Elliott, D. (1986). Foundations for news media responsibility. In D. Elliott (ed.), *Responsible journalism.* (pp. 32–34). Newbury Park, CA: Sage Publications, Inc.

————. D. (1991, Autumn). Moral development and the teaching of ethics. *Journalism Educator,* pp. 19–24.

Ellul, J. (1965). *Propaganda* (Trans. by K. Kellen and J. Lerner). New York: Alfred A. Knopf.

Emery, E., & Emery, M. (1978). *The press and America: An interpretative history of the mass media.* (4th ed.) Englewood Cliffs, NJ: Prentice-Hall.

Encabo, N. (1995). Ethics of journalism and democracy. *European Journal of Communication, 10* (4), pp. 513–526.

Epstein, E. J. (1974). *News from nowhere.* New York: Random House.

Etzioni, A. (1993). *The spirit of community.* New York: Crown Publishers, Inc.

Fallows, J. (1996). *Breaking the news: How the media undermine American democracy.* New York: Pantheon.

Farrow, B. (2000, April 06). Connected: Taking the movies to market. *Daily Telegraph,* London, p. 8.

Fenton, D. (1989, October 3). Personal conversation with the author.

Fink, C. (1988). *Media ethics:In the newsroom and beyond.* New York: McGraw-Hill.

Fischer, C. T. (1980). Privacy and human development. In W. C. Bier (ed.), *Privacy: A vanishing value?* (pp. 37–46). New York: Fordham University Press.

Fitzgerald, M. (1995, November 11). Decrying public journalism. *Editor and publisher,* p. 20.

Fletcher, G. P. (1993). *Loyalty: An essay on the morality of relationships.* New York: Oxford University Press.

Fore, W. F. (1987). *Television and religion.* New York: Augsburg Publishing House.

Fry, D. (ed.), (1983). *The adversary press: A modern media institute ethics seminar.* St. Petersburg, FL: The Poynter Institute.

Fuss, P. (1965). *The moral philosophy of Josiah Royce.* Cambridge, MA: Harvard University Press.

Gans, H. (1979). *Deciding what's news: A study of CBS evening news, NBC nightly news, Newsweek and Time.* New York: Vintage.

Gerbner, G. (1987, Summer-Fall). Television: Modern mythmaker. *Media and Values,* pp. 8–9.

Gert, B. (1988). *Morality, a new justification of the moral rules.* New York: Oxford University Press.

Gilligan, C. (1977). In a different voice: Women's conceptions of self and morality. *Harvard Educational Review, 47,* pp. 492–505.

———. (1982). *In a different voice: Psychological theory and women's development.* Cambridge, MA: Harvard University Press.

Godwin, M. (1995). The shoddy article. *JournoPorn on HotWired (Online).* Available: http://www.hotwired.com/special/pornscare/.

Goffman, E. (1959). *The presentation of self in everyday life.* New York: Anchor.

Goldberg, J. (2000, January 28). Benetton's death-row ads drawing criticism, campaign makes no mention of crimes. Victims. *Charlotte Observer,* p. 1B.

Goldstein, P. (2000, January 1). The year of unconventional wisdom. *Los Angeles Times,* p. 1F.

Goldstein, T. (ed), (1989). *Killing the messenger: 100 years of media criticism.* New York: Columbia University Press.

Goodman, E. (1991, March 2). To libel lettuce. *Syndicated column.*

Gormley, D. W. (1984). Compassion is a tough word. *Drawing the Line,* pp. 58–59. Washington, D.C.: American Society of Newspaper Editors.

Grcic, J. M. (1986). The right to privacy: Behavior as property. *Journal of Values Inquiry, 20,* pp. 137–144.

Greenfeld, K. (2000, Oct. 2). Meet the Napster. *Time,* pp. 60–68.

Gross, L., Katz, J. S., & Ruby, J. (eds). (1988). *Image ethics: The moral rights of subjects in photographs, film and television.* New York: Oxford University Press.

Grunig, J. E., & Hunt, T. (1984). *Managing Public Relations.* Fort Worth: Holt, Rinehart and Winston.

Gurevitch, M., Levy, M., & Roeh, I. (1991). The Global Newsroom: Convergences and Diversities in the Globalization of Television News. In P. Dalhgren and C. Sparks (eds.), *Communication and Citizenship.* London. Routledge.

Haddix, D. (1990, March/April). Alar as a media event. *Columbia Journalism Review,* pp. 44–45.

Haiman, F. (1958). Democratic ethics and the hidden persuaders. *Quarterly Journal of Speech, 44,* pp. 385–392.

Halbert, D. J. (1999). *Intellectual property in the information age.* Westport, Conn.: Quorum Books.

Hanson, K. (1986). The demands of loyalty. *Idealistic Studies, 16,* pp. 195–204.

Henry, W. H., III. (1994). *In defense of elitism.* New York: Anchor Books.

Hersey, J. (1989). The legend on the license. In T. Goldstein (ed.), *Killing the messenger: 100 years of media criticism.* New York: Columbia University.

Hersh, S. (1991). *The Samson option: Israel's nuclear arsenal and American foreign policy.* New York: Random House.

Hess, S. (1981). *The Washington reporters.* Washington, D.C.: The Brookings Institution.

Heston, C. (1992, August 17). Just a song? *National Review,* pp. 37, 53.

Hixson, R. F. (1987). *Privacy in a public society.* New York: Oxford University Press.

Hobbes, T. (1958). *The Leviathan* (Reprints from 1651). New York: Bobbs-Merrill.

Hodges, L. W. (1983). The journalist and privacy. *Social Responsibility: Journalism, Law, Medicine, 9,* pp. 5–19.

———. (1986). Defining press responsibility: A functional approach. In D. Elliott (ed.), *Responsible journalism.* (pp. 13–31). Newbury Park, CA: Sage Publications, Inc.

———. (1989, October 3). How a PR firm executed the Alar scare. *Wall Street Journal,* p. 9.

Hoyt, M. (1990, March-April). When the walls come tumbling down. *Columbia Journalism Review,* pp. 35–40.

Hughes, C. (2000, April 29). Benetton, Toscani End Partnership. *Associated Press.*

James, C. (2000, Dec. 3). In a gay world, without the usual guides. *New York Times,* Section 2, p. 27.

Jamieson, K. H. (2000). *Everything you think you know about politics...and why you're wrong.* New York: Basic Books.

———. (1992). *Dirty politics.* New York: Oxford University Press.

Jamieson, K. H., & Campbell, K. K. (1992). *The interplay of influence: News, advertising, politics and the mass media.* (3d ed.). Belmont, CA: Wadsworth, Inc.

Johannesen, R. L. (1990). *Ethics in communication.* Prospect Heights, IL: Waveland Press.

Joy, D. M. (1983). *Moral development foundations.* Nashville: Abingdon Press.

Junas, L. (1980, February 23). Tragedy and violence photos dominate in news prizes. *Editor and publisher,* p. 17.

Kaid, L. L. (1992). Ethical dimensions of political advertising. In R. E. Denton (ed.), *Ethical dimensions of political communication,* (pp. 145–169). New York: Praeger.

Kant, I. (1785). *Groundwork on the metaphysics of morals.*

Kerrigan, M. (2000, January 28). Death row adverts could put Benetton in the frame. *The Scotsman,* p. 22.

Kessler, L. (1989). Women's magazines' coverage of smoking-related health coverage. *Journalism Quarterly, 66,* pp. 316–22, 445.

Klein, J. (1992, June 8). Whose values? *Newsweek,* pp. 19–22.

Kohlberg, L. (1968, September). The child as a moral philosopher. *Psychology To-day,* pp. 25–30.

―――. (1973). The contribution of developmental psychology to education. *Educational Psychologist, 10,* pp. 2–14.

Kroeger, B. (1994). *Nellie Bly.* New York: Random House.

Kurtz, H. (1990, March/April). Dr. Whelan's media operation. *Columbia Journalism Review,* pp. 43–47.

Lambeth, E. B. (1986). *Committed journalism.* Bloomington, IN: Indiana University Press.

―――. (1992). *Committed journalism: An ethic for the profession* (2d ed.). Bloomington, IN: Indiana University Press.

Landsman, S. (1984). *The adversary system: A description and defense.* Washington, D.C.: American Enterprise Institute.

Lasch, C. (1979). *The culture of narcissism.* New York: Warner Books.

Lebacqz, K. (1985). *Professional ethics: Power and paradox.* Nashville: Abingdon Press.

Leiss, W., Kline, S., & Jhally, S. (1986). *Social communication in advertising: Person, products and images of well being.* New York: Methuen Publications.

Leland, J. (1999, August 16). The Blair Witch Cult. *Newsweek.* p. 44.

Lester, P. M. (1992). *Photojournalism: An ethical approach.* Hillsdale, NJ: Lawrence Erlbaum and Associates.

Lester, P. M. (1996). *Images that injure.* Westport, CT: Greenwood Press.

Linsky, M. (1986). *Impact: How the press affects federal policymaking.* New York: W. W. Norton.

Lippmann, W. (1922). *Public opinion.* New York: Free Press.

―――. (1982). *The essential Lippmann.* Cambridge, MA: Harvard University Press.

Lippmann, W., & Merz, C. (1989). A test of the news. In T. Goldstein (ed.), *Killing the messenger: 100 years of media criticism.* New York: Columbia University.

Long, E. V. (1995, July 3). To our readers. *Time,* p. 4.

Lont, Cynthia M. (1995). *Women and media: Content/careers/criticism.* Belmont, CA.: Wadsworth.

Lowery, S., & DeFleur, M. (1988). *Milestones in mass communication research.* (2d ed.). New York: Longman.

Madison, J., Hamilton, A. & Jay, J. *The Federalist papers.*

Malcomb, J. (1989). Reflections: The journalist and the murderer. *The New Yorker,* pp. 38–73.

Mander, J. (1979). Four arguments for the elimination of advertising. In K. Retzell (ed.), *Advertising and the public* (pp. 17–28). Urbana-Champaign: University of Illinois Dept. of Advertising.

Martin, E. (1991). On photographic manipulation. *Journal of Mass Media Ethics, 6,* pp. 156–163.

Marzolf, M. T. (1991). *Civilizing voices: American press criticism 1880–1950.* New York: Longman.

Matsuda, M. (1989). Public response to racist speech: Considering the victim's story. *Michigan Law Review, 87,* pp. 2321–2381.

McCarty, J. F. (1996, February 23). Son's new evidence in Sheppard case is put before the judge. *The Cleveland Plain Dealer,* p. 1A.

McChesney, R. (1997). *Corporate media and the threat to democracy.* New York: Seven Stories Press.

Medved, M. (1992). *Hollywood vs. America.* New York: HarperCollins.

Meislen, A. (1994, December 14). Blunting TV new's sharp edges. *New York Times,* p. 20.

Merrill, J. C. (1974). *The imperative of freedom: A philosophy of journalistic autonomy.* New York: Hastings House.

Merritt, Davis. (1995). *Public journalism and public life.* Hillsdale, NJ: Lawrence Erlbaum Associates.

Meyrowitz, J. (1985). *No sense of place: The impact of electronic media on social behavior.* New York: Oxford University Press.

Mill, J. S. (1859). *On liberty.*

———. (1861). *Utilitarianism.*

Miller, E. D. (1994). *The Charlotte Project: Helping citizens take back democracy. The Poynter Papers: No. 4.* St. Petersburg, FL: The Poynter Institute.

Miller, K. (1992, December). Smoking up a storm: Public relations and advertising in the construction of the cigarette problem, 1953–1954. *Journalism Monographs, 136.*

Mills, C. W. (1956). *The power elite.* New York: Oxford University Press.

Mills, K. (1989, Winter). When women talk to women. *Media and Values, 12.*

Mitchell, W. J. T. (1995). *Picture theory.* Chicago: University of Chicago Press.

Molotch, H., & Lester, M. (1974). News as purposive behavior: On the strategic use of routine events, accidents and scandals. *American Sociological Review, 39,* pp. 101–112.

Montgomery, K. C. (1989). *Target: Prime time. Advocacy groups and the struggle over entertainment television.* New York: Oxford University Press.

Moore, G. F. (1903). *Principia ethica.*

Moyers, B. (1988). Quoted in *'The promise of television,'* episode 10. Produced by PBS.

Mullaney, T. J., & Ante, S. E. (2000, June 5). Info Wars. *Business Week,* pp. EB 107.

Mundow, A. (2000, January 29). Ad Men Walking—Benetton is facing its biggest U.S. advertising backlash yet, with a new campaign about Death Row. *The Irish Times,* p. 61.

National Association of Broadcasters. (1985). *Radio: In search of excellence.* Washington, D.C.: NAB.

Nelkin, D. (1987). *Selling science: How the press covers science and technology.* New York: W. H. Freeman.

Neville, R. C. (1980). Various meanings of privacy: A philosophical analysis. In W. C. Bier (ed.), *Privacy: A vanishing value?* (pp. 26–36). New York: Fordham University Press.

Newsom, D. (1993). *This is PR.* Belmont, CA: Wadsworth.

Newsom, D., Turk, J. V., & Kruckeberg, D. (1996). *This is PR: The realities of public relations.* Belmont, CA: Wadsworth.

Nimmo, D., & Combs, J. (1985). *Nightly horrors: Crisis coverage in television network news.* Knoxville, TN: University of Tennessee Press.

O' Marcaigh, F. (1999, September 6). Sects, lies and Internet hype. *The Irish Times,* p. 12.

O'Toole, J. (1985). *The trouble with advertising.* New York: Times Books.

Oldenquist, A. (1982). Loyalties. *Journal of Philosophy, 79,* pp. 73–93.

Olsen, Jack. (1985). *Give a boy a gun.* New York: Delacorte.

Oran, D. (1975). *Law dictionary for non-lawyers.* St. Paul, MN: West Publishing Co.

Palmer, E. L., & Door, A. eds. (1980). *Children and the faces of television: Teaching, violence, selling.* New York: Academic Press.

Patterson, T. E. (1980). *The mass media election.* New York: Praeger.

Patterson, T. E., & McClure, R. D. (1972). *The unseeing eye.* New York: G. P. Putnam's Sons.

Perry, W. O. (1968). *Intellectual development in the college years: A scheme.* New York: Holt, Rinehart and Winston.

Piaget, J. (1965). *The moral judgment of the child.* Translated by Marjorie Gabain. New York: Free Press.

Plato. *The republic.*

Postman, N. (1986). *Amusing ourselves to death: Public discourse in the age of television.* New York: Penguin Books.

Powell, T. F. (1967). *Josiah Royce.* New York: Washington Square Press, Inc.

Price, M. (2000, Dec. 10). Showtime's "Queer as Folk" gives voice to a love that dared not speak its name on TV. *Charlotte Observer,* p. F1.

Protess, D., et al. (1991). *Journalism of outrage: Investigative reporting and agenda building in America.* New York: Guilford Press.

Rainville, R., & McCormick, E. (1977). Extent of covert racial prejudice in pro football announcer's speech. *Journalism Quarterly, 54,* pp. 20–26.

Raissman, B. (1999, October 27). In baseball vs. Rose, Gray is not a player. *New York Daily News,* p. B1.

Rather, D. (1987, March 10). From Murrow to mediocrity? *New York Times,* Sec. I, p. 27.

Rawls, J. (1971). *A theory of justice.* Cambridge, MA: Harvard University Press.

Reaves, S. (1987, Spring-Summer). Digital retouching: Is there a place for it in newspaper photography? *Journal of Mass Media Ethics,* pp. 40–48.

———. (1991). Personal correspondence to the author quoted in Digital alteration of photographs in consumer magazines. *Journal of Mass Media Ethics, 6,* pp. 175–181.

Rieder, R. (1996, July/August). The admiral and the 'V' clips. *American Journalism Review,* p. 6.

_____. (1999, November/December). A costly rookie mistake. *American Journalism Review*, p. 6.

Robertson, N. (1992). *The girls in the balcony.* New York: Random House.

Robinson, M., & Sheehan, G. (1984). *Over the wire and on TV.* New York: Basic Books.

Rogers, E. M., & Chang, S. B. (1991). Media coverage of technology issues: Ethiopian drought of 1984, AIDS, Challenger and Chernobyl. In L. Wilkins and P. Patterson eds., *Risky business: Communicating issues of science, risk and public policy,* pp. 75–96. Westport, CT: Greenwood Press.

Rosen, J. (1995). What should we be doing? *The IRE Journal, 18,* pp. 6–8.

Rosen, J. (2000). *The Unwanted Gaze: The Destruction of Privacy in America.* New York: Random House.

Rosenthal, A. M. (1989, October 10). Trash TV's latest news show continues credibility erosion. Syndicated column by *New York Times* News Service.

Ross, W. D. (1930). *The right and the good.* Oxford, England: Clarendon Press.

Rothmeyer, K. (1991, September/October). The media and the recession. *Columbia Journalism Review.* pp. 23–28.

Royce, J. (1908). *The philosophy of loyalty.* New York: The Macmillan Co.

Russell, B., (ed.). (1967). *History of Western philosophy.* New York: Touchstone Books.

Ryan, B. (1999, October 27). Rose's case doesn't deserve your sympathy. *Boston Globe,* pp. C1.

Sabato, L. J. (1992). *Feeding frenzy: How attack journalism has transformed American politics.* New York: Free Press.

Safer, M. (1992, January 30). Keynote address at the annual Alfred I. DuPont—Columbia University Awards ceremony.

Sandel, M. J. (1982). *Liberalism and the limits of justice.* Cambridge, MA: Harvard University Press.

Sanders, M., & Rock, M. (1988). *Waiting for prime time: The women of television news.* Urbana: University of Illinois Press.

Schaffer, J., & Miller, E. D. (1995). *Civic journalism: Six case studies.* St. Petersburg, FL: The Poynter Institute.

Schoeman, F. D., (ed.). (1984). *Philosophical dimensions of privacy: An anthology.* Cambridge, MA: Harvard University Press.

Schoenbrun, D. (1989). *On and off the air: An informal history of CBS news.* New York: E. P. Dutton.

Schudson, M. (1978). *Discovering the news.* New York: Basic Books.

———. (1984). *Advertising: The uneasy persuasion.* New York: Basic Books.

———. (1995). *The power of news.* Cambridge, MA: Harvard University Press.

Schwartz, T. (1973). *The responsive chord.* Garden City, NY: Anchor Press.

Seldes, G. (1989). The press and the individual. In T. Goldstein (ed.), *Killing the messenger: 100 years of media criticism.* New York: Columbia University Press.

Shaw, D. (1999, December 20) . Journalism is a very different business—Here's why. *Los Angeles Times,* p. V3.

Sheehan, M., & Robinson, M. (1984). *Over the wire and on TV.* New York: Russell Sage Foundation.

Sheer, R. (2000, October 23). How the New York Times convicted Wen Ho Lee. *The Nation.* pp. 11–20.

Shilts, R. (1987). *And the band played on.* New York: St. Martin's Press.

Siberner, J. (1989, March 27). The great global food fright. *U.S. News and World Report,* pp. 56–59.

Sieh, P. *Campaigns and conscience: The ethics of political journalism.* Westport, CT: Praeger.

Siebert, F. S., Peterson, T. & Schramm, W. (1956). *Four theories of the press.* Urbana: University of Illinois Press.

Silver, R. (1989, Winter). The many faces of media women. *Media and Values,* pp. 2–5.

Smith, C. (1992). *Media and apocalypse.* Westport, CT: Greenwood Press.

Smith, D. (2000, Dec. 19). Flap over gay kiss photo proves instructive. *Charlotte Observer,* p. 17A.

Smith, R. (2000, Jan. 13). Critic's Notebook: An Ugly Legacy Lives On, Its Glare Unsoftened by Age. *New York Times,* p. E1.

Sperber, A. M. (1986). *Murrow: His life and times.* (4th ed.). New York: Freundlich Books.

Squires, J. (1997). *Read all about it! The corporate takeover of America's newspapers.* New York: Basic Books.

Stamper, C. (1999. July 15). Blair Witch, a scary home brew. *Wired News.*

Stein, M. L. (1986, June 21). Covering a disaster story. *Editor & publisher,* p. 17.

Steuver, H. (2000, January 25). Radical Chic: Benetton Takes on the Death Penalty. *The Washington Post,* p. C01.

Stone, I. F. (1988). *The trial of Socrates.* Boston: Little, Brown and Co.

Szarkowski, J. (1978). *Mirrors and windows.* New York: Museum of Modern Art.

Thoman, E. (1987, Summer-Fall). How well does television handle social issues? *Media and Values,* pp. 20–22.

Thomas, B. (1990, January 19). Finding truth in the age of 'infotainment.' *Editorial Research Reports.* Washington, D.C.: Congressional Quarterly, Inc.

Tomlinson, D. (1987). One technological step forward and two legal steps back: Digitalization and television newspictures as evidence in libel. *Loyola Entertainment Law Journal, 9,* pp. 237–257.

Toufexis, A., & Garcia, C. (1989, March 6). Watch those vegetables, Ma. *Time,* p. 57.

Toulmin, S. (1988, Summer). The recovery of practical philosophy. *The American Scholar,* p. 338.

Warren, J. (1989, March 26). How 'media stampede' spread apple panic. *Chicago Tribune,* p. 1.

Watkins, J. J. (1990). *The mass media and the law.* Englewood Cliffs, NJ: Prentice-Hall.

Weaver, D. H., & Wilhoit, G. C. (1986). *The American journalist: A portrait of U.S. newspeople and their work.* Bloomington: University of Indiana Press.

Weinberg. S. (1995, Nov/Dec.). ABC, Philip Morris and the infamous apology. *Columbia Journalism Review,* pp. 29–37.

Wengraf, A. (1989). Property and ideas, *13 Legal Studies.* F. 341, 341–42.

Werner, M. R., & Starr, J. (1959). *Teapot Dome.* New York: Viking.

Westin, A. F. (1967). *Privacy and freedom.* New York: Atheneum.

Wicker, C. (1990, March 7). Awhile back, everyone was doing it—but not anymore. *Dallas Morning News,* pp. 1–2C.

Wilkins, L. (1987). *Shared vulnerability: The mass media and American perception of the Bhopal disaster.* Westport, CT: Greenwood Press.

Wilmington, M. (2000, October 25). Bamboozled. *Metromix and ZAPZIT.com.*

Wilson, E. (1940). *To the Finland station.* New York: Doubleday & Co.

Wolk, J. (1999, July 12). Scare tactics. *Entertainment Weekly.*

Woods, G. (1996). *Advertising and marketing to the new majority.* Belmont, CA: Wadsworth.

INDEX